MODERN SICILY

A HISTORY OF SICILY

MEDIEVAL SICILY: 800–1713
MODERN SICILY: After 1713
By D. MACK SMITH

A
HISTORY OF SICILY

MODERN SICILY
AFTER 1713

Denis Mack Smith

DORSET PRESS
New York

This edition published by Dorset Press,
a division of Marboro Books Corporation,
by arrangement with Viking Penguin Inc.
1988 Dorset Press

ISBN 0-88029-238-5

Printed in the United States of America

M 9 8 7 6 5 4 3 2

CONTENTS

MAPS

ILLUSTRATIONS

PART 7

Three Experiments in Foreign Government
1713–1765

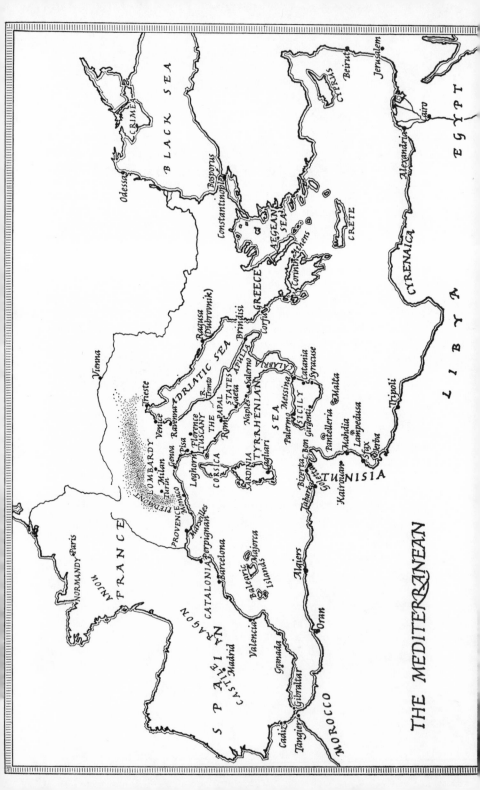

THE MEDITERRANEAN

Chapter 24

RULE FROM TURIN

The sudden reversal that removed Sicily from Spanish rule and attached her once again to an Italian power was partly to be explained by the attitude of England. The Austrian Habsburgs who now occupied Naples would have liked also to take Sicily for themselves and so restore the *Utriusque Siciliae Regnum*, but England preferred the island in weaker hands, and argued that the Duke of Savoy-Piedmont had earned a reward by prudently changing sides during the war and helping to defeat his Bourbon relatives. When Queen Anne anachronistically demurred to a country being bartered around without its consent, her ministers pointed out the incidental diplomatic and political advantages. The Duke himself was delighted. He came from an ambitious family which set particular value on territorial acquisition, and it seemed a worthy outcome of a costly war to obtain a regal title and be able to call himself King of Sicily and Jerusalem. He merely had to promise England that he would maintain free trade and satisfy Sicilians that their laws and privileges would remain intact.

His new subjects were left to make the best of it. After thirteen years under the Franco-Spanish Bourbons, they were now to be ruled for five years by the Piedmontese, then for fourteen by the Austrians, and thereafter by the Neapolitan Bourbons. In April 1713, when news of the Treaty of Utrecht reached Palermo, the artisan guilds at first showed some annoyance; but the leading noblemen were chiefly anxious that their new King would set up court in Palermo and revive the glories of a distant past. Some of the aristocracy sped to Turin to pay homage and be the first to obtain his ear. Most other Sicilians, according to Bourbon officials, accepted the change with the fatalism of those who were now accustomed to being cast as the playthings of fortune.

When Victor Amadeus was brought to Sicily by an English ship in October 1713, this was the first royal presence in the island since 1535. Six thousand soldiers were also carried from north Italy by the English, to replace the Bourbon garrisons. The new King stayed for a year, during which he visited the main coastal cities and made an effort to understand local problems. He brought a good deal of cash with him to subsidise the Sicilian budget. He instigated enquiries into most areas of national life, and the first attempt for a long time was made to think out a programme of administrative reform. Yet up to a point he also tried, and with reason, not to antagonize vested interests unnecessarily. The

243

university of Catania was revived and given new endowments and professors. At the same time he restored to the civic senate of Messina something of its old dignity, with the togas, the incense and the velvet-covered bench that meant so much to the city authorities; and Messina was again allowed to take precedence immediately after Palermo.

Improving the economy was made a first priority. Encouragement was given to a paper factory using local raw materials, and skilled workers were summoned from Piedmont and France to start a glass industry and to improve the quality of local woollens and silks. The Palermo arsenal was also stirred into life by Piedmontese shipwrights who made a survey of the timber resources still available in the mountains. Something was done to build up a register of existing roads and bridges, with a note in each case of who was responsible for their upkeep, and there was an attempt to revive the mining industry near Messina. An enquiry was ordered into why so many idle unemployed could exist in Palermo at a time when in the countryside there were not enough people to cultivate the fields: the main reason was said to be the thoroughly inequitable contracts of labour forced on the poor by the rich. The King wanted to bring in new types of labour-contract from Piedmont. He was advised of the need to force rich landowners to pay their debts and to make them sell parts of their large estates, so creating many more middle-sized farms. It was thought that a great deal could be done by the government to introduce proper methods of animal husbandry. There were also plans to re-possess sources of water which had been illegally converted into private property, and to build windmills as the basis for a proper system of irrigation for fruit trees.

The Piedmontese did not make themselves popular by their often accurate but also critical and condescending approach to these economic problems. Moreover, Sicily now belonged to a small state instead of to a grand empire, and Sicilians who were accustomed to the pomp of Spanish Viceroys found Victor Amadeus mean and parsimonious. He did not wear gold and lace, but undyed wool, large boots and a casual travelling wig. His sword was even a bit rusty and he preferred a rough walking stick. Nor was the palace so freely open on festive occasions to the local aristocracy. Dislike of this somewhat puritanical northerner went so deep that, a hundred years later, children were still playing a game in which stones were thrown at a dummy called Victor Amadeus.

At the end of 1714 he returned to Piedmont and never revisited the country which provided his kingly title. Perhaps he was disappointed with what he had found, or perhaps he had never valued it except as a stepping stone to yet further expansion. Sicily was henceforward to be governed through a special council in distant Turin. The Viceroy at Palermo, Count Annibale Maffei, was a northerner and had to refer to Turin for all important matters. The allocation of pensions was henceforward to be much stricter than before. Peremptory orders came about reform of the diverse and sometimes conflicting courts which interfered with application of the law. The King pointed out that, since Turin was nearer than Madrid to Palermo, there was now less need than before for any local autonomy.

A number of interests thus felt themselves threatened; and when other northerners were freely chosen to be ministers and judges, the implication that Sicilians were either corrupt or incompetent gave offence. Maffei reached the unwelcome conclusion that the sheer multiplicity of officials had been a major reason for the slowness of business and the difficulty of getting action. Accounts were not being checked, and this led to a great loss of revenue. The award of office by purchase and not merit reflected the fact that public life was all too often regarded simply as a way of making money. Civil servants were therefore sent from Turin to supervise the finances and to administer the army and navy. Officers were even brought from Scotland to help man the three sailing ships which were introduced to supplement the five expensive but not very useful Sicilian galleys—the first new sailing vessel was specially built in England to serve as a model. Other Piedmontese were introduced into the civic administration of Palermo, though they found Sicilian methods of government hard to understand. The King hoped that the local notables would give up their Spanish-style clothes and adopt the uniforms of Savoy, but naturally this kind of regimentation was resented. So was the fact that the censorship of books became more severe or at least more efficient. Moreover the military and disciplined traditions of Turin were quite alien in a society which despised the life of a soldier and possessed so few traditions of public service; nor did ideas of absolutist government square easily with the traditional laxity allowed by Spain.

The sense of dissatisfaction was never allowed to reach the point of open revolt. A few of the barons received a job after a short list had been drawn up with details about their individual weaknesses and capabilities; and the rest were in general allowed to go on enjoying their privileged immunities, for on this condition they would loyally serve whatever dynasty the Concert of Europe might impose on them. The King, who was quite aware of the injustices of the baronial courts and the economic disadvantages of unfettered baronial rule, could not afford in practice to give more than the most general consideration to reducing feudal abuses. His cryptic advice to Maffei was not to stir up the barons against each other, but if possible to ensure that they were not too much united. Any change in ownership of a fief had to be by royal permission and after payment of dues to the crown. In 1716 it was also ruled that all barons who had founded new villages without first buying a license should forfeit them; but this was not enforced very rigorously.

Other laws, equally ineffective, were made against extravagant living and gaming; for although some nobles were considered rich, many others were still being driven into bankruptcy by the desire to keep up appearances; almost all of them lived on credit, and the whole economic life of the country was threatened if ever they did not or could not pay interest on their debts and mortgages. The Prince of Butera, for example, who 'owned' 50,000 people in ten towns (apart from about eighty other large farms as well as considerable properties in Naples), was now paying 63,000 *scudi* a year in interest, nearly as much as the annual cost of the Sicilian navy. This kind of fact was not unconnected with the decline in Sicilian agriculture. Yet there was little the government could do except try to limit aristocratic extravagance. Thus another sumptuary law prescribed that no one should have more than one carriage, and the number of horses to a carriage was also limited; but the King weakly allowed certain favoured nobles a little latitude here, and soon it became a point of honour to secure a special exemption. Ladies, too, had to register their fine dresses with the authorities: three years' grace would be allowed during which existing dresses could be worn, but thereafter a limit would be imposed on the use of foreign silks and laces.

The government as well as the barons had recently been falling further into debt, and when the Piedmontese arrived they found the island's finances completely disorganised. In order to restore government credit they cut down on minor extravagances. They carried out a new census for tax purposes, since the existing figures were quite unrealistic and some areas had been escaping tax altogether. The parliamentary *donativi* were heavily increased; and if people who could afford to pay continued to delay payment, the King was prepared to distrain upon their goods and those of their relatives. This attempt to bring the finances into line with those of Turin was bound to arouse indignation. What was worse, he showed that he was ready to reduce the authority of the parliamentary Deputation over the allocation of *donativi*. This committee, in 1714, consisted of four princes representing the baronial House, three princes and a duke representing the lower House, and an archbishop, a prince, a duke and a marquis representing the ecclesiastical House: it was obvious that this was merely a mouthpiece of the higher aristocracy, and equally obvious that they were using it to reduce their own obligations. Efficiency in revenue collection was something which Victor Amadeus particularly required. In the customs department, for instance, he found that officials were taking heavy bribes in return for altering bills of quantity, while dockers were losing or delaying merchandise if they were not adequately tipped. Another common fraud was that merchants, to avoid paying their debts, would seek asylum in churches or declare themselves bankrupt, and it was almost impossible for strangers to steer their way through half a dozen different and rival law courts to gain redress. This was one reason why foreigners were avoiding Palermo, and hence other parts of Sicily were not sending their goods into the capital city for exchange against imports. Maffei secured the condemnation for peculation of the nobleman in charge of the Palermo customs, and introduced Piedmontese officials instead. He insisted that a precise tariff of charges and tips should be posted at the landing quays where all could see. Duties now had to be paid in the customs house and not when merchandise was sold, with the result that evasion became harder. At every stage, payments of tax had to be checked and double-checked, and officials had to present their books each day for signature. They could not give the work to subordinates; they were not allowed to receive presents; and it was forbidden ever to leave the customs house unattended. The immediate consequence of these new measures was a doubling of customs revenue.

Efficiency, however, also had some disadvantages. It meant an increase in prices, especially of salt and tobacco which carried a high duty. If illicit perquisites were stopped and some sinecures abolished, this was unwelcome to the more privileged members of the privileged classes; if mulberry and olive trees were precisely enumerated, it was harder for farmers to avoid tax; and if trained archivists were appointed to the various government departments, there were bound to be fewer opportunities for profitable cheating. Crown officials, who hitherto had exempted themselves from contributions to the *donativi*, suddenly found that they had to pay. Even the erudite historiographer Canon Mongitore, who saw the need for reform, who knew that the previous administration had not even had the money to pay basic salaries, shared the general anger at such a challenge to the Sicilian way of life; because equity and efficiency were not particularly valued in this feudal environment, and avarice in a sovereign was despised. This five years' experiment in Piedmontese government therefore met with considerable and growing displeasure. What it proved, among other things, was that deeply entrenched methods of thought and behaviour would always interfere with any serious attempt at reform.

In the vital matter of crime prevention the King's intentions were equally good, but again he came up against the inflexible *immobilisme* of a complex society with ways of behaviour that had persisted for centuries. He was indignant to find vendettas and banditry so common. Effective punishment of homicide was the first of eleven practical suggestions for the improvement of trade which were addressed to him by the English consul at Messina. Another report, drawn up for him by a Sicilian, pointed out that churches, because of their rights of asylum, were active bases for criminal activity; and indeed this privilege of sanctuary for thieves and murderers had become quite a tourist attraction in Palermo. The local Captains at Arms, whose job was to put down crime, were frequently ex-convicts themselves and presumably had been selected for the very reason that they were familiar with the underworld: these Captains had to hire companies of police at their own charge; and there was no one to stop them levying protection money or penalising those who would not pay. Equally to be feared were the armed peasant bands which, as an English visitor noted, were maintained by some of the magnates for use as occasion demanded.

The new administration was bold enough to imprison one prince who was a notorious harbourer of brigands, and sequestered his income to pay off some of his 180 creditors. At the same time the Viceroy executed a leading member of the Palermo silk workers for insubordination, because the authorities had been particularly warned that rioting by the guildsmen might be fomented by some of the nobility for criminal purposes of their own. Maffei also confirmed the old rule that, if the Captains at Arms failed to prevent crime, they could be held liable to pay personally for unpunished thefts. The carrying of arms by any except officers of the law was forbidden once again, but this was as unenforceable as ever in a society which placed such value on honour and prescriptive right.

It was the privileges and immunities built into society at every level which chiefly frustrated reform. One of the most intractable and debilitating immunities was that created by article ten of the Treaty of Utrecht about the personal property which, somewhat anomalously, had been retained by Philip V in Sicily even after he had surrendered his sovereign rights there. Still more anomalously, this retained property was held to comprise any land confiscated by the crown from private individuals before 1713: it thus included the vast County of Modica as well as Alcamo and other towns, and a case was even made out for including the goods confiscated from Messina in 1678–80. One estimate gave Philip personal property rights over as much as a tenth of Sicily. His 'states' continued to be administered by a Spanish official, and this man exaggeratedly claimed freedom from ordinary laws and exemption from national taxation and military service for all Spaniards remaining in the island; he also employed a separate police force and tried to refuse access to Piedmontese troops; he claimed the right to export wheat from Modica without paying duty, and salt from Trapani. Most of these claims were rejected by the Piedmontese with an equal or even greater wealth of historical learning. Probably Philip was keeping them alive as possible grounds for an expedition of reconquest at some future date. Since the Austrians also still had their eye on Sicily—and in 1715 put out more feelers for English assistance in taking it—the future of the Savoy dynasty was thus more than uncertain.

As much as anything it was a clash with the Church that under-mined this experiment in government from Turin. Controversy was touched off by a minor incident in Lipari, an island which had belonged only for a hundred years to the kingdom of Sicily and where there was hence considerable doubt about the King's powers as Apostolic Legate. In 1711 the Bishop of Lipari excom-municated certain local officials who had taxed a consignment of beans without realising that it was episcopal property and thus exempt from excise duty. The officials quickly apologised, but the Bishop did not want to back down. The case thus came before the clergy in the office of the Apostolic Legateship, who reversed the excommunication. When the Pope supported the Bishop, the Spanish Viceroy produced a statement by some dozens of theo-logians pointing out that the Pope's authority in Sicily was limited by ancient custom and would always require validation by the crown. For five hundred years both sides had avoided this kind of jurisdictional conflict, but, perhaps inadvertently, they had now allowed a full scale battle to grow up out of nothing, with interdict on one side, arrest and deportation on the other.

Victor Amadeus inherited this conflict from the administration of Philip V. The extreme papalists then seized the opportunity of his accession to raise the old claim that he should first ask Rome for feudal investiture, but the King had sworn to preserve Sicilian privileges and therefore would not submit to these papal demands; on the contrary, he insisted that, by law and tradition, even papal dispensations for marriages, let alone excommunications, were invalid in Sicily without the royal *exequatur*. He was privately encouraged in this view by the King of Spain, who may not have been averse to creating trouble for his successor.

In 1715, a papal bull, *Romanus Pontifex*, therefore declared at an end the 600-year-old concession by Pope Urban that Kings of Sicily could exercise legatine powers. The Pope also refused to sanction the crusade tax or let the clergy pay their share of the *donativi*. Hundreds of priests were exiled or imprisoned for obeying this papal order, and their goods were confiscated. Bishoprics were left vacant, their revenues declared forfeit, and in many places the public exercise of religion came almost to a halt. Released by the Pope from their allegiance, citizens were encouraged to defy royal authority, and the monks of Girgenti even prepared to repel royal officers with boiling oil from the walls of their monastery. Proud though Sicilians had always been of the Apostolic Legateship, this interdict soured their loyalty to the new regime much more than it did to the spiritual authority of Rome.

Chapter 25

RULE FROM VIENNA

Victor Amadeus did not take long to learn how little he could do for Sicily and how little of an asset it was to him, so he began to think of exchanging the island for Milan or Florence, and with this in mind prepared for war against his late ally, Austria. He secretly informed Spain of this intention, and withdrew troops from Sicily for what he hoped might become a joint attack on the Austrians. His Viceroy in Palermo was intercepting letters between Spain and Sicily, and was thus able to warn Turin that the Spaniards were secretly hostile; but when, in June 1718, Spanish naval ships approached, he was told to welcome them as allies. He, at least, was not entirely surprised when they landed an army to recapture the island of which they had been deprived in 1713.

The Piedmontese had vague contingency plans to cut off the food and water supplies of Palermo, but the large Spanish fleet made it quite impossible to blockade the port. Against twenty thousand soldiers, far more than Spain had ever used in Sicily before, Maffei was powerless. He was fairly sure that the local nobility, even those who favoured Spain, would remain completely passive until the fighting was over. Far more ominous, the Palermo artisans were meeting in secret *conventicole*, since the mere rumour of a possible Spanish invasion opened up the possibility for them of yet more profitable rioting and another tax holiday.

The Viceroy, not very hopefully, summoned the barons to military service, but they did not obey. His receptions were suddenly deserted; the senior aristocrats and the senate of Palermo met at the behest of the praetor, but chose to send humble messages of loyalty to Spain, while the praetor himself set an example by refusing to pay his quota of tax. With the cry of "Long live Philip and the Pope", popular riots broke out to exploit this welcome hiatus in public authority, and prisons and arsenals were raided by malcontents who had suffered from the strict security measures of the Piedmontese. Sometimes the nobility helped to repress these popular movements, but not from any love of Savoy. Only the two Inquisitors accompanied Maffei as he hastened to leave Palermo; but the Spanish General Lede, when he appeared outside the gates, was welcomed by nobles and *maestranze* alike, and the senate once again donned their Spanish clothes and proclaimed the indissoluble ties which bound them to

Madrid. All they wanted was assurance that Lede intended to maintain their privileges and not use their houses for billeting. A large shipload of bullion from Spain then made his arrival still more palatable. In order to restore church services he accepted the Pope's abolition of the Apostolic Legateship. Philip V had been the one to begin this conflict with Rome, but now Cardinal Alberoni, Philip's minister in Madrid, needed papal support against the Piedmontese and Austrians, and incidentally was glad of an excuse to sequester the property of a rival cardinal who held the rich archbishopric of Monreale.

Victor Amadeus desperately called upon the rest of Europe to support the Treaty of Utrecht, and now offered to cede Sicily to Austria in return for Tuscany or Sardinia provided that he could go on calling himself a King. The Austrians, however, had already decided to fight Spanish aggression. The first move in the War of the Quadruple Alliance was that the British fleet, the strongest force in the Mediterranean, annihilated the Spanish navy off the Sicilian coast, and this cut off Spanish reinforcements at the same time as it gave Austrian soldiers free passage across the straits to Messina. Two large armies, Austrian and Spanish, then ravaged the island for a year as they chased each other: their engagement at Francavilla in 1719 was probably the biggest battle fought in Sicily since Roman times. Some areas recognised Philip V, some Victor Amadeus, and some the Archduke Charles who was now Charles VI of Austria; but the Austrians had the advantage that their British ally controlled the sea approaches and could keep them supplied. The retreating Spanish troops carried off cereals and cattle, cut down fruit trees and mulberries, and set fire to the woods. Near Palermo "everything was cut down and destroyed", said an English officer, "and not a house escaped." Not until February 1720 did Philip acknowledge defeat, and even after the armistice a good deal of damage was done by soldiers of both sides. Some towns avoided sack by paying large sums of money. Palermo escaped only by negotiating simultaneously with both Spain and Austria.

The Emperor Charles had been Habsburg claimant to Sicily for over fifteen years, and now he was also King by conquest. The European diplomats drew up the Treaty of London which confirmed his accession. The interests of Sicily bothered no one. A large Austrian army tried to impose firm government, confiscating weapons and forbidding the Palermo guilds to man the city fortifications. Victor Amadeus, now compensated with the kingdom of Sardinia, took away with him some of the Sicilian navy, all the archives of his own reign and some of previous reigns; and a number of the more talented Sicilians went at his invitation to take up jobs in Turin.

The lack of active resistance did not mean that Sicily would readily accept government by yet another foreign power. Some of the best of Victor Amadeus's civil servants were retained by Charles, for example Ignazio Perlongo and Placido Marchese who were responsible for a number of the administrative reforms attempted between 1713 and 1734; but "the Germans never became familiar with Sicilians," wrote Mongitore, "and their barbarous language was unintelligible." Some citizens were scandalised that the new Austrian-appointed Viceroy lived apart from his wife and employed some non-Catholics. His foreign soldiers were soon accused of black marketeering—no doubt correctly, because no army ever had much patience with the excises and control points which made food supply so difficult and expensive. The fact that he did not restore the easy-going ways of Spain told against him, and so did his revocation of titles and jobs granted in the previous year by Philip.

The breaking point came over a simple point of status. Representatives of the privileged classes used to call upon the Viceroy every Christmas, but in 1721 he was suffering from an ulcerated leg: his bedroom was too small for all his visitors to sit down, yet he was unable to stand up. The ecclesiastics and most of the grandees swallowed their pride and did not insist on their right to sit while he was sitting, but the Prince della Cattolica led the city senate in refusing to submit to such an indignity. The elderly Viceroy, who was connected with the Sicilian family of Terranova and knew about the requirements of honour, arrested four senators for their 'criminal obstinacy'. Vienna tried to pacify the parties, but the senators revenged themselves by informing the Austrians about the Viceroy's tax dodges and inefficiency, and he was soon withdrawn.

His successor, a Spaniard who had remained loyal to the Habsburgs, realised that much more tact was needed. Some of the barons were made Princes of the Holy Roman Empire, while the mayor and senators of Palermo were properly recognised as 'grandees of Spain first class', a rank which carried the coveted title of *eccellentissimo*. Any barons accused of harbouring bandits were now treated more leniently than before, and in response to repeated petitions a school was to be set up at government expense where young nobles could be educated free. Furthermore the Church was pacified to the point where Benedict XIII in 1728 repealed the bull of 1715 and allowed a modified version of the Apostolic Legateship to be restored 'in perpetuity'.

The Spanish Inquisition, despite complaints at its excesses and a slight curtailment of its legal powers, was now given its head once again in matters of religion. Contemporary pictures of an *auto da fé* in 1724 show the 'theatre' erected in the cathedral square of Palermo, with the victims wearing conical dunces' hats, while boxes were set up for titled ladies and the clergy, and standing room only for ordinary citizens. People came from afar to see Brother Romualdo and Sister Gertrude burnt alive. On another occasion a victim was about to be treated in the same way for doubting the Trinity and calling the Pope a *pulcinella*—and perhaps even more because he succeeded in corrupting the theologians who tried to instruct him—but at the last moment grace was given this man to repent, and to the great joy of the whole town he sang a Te Deum in front of the Inquisitors who then embraced and kissed his feet; but he lapsed when back in prison, and in 1732 Antonino Canzoneri was the last Sicilian to be burned alive at the stake.

The chief stumbling-block to any government of Sicily was likely to be taxation. Even though the Austrians were ready to pay most of the expenses of their invasion, they expected local contributions towards the cost of a garrison and of additional warships to protect commerce. They also wanted 30,000 *scudi* a year paid to the imperial general, Prince Eugene. The Austrians, like the Piedmontese, were accustomed to more expenditure and more efficient tax collecting than was the practice in Sicily. They wanted new bridges to make the interior more accessible. For the first time ever, and for the last time until the British occupation in the next century, a detailed map of the island was prepared by government engineers. Attempts were also made to make the tax system fairer and less damaging to the economy. In other words, this was in many ways an enlightened administration. Some Sicilians took advantage of the fact to advocate certain particular reforms; but they were a tiny minority, and the general consensus seems to have preferred inaction and low taxes.

The new proposals certainly looked expensive. Parliament met in 1720 after a six-year gap, and, apart from the ordinary *donativi* which had long since passed out of the area of parliamentary decision, the Emperor was granted an extraordinary *donativo* of 600,000 *scudi*—as compared with 400,000 asked by Victor Amadeus in 1714 and only 200,000 by Philip before that. In 1723, another parliament granted 600,000 again; a third in 1728 granted 400,000; in 1732 a fourth voted fully 800,000 *scudi*. Despite protests that the kingdom was very poor, there was apparently no great difficulty about getting these grants accepted, partly because they were only nominal statements of intent to pay, and partly because the leading parliamentarians by now had become skilled in putting a relatively light load on themselves.

The barons, in any case, hardly took parliament seriously

except as a festive occasion; those who turned up could be few enough to ride in a single carriage, and a royal official in 1732 obtained the proxy votes of thirty-six of them who preferred not to attend. By 1720 the number of parliamentary baronies had grown to 229, owned by 99 barons. The five most prominent barons owned 52 votes between them, and controlled many more through their family connections. But they used their influence to resist reform rather than to oppose the Viceroy's financial demands. The barons still contributed nothing to many of the *donativi*, and had the further assurance that the census still could not claim to assess all feudal property; while in the last resort they could always increase the *octrois* on their estates to meet any residual tax liabilities. To make doubly sure, almost all of them now lived in Palermo, and this town was taxed at a tenth and sometimes even less than a tenth of the gross national figure, though its accumulated wealth was such that it was thought to consume about a third of everything produced in the island. Other towns, moreover, were prohibited by parliament from taxing land owned in their areas by residents of Palermo, and it was common knowledge that many individuals who lived elsewhere took out nominal citizenship of Palermo to obtain the benefits of this invaluable privilege. To make up for what these landowners did not pay, foreign residents, royal officials, and a growing body of rentiers were now made into new categories of contributor to the *donativi*, and the clergy's share was increased to what at one point was over a quarter.

Parliamentary taxes were easily granted, but the Viceroy Sastago after 1728 complained that the sums voted bore no relation to the amounts collected. The accounts were "completely irregular and confused"; indeed the Exchequer kept no record at all of many of its payments, and some thought that a more accurate supervision would by itself have doubled the revenue. The Emperor was advised that the incidence of taxation should be changed so that it fell on those who had money to pay, for example by placing a surcharge on luxury imports and by taking a new census to cover all feudal property; what he should not do, said these advisers, was to penalise the poor who had no margin of resources which could still be taxed. Sastago reported that an unbelievable amount of money was spent on extravagant novelties from overseas; and every occasion, from a royal birthday to the opening of parliament, was taken as an excuse by ladies of high society to buy new dresses from abroad. Why these dresses could not be made in Sicily he could not understand.

Another attempt was therefore made to raise more money from the rich. Owing to the inflation of honours, the price of titles had not gone up with the cost of everything else: a dukedom now cost about 4,000 *scudi*, a princedom 7,000; but this could still be an appreciable contribution towards an annual revenue of about a million and a half *scudi*. The King's regalian rights over the cereal storage depots, over the customs, the tunny fisheries, the tobacco monopoly and the sulphur mines, all these could be sold or leased, and there did not lack men of means who looked on them as a good investment. The Prince of Villafranca in 1734 paid a large sum in return for being enfeoffed with the postal service. Other methods of raising money were not so popular. Another forced loan was collected from the bank of Palermo, and the accounts of the civic administration were incidentally submitted to an embarrassing analysis. The King also confiscated the possessions of certain nobles who had followed Philip to Spain and Victor Amadeus to Piedmont. He allowed the barons to compound for their feudal obligation of knight service at 25 *scudi* a head, and this could bring in about 40,000 *scudi*.

Most of the tax revenue still derived in one way or another from cereals. The Austrians even increased the cost of export licences for wheat and put pressure on merchants to buy these at the inflated rate. This helped to lift prices to the point where, as parliament protested in 1728, "our grain lands are abandoned, the workers lack the basic requirements of life, and the feudatories can neither support their workers nor pay the interest on their debts". But the export dues were negligible compared to the excises on flour paid by the Sicilian consumer. These excises were now said to amount to a million *scudi* a year. Here was the chief cause of unemployment and vagabondage. This as much as anything explained the unprofitability of agriculture.

Chapter 26

TRADE AND INDUSTRY UNDER THE AUSTRIANS

The Austrian Viceroys knew that the profitability of their Sicilian venture depended on a radical improvement in the island's economy, for merchants even in Austrian Naples found wheat cheaper to buy in the eastern Mediterranean, and this fact bore hardly on almost everyone in Sicily. Unable to diagnose exactly what was wrong, the government tried as one experimental remedy to make commercial treaties with the rulers of Tunis, Tripoli and Algiers, rejecting what were called "superstitious considerations of affected Christian piety"; and this *rapprochement* with the Barbary powers may have helped wheat exports as it possibly diminished the privateering which had deterred slower-moving ships from visiting Sicilian waters.

They also made a serious effort to revive the commerce of Messina. This town was still under military government and less than half its former size. Most of the silk workers had left, and as tax discrimination lifted the cost of living well above that of Palermo, the exodus continued. Foreign tourists were struck by how many houses at Messina remained empty. Millions of ducats-worth of foreign trade had disappeared, and the customs revenue fell to almost nil. The blame for this was placed by the Messinese on the "pernicious rivalry of Palermo" and on a deliberate attempt by the rest of Sicily to impoverish them. Letters were sent to Vienna insisting that Messina was far more loyal and submissive than Palermo, but begging for her monopoly of silk export once again, since only with an assured monopoly would her factories be able to reopen; the extra inducement was held out that this would enable the King to tax the Sicilian silk industry more heavily than ever, since the export taxes were higher at Messina than elsewhere. Privilege, monopoly and protection, these were the remedies envisaged in this proposal, and there was little thought for the country as a whole or for the wider interests of the silk trade.

Charles duly agreed to give Messina greater privileges as a free port; he agreed to reduce her taxes and to attract newcomers by promising some immunity for crimes committed elsewhere. He allowed the Jews to have a synagogue, though they still would have to wear a yellow badge and return at night to the ghetto. The surrounding villages were also bought back cheaply from those who had bought them after 1680, and were then restored to Messina. The Viceroy was instructed to live there more often. On this last point, Sastago replied to the Emperor with a firm memorandum on how such repeated movement of the Viceroy's court would cause administrative chaos. The continual shifting of the tribunals and archives led to documents being mislaid, and this had allowed the nobility to assert pretended rights and privileges in defiance of central authority: so much so that people as a matter of course now used to wait for the Viceroy's absence before initiating a legal process or trying to bribe some official.

Messina in the end gained much less than she had hoped from these reforms. Foreigners would not so easily be lured back there, and perhaps they were now convinced that the Sicilian market was unprofitable. Silk was bought more cheaply in China. The port dues were infinitely cheaper at Leghorn and Reggio, for Messina was so heavily in debt and so restrictionist in outlook that heavy local taxes made its commerce uncompetitive. The Austrians, too, did not entirely believe in free trade: though commerce was encouraged with Trieste and Austrian Flanders, English cloth merchants met serious discrimination, even to the extent that England began to think of trying to restore the more easily influenced Victor Amadeus. An attempt was made, apparently without much success, to attract capital from Antwerp and Vienna for investment in Sicily. At the request of seventeen Messinese merchants, a joint stock trade company was also projected to operate with government support; but there was too little mutual trust in the mercantile community for it to succeed, and the Viceroy became more pessimistic than ever about the commercial sense of the city fathers. Palermo, not to be outdone, first protested against this company, and then quickly planned a rival trade corporation of their own: its promoters tried to bargain with the government, asking that they and their employees should be exempt from paying parliamentary taxes; they also demanded a twenty-year monopoly over trade in western Sicily.

Sicilians evidently feared to put up risk capital without fairly precise guarantees of success. Above all they required preferential legal privileges. Both these companies thus wanted their own law court with jurisdiction superior to all other courts. A complex of different *fori* and legal systems had grown up gradually over the centuries. Not only the Church courts which gave all the clergy a special immunity, but the Inquisition and the Apostolic Legateship, the Chancellor, the Protonotary, the Royal Mint, the Auditor General of the army, the Admiralty, the tobacco tax collectors, the wheat export council, the crusade tax, the customs, the British and French consuls, even to some extent the *maestranze*, all had a jurisdiction of their own; and members of each *foro* busily tried to establish their own exemption from jurisdiction by the others. In addition, of course, many barons had the *merum et mistum imperium* in their fiefs. Even the general commanding the artillery possessed a special court for his apprentice gunners, and as he had a financial interest in magnifying its competence, he used to sell licenses to anyone who wished to register as an artillery-man and escape the jurisdiction of other courts. Occasionally the government was forced to issue decrees which overrode the 'rights' of *foristi*, and Victor Amadeus had curtailed those of the army, the Inquisition and the Apostolic Legacy; but these regulations were not easy to enforce, and great numbers of lawyers had an interest in preventing reform of such a wonderfully cumbrous system. Nowhere in Europe, commented the Viceroy, were lawyers so artful and slippery, nowhere were cases so long-drawn-out and decisions so hard to reach.

These competing courts systems were an enormous incubus on trade. Merchants and shopkeepers figured prominently among the 'cannon cleaners' licensed by the general of artillery, because this license made it very hard to enforce contracts against them or make them pay their debts. The sponsors of the two projected joint-stock companies explained that commerce needed speed and assurance of contract enforcement, otherwise foreigners would stay away and merchants would neither put up the money for buying raw materials nor give credit to shopkeepers and artisans. Instinctively, however, these sponsors could only suggest making the system still worse by creating an additional *foro* of their own, to which even the tax collectors and the Inquisition would presumably have to submit.

Repeatedly Sastago in 1728–30 complained that 'bad faith' was what made lawyers so flourishing and commerce so depressed. He explained that ministerial departments in charge of commerce had multiplied their staffs to the point where inefficiency was inevitable and cheating positively encouraged: some merchants exported wheat tax-free by means of forged permits; and others, after bribing the right officials, were able to export a hundred thousand bushels although they paid tax only on twenty thousand. One spot check produced fifty people who had improperly secured the exemption from excise duty allowed to fathers of twelve or more children. It was notorious that a vast quantity of goods was also being brought in to Palermo tax-free by ecclesiastics under cover of their clerical immunity, while the illicit manufacture of tobacco by the clergy and their large-scale smuggling operations from Malta were seriously affecting the tobacco tax. Sastago concluded that the "diabolic chaos" of national and local tolls had created a confusion which in itself blocked any increase in the revenue or in trade; and too many people gained from this for there to be much chance of reform.

For a long time people had known about the silver and alum mines of Sicily, and about its deposits of sulphur, lead and 'petrol oil'. At least three times since the 1560s a contractor had been given monopoly rights over all known and unknown minerals in the island, with his own *foro*, and with the right to mine even on private property and to requisition wood for smelting. In the mountains above Messina both Savoyards and Austrians attempted to revive this industry, but here was another field where the environment of feudal Sicily proved unfavourable. Local finance was not forthcoming, and skilled labour had to be imported from Saxony and Hungary. Neighbouring landowners also stirred up their peasants against the foreign miners. Most serious of all were the difficulties encountered over transport, particularly the transport of fuel. Some locally mined silver was used to make coins, but it did not justify the enterprise, and iron was more cheaply imported from Sweden.

These were the last years of the Sicilian sugar industry, an industry which in its time had been so very profitable. Four refineries were still working, each apparently with about four hundred workers, but the closing of sixteen others in the fairly recent past had caused serious unemployment, and the requisite skills once lost were hard to recover. Taxes on export had discouraged production, but the chief factor was probably climatic, since sugar cane in Sicily rarely grew higher than four feet. Brazilian sugar had progressed to the point where it could now undercut Sicilian in price and quality, and 100,000 *scudi* were therefore spent on imported sugar each year. The owners of the surviving refineries went to Vienna in the hope of obtaining help in getting their capital out of the industry, for its survival depended on improved equipment and techniques which they were not prepared to risk. The Austrians, on the other hand, hopefully estimated that at least six more factories could be made economic so long as borrowing was possible at 7 or 8 per cent, and they felt that the saving of foreign currency would be very much in the national interest. A heavy surcharge was therefore placed on imported sugar. But before this tax could have any effect, the wealthy few who were the main consumers of sugar in iced drinks and sweetmeats persuaded the government to rescind it, and sugar cane soon ceased to be grown commercially.

The Austrians optimistically thought that there existed the raw materials and a sufficient market for quite a number of other industries, and the presence of so many beggars indicated that labour was abundant; it therefore seemed to them that Sicily was allowing herself to remain poor unnecessarily. A textile industry hardly existed. Wool was exported raw for lack of home demand,

and for the same reason there was little readiness to exploit natural advantages and grow cotton and flax instead of wheat. Half a million *scudi* a year now went on imported foreign cloth, said a report by di Robilant in 1718, and this took no account of the huge smuggling trade. Even the habits of monks and nuns, indeed everything except the peasants' clothes, had to be imported; so had hats, though these were worn by everyone, and although skins used in making them were exported from Sicily. Some silk stockings were made locally, but most Sicilian silk was now not even spun before export. There were complaints that Sicilian silk cloth was too expensive and of the very worst quality, so that anyone who could afford it bought imported goods. "Every day," said di Robilant, "more people are giving up the habit of wearing silk which prevailed under Spain." The Austrian Viceroy planned a new cloth factory, and hoped to bring in Milanese workers to revive the silk industry at Palermo and Messina; but fourteen years was too short a time to effect any significant change. Some bitter consolation was found in the fact that only if foreigners came to sell cloth would they have any inducement to take back a balancing cargo of Sicilian farm produce.

Other manufactures also languished. A little paper was made in a mill set up at Monreale by Maffei, and there was said to be plenty of water available for other paper factories, but another 100,000 *scudi* a year were spent on paper imported in Genoese ships, and this was an unnecessary expenditure which Sicily could scarcely afford. Only the coarsest glass was made locally, yet some of the main raw materials were exported from Sicily to Venice, and manufactured glass and mirrors were then imported, again at considerable expense. Gunpowder was bought in Genoa, though sulphur, saltpetre and charcoal had been exportable commodities in Sicily itself; and likewise several vegetable colours and fixatives were exported for the dyeing industry which could easily have been used at home. Wine-making was not yet taking advantage of local conditions, though Frenchmen had already discovered that they could buy poor local wines and transform them into something far more saleable. Shipbuilding was on such a small scale that Sicily possessed only about twenty ships capable of reaching Genoa, and cargoes for longer journeys then had to be reshipped out of Genoa in foreign vessels. Northerners were surprised to find so few merchants. There was some coastal trade in large open barges, but "scarcely a decked vessel", wrote Leckie at the turn of the century; Sicilians were unwilling and inexpert navigators who allowed foreigners to take most of the profit which could come from exporting local goods.

Chapter 27

NAPLES AND THE SICILIAN PARLIAMENT

The governments of Turin and Vienna confronted local problems with some initial enthusiasm, but both of them lacked the patience, the tact and the sheer physical force to make much impact on such a traditionalist and static society. Concessions to Messina did not result in rescuing the town from its depression. Improved methods of taxation could be suggested but not easily applied, nor could economic resources be mobilised in a world where most changes were feared and resisted at many different levels of society. Rulers and ruled therefore became disenchanted very quickly with each other. In comparison with Austria or Savoy, Spain could be called decadent, and yet Sicily had become accustomed to the distant and easy-going Spanish government that allowed the nobility a free hand to govern and misgovern their serfs as they wished.

When international tensions momentarily isolated Austria in 1734, another Spanish expedition therefore found it an easy task to retrieve the kingdom which Spain had lost in 1713. There seems to have been no Sicilian rebellion against the Austrians, no organised group which called on Spain for deliverance; but at the first news of a successful Spanish landing, another deputation of nobles from Palermo hurried to meet the invading general and assure him of a welcome just as in 1718. The Austrian army did not put up much of a fight, and what now took place can hardly be called a serious invasion. Sicilians suddenly found their country joined once again to Naples and made into an apanage for Don Carlos, an *Infante* of Spain, who became King with the title of Charles III.

The victory of Charles with so little bloodshed was greeted with what was called "extraordinary enthusiasm". It flattered people to have another real King arrive in person and swear to preserve their laws—though in fact Charles was the last ruler to bother with this empty coronation ceremonial. Palermo was delighted to have him reject the suggestion that he should rightly be crowned in Messina, while the Messinese in compensation were relieved of the last remaining financial penalties imposed in 1679–80. Charles opened up the royal palace, and Palermo half came to life again as the centre of court receptions. After a week, however, he left. All that Sicilians were to see of him in the future was his statue, and this for cheapness' sake was made out of the melted-down bronze from a statue of the Austrian Emperor (and used for previous Kings before that). He had not even remembered to call a parliament to confirm his accession, and there was no doubt that he meant to be primarily King of Naples and govern from a distance. Swiss regiments came to replace German, and strange Neapolitan coins became current. All of this was accepted with resignation.

Even though Sicily was now to be ruled from Naples, the influence of Spain remained strong until the middle of the century. There had been Spanish Viceroys even under the Austrian Habsburgs, and Spanish fashions in dress had again been accepted. Though the Austrians tried to introduce a new note by holding grand balls in the Viennese manner, they quickly gave up the idea when the nobility were too shocked or too shy to turn up. Spanish manners and behaviour were still accepted as the outward sign of gentility, and masquerades and carnivals remained a permanent part of Sicilian life; bull-fights, too, were much enjoyed by all classes throughout the eighteenth century and were not unknown in the nineteenth. Although trade with Spain diminished, Spaniards continued to own large areas of Sicily, and Spanish was still commonly the language of official documents until the 1760s. But the solid undercurrent of Italian cultural influence had always persisted and now became much more marked. Many Viceroys even under Spain had been Italians. The architects of the eighteenth-century Palermo villas had mostly been educated at Rome, and use of the Italian language had become increasingly common alongside the Sicilian dialect. In 1741 the Viceroy opened parliament with a speech read in Italian, though in 1738 he had used Spanish.

When Charles was promoted in 1759 to the throne of Spain, the rest of Europe would not let him keep Sicily and Naples as well; so he presented these two kingdoms to his eight-year-old third son, who became Ferdinand IV of Naples and Ferdinand III of Sicily. Once again the old laws and privileges of the island to which Charles had sworn did not prevent the realm being treated as personal property and the succession being governed merely by dynastic convenience and the balance of power. Some of the Sicilian nobility followed Charles and went to live in Spain. The new King Ferdinand was to call himself an *Infante* of Spain and at first took orders from Madrid; but during his long reign of sixty-six years Sicily more and more developed the links which bound her to Italy.

The Neapolitan Bourbons at first hoped that they might succeed where Austrians and Piedmontese had failed. Charles III, for example, set up a Supreme Magistracy of Trade with wide powers of intervention in economic affairs and with a governing body on which the nobles could be outvoted by merchants and officials. This body had to look after shipping and ship-building. It was intended to control the collection of customs duty and internal communications in general, as well as mines, the salt industry and the fisheries. One of the tasks laid upon it was to collect the statistical information on which economic policy could be based, and this was a very promising line of development. Another obligation was to tackle questions of private indebtedness and insolvency, which were having such harmful effects on trade and the provision of credit.

But instead of welcoming this institution, every vested interest in Sicily was immediately mobilised against it. Parliament repeatedly begged the King to put things back as they were before. So did the Palermo senate. Palermo and Messina in particular disliked the fact that the Magistracy of Trade had also been given authority over price-fixing, food supplies and the urban guilds, for this deprived the towns of much of their power and autonomy. Parliament, among other things, did not like having to surrender control over public works, especially roads and bridges. Many private *fori* found their jurisdiction curtailed and hence less profitable. So did the main tax authorities. Altogether this new institution was far too revolutionary an intrusion into Sicilian politics, and after seven years the King decided to take most of its authority away. His experiment in 1740 of letting the Jews return —he had even allowed them to own Christian slaves—also had to be revoked in 1747 because they were thought a danger to religion.

Such experiences destroyed much of Charles's interest in the development of Sicily's economic potential. He decided rather to play up to the barons with a less active and less interfering administration than that of Turin or Vienna. The extraordinary *donativi* were reduced from 800,000 to 200,000 *scudi*, and little more was heard for a time of any serious schemes of tax reform or social reform. In Naples the monarchy was now developing a stronger centralised state, but the Sicilian *notabili* were allowed to continue behaving as though their privileges were the best guarantee of happiness for their fellow countrymen.

Parliament was an institution which, if it did nothing else, kept alive the nostalgia for a romanticised and to some extent imaginary past, and thus slowed up the process of change. This in part explains the pride in parliament's continued existence and the erudite antiquarianism which invented for it a fictitious ancestry back to Roman times. The three *bracci*, or Houses, were proudly assumed to have been the champions of Sicilian liberties against Spain, Savoy and Austria in turn. So long as these foreign governments remained a convenient scapegoat on which to blame the country's poverty and backwardness, no Sicilians were disposed to suggest that it was rather parliament itself, and the attitude of mind it typified, which were their undoing. As an institution,

Auto-da-fé, 1724, in front of the Archbishop's Palace and Palermo cathedral: the Inquisitors are to the right, and boxes are provided for the
Viceroy and the aristocracy. (From Antonino Mongitore)

Tim Benton

Stucco figure by Giacomo Serpotta in the Oratorio della Compagnia del Rosario di Santa Zita, Palermo: relief of the battle of Lepanto in the top background

parliament had hardly developed at all since the sixteenth century. Several times it had seemed near to taking a real political initiative: many years earlier it had once resisted the arrest of its members, as it had once tried to resist an edict of dissolution, and there had been vague talk of no taxation without representation; but isolated attitudes and talk had never developed in the direction of parliamentary government. The three Houses were made up exclusively of privileged people who had far more to lose than gain from challenging a Viceroy so long as he did not stray too far outside the rules.

The parliamentary barons still flattered themselves, in Mongitore's phrase, that they were "associates of the sovereign" in governing the state. Of all the three *bracci*, the barons constituted, as one Englishman observed "the only order which requires some management"; and whenever parliament assembled, "a profusion of stars, ribbons, and gold keys is therefore distributed" to reward their vanity and maintain their subordination. The other two Houses were of less importance, and consequently had to pay a high proportion of the taxes. The office of representative for a royal town carried no power and led nowhere, so few people wanted it. Representatives were appointed by the town corporation nominally, but in practice usually by the King or some local baron. For convenience they were often lawyers resident in Palermo: the same man might even represent a number of towns. The leader of the domanial House was the only member ever worth recording by name, and he was an aristocrat nominated to this post by the government. Of this man, Lord Valentia commented some years later that, out of forty members, he "has usually 17 or 18 proxies in his pocket, so that he can at all times command a majority". Most Sicilian towns were anyway in the baronial fiefs and so were represented only by their landlords in the baronial *braccio*. Hence the towns and the third estate had no experience of common interest or common action.

The Deputation, the committee which theoretically represented parliament between sessions and was claimed as another palladium of Sicilian liberties, had long since become hand-picked almost exclusively from a few dozen aristocratic families. Since membership still carried the title of 'Excellency' and the right to wear a hat in the Viceroy's presence, mere commoners were discouraged; and the fact of nomination by the Viceroy seems even to have been welcomed by the select few just because it was a convenient means of excluding everyone else. This committee retained some function in tax collecting and managing the census. It was, in theory, under instruction to avoid taxing the really poor and to ensure that the truly rich paid proportionally to their wealth; it was also charged not to allow personal friends to escape nor enemies to suffer unfairly; but there was no force behind these general admonitions. The delaying power exercised by the Deputies was sometimes not inconsiderable: for instance, whereas the census of 1714 took only two years to complete, that of 1747 took them twenty-three years, after which time its figures were quite out of date (and yet the barons formally objected to having another one).

One block to constitutional development was that so much of the revenue lay outside the competence of parliament; hence members of parliament had little leverage and so were less preoccupied with power than with status. Of the taxes for which their consent was nominally required, all the ordinary *donativi* were in fact accepted automatically by each parliament; once granted they were never challenged again. Only the King's demand for a large extraordinary *donativo* gave them any chance to assert themselves, and here the almost absolute power which the barons wielded in their fiefs left them little incentive to develop their nominal right of objection; nor did their right of petition ever blossom into a truly legislative activity. Petitions were occasionally serious and responsible, for instance those which requested more roads and more protection against the corsairs; but for the most part they continued to be at the level of asking the King to choose more noblemen as army officers or to appoint more Sicilians as bishops. In any case the King had absolutely nothing to fear if he refused to accept parliamentary requests. Victor Amadeus had derisively spoken of the "ice-cream parliament", since eating ice-cream seemed to be the members' most noticeable occupation during sessions.

Parliaments were still very short. The business accumulated in three years of recess could sometimes be completed in two or three meetings, after which the Viceroy might graciously invite members (not of course the representatives of the towns) to music and refreshment. Sessions were taken up not so much in deciding what petitions to present, nor about the amount of tax—indeed the King now confirmed that the *donativi* were no longer to be thought of as voluntary gifts—but the debates were rather over who should pay. On one occasion there was a heated discussion over the 'solemn' matter of the order of precedence for coaches at the opening of parliament. Sometimes more serious issues must have been debated, but we rarely hear much about them. In 1741, when discussion went on for some days, this was because the president of parliament was on this occasion the Bishop of Syracuse who was a notoriously litigious and independent character, and Sicily was being called on to support Philip's purely Spanish policy in north Italy. On another occasion, in 1746, the royal towns were bold enough to complain that they carried an unfair share of the agreed burden, but their complaint was not taken seriously.

Yet another hitch in the usually prearranged performance occurred in 1754, when the Viceroy obtained the amount of tax he had requested but was thought to have used too much coercion. A contemporary diary explained that the Marquis of Spaccaforno

> was the only person to protest, and he told the Viceroy that the King would not be well served by putting a burden on the country which it could not stand; nor was it proper to restrict the freedom of parliamentary discussion. The marquis therefore invited a number of barons to attend private meetings in his house so that they could consider what answer they should make to the government and how they should spread the taxes. . .; but in the end the King's wishes were agreed to, and no one did more than murmur against it.

The Marquis was in fact sent to prison for being rude to the Viceroy, and we are told that no one protested against the fact.

An equally serious subject of debate would have been the system of tax apportionment, for this could be attacked from many directions as being at the same time cumbersome, unproductive and unfair. Not only was there still no properly funded debt, but in a sense there was no national system of taxation at all. As far as the parliamentary taxes were concerned, every area and township was allocated its quota by the parliamentary Deputation, and then the local *notabili* still had uncontrolled discretion to decide how and from whom they should find the money. Moreover, the censuses of population and property were very unreliable as a basis for this procedure, as can be seen by the variations from one to the next.

It was remarkable that any census could be taken at all, but the usefulness of the figures obtained was limited by the fact that they were based on voluntary declarations of income for which there could be little if any check. Many people must have been left out altogether, quite apart from the privileged classes who were given special exemptions, and the Deputation sometimes found the figures so grossly and obviously inaccurate that they arbitrarily 'corrected' them before making their final returns. In thus fabricating the census figures, they assured the Viceroy that they "put all prejudice aside", but they still did not escape being accused of favouring their rich friends and the baronial towns. One of the basic and most inequitable divisions for tax purposes was still that between royal and feudal territory. By the 1747–70 census there were, not counting Palermo, 780,000 people officially registered in feudal territory compared with 395,000 outside; yet each of these two groups had to find much the same amount of tax, and one royal town might thus pay half as much again as a nearby feudal city which had twice its population.

At a time when reforms in Naples were making the incidence of tax more equitable and less economically harmful, in Sicily the exemptions established by each House of parliament were an obstacle in the way of any similar development. No interested party wished to stir up trouble by protesting against the excessive number of different taxes which had grown up piecemeal over the centuries, or against the different criteria used in their collection, or the different courts responsible for enforcing them, nor against the fact that some taxes cost more to collect than they were worth. If export duties on wheat were disliked by the landed proprietors, if taxes on domestic silk manufacture and export were resented by the merchant aristocracy, the sufferers never took their opposition beyond a certain point, for on balance the existing system treated them favourably enough to make any radical change unwelcome.

PART 8

Society and the Enlightenment:
The Eighteenth Century

Chapter 28

CEREALS AND THE ECONOMY

In the first half of the eighteenth century, Sicily in a good year may still have produced twice as much wheat as she consumed, but on average the amount exported was declining, and the annual variations in production were enormous and almost certainly much larger than they used to be. After two good harvests in succession, growers might have surplus wheat to feed to their pigs, and the next year would let land go out of cultivation; after a bad harvest, however, high grain prices could lead to ploughing more land, even to killing off herds of cattle for this purpose and burning down scrub on the mountainside. In very bad years, less wheat was grown than was needed for domestic consumption and supplies would have to be imported. Although landowners complained in 1706 against people being allowed to buy foreign cereals, some imports seem to have been needed and permitted in about one year out of ten.

Many explanations were suggested why Sicily, when agriculture elsewhere was beginning to experience a great development, could no longer regularly balance her economy by selling grain to the outside world. Wheat had been invented in ancient Sicily, said Mongitore, and so had all the basic agricultural implements, but too little had been done since then to keep abreast of changing techniques and circumstances. Primitive methods of cultivation, landlord absenteeism, unremunerative contracts of labour, these were possible explanations of why things had changed. One remedy proposed by a foreign resident at Messina in 1713 was to "make the *titulati* treat their tenants better and so encourage cultivation of the countryside"—and to stop the nobles from protecting bandits, he added. An increasing intensity of drought was another possible factor. Climatic changes in North Africa were possibly responsible for the fact that great armies of locusts used to descend on Sicily for years at a stretch, clogging the water supplies and leaving not a green leaf anywhere. The Church developed a special ceremony to curse these locusts, and bounties were given for them to be swept up in sackloads. Possibly, however, their visitations were no more frequent than before, only more dangerous to a community that was outgrowing its food supplies.

A population of probably not much more than a million in 1700 was half as much again by the end of the century. According to the Marquis of Villabianca, whose diaries are a major source for the history of these years, domestic food requirements seemed in 1775 to have doubled in living memory; yet production was not keeping pace, and the agronomist Balsamo insisted that Sicilian wheat production even in quite good areas was no more than six times the quantity of seed. The changing distribution of population made things still more difficult, because people were moving in to the cities and left the agricultural areas impoverished. Judging by the census returns, some villages lost half their population in the course of a century, and others altogether disappeared. A seasonal shortage of labour necessitated workers coming from Calabria, and on at least one occasion landowners were recruiting labourers as far away as Dalmatia.

Government policy only added to the difficulties. As a parliamentary petition complained in 1742, "agriculture is generally self-regulating and needs no more than the hard work of farmers; but when the government tries to interfere, the result is complete confusion; expenses increase all round, the normal pattern of farming is overthrown, many people go bankrupt and give up altogether". Yet the government could not help interfering. In the first place it needed revenue, and the flour excise was not only the easiest tax to collect and the hardest to evade, but it fell mainly on the poor and so was much more acceptable to parliament and civic authorities than a land tax would have been. One British vice-consul thought this the most fundamental reason of all for the backwardness of the Sicilian economy, since the tax system "has been invented to make the poor pay for the rich". These *octrois* depressed standards of living, and the numerous excise barriers and the officials which they required were a potent obstacle to trade. They restricted consumption and led to unfortunate reprisals between one village and the next. Their collection was leased out to private individuals who bid for them at a certain price; the successful contractors then tried to recoup the cost as soon as possible, and were allowed to enlist private bodies of armed police for the purpose.

The government also took upon itself the responsibility of ensuring that enough food was retained in Sicily to meet any emergency. Every consignment for export still needed government permission, so that sometimes, as Balsamo complained, the Sicilian farmer was penalised rather than rewarded for his pains. The procedure of control had changed little. The 'third part' of the harvest had to be surrendered at a controlled price to local authorities, and the rest had to go to the royal *caricatoi* for storage. Each year in December the *Maestro Portulano* calculated how much had been deposited, how much seed would be needed for the winter sowing, how much flour for feeding the population until the next June, and then he decided how much could be exported. Again in

April he made another estimate in the light of prospects for the harvest. On each occasion, if there was enough grain to spare, he would invite applications to buy the *tratte* or export licences, and these would vary in price according to supply and demand. If he allowed too much to be exported, the country would starve; if he asked too high a price for the *tratte*, exports would collapse and farmers might be ruined.

The chief beneficiaries of this system were the grain brokers at Palermo who sometimes bought a crop *sur souche* or before it had even been planted. Occasionally they could raise and lower prices in a single day and so manipulate both growers and exporters simultaneously. These were the people who could afford export licences, and in their hands the *tratte* became a negotiable currency. It was said in 1726 that almost the whole trade was controlled by half a dozen brokers. In the 1760s a single man, Gazzini from Genoa, was able by himself virtually to regulate the price of wheat and so the cost of living. His interests were neither those of the consumer nor of the farmer. If he could persuade the *Maestro Portulano* that there was not enough wheat for export, an embargo might be declared, with the result that the price would fall and he could buy cheaply; then if subsequently he could give exaggerated reports of the harvest, the government might permit more than the safe amount of exports and the consequent rise in prices was sheer gain.

Often there was some official who would help the brokers make this double killing. The corn laws needed a large bureaucracy, mostly of lawyers who knew little about commerce, and foreigners reported that to obtain a licence from these officials one might have "to bribe through thick and thin". One Viceroy, Prince Corsini, made a good deal of money out of the grain trade in the 1740s, and of course was accused of using his position improperly. Similar criticisms were also made against the family of one of his successors, Fogliani. More to the point, the *Maestro Portulano* after the 1720s stopped his regular inspections of the *caricatoi*, and this opened the way to all kinds of sharp practice. Hard wheat was mixed with soft, or was diluted with chaff and otherwise adulterated, or else was soaked to increase its weight. One British ambassador reported that "in no case are the injunctions as to the quantity of corn to be exported strictly adhered to". Another ambassador, Sir William Hamilton, reported that "sometimes the excess will amount to ten times the quantity limited, especially when the corn is loaden at many different ports. Hence it sometimes happens that a year of real abundance becomes in the end insufficient for the internal consumption."

One effect of artificial prices and controls was to make smuggling

highly profitable. Inevitably the evidence for this is more circum-
stantial than statistical. Some landowners, the so-called 'grain
barons', had the privilege of exporting without licence from their
own private ports or *scari*, and it is likely that other people took
advantage of this loophole in the system. The French Dominican,
Père Labat, observed at Messina in 1711 that the customs boats
while pretending to control contraband were really engaged in it
themselves. A British consul was accused of smuggling in 1717, but
managed to put the blame on his servants; and in 1768 the French
consul at Palermo was actually arrested for the same offence.
Part of the trouble was that the customs, like the excises, were
rented out and so became a private perquisite. Lack of supervision meant that the Palermo customs office—at least for three
years when we have information, in 1714, 1723 and 1767—was
full of pay-offs, kick-backs and feather-bedding; and one may
guess that this was true for many other years and other offices
where the relevant figures are less well known. One report to
Victor Amadeus estimated that, if only frauds could be eliminated,
the prevalent rate of customs could be reduced by two-thirds and
still bring in the same amount of money.

Nothing had changed by the end of the century. In 1790,
another British consul thought that a third of Sicilian cereal
produce was "occulted by the growers and not reported", and
some landowners told the jurist di Blasi that they regularly concealed a half or even two-thirds of the harvest. Merchants trying
to buy grain for England after 1789 discovered that it was
enormously more profitable for the brokers to forge permits and
export illegally to France in return for church plate confiscated by
the French revolutionaries: indeed it was then estimated that well
over a million bushels on average were leaving the island each
year as contraband—in other words as much as might go in legal
export. Meat, animals, barley, vegetables, wine and silk were also
smuggled out of the country to avoid export tax, just as silks and
tobacco were smuggled in the other direction. Moreover public
opinion was strongly behind the smugglers on principle and from
economic interest. When the Marquis della Rajata was murdered
in church by a smuggler he had punished, the assassin was
publicly applauded. On another occasion, after the Knights of St.
John from Malta had thrown some of the tobacco control police
into the sea, bystanders were only too happy to help in smuggling
their illicit cargo into Palermo.

That the whole traffic in commodities was under severe strain
can be best seen in the difficulties of providing Palermo with food.
In 1683 the city set up the *colonna frumentaria*, a buying and selling
organisation for stabilising the supply and demand of flour.

Citizens were forbidden to bake at home, and to the Viceroy's agreeable surprise they apparently accepted this prohibition without much fuss; instead, the municipality was given monopoly rights to sell bread at a fixed price and weight. The same policy of subsidised price stabilisation was applied to oil, meat, cheese and charcoal. This was meant to ensure cheap supplies and prevent big price fluctuations. In normal years it also was intended to accumulate a profit which could be used in times of dearth. Of a municipal income which just tipped 300,000 *scudi* in 1717, 250,000 *scudi* came from wheat and flour, 2,000 from meat. As inflation progressed, however, Palermo found herself tied to a selling price which for political reasons could not be raised as fast as the cost price of flour, and the *colonna* was soon running at a loss.

This did not become obvious until the catastrophic harvest of 1763 when stocks failed in the countryside and peasants poured into the city to find cheap subsidised food. Living and sleeping in the open streets, they spread disease, and there were bitter clashes between them and the townsmen. The attempt by Palermo to seize provisions in the countryside by force sent purchase prices rocketing still further, and emergency supplies of food had to be sought from as far away as England and the Levant. A million *scudi* were spent on buying abroad; yet thirty thousand people were reported dead of disease or starvation. Desperately the Viceroy offered to pardon hoarders who produced hidden stocks. He asked landowners to take responsibility for feeding their own peasants and prevent them entering town, while guards were posted round the city walls to stop bread being thrown to friends waiting outside. Nevertheless, even in these conditions of famine, the Prince della Cattolica was able to export 20,000 bushels from his feudal estates at Siculiana by a privilege dating from 1450; and at current prices this must have been immensely profitable.

Only in June 1764 did the new harvest bring prices down, and the one limiting factor in the summer drought was a lack of water to work the mills. The 1765 harvest was even better. Some growers and merchants at first tried to pretend the contrary so that they could keep prices up, but eventually *tratte* seem to have been granted for as much as four million bushels. Sudden cash sales made people forget the previous shortage. It had become profitable to plant quite poor marginal land with wheat, yet with existing methods of cultivation this caused further land erosion, especially on the hillsides; it also meant that more pasture was brought under tillage, and this once again meant fewer draught animals and less manure, both of which in the end helped to make wheat production more difficult. Each swing of the pendulum thus brought its own losses, and some of them would have been impossible to repair without a fundamental change in agricultural techniques.

Arnolfini, an economist from Lucca who visited Sicily in 1768, did not believe those farmers who thought that cereals were still profitable. In years of real abundance, too much wheat was produced, and it sometimes did not even pay to reap it; whereas in a scarcity the profits were limited because of fixed prices and a prohibition of export. Nor was his pessimism more than a little exaggerated. In 1772–3 very little export could be allowed and only through a few favoured merchants; in February 1774 all exports were stopped; again, in 1775, Palermo put pressure on the Viceroy and halted exports so that prices would fall and permit restocking of the municipal granaries. Palermo and consumers in general strongly favoured this system of controls and protection. The grain barons and many government officials also gained from it.

The effect on the economy as a whole, however, was not so beneficial. Naturally the growers reacted to increasing controls by if possible avoiding, or at least delaying, despatch of their produce to the *caricatoi*, and this vitiated the whole system just because it upset the calculation of what stocks were available for export. Lying at Palermo harbour in July 1775 were a hundred and fifty cargo vessels hoping for export licences, but after months of waiting they had to depart empty to the Levant with their much-needed foreign currency. For the third successive year, the British consul expressed the disappointment and anger of foreign shipowners with the uncertainty of this system of *tratte*. It seemed to him an obvious reason why alternative markets were gaining ground and why some Sicilian wheatlands were only spasmodically in production.

He might have added that the hard Sicilian wheat was difficult to mill and so was losing favour in overseas markets, while soft wheat, which the arid areas of Sicily could not grow nearly so well, produced far bigger yields in milder climates and so could now be bought much more cheaply. The main advantages of *grano duro* were, first its ability to grow in a climate of great heat and dryness, secondly its keeping qualities in the deep rock storages of the *caricatoi*—where there were recorded instances of it lasting for twenty-five years in perfect condition. By comparison, the soft wheat of the Crimea and northern Europe was more liable to rot on long sea voyages. Already, however, faster journeys and better storage methods were beginning to make this ancient advantage less important. At the same time, moreover, the higher costs in Sicily of production and transport, together with the export tax, not to speak of excises, bribe money and the merchants' rigging of prices, all these were adding to the prime costs of agriculture and allowing other countries to overtake Sicily in the grain trade. Russian ships were soon being allowed through the Bosporus into the Mediterranean, and the higher-yielding, low-cost wheat from the Ukraine and the Crimea would soon be sold even inside Sicily itself. Natural and man-made causes were combining to destroy the main economic advantage which had supported the island through so many centuries.

In 1775 the Prince of Castelnuovo made a report to the Viceroy which, while accepting that the government had to make money out of wheat export, pointed out that controls must be effective to be justified. What with smuggling, the baronial *scari*, the corruption of civil servants, and the difficulty of supervising storage magazines, the existing procedures just did not meet the needs of a growing population. Castelnuovo wanted fewer *caricatoi* and severe penalties for malfeasance; but this suggestion, to say nothing of his proposal for regular inspection of the *caricatoi* and for not selling any office to do with wheat control, cut too close to the bone. From Villabianca's diary we know that a number of landowners were managing to profit from the difficult years after 1763, and this is also suggested by the size of the villas and palaces they were building: these men were not eager for reforms which would merely benefit the community as a whole. When a rich Sicilian landowner, the Marquis della Sambuca, became the King's first minister at Naples, obviously such a man had no interest in challenging the privileged classes. Castelnuovo, therefore, though he sent frequent protests to the government about the fraudulent practices he had discovered, did not receive so much as a reply.

Nevertheless his report shows the existence of some disquiet among the more enlightened of the aristocracy; and even a man of the old school like Villabianca, as a member of the Palermo senate, was beginning to understand that protectionist doctrines and fixed prices could result in starvation and the bankruptcy of the city government. This common sense view was no doubt reinforced by the private criticisms of Arnolfini and other visitors; one or two people may even have been impressed by the reasoning of the Physiocrats and Adam Smith. The *tratte* were obviously a defective tax now that there was no longer a guaranteed overseas market for Sicilian wheat. They varied too much from year to year to be a satisfactory revenue-producer, and by being so easily evaded they were a positive encouragement to bribery and contraband. Their injurious effect on agriculture was obvious when they dissuaded foreign buyers and when their very irregularity encouraged woodland to be first ploughed up and then abandoned to the ravages of soil erosion.

Chapter 29

LAND TENURE AND THE ROAD SYSTEM

Contracts of labour and land tenure were coming to present a special problem of their own for the farming community. In the seventeenth century there had been an increase in the number of *enfiteusi*, the long-term leaseholds or permanent copyholds by which landowners attracted labour to their estates; and in some villages almost everyone thus acquired a little land of their own. Clearly there had been good economic reasons for this. Landowners obtained rents from hitherto barren land, as well as profitable rights of jurisdiction and miscellaneous payments in money or kind. As for the tenant farmers, instead of single-year contracts which encouraged disastrous over-cropping of the land for the maximum immediate return, they themselves would receive the value of any long-term improvements they might introduce. It paid them to work hard, to invest in the land, and in some areas to plant more profitable but more difficult and longer-term crops than wheat.

This trend towards longer leases was not maintained through the eighteenth century. Some *enfiteusi* were abandoned by un-enterprising tenants or when times were hard; the kind of harvest failures which occurred in 1728, 1746 and 1763 forced many farmers into debt to keep their families alive, or they had to sell their oxen and farm implements. Absentee landowners, too, no longer had quite the same incentive as before to found new villages or the same interest in attracting labour by granting long leases. On the contrary, inflation was reducing the value of fixed *enfiteusi* rents, and leasehold farms were being divided between heirs to the point where rent collection and good farming were alike difficult or impossible. While the more successful copyholders were being provocative enough to compete with the baronial *latifondi* in selling wheat, the less successful caused equal offence by defaulting on their payments, and many laws testify to the difficulty experienced by landowners if they lent money or animals and tools to their tenants.

When *enfiteusi* contracts were unilaterally cancelled by land-owners, the government made no objection, for it was politically expedient to allow the barons wide powers in their fiefs. Economi-cally, too, the indebtedness of many aristocrats was a serious problem which threatened the whole economy and had if possible to be alleviated. Hence the King in 1752 formally confirmed the arbitrary abrogation of these copyholds and did not even stipulate that tenants should be compensated for any capital improvements they had introduced. In this casual way, one vital incentive for agricultural development was lost; the growth of smaller farms was arrested, and a preference was shown instead for day labourers and share croppers who had little interest in long-term betterment. Further legislation in 1769–72 against the accumulation of land by the Church had a similar effect unintentionally, for when holders of *enfiteusi* on ecclesiastical lands were made freeholders, the Church understandably ceased granting leaseholds, and here too the result was to encourage less intensive and more inefficient methods of agriculture.

The preferred contract now was what was called the *gabella*, something which had been known before 1600 and was common a hundred years later. A *gabella*, since it comprised a large area, fitted easily into a world of fiefs and large ranches. Especially now that the barons lived in Palermo, they preferred a single *gabelloto* who would supervise a large estate, who would pay punctually, in advance, and would relieve them of the bother and indignity of dealing with individual peasants. The *gabelloto* was sometimes a very rich man. Occasionally he was a foreigner, and in the seventeenth century the Salaparuta estates had been farmed by a Genoese who even owned a Van Dyck. Usually, however, he was someone who had emerged from the peasantry, either by clever farming, or money-lending, or by using strong-arm measures to assert his authority in a neighbourhood. He may originally have been the chief of the force employed by a baron as a rural police on the large estates: becoming a field guard was a familiar way of acquiring local power and influence. By the 1770s these *gabelloti* were referred to as the new tyrants of the countryside; some were already rich and aspiring to become aristocrats themselves. They had the reputation of being more ruthless than the landlords, more anxious to repudiate the earlier *enfiteusi* contracts, and this helped to reduce the peasants to a status of absolute dependence with a day-to-day or at most a yearly contract.

The *gabella* was usually for three years or possibly six, because landlords found that short tenancies were the least troublesome way of keeping abreast of inflation; but this of course carried the incidental disadvantage that few practising farmers would have much interest in capital-intensive agriculture, for instance in planting vines, citrus or olives. Managers and labourers alike, lacking security of tenure, would be looking for quick returns. Being forced to pay rent in advance, a new tenant would be encouraged to slaughter animals and cut down timber, both of which processes had already gone much too far. His interest was in ploughing up virgin soil, overcropping it with wheat year after year and leaving it abandoned after expiry of his contract. This was the easiest kind of farming on a *latifondo* whenever a landlord had lost interest in developing his estates. It rarely produced more than nine bushels an acre, and, in the absence of proper crop rotation, the land was left wastefully uncultivated every other year.

Balsamo lamented that, when English agriculture was being transformed by leaseholds, the *gabella* contract was regressive, while the *gabelloti* themselves had as their objective to live as gentleman capitalists remote from the land. He would have been quite happy with large estates if only they were well cultivated, for in his view *enfiteusi* had often been too small for efficient farming. But from what he could see in 1792, hardly a single landowner in all Sicily was an active farmer: not only would they not invest in the land themselves; they would allow only the kind of contracts which discouraged other people from doing so. Share croppers were expected to provide most of the working capital on the farm, even though they themselves could hardly make ends meet and had no interest in what Balsamo called efficient agricultural methods. A large class of industrious people was thus made useless to the state. At a time when there was an agricultural revolution at work in northern Europe, in Sicily you could ride for hours without seeing a farmhouse, a road, or even a tree, since nearly all the profits of agriculture were spent in the towns where the landlords lived. Here was a fundamental reason why Sicilian agriculture was becoming uncompetitive. The rents taken by these absentee landlords ought either to have been invested productively, or else reduced by half; yet either alternative was, for social and political reasons, unacceptable.

Towards the end of the century, a small class of intellectuals was beginning to recognise this impasse. Not only Paolo Balsamo, but Sergio, Guerra, Giarrizzo and de Cosmi drew attention to different aspects of it. Much fertile land was regularly left fallow and uncultivated; much was producing a feeble crop of wheat though conditions were far more suitable for olives and mulberries. The smaller farms which the Piedmontese had wanted to introduce were now being positively discouraged, and most Sicilians were thus condemned to a half-time job on the sparsely cultivated *latifondi*. Guerra said that two-thirds of Sicily was absolutely barren and the rest cultivated only by the most primitive means.

The *latifondisti* could argue with some justice that drought, as well as the absence of roads and capital, made this the easiest kind of agriculture for them, but in part they were merely trying to justify a way of life they preferred. Longer leases and greater security of tenure could have made agriculture much more productive at little cost to anyone, and this would not have been

The baroque church of San Giorgio, Ragusa,
by Rosario Gagliardi: consecrated 1738

Tim Bent

The Chiesa Madre at Palma di Montechiaro, a town founded in the 17th century by the Lampedusa family

The church of San Antonio at Buscemi, near Syracuse: an 18th-century example of the vernacular baroque

Tim Bent

incompatible with the system of *latifondi*. A simple change by which beans were planted every third year could have had important results, but it would have also needed a radical change of outlook. The Austrians in the 1720s had concluded that Sicily was poor when there was no reason for it to be; and now Balsamo and de Cosmi confirmed that Sicilian agriculture should be giving four times its present yield; Niccolò Palmeri, a few years later, said six times.

Better roads and bridges would have been the first requisite of a prosperous agriculture. Communications were probably not as good as they had been in Roman times. Except for a few miles of paved road outside Palermo, the only means of travel by land in 1700 was along circuitous mule tracks or *trazzere*, the wide sheep runs used by wandering herdsmen; and these had to traverse river beds which in winter could be impassable. The number of people drowned fording these rivers was said to be greater than that lost at sea. Wheeled transport was impossible, because the few bridges were high one-arched constructions wide enough only for a *lettiga*, which was a travelling *vis-à-vis* slung between one mule in front and another behind.

Much of the island was therefore more or less inaccessible. Sergio and Guerra commented distantly on the almost savage aspect of the 'mountaineers' living out of touch with civilisation and sometimes at a primitive level: the landowners knew little about these people, and little enough even about their own villeins, for they rarely faced the inconvenience of travelling to their estates. The high cost of transport from the *latifondi* to the coast was a major reason for the increasing uncompetitiveness of Sicilian wheat exports, and there was a public complaint that agricultural prices in 1711 barely paid for more than transporting produce to the ports. This problem of communications explains why fuel was so expensive in the towns, why industry in consequence was so limited, and why building materials—including road-building materials—were so difficult to obtain inland. Transport costs also help to explain the poverty and ignorance of the peasants, why they often had no option but to sell their produce to the local boss, why there was so little incentive to grow a marketable surplus of anything, why they usually had to waste up to six or seven exhausting hours a day travelling over bridle paths to their work and could carry with them only the most primitive and ineffective kind of plough.

Because of poor communications, the Viceroy and his staff were unfamiliar with the inland provinces, even though the most remote areas were no more than forty-five miles from the coast. Officials usually preferred to travel by boat. In 1727, the Viceroy was riding by the coast road to Messina in October, but had to turn back because mud and swollen streams blocked his path. In 1734, when a rough sea forced him once again to go to Messina by land, he managed to get through at a rate of twenty miles a day, but the army reckoned that ten miles a day was good going along this most frequented of all Sicilian routes. From Trapani in the west to Messina 225 miles away in the east was generally a three-week journey. The different regions of Sicily therefore knew surprisingly little of each other. In 1743, when the plague did not spread from Messina, this was because the main commercial port of Sicily was easily cut off from the rest of the island. Far more remote still was the interior, without schools, without money, almost always without police, where the government writ did not run, and where gangs of malefactors obeyed a code of justice and behaviour all their own.

A proper network of highways would have done more to change economics, politics and even morals than any other reform, and the Marquis Giarrizzo thought over-optimistically that with good will it would take only five years of serious work to achieve. The obstacles were as much social as financial. Proper roads would have been expensive, given the nature of the country, and would also have needed a more than conceivable efficiency and honesty in the barons of the parliamentary Deputation who supervised the tax money allocated to public works. A proper road system thus presupposed a reduction in parliamentary privilege and an altogether more forceful attitude by the Viceroy. It would have needed either more private enterprise by individual landowners, or at least the much readier acceptance by them of communal responsibility and higher taxation. The annual sum allocated for the purpose by government and parliament was still only eight thousand *scudi* in the 1740s, the same as it had been a century and a half before, and this was only a bare fifth of what were now the Viceroy's personal emoluments; such an exiguous sum (to which the leading barons did not contribute) disappeared with little trace. Since every rich person lived on the coast where they could move by boat, the expense of road-building must have seemed excessive to them. It was even suggested that some barons might have no wish to make their estates more accessible to the disruptive forces of public law and a market economy.

Only in the immediate neighbourhood of the big towns was any trouble taken, for here there was at least a call for carriageways to the suburban villas which were now an essential appurtenance of town life. When King Victor Amadeus arrived in 1713, a little road-levelling was quickly done on the routes he was expected to follow; though a few years later some of these very same places were once again impassable on horseback. On the main western track to Trapani, barely eight miles outside the capital, muleteers in 1750 were losing animals every day on the slippery mountain path. To the east of Palermo, Butera and the other nobles who lived ten miles away in the fashionable resort of Bagheria were able to insist on adequate road maintenance. To the south, the Archbishop of Monreale in the 1760s at last made a five-mile-long carriageway to his cathedral, using gunpowder to cut into the rocky hillside; but beyond that point wheeled traffic could not go. Near Catania, Prince Biscari in 1777 built a bridge over the river Simeto, but after four years it was carried away in a storm, and, fifty years later, travellers on this main highway still had to ford the largest river in Sicily.

Not until the 1770s did road construction become a question of serious public interest. Parliament itself then complained that "as no money penetrates inland, agriculture suffers, the labourer cannot become a proprietor, and the land is not divided up into smallholdings". The King therefore ordered a Neapolitan military engineer, General Persichelli, to draw up plans for a main road inland between Palermo and Catania, with other radial roads running to Messina and the main *caricatoi* on the south coast. The annual parliamentary grant was trebled to pay for this, and towns were allowed to set up toll barriers to finance local construction. Convict labour and troops could be used, and permission was accorded for the compulsory purchase of land, while even the privileged classes were told that they would have to forfeit any tax exemptions and pay their share.

Obstructionism, however, made Persichelli's job impossible, and perhaps as an outsider he never quite realised the difficulties. Even if the bureaucracy had been more efficient, the problem would still have remained that the department of road construction did not want certain irregularities exposed, and some of its favoured contractors had no qualifications at all for the job. Towns and landowners sometimes fought each other over alternative routes, and created trouble over any project which was not to their advantage. Palmeri remarked that one could deduce from the routes chosen the names of the landowners serving on the Deputation. Even the basic difference between those who wanted a coast road and those who preferred Persichelli's scheme was not resolved. Once again the Viceroy's authority was insufficient to carry out government policy against local non-co-operation, and the century ended without Sicily having any roads worthy of the name.

Chapter 30

THE NOBILITY

Baronial influence was as strong in eighteenth-century Sicily as anywhere in Europe. The barons owned most of the land even though they paid only a fraction of the taxes. They possessed feudal lordship over about 280 out of 360 villages, so that most Sicilians lived under their direct jurisdiction; while the minuscule middle class relied utterly on them and seldom showed much independence. At the end of the eighteenth century the titled aristocracy consisted of 142 princes, 788 marquises, and about 1500 other dukes and barons, quite apart from the boasters of pretended titles that were sufficiently common to be legislated against. About twenty families among this nondescript proliferation possessed overwhelming economic power.

The *titolati* had multiplied much faster than the rest of the population despite the fact that their birth rate seems to have been lower than the average. The selling of titles had been a method of taxing the rich. It might conceivably have provided a beneficial element of social mobility except that the latest comers tried hard to identify with their predecessors. This was a closed world only in attitude, not in composition. A penniless lawyer, Joppulo, became immensely rich after a few years as a senior civil servant, and married into the aristocracy. Another humble official suddenly emerged as the Prince of Campofiorito. A few merchants and even some *gabelloti* could aspire to buy up the titles of insolvent aristocrats. By 1800 the nominal price of a barony was perhaps no more than a hundredth of what it had been two centuries earlier, but though this in one sense debased the currency of peerage, in another it whetted the appetite for honours as more people needed to buy promotion out of a constantly depreciating caste. The Neapolitan historian Colletta, after his experience as military governor at Palermo, was to remark that "nowhere in the world is a title or medal so much prized as in Sicily". The head of the most senior of the twelve branches of the Ventimiglia family, the Marquis of Geraci, portentously invented for himself the title 'by the Grace of God, Chief Lord of the Sicilies and First Count of Italy'; which still did not save him from arrest by the police, who inadvertently came upon him when they were raiding the house of an actress in Naples.

Although for convenience one may speak of 'the aristocracy', this was of course not one indistinguishable group. Try though they might to identify, the owners of new creations were still divided by a special degree of snobbery from older titles, and Viceroys disregarded this difference at their peril. Some nobles were very rich indeed, most were poor; a very few were cultivated *grands seigneurs*, many more were entirely illiterate. There was a down-at-heel provincial nobility who failed to afford life at Palermo, as well as a new and more mercantile aristocracy in the growing town of Catania. Most prominent of all, however, were those who lived grandly in the capital and were the petty sovereigns of some feudal estate which they perhaps never visited. A sense of obligation made some of them endow orphanages and monasteries, as it made others join the confraternity of *Bianchi* who dedicated themselves to comforting condemned prisoners before execution. The Prince of Niscemi about 1710 was a hard-working man of affairs, and the Prince della Roccella was a rich merchant, while the Baron of San Giaime e Pozzo produced a manual of agriculture in 1735. Prince Biscari at Catania not only had a reputation of being benevolent to his servants and tenants, but built up one of the finest private museums in the world. His family had shown that they could be good farmers whose acquisitive instincts harmonised not too discordantly with those of the general public. He introduced foreign artisans to encourage linen and rum manufacture, and in one emergency, at his own expense, he virtually fed the whole town of Catania for a month.

These were, however, a small exception, for the general impression given by the baronage as a whole is one of fecklessness and inadequacy, and singularly few of these leaders of society left a name behind for the admiration of posterity. There was almost nothing to compare with the sense of duty and public service which prevailed among so many of the gentry in Piedmont. As Victor Amadeus was told on his arrival in 1713, "the Sicilian nobility do not do any work" but were "soft and effeminate". Their old castles were empty and going to ruin. Those who could afford it often escaped abroad to live on their rents in Spain or Naples.

Most were heavily in debt, and often over half their income went on mortgage payments. This was true of Geraci, as it was true of Butera the richest of all, whose income had grown until it was nearly 10 per cent of that of the Sicilian government. No inheritance, in other words, was so large that a Sicilian baron would not regularly overspend it. Moreover, since many other individuals and institutions made a living out of loan and mortgage interest—and so were parasitically dependent on feudalism—any big dip in agrarian profits produced widespread results. In 1747 therefore, the Viceroy, not for the first time, declared a moratorium on debt repayments in order to prevent bankruptcy ruining the main pillars of society. Even though this aroused opposition, creditors lacked political power; what was more, they lacked any interest in destroying the system from which they obtained their livelihood. The law of 1752 which allowed the nobility to repossess leasehold property was another move to make life easier for the *latifondisti*. As the Viceroy explained, forcing the nobles to pay their debts would reduce them to beggary, and this must be avoided as it would upset the basic bonds of society.

This indebtedness was largely due to sheer improvidence, but some historians have also inferred a decrease in the profitability of cereal farming. Others have countered this by arguing that there took place a considerable increase in grain prices over the years, and any efficient landlord would have seen to it that this outstripped the rise in his living costs. Some rents doubled in the eighteenth century. Land values were also going up, mainly because land was sought as the most tangible sign of status, at once an inflation hedge and the quickest passport into the aristocracy.

But this is not to say that wheat production on the *latifondi* was all that profitable; on the contrary, the profits of agriculture were evidently slow to reach all but the most enterprising of landlords, and enterprise in this conformist society was unusual. Sergio asserted that the increasing resort to *gabelloto*-management led to a decline in production, just because short leases inevitably diminished incentive. Moreover landowners in time found the *gabelloti* to be somewhat intractable subordinates, and the difficulty of compelling them to pay their rent was given by the Deputation as one reason why creditors went unpaid. Any increase in agricultural incomes now had to be filtered through this new managerial class who, legally or illegally, sometimes took a good 50 per cent of the profits for themselves. Costs also increased in proportion as more marginal land was cultivated and distant fields came into production. We have the evidence of Balsamo and Arnolfini that much current wheat production was uneconomic, and that, because of landowner absenteeism, no more capital was being invested in the *latifondi*: this spelt diminishing returns for all but the luckiest.

The *latifondi* were therefore not proving as remunerative as the increase in wheat prices would suggest; and possibly those nobles who showed a profit did so less from agriculture than from speculation in commodities and export licences, or from smuggling and the ability to obtain special privileges. Real success needed influence with officialdom, ruthlessness in dealing with tenants, and evading the law; whereas those who relied on the profits of agriculture would have had to be more industrious and enterprising than social habit would easily permit. Despite higher agricultural prices, the Marquis Giarrizzo in the 1780s suggested that landowners as a whole were becoming poorer. They usually lacked the money to buy export licences. It was rather the wheat brokers who controlled this particular market and took perhaps another quarter of the profits of cereal cultivation.

Most of the nobles seem to have had little idea how to retain or improve their family fortunes. Efficient methods of estate management were outside their knowledge and would hardly have been permitted by current *mores*. As they had almost no education at all, the calculation of profit and loss on a sufficiently large scale was beyond them, and they did not welcome sharing family secrets about their income with their managers. Commerce and industry offered no attractions, and piracy was becoming less rewarding and more dangerous, while government hand-outs were bestowed rather at Naples than Palermo. Selling land in order to be released from debt was not always easy: feudal custom was against it; so were entails with all the legal obstacles they involved, and so were the immemorial 'promiscuous rights' of grazing possessed by villagers in the *latifondi*; while hazily remembered regalian rights of suzerainty over the baronial fiefs could make conveyancing somewhat problematic. The feudatories therefore, while they undoubtedly kept power and prestige, had lost much of the economic basis of their authority. Furthermore their failure to adjust was an increasing burden on the rest of the nation. A strong case was therefore building up for radical reform, for freeing the market in land and abolishing the corn laws, because the restrictive practices by which the aristocracy held on to power were also a fundamental cause of their poverty and that of Sicily as a whole.

The complaint of personal impoverishment was often no doubt deliberately exaggerated in order to keep taxes low and creditors at bay. Sicilian economic backwardness cannot simply be explained by poverty, for the extravagant rebuilding of Catania, Noto and other towns after the earthquake of 1693 tells a more complicated tale. The parliamentary taxes, say nearly half the tax burden, were estimated as being under 1 per cent of the declared value of property in 1748 and even less of its real value. Parliament in 1754 thought that a subsidy of 80,000 *scudi* would be very high, yet the Archbishops of Palermo and Monreale earned as much as this between them, and in 1738 even a retired archbishop was receiving a pension of 20,000. Arnolfini discovered that the Prince of Valguarnera in the 1720s paid 180,000 *scudi* for his villa in Bagheria; the Prince of Palagonia, who had recently been fleeing from his creditors, was thought to have paid 200,000 for his; and the Marquis della Sambuca seems to have spent a quarter of a million buying up the nationalised property of the Jesuits. One Jesuit fief alone found a buyer at 92,000 *scudi*. Plenty of money seems to have existed somewhere; the important fact was that it was spent on prestige rather than productive investment.

Since family pride was one of the most impelling motives in this society, the great estates continued to be kept intact wherever possible by deeds of strict settlement. Daughters and younger sons were commonly put into convents and monasteries about the age of ten (nunneries would accept girls even at four or five) so as to keep the family possessions in one hand; the ecclesiastical life at least had its own privileges and would not mean loss of caste, and John Dryden's son in 1701 found that any monk of quality was allowed his own retinue of servants. The head of the family and the eldest male child alone were of much importance. Northern visitors such as Houel and the Count de Borch were surprised that in years of visiting the gentry they so seldom met the wife of their host. Younger sons were discouraged from marriage and were not permitted by the code of gentility to make their own fortune; hence one potential ingredient for a challenge to this patriarchal way of life was lacking. Moreover poorer people tried to copy this fashion of setting up family entails and sending younger sons into the Church. Parliament repeatedly protested about the growing number of ecclesiastics. Putting one's daughter into a nunnery suitable for gentlefolk cost a thousand *scudi* in 1768, since fashion dictated peremptorily that the immuring should be celebrated with a certain panache; and yet parliament, in other words the baronage, feebly petitioned the King to stop this convention which was pushing so many conformist parliamentarians into insolvency. The only alternative to a nunnery, however, was for a father to provide a dowry, since without a dowry no girl in any class was likely to find a husband: dowries were themselves so expensive that they were called a prime explanation of the low birth rate, and not without reason did reformers suggest that they were as much an impediment as primogeniture to the development of a more mobile and liberal society.

Extravagance was socially unavoidable once the aristocracy had come to live in Palermo, where those with regular access to the Viceroy's court laid down rules of behaviour for every aspirant to follow. Their estates had to be neglected, except possibly for quick visits to collect rent and receive homage; expenditure had to be on expensive private luxuries rather than on the roads which might have halved agricultural prices and made exports profitable again. Farm labourers were left to fend for themselves, without capital and without education. Agriculture suffered in consequence, but so did the aristocracy themselves, for their lives became much more expensive just when they were surrendering to the *gabelloti* many of the profits of ownership. By the 1770s, according to the traveller Denon, some of them were borrowing from their own *gabelloti*, and some were reduced to selling their wheat a year ahead at a 40 per cent discount.

"Luxurious living and gambling have always been the dominant passions of the Sicilian aristocracy", so wrote one aristocrat in 1790; and in this century there were half a dozen laws against gambling because it was ruining so many families. The nobility themselves begged the King to make their extravagance illegal, since the competition for status made it hard for them to save their fortunes by voluntary action. They continued to grumble that the extravagance of dowries and funerals was spiralling competitively, and that people of lower condition were aping this extravagance so that it cost too much for the nobles to maintain their proper distance in the social round. Yet although they complained, they still went on trying to outdo the next man in expenditure, because to stand still was to lose caste and that meant to lose everything. For the same reason, according to a report in 1714, they could not afford to educate their children, and sometimes said that they could not afford even to get married.

The number of palaces at Palermo, so thought one foreigner, was greater than in all the cities of the British Empire put together. As well as a palace, however, it was by 1700 becoming fashionable to have a splendid villa outside the walls to which one could retreat between the St. Rosalia festivities in July and the autumn rains. Prince Butera had begun this fashion in the 1650s, and one of his motives had been to provide another means of distinguishing real aristocrats from counterfeit title-hunters. Over two hundred of these villas were begun in the eighteenth century, often quite regardless of cost. Dozens of them were never completed but existed only as splendid façades. It is possible that nothing contributed more than this to the indebtedness of the aristocracy as a class. These villas remain as monuments to their taste in luxurious living, as reminders of the family tyrannies which spent so much of the national income on the upkeep of enormous patriarchal households. In Palermo itself "their time is wasted in balls, masquerades and such like dissipation", commented an Englishman. Every family of note, even apparently in provincial towns, still felt obliged to possess a slave; and a lady of real birth, said Arnolfini, required a dozen servants for herself alone. The government tried to come to their rescue by forbidding so many servants, by restricting dowries and nunnery charges, by ordering the courts to speed up family lawsuits, and by several enactments against excessive funeral expenditure; but this was battling against the tide of social custom, and soon a special status was accorded to whoever could evade or buy exemption from these restrictive laws.

Keeping up appearances was a costly and time-consuming activity. A carriage, or preferably two, was obligatory, and by the 1740s this fact was causing serious traffic problems in Palermo: there were already penalties for disobeying the traffic police and not using the designated parking lots. The most strenuous resistance was mobilised against any suggestion that carriages should be taxed. Balsamo vainly wished that the nobles would occasionally ride through their own farms on horseback instead of taking their daily boring journey along the marine front with their liveried equipages; but the afternoon drive was mandatory, and even the most indigent lady of breeding would take advantage of the fact that carriages, like dresses, could be hired by the hour without too much loss of face. When Marquis Regalmici was detailed to carry urgent relief to areas damaged by an earthquake, he insisted on waiting until he could leave with appropriate dignity accompanied by a large and brilliant cortège, and so arrived a fortnight after the disaster. When Goethe visited Palermo and asked why no one ever swept up the dung in the streets, the answer came that the gentry liked a soft path for their carriages.

Such details fascinated the foreign travellers now attracted to Sicily by the current enthusiasm for the antique and the strange. The magnificence and hospitality of aristocratic Palermo impressed most people, and French cooking was one more social habit which entered into the competition for prestige. Foreign visitors observed that stables on the big ranches were more commodious and comfortable than the huts of the peasantry. Hunting, which had been a genuinely popular sport, was becoming more a perquisite of the rich: the law said that partridges could be taken with falcons, and hares by dogs (except between March and August); but using the more plebeian means of nets, traps or catapults was punishable by two years in the galleys for a poor man and a fine for the rich. The nobility had long since begun to enclose common lands for hunting. Even in the outskirts of Palermo they were now building walls everywhere and using their *guardiani* to keep out intruders. The citizens of Palermo in 1769 momentarily persuaded the Viceroy to halt this process, but the courts increasingly ratified the enclosure movement and made trespass a very serious offence.

Another social habit which struck outsiders was the great consumption by rich people of sugar, confectionery and ice-cream. Very common indeed even among poorer people was the use of snow for cooling drinks. In the eighteenth century the export of snow was an industry of some size and even subject to piracy because of its value. The Bishop of Catania earned a considerable revenue from it; so did the Viceroy himself, and in 1717 it provided a twentieth of the municipal income of Palermo. The snow was collected in March up in the mountains; then it was beaten into hard ice with sticks and rolled down into caves; from here it was brought down each day by donkey into the towns wrapped in straw and salt. Even in the winter there was an enormous consumption of it, especially since it came to be considered a medicine for giving tone to fibres relaxed by the sun. The Austrians thought of increasing the tax on snow as well as on sugar, but this met with immense resistance. If stocks ran out, or if the contractors raised prices by pretending that there was a shortage, soldiers might be sent into the mountains with powers of life and death to remedy the matter.

The fact that the Sicilian aristocracy consumed a great deal and produced nothing was fundamental in explaining the problems of the island. To some extent, however, their social preponderance continued to conceal their economic debility. Indeed, even at the cost of keeping Sicily poor, they naturally did what they could to twist the social relationships of feudalism still further in their own favour. On the mainland, except perhaps in Calabria, the Bourbons usually managed to appropriate fiefs for failure to pay feudal dues or when a line of succession died out; but in Sicily, at at least after the temporary confiscation of several 'states' early in the eighteenth century, these regalian prerogatives dwindled away.

The lawyers, moreover, elaborated a sophistical justification of this resurgent, bastard feudalism. A clever advocate, Carlo di Napoli, won a famous case in the 1740s against the village of Sortino which wanted to buy itself back from its prince into the royal demesne. The argument which prevailed was that the original Norman barons had strictly been not feudatories of Count Roger, but rather his *commilitones* who by helping him to conquer Sicily had won for themselves a share of sovereignty in the land; and the thirteenth-century laws, *Si aliquem* and *Volentes*, were held to have confirmed this by admitting that fiefs could lapse to the crown only in quite exceptional circumstances. Di Napoli, with more forensic than historical persuasiveness, argued that fiefs were private property. As an even more extravagant extension of this view, tenants were sometimes said to owe allegiance to their feudal lord rather than to the monarch. No wonder that a monument was erected to di Napoli at Palermo by a grateful baronage; no wonder that the personal links of vassal and client were considered to be of paramount importance; no wonder the liberties of Sicily came to be confused with baronial privilege.

Even towns on the royal demesne were, for good or ill, frequently bossed by the local aristocracy. At Catania, for example, Prince Biscari, as the leading citizen and chief employer, was more important than any royal judge, and local government was invariably in aristocratic hands. At Caltagirone the nobles bought from the King the right to monopolise the civic administration. At Syracuse the local nobility even rebelled against allowing any power to those whose family had not been noble for more than two hundred years. In minor towns and villages, the poorer relatives of a baron would commonly share out the perquisites of office among themselves. They and their friends might pay no tax; their daughters would be comfortably placed in public 'orphanages'; civic charities would disappear and municipal revenues would be diverted to private purposes.

"The poorer the nobles, the greater the frauds they commit", remarked one report to Victor Amadeus, and he discovered that the whole burden of local taxation was placed on poor people who could not resist. Many royal forests, villages, castles and mines were from time to time encroached upon or even annexed outright by the rich. They took over the foreshore and public rights of fishing, to the point where fishermen were forced to give up their jobs and take to brigandage. In the countryside the peasants could find themselves virtually bound to the soil, compelled to owe *corvées*, to use the baron's mill and olive press, prevented from undercutting him on the market or selling before his produce had been sold. Spanish Viceroys had forbidden these practices as they had also forbidden the nobles to interfere in urban administration, but any serious attempt to enforce such laws would have stirred up too much trouble. Even in the early nineteenth century the Prince of Palagonia went on collecting a marriage tax from his vassals in commutation of his seigneurial right to sleep with their daughters.

Strong Viceroys had always claimed the right to override any feudal privilege; occasionally they took cases away from the baronial courts; they sometimes forbade the export of cereals from Modica, and insisted that even the Prince of Butera should ask their permission before leaving Palermo. Just occasionally, if for example a feudatory incorporated public water supplies and irrigation rights, a lawsuit might be initiated against him in the royal courts. But usually royal officials were helpless even if they did not actively assist baronial misgovernment. Strong Viceroys were few. The baron or his *gabelloto*, on the other hand, had a private army of *guardiani* whose job it was to compel obedience from recalcitrant peasants. The government recognised and even had to employ these private armies. The Duke of Terranova had one for each of his eight 'states'. Villabianca referred to "the company of twenty-four dragoons employed by Prince Butera, who had their own flag and their own military band of trumpets and drums; and frequently they could be found riding through the kingdom with as much liberty and authority as a company of royal troops".

The Bourbons of Naples by no means always favoured the nobles, and at Naples they almost eliminated feudalism during this century; but they knew that keeping Sicily submissive would be infinitely less expensive if the baronage could be persuaded to co-operate. The barons were cheaper than royal officials in local government; with their assistance any movement for Sicilian independence could be checked; and they could be used to help inculcate respect for the established order in Church and State. The Bourbon government, in return for their political subservience, was usually ready to excuse their malpractices. "If only other Kings would follow such a good example!", apostrophised the Marquis of Villabianca.

The nobles therefore received official assistance against their tenants and creditors. They were sometimes given jobs and some of their children a subsidised education. To stop the runaway marriages which threatened to undermine certain important families, a savage law in 1767 threatened even the witnesses to such marriages with five years in the galleys. Though in Naples the Bourbons showed how isolated was the nobility without monarchical support, and though many Sicilian Viceroys were persuaded that a similarly forceful policy should be adopted at Palermo, political considerations ensured that the autonomy of the island and its own different social tradition should up to a point be respected.

Chapter 31

BANDITS AND THE LAW

As Sicily was left so much to herself, law enforcement remained much the same problem as in previous centuries. Over most of the island, smugglers, cattle rustlers, highwaymen and robber barons had each other to fear rather than the authorities. Viceroys spasmodically tried to control banditry, and occasional military expeditions were sent through the countryside with full powers to carry out torture of suspects and garrotting of those thought guilty; yet if one gang was destroyed, a rival or subordinate gang was always ready to take its place. The Historiographer Royal of the Bourbons, Giovanni Evangelista di Blasi, when describing the violence, the vendettas and the legendary robber heroes of this time, remarked on them as showing "characteristics which we can rightly call part of the national character, and which remained the same whether under Spain, Savoy or Austria".

Early in the eighteenth century a group of outlaws led by a certain Catinella was the most feared of all; one of his specialities was capturing rich men for ransom and then winning popular connivance by distributing some of the proceeds to the poor. He was active all over the island, for brigandage still seems to have been as common in the east as in the west. The great bandit Foti had come from Messina. Again in the 1720s this town was tyrannised over by four brothers who led a gang of assassins and were quite outside police control. In Palermo the Austrians had momentarily deluded themselves that they were eliminating crime. Yet nothing stopped large bands of outlaws roaming the countryside; for the brigands, even though they sometimes levied a contribution on the peasants, were supported by a strong conviction that breaking the law was an entirely respectable activity.

Perhaps it was one index of this mixed fear and admiration for crime that there existed a vigorous popular religious cult of the *Decollati*, in which prayers were offered to executed criminals, and shrines were set up in which their dismembered relics were accorded supernatural powers (pieces of the hangman's rope were considered specially efficacious). Co-operation with the police was almost unknown except when the privileged classes wished to put down social revolution. The Austrian authorities had been baffled to discover that "to be a witness in any kind of criminal action brought unspeakable disgrace even on the most abject member of society". Much the same had been said by Spanish Viceroys, and for each successive administration this was to remain as serious a problem as any.

Another fact which inevitably reduced the respect for public law was the continued existence of all the many different legal systems or *fori*. Ecclesiastics still claimed exemption from the ordinary courts as did members of the Inquisition from the bishops' courts, and so forth. Hundreds of churches went on granting a legally recognised immunity to any criminal fleeing from justice, and sometimes the parish priest was able to extend this immunity to an area forty paces around his church precinct. About 1726 a seminarist named Don Sferlazza formed a gang in pursuit of a family vendetta, and the government finally charged one prominent aristocrat to organise what amounted to another gang against him. The criminal was eventually caught, but his clerical privilege exempted him from punishment, and after his release he continued to spread terror through the land. Terrorism was, of course, a tactic always used by these gangs, and Sferlazza's victims were, with reason, much too scared to give evidence.

The traditional lawlessness of the upper classes was yet another factor in encouraging the spread of crime. Everywhere, said the early nineteenth-century historian Palmeri, there could be found nobles who protected banditry either out of fear or from covetousness, and some landowners deliberately attracted labour to their estates by offering asylum to outlaws: this kind of complaint had been found in every century of Sicilian history. In their own territory the nobles could, within broad limits, behave as they liked. They still had powers of life and death, and Victor Amadeus was told that in their courts injustice was the rule, for innocent people could be punished out of mere caprice. Baronial prisoners were kept either in the underground water-logged *dammusi* to which they might have to be lowered on ropes, or else at public expense in the royal prisons where, incidentally, they would not normally be eligible for a royal amnesty. Modica had retained not only its own courts, but was large enough to boast a court of appeal, and its Grand Justiciar could imprison people with no further explanation than 'for reasons well known to us', something which not even the Viceroy could do. In these enclaves it was not unusual for the insignia and effigy of the baron to replace and exclude that of the King, while any right of appeal to the sovereign could be only fitfully maintained.

In practice even the royal courts treated nobles quite differently from ordinary citizens. The Prince of Villafranca, who had tortured boys with burning irons because they taunted him for his eight-horse carriage (in fact four horses was the maximum now allowed by law to anyone except the Viceroy), effectively contended in 1731 that the royal courts had no jurisdiction in the matter. The Duke of San Filippo openly engaged in contraband at Palermo, protected by the authorities. The Prince of Santa Margherita, who had killed his mistress, was merely fined 1,200 *scudi*. When in 1771 a nobleman was executed for murder, it was the first time this had happened for nearly a century; and, even so, strong representations for a reprieve were made by his peers, one argument being that the executioner had no experience with a guillotine and would first need some practice. The victim was in this case too poor to buy a reprieve, and, as he was expected to pay for his own execution, Palermo had to forgo the pomp and ceremony which such an occasion would once have required; yet it was accepted as axiomatic that he could not be strangled like any ordinary murderer. A few years later another aristocrat, after being found guilty of killing his wife, was charitably pardoned by his fellow nobles of the *Bianchi*, who claimed this act of mercy as their privilege; but when the same man subsequently killed his second wife, they agreed to let the law take its course.

The most successful governments at dealing with crime were those which suppressed their indignation and came to terms with the underworld. Setting a thief to catch a thief often achieved a fair amount of success. That was why notorious criminals were still employed as Captains at Arms and to staff the private forces recruited by the tax contractors. Like many brigands before him, the famous Testalonga was caught in the 1760s only by disaffection and treachery inside his own gang. This bandit was making travel and commerce hazardous for anyone who did not buy a safe conduct from him, and the fact was having a seriously restrictive effect on agriculture. The Prince of Trabia was therefore charged to raise a posse of irregulars against him, but the criminal was brought to book only when printed notices reached his accomplices offering them rewards and a free pardon in return for his capture. Police action was often a freelance operation undertaken for a reward; and frequently it was carried out by criminals who understood the underworld and had few of the scruples about honour which they liked to encourage in the rest of the population.

The problem faced by successive governments was not simply these isolated gangs of highwaymen; it was rather a way of life shared widely throughout society. The public good was a meaningless phrase. Here was a kind of tribal society where separate *fori* and the relations of patron to client were far more immediate and real than the state, and where the family counted most of all. Despite repeated prohibitions, almost everyone carried arms and was ready to use them. Sometimes there seemed to be a widespread underground conspiracy against the law; and a number of

Fosco Maraini

The Villa Valguarnera at Bagheria, near Palermo, built by
Tomaso Napoli in 1721

Garden front of the Villa Palagonia, Bagheria, also by
Tomaso Napoli, 1715

Tim Benton

Tim Benton

The 'sitting-out' room in the Gangi palace,
Palermo: mid-18th century

writers in the eighteenth century boasted that Sicilians had a secret sign language which since the time of the Greek tyrants had been a means of resistance against foreign rule.

Enterprising visitors from overseas were told of criminal organisations which were in collusion with each other and which sometimes boasted an aristocratic protector. Certainly one must allow here for exaggeration and rumour, since there was a desire to impress foreigners, as there was also a desire by gullible foreigners to be impressed. The *Beati Paoli* and the Revengers may or may not have been serious organisations, but some delinquent groups undoubtedly did exist which levied a tax on peasants and landlords alike. They had their own system of justice, which could be more effective than the normal courts, and it was said that members were sworn to execute their secret judgements without question. Rarely was a foreign traveller molested by these criminals, but it is impossible to argue from this, and against abundant evidence to the contrary, that they did not exist. The truth was rather that they were mainly concerned with local conflicts for power into which foreigners did not enter. Travellers in any case were advised not to move without hiring three or four guards from this penumbral underworld and making proper payment in the right quarter.

From an amnesty granted in 1778, something can be learnt of the state of law and order. Apart from false coining and having sexual relations with nuns, the offences which were excluded from pardon as particularly heinous all related to gangsterism in the countryside: these included blackmailing, obtaining money by the threat of destroying crops and animals, stealing livestock, giving false testimony, kidnapping and acting as go-between to collect money from the relatives of a kidnapped person. These were a kind of offence which the authorities could rarely control and which remained for centuries as a crippling deadweight on the development of rural Sicily. Such crimes could in a sense be regarded as the protest of a subject people who lacked any means of organised political opposition. In the absence of other kinds of social cohesion, the gangs had a special function in the countryside by establishing boss rule over one or more villages. Perhaps they were also a means of making money; at all events one gang leader offered his judges 10,000 *scudi*, which was more than the annual income of quite a rich man. In addition, the many excise duties must have helped to make crime profitable and to familiarise criminals with the practice of forming underground associations.

The sheer variety of laws and regulations helped to make delinquency easier, because the many foreign invasions of Sicily had left behind them a labyrinth of uncodified legislation which was extremely hard to understand or apply. Some laws completely contradicted each other. This is another reason why public justice was disobeyed and even derided. In a world of overlapping and conflicting jurisdictions, of privileged exemptions from the ordinary courts, of judgeships being sold and witnesses intimidated, frequently the local boss or the local landowner was more important for law enforcement and even for law-making than the central government. The magistrates often depended on him, and so took his part against his tenants. A leading landowner such as the Duke of Terranova could have a dozen of the best lawyers and at least some of the royal judges on an annual salary. As Palmeri told parliament, the stronger man was therefore bound to prevail in the courts: judges were paid little, and had to rely on what they could obtain either from their protectors or from suitors and prisoners.

The enormous litigiousness of all classes had astonished many foreign Viceroys and was accounted by them a great bar to efficiency and prosperity. Often a Viceroy on his first arrival tried to speed up the process of justice: the Austrians did so in 1720, likewise the Marquis Fogliani in 1747, and the latter even went so far as to instruct the judges to work a full six-hour day; but the lawyers always triumphed over this unwelcome urge for reform and had a strong interest in keeping cases alive and undecided. Some foreign merchants avoided coming to Sicily with their merchandise just because contracts could not be enforced quickly and cheaply, and they would also have needed a good deal of fairly esoteric knowledge about the different court systems. The creaming off of local talent into the legal profession was reckoned by the economist Scrofani to be one reason for the backwardness of everything from intellectual life to farming, and in practice a large slice of the national income was continually being taken out of agriculture and spent on this parasitic class of lawyers in Palermo. The Prince of Villadoro in 1810 was engaged in twenty-two lawsuits simultaneously.

More important still was the fact, as Viceroys themselves complained, that the law was positively discredited by its deviousness, its complexity and its delays. Individuals were therefore inclined to seek redress by other means. Many quite poor people, according to the poet Meli, were ruined by protracted lawsuits, and this kind of fact put another premium on gangsterism; for everyone, whether peasant, landlord, priest, businessman or criminal, had an added incentive to commend himself to any quasi-legal organisation which could show that it was more practically effective than the regular forces of law. The courts imposed harsh deterrent penalties which included branding, public torturing and the strangling and disemboweling of criminals; but all this, to say nothing of the permanent display of severed heads and members (hung up on hooks like ham, said a visiting Englishman), was a futile attempt to conceal the ineffectiveness of these same courts in supporting law and order.

Chapter 32

INTELLECTUALS AND REFORM

An important reason why the voice of reform was muffled in Sicily can be found in the ties which bound the small class of intellectuals to an essentially conservative world. Anyone with genuine originality was tempted to move away from this closed, patriarchal society to find employment elsewhere: the most celebrated Sicilians of the century, the architect Juvara, the composer Alessandro Scarlatti and that talented impostor Cagliostro, lived and died abroad, as did many others of lesser fame. At home there were few jobs, and any posts which carried a good salary often went to non-Sicilians.

The main hope of preferment, apart from in the Church, was through the patronage of some baron, and this is one reason why there was so little open criticism of the established order. Criticism was rather directed against any attempts at reform. It was thus fashionable to blame the Bourbons of Naples for what was wrong in society, even when the Neapolitan government was relatively enlightened. In Naples itself many lawyers supported the crown against feudal usurpations, but in Sicily the legal profession looked rather to the nobility for their living. If they ever became rich it was likely to be through lawsuits over the collateral succession to feudal estates. Dozens of these lawyers could now afford to build country villas not far from those of the aristocracy, and Carlo di Napoli owned the Cuba palace where Kings had once lived.

When the *ancien régime* came under attack, the impetus was derived not from these people but from a new generation of reforming administrators at Naples. The first and easiest target for a reformer was the Jesuits. This religious order had, along with the Theatines, almost a monopoly in the field of education, and here it was the resolute champion of scholasticism against the Enlightenment. As such it was heartily disliked by the progressives. Some lay landlords also realised how they could use this chance to secularise and share out the great Jesuit estates. In 1767, following the example of other countries, and on the pretended grounds of worldliness and corruption, Ferdinand expelled the order and confiscated their property. Culturally this was an act of liberation, though less than some people may have hoped. Another expressed intention, to experiment in social and economic reform by breaking down some Jesuit *latifondi* into smallholdings, was not so successful, for the peasants either were never allowed to hear about it, or else were too frightened to submit their claims as the law intended. Instead of these estates being divided into small lots, the land went to enlarge existing lay *latifondi*. The exchequer profited, but much hardship was caused to the eight hundred Jesuits; and though a few rich men took advantage of the occasion to become even richer, Sicily was no better off economically.

The Neapolitan reformers intervened in many other small ways, legislating about abortion, trying to stop the scandalous breaches in the rules on visiting hours in nunneries, and yet also trying to moderate what they considered to be excessive religious zeal in Sicily. When for hygienic reasons they encouraged the creation of cemeteries, offence was caused to those who assumed that burial inside churches was necessary for salvation, just as others were annoyed who were accustomed to buying a certain remoteness from their peasants in death as in life. Ferdinand also revived ancient legislation against the Church acquiring property in mortmain, and he dissolved some of the smaller monasteries. He also abolished the archbishopric of Monreale, arguing that the enormous revenues of the often non-resident archbishop would be more usefully spent in defending the coast against pirates. There was a widespread feeling that far too many people were entering religious orders. It was said that there was an ecclesiastic in every house in the kingdom, whereas the King would have preferred fewer "parasites on society" and "more men able to bear arms and cultivate the soil". He ordered the monasteries to open free schools for the poor, since their endowments were held in trust for society: writing, reading and arithmetic should be taught for four hours a day to the *basso popolo*; it was added that the instructors should not receive bribes from parents nor become too friendly with the boys.

A slight impetus was given to higher education. Messina university had been suppressed long ago; that of Catania had been temporarily destroyed in the earthquake of 1693. Once the Jesuits had gone, Palermo was less than ever a place of scholarship or research. Outdoing Cagliostro, the Abbè Vella, without even knowing the Arabic alphabet, could build up a reputation as an Arabist by forging documents in a language that none of his colleagues understood, and so became rich as Abbot of San Pancrazio. Not only was nearly everyone in Sicily illiterate, but higher education concentrated on theology and law, and both these disciplines were geared to an obsequious respect towards tradition and authority. Degrees in medicine were obtainable, but they could evidently be bought without much serious study.

Among cultured aristocrats, interest rarely stretched beyond antiquarianism, numismatics and archaeology. Messina in the fifteenth century had been one of the earliest places in all Italy to print books, but, three hundred years later, publications in

Sicily could expect a circulation of only a few dozen. Scholastic philosophy was therefore slow to be questioned. The Marquis Natale once broke through the current traditionalism so far as to write a poem on Leibnitz, but the Jesuits had it censored by the Inquisition as heretical and its non-noble printer was imprisoned. Villabianca acidly dismissed this poem as something not written to acquire reputation (a motive he could have accepted) but composed with the unworthy and dangerous purpose of instructing the public "as they do in England". He need not have worried, because the public remained in ignorance, and among professional philosophers the old school held its ground for another half-century. Though the names of Descartes and Newton were familiar in certain circles, there was not much understanding let alone acceptance of either rationalism or the experimental method.

King Ferdinand had a little more sense and open-mindedness than his later historical reputation allowed, and a number of his ministers were men of outstanding ability and rectitude. At the request of the Sicilian parliament—the nobles dissenting—he agreed that some of the money confiscated from the Jesuits should be used to start an academy in one of their ex-churches at Palermo, though full degree-conferring privileges were denied to it because Catania once again jealously asserted her ancient right to prevent any other town having a university. A committee of nobles was appointed to govern this Palermo academy, and some twenty chairs were endowed by the government. A surgical theatre was built for it. Equipment was installed for teaching physics. Telescopes were purchased in Paris and London, and students sent overseas to study agriculture and veterinary science. One or two other Jesuit houses were converted into technical schools where poor children could learn to weave and make glass and ceramics: this, at least, was the intention. After another request by parliament—with the nobles this time enthusiastic—three free schools were set up at state expense for young noblemen; since it was thought especially dangerous that so many aristocrats were illiterate. The government agreed that children whose family title went back over a century were to be accepted first. General Cockburn, when he visited one of these schools a few years later, thought it "far superior to Eton".

These few changes were possible because some individual Sicilians were becoming aware that in education, law, economics and politics, the established order could be modified with advantage. If the Jesuits and the Church were the easiest target, that was because the privileged classes were not united in their defence. The baronial and domanial Houses of Parliament both protested that ecclesiastics were becoming too wealthy and were escaping their full share of tax. Pious legacies, so it was asserted, had reached the point where they could be said to be impoverishing the lay aristocracy, and towns complained of being unable to pay their quota of tax because so many laymen were temporarily vesting their goods in ecclesiastical trusts so as to profit from clerical tax exemption. The fact that envious eyes were cast on ecclesiastical land must also have helped to make anti-clericalism moderately, or even immoderately, respectable.

Other projects of reform had only individual champions, and the reformers were often impractical or half-hearted. The legal reformer, Francesco Paolo di Blasi, wanted a new legal code and the abolition of primogeniture; he favoured women's education and compulsory free instruction for the poor, while he also had revolutionary ideas about replacing the excises by a graduated income tax. Tommaso Natale was strongly influenced by the Neapolitan reforming intellectuals; his book on the efficacity of punishments, published in 1759, questioned both the death penalty and the use of torture as a method of investigation. Yet Natale was at heart a conservative. Torture when used as a punishment was quite acceptable to him: indeed amputation or putting out an eye, he thought, might have a salutary effect on spectators, and he believed that poor people should be punished more severely than the titled. Sergio, the best-known Sicilian economist of his day, accurately criticised the many internal excise barriers and the restrictive privileges of the town guilds; nevertheless he accepted much of contemporary mercantilism and shied away from some obvious conclusions which might have threatened the established order of society. If new ideas could now be discussed, it was only by a few exceptional individuals or as an elegant pastime in the Palermo salons, and certainly not with much serious intent of practical application. When di Blasi said that most crimes were attributable to poverty, when he recommended that a suitable punishment for nobles would be to make them sweep the streets, and when he denounced illiteracy even in the lower classes as inefficient as well as wrong, his voice was isolated and he spoke only as a theorist.

Much more effective than individual Sicilian reformers was the fact that Sicily was exposed more directly than before to the main currents of European thought. Suddenly it was beginning to acquire the reputation of being a highly romantic island which foreigners ought to visit. Dryden's son was there in 1700, but above all it was Patrick Brydone's travel volume, published in 1773 and at once translated into German and French, which publicised its charms, and there was a sudden spate of perhaps fifty other such volumes in the next half-century. Sicily contained something for everyone with a taste for adventure: it had earth-quakes, volcanoes, bandits, all manner of discomforts and quaint local customs, as well as splendid memorials of classical antiquity and a notable hospitality towards foreigners.

These overseas visitors helped a little to shock local culture out of its fairly considerable self-esteem, out of its liking for repetitive metaphysical dissertations and purely erudite scholarship. A French bookseller opened a shop in Palermo. Private tutors and family librarians were imported from Tuscany. Brydone found many English books in family libraries, and translations were beginning to appear of Arthur Young, Pope, Hume and even Locke. Northern travellers were astonished to be served iced punch and porter, to find people following the English fashion of frock coats, and to encounter the hands-in-the-pocket affectation which English nonchalance was thought to demand. Severe penalties were threatened in 1769 against those who possessed books by Voltaire, Bolingbroke and 'the so-called philosophers', but in practice the smuggled writings of Voltaire, Diderot and Montesquieu were bringing the European Enlightenment to the fascinated attention of a select few. Of the Italian reformers, Beccaria and Genovesi had some following. At another level the Freemasons also found dilettante support especially among the high born; they recruited Benedictine monks as well as the poet Meli and at least one Viceroy, and the masonic Lodge at Palermo was run for a time by an Irish colonel.

Only a handful of Sicilians, on the other hand, travelled in Europe. Villabianca, for instance, never left the country. Books, moreover, were possessed rather than read; the new ideas were not genuinely assimilated, nor was their impact anywhere near sufficient to awaken the conscience of the privileged classes. Sicily might be an interesting place for foreigners to visit, but only because of the very isolation and idiosyncrasies which were such a handicap. Its people had the reputation of being completely ignorant about other countries and not wanting to know more. Northerners therefore half-accepted the idea that Europe ended at Naples, while Sicily was part of a different semi-African world. Few visitors were as enterprising as Goethe, who made a brief excursion inland; and Palermo seemed so remote that an article in the great French *Encyclopédie* described it as ruined by an earthquake in the previous century. Other Italians, except those from Naples, knew almost nothing of the island, nor did Sicilians themselves know it well; and without knowledge there could hardly be any serious or successful reform.

PART 9

Revolution and Reform 1770–1800

Chapter 33

THE PALERMO REVOLT OF 1773

The concentration of public life on Palermo became more pronounced than ever after the partial eclipse of Messina. Not only had Messina been overcome by military defeat in 1678, but she suffered a terrible plague in 1743 which halved the population again—two shiploads of convicts had to be sent from Palermo to clear the dead from the streets and burn all infected chattels. Then an earthquake struck the town in 1783 just when recovery was beginning, and a huge fire burnt for over a week. Pamphlets went on being published with the brave message that Messina was by rights the true capital of Sicily, but physical disasters had by now taken the heart out of this controversy except with a few dedicated antiquarians.

Palermo, on the other hand, was the largest town except for Naples in all Italy, and growing faster than Rome, Milan or Turin. Speculation over building and illegal construction were already a problem by 1738. At a rough estimate its population doubled or almost doubled to about 200,000 in the course of the eighteenth century, in other words to four times the size of Messina. The territory round Palermo was fairly well colonised, and the town's jurisdiction well established over the near-by villages. Most of the aristocracy lived at Palermo; so did a growing slum population in shanty towns. The Viceroy's main concern was to indulge these aristocrats with honours and frivolity, and the urban proletariat with doles and cheap bread. Sicily was then easily governed.

Hence, as consul Leckie could put it, "the welfare of the whole has been sacrificed to the capital". At a time of recoinage, to take one example, only at Palermo could one exchange bad coins for good at par. The census still omitted Palermo, to its great profit. The proceeds of local *octrois* went to the city and not to the government, unlike those of Messina after 1678, and Palermitans still paid no *donativi* on their property elsewhere. Palermo was where government income was mostly spent and where the lawyers and civil servants were concentrated. Probably most members of parliament always came from this one town. If Palermo lacked food, exports might be forbidden from other coastal towns, and even in normal years Catania and Syracuse could not break Palermo's virtual monopoly of wheat brokering. The mayor and senate of the capital even took a leaf out of Messina's book and wanted to have it recognised that they could scrutinise projected laws to prevent infringement of their privileges.

Palermo was far more a town of administrators than of industry. Its dangerous harbour had by now been made larger and safer, but the Austrians had commented on its small share of overseas trade, and Sir William Hamilton in 1769 was surprised to find no ships there. Later in the century another northerner, the traveller Bartels, observed that the few ships at Palermo were foreign. The citizens took great pride in the *Senatus Populusque Panormitanus*, as their corporate self was grandiloquently styled, though to become a senator, commented the Frenchman Denon, was desired as an occasion for pride and display, not because of any notions about public service. A senator had considerable patronage; if he could also become a governor of the city bank or of the pawnshop he could find many ways of becoming rich as well as powerful. City entertainments were organised with immense zeal. Bull-fighting continued to be a favourite pastime, the bull-fighters still wearing Spanish costume; and carnival activities were most elaborate, with floats, masquerades, right down to mock executions with appropriate dirges and hooded processions.

Still more striking was the festival of St. Rosalia, one of the few occasions when a genuine collective effort overrode the individualism which inhibited public life. This July festival had some elements of a harvest thanksgiving after the wheat was gathered and food supplies were hopefully assured. For most citizens it seems to have been the peak moment of the year, as it also constituted the second biggest item in the city budget. The festivities lasted for five or even six days, during which work came to a stop, and were preceded by weeks of preparation. Each mayor had to outdo his predecessor with yet more expensive gaiety to fix the glory of his name upon the memory of a demanding populace. In 1746 the Prince of Lampedusa completely unbalanced the accounts through all the fireworks with which he signalised Palermo's gratitude to her protectress for being saved from the Messina plague; and the Viceroy gave qualified approval, for it was pointed out that the common people were thus distracted from less innocent pleasures.

The seventy-two *maestranze* or workers' guilds played an important part in the ceremonial life of Palermo and even its politics. Normally their internal affairs came under close supervision of the mayor and senate, but their cohesion and habitual discipline, together with the skills which were necessary for the smooth working of city life, could give them considerable power in an emergency. If food supplies broke down they could make or break the city government and challenge the authority of the Viceroy himself. As regulators of their trades, the guilds were closed monopolies devoted to the selfish perpetuation of privilege. They were thus essentially restrictive. They interpreted their interest as being to keep production on a small scale, to prevent undercutting in price, and to restrain tradesmen from getting ahead of their fellows by investing more capital or employing more labour. In politics, too, their tastes were anything but radical. Flattered by the government and city magnates, their members were sometimes permitted the valued privilege of carrying weapons, and usually were allowed hunting rights near Palermo, with the not unimportant result that they had some practice in arms. They were equally flattered by being allowed to act as auxiliary police and in times of emergency to man the city fortifications: this service was the more gratefully undertaken in that it was well paid. By being brought inside the circle of privilege, they too were given a status to defend against any insurrection of the *basso popolo*.

In 1773, when a revolt broke out in the capital, these artisan corporations suddenly found themselves to be, as they had been before in 1647 and 1708, the chief effective force in the island. The city aristocracy had been accumulating certain grievances against the Marquis Fogliani, who was then Viceroy, and this fact temporarily weakened the established order. Fogliani had begun by dutifully favouring the nobles as the chief prop for Neapolitan rule, and had even helped to conceal certain financial irregularities in their conduct of the city administration, but in his unusually long eighteen years of office he became a little impatient with aristocratic pretensions and pretentiousness. His friendliness towards the common people nettled Villabianca, who was terrified by the possibility of a "reduction in the importance of the feudal element". Fogliani had exhausted his powers of patronage, and many people would thus have been quite glad of a change. Most challenging of all, he had dared to attack certain tax immunities of Palermo and other privileges which concerned the parliamentary *donativi*. As increasing prices were bankrupting the *colonna frumentaria* and threatening to undermine the policy of subsidised bread on which the peace of Palermo depended, in 1770 he also imposed new taxes on luxuries, on windows, balconies, wine and the consumption of snow. There was an outcry: his notices were torn down, and most people flatly refused to pay. The rule had to be learnt once again that rich people simply would not accept this kind of graduated taxation; but meanwhile the alliance which normally bound the aristocracy to the government was momentarily snapped. A tax was also placed on coal, and this caused disaffection among some of the industrial guilds.

The failure of another harvest in 1773 then triggered off a popular explosion. When food supplies began to run short, some of the leather workers and gunmakers were processing barefoot in penitence, wearing crowns of thorns and whipping each other with chains in the usual manner; but once again intercession unexpectedly changed into violence. Hunger kindled a religious excitement which led to desecrating the images of saints and then to something like social revolution. A few boys began throwing stones—later they were conveniently labelled ringleaders of the 'revolt', and for this they were eventually torn to pieces publicly by the executioner. Others broke into houses and shops. Many nobles escaped hurriedly to their country villas, a fact which only aggravated unemployment and class antagonism. When finally the Swiss guard were provoked to the point of shooting, certain groups of citizens reacted by taking what was traditionally the first organised step on such occasions: they broke into the prisons, burnt the police files and set some of the convicts free. They also demolished the gallows, sacked the hangman's house, and tore the red and yellow uniform off his back. A hysterical crowd then proceeded to the Archbishop's prison, where the prostitutes were set free to add what they could to this moment of popular frenzy. Nevertheless there was still apparently little theft or bloodshed.

At this critical moment the Mayor, a man much trusted and liked, died after a dramatic and painful operation for stone; and the whole town, which had followed his sickness in detail, suffered an emotional shock. No more was needed than a rumour to spread that the Viceroy was bringing more troops into Palermo, and the *maestranze* then ran to the bastions, claiming their ancient right to defend the town gates. The sailors and coachmen took their traditional position at the Porta dei Greci, the barbers and tailors at the Porta di Vicari and so forth, the object being to prevent nobles leaving or soldiers entering. From several of these bastions they could direct cannon on the palace. Meanwhile the common people, seeing the normal forces of conservatism divided, quickly attacked the city armouries to exchange their sticks and billhooks for something more substantial; and—another fact with close parallels at other moments in Palermo history—Monreale, Montelepre and other near-by villages, as though by prior arrangement, broke out in gang warfare against the authorities.

Finally the palace was attacked, to the familiar cry of "Long live the King and out with the Viceroy". Fogliani humanely capitulated rather than order his troops to fire, and was escorted ignominiously down to the harbour by the consuls of the guilds. Thence he sailed for Messina, judging that Messina would see this as a chance to re-establish herself against Palermo; and in fact he was given a great welcome there and showered with gifts. But at Palermo the delighted rabble lost all control. The English consul and the Genoese Gazzini, both of them grain brokers, had their establishments ransacked. The mob also sought out a Sicilian suspected of rigging the coal trade and another who had bought the invidious right to collect some of the city food taxes. Some citizens took advantage of the situation to pursue private vendettas. Threatening broadsheets against the nobility also began to appear.

Only the *maestranze* saved the day, just as in 1647, for they had good reason to want law and order restored. Artisans and shopkeepers needed the nobles back in town. Cannon were therefore set up in the streets and the rioters disarmed. The guildsmen then acted as police and self-appointed magistrates, refusing to accept help from the troops and adamantly preventing the Archbishop bringing back the ordinary police as he would have liked. Within a few hours the 'idle vagabonds' were cleared out of town and sent to the galleys or the penal islands. It was said—and others had reported much the same in 1647 and 1708—that never before had there been such freedom from crime. Some anonymous delations were made against individuals accused of instigating the original revolt, and perhaps some private feuds were here being pursued. A few executions even took place, on not very much proof: if the intention was to inculcate fear, no doubt it succeeded, since the novice executioner botched his job, and even the hardened Palermo mob watched him in grim silence.

For a full year this emergency lasted. Food supplies were quickly reorganised, which suggests that the shortage had largely been due to illegal concealment; and, under the lead of the Archbishop, the city government gradually reasserted its authority over the countryside so that supplies could be better assured. As one measure of social reform, proclamations were sent to the villages encouraging peasants to apply for land under provisions of the law which had nationalised Jesuit property. Richer citizens and monasteries were taxed to provide doles to tide over the emergency and were obliged by law to provide more employment. Nobles who delayed their return to town were penalised.

Little by little the aristocratic establishment regained its lost authority, and "on orders from Spain confirmed by the Neapolitan court" the *maestranze* were deprived of their police powers. At once, so we are told, theft and assassination became common again, whether because the criminal classes were thereby turned once more against the government, or because the official police went back to their traditional policy of partial collusion with crime. Five thousand troops took over the fortifications, and the hundred cannon belonging to the city authorities were finally confiscated. There was little opposition, because the city magnates supported the Neapolitan government. They had signally lost face at the hands of this irregular army of workmen, and there was a strong desire to destroy the guilds as a serious political force. When a non-noble tried to become a Palermo senator, the very idea was now treated as scandalous. A senator's office carried no salary, but notoriously a great deal of money could be made on the side; and, in a society where status meant power, the senatorial entitlement to be considered a grandee of Spain, first class, could not be allowed to depreciate beyond a certain point.

The revolt therefore came to an end with the town aristocracy fully restored to power, but they were now heavily in debt to the government instead of the other way round. The experience of 1773 indicated to Ferdinand and his ministers that Sicily was slightly uncivilised and even dangerous; hence the government would be compelled to intervene more directly in future to prevent any recurrence of revolt. Some kind of initiative from Naples was seen to be required in order to help reduce class tensions, improve food distribution and diminish the chances of a yet more dreadful blend of town riots and a peasants' revolt. A Neapolitan, the Prince of Stigliano, was sent as Viceroy to see what could be done. At this prospect of further outside interference, Villabianca was provoked to comment that "Sicilians now find the Neapolitan nation very antipathetic".

Stigliano brought a less protectionist attitude to the basic problem of food supplies and wheat exports. Finding that contraband in small ships from the smaller ports was quite out of control, he lifted some restrictions so as to let the Palermo *colonna* buy at market prices; smuggling therefore suddenly became less profitable, and supplies unexpectedly became available on the open market. Although the cost of living went up, to people's astonishment there was little criticism of a move which so many previous governments had feared to take. So in 1777 the Viceroy advised introducing complete freedom of trade in cereals. He began by offering export licences to a wider circle of merchants than usual, only to discover that there was little demand. Intimidation may have been at work here, but it may have been merely that most rich Sicilians despised grain broking: they preferred to leave this type of business to foreigners, and foreigners were learning to buy cereals cheaper elsewhere. Nor had the government by any means entirely abandoned its restrictive policy. When Naples needed an emergency consignment of flour, the Viceroy commandeered the mills round Palermo, and in order to work them he stopped people using water for irrigation: the local reaction was such that the sacks of flour, when they arrived at Naples, mostly contained grass seed.

Passive obedience or disobedience had proved effective weapons against strong rule from Turin and Vienna; yet Fogliani, Stigliano and, above all, the next Viceroy Caracciolo, all in turn realised

Curved staircase of the 18th-century Villa Malvagno,
near Palermo

The Convento dei Benedettini, now a school, at Catania:
late 18th century

that Sicilian interests required another attempt at firm government. It was important to make the nobles set a better example and show more sense of responsibility; their growing indebtedness had to be curbed, if necessary by the threat of very severe penalties; they had to be brought more under the law if the law were ever to be respected. More frequently, therefore, the titled nobility were now sent to prison for their misdemeanours, not of course to the ordinary prisons, but to more decorous incarceration in a royal castle. Occasionally they were punished even for offences against people of lesser rank, for wounding a magistrate, or assaulting a ballet dancer who happened to possess powerful friends. More usually they were brought to book for offences against their own kind, whether for eloping with the daughter of a yet more lordly family, or after a family quarrel when a wife had relatives well enough placed to obtain redress. One duke was imprisoned for throwing another duke into the sea and damaging his face on some rocks. Such instances are trivial enough, but they show that the Bourbons had no intention of abdicating entirely to the feudal classes.

Chapter 34

THE VICEROYALTY OF CARACCIOLO 1781–1786

The Marquis Domenico Caracciolo was another Neapolitan, though born in Spain and of a Spanish mother. He had lived in Paris and London, and especially in the France of Turgot, Diderot and Helvétius he had learnt to dislike all he was to encounter in Sicily. So reluctant was he to take the appointment that he delayed his arrival for a year. He was appointed as a man of the Enlightenment and as someone who had no private axe to grind. Unlike some of his predecessors he was not so frightened of dismissal that he always waited for the King's approval before taking an initiative. Nor was he open to bribery. Being an honest man, possessed of courage, persistence and a sophisticated intelligence, he was able to initiate a more radical programme of reform than any since the thirteenth century.

His first move was to tackle the most vulnerable symbol of the old regime, the Inquisition—a relatively easy task because the Holy Office was no longer the institution which had once challenged even viceregal authority. When Caracciolo suppressed it in 1782, only three old witches were found in its prisons. The punishment of burning alive had fallen into disrepute and disuse over the previous half-century, and although homosexuals and other of the more vicious kinds of criminal were still publicly cremated after execution, this too was beginning to be thought distasteful because of the smell, if for nothing else. Like many of his predecessors, Caracciolo held against the Inquisition that many laymen owned the privilege of its *foro* with exemption from the ordinary courts. Protests had also reached him against its reliance on secret denunciations and secret testimony. On the other hand a number of aristocratic families appealed against Caracciolo's decision to suppress it, for they enjoyed lucrative sinecures paid out of the funds of the Inquisition; but the King overruled them and supported his minister.

Popular celebrations suggested that this was a welcome step, and many secular lawyers and ordinary clergy were delighted at the disappearance of a rival jurisdiction. The Inquisition had accumulated considerable wealth, some of which was now used to pension off the Inquisitors, and demands also poured in from other individuals who thought that they might like a share. Some of the money was used to boost the endowments of the Palermo academy. A year later, on the appeal of the last Grand Inquisitor, the King ordered that all the papers of the Inquisition should be burnt; they contained too many secrets about both Church and State; moreover some families might otherwise have risked exposure to unwelcome publicity over faith or morals, or because they had used the Inquisition to harass their private enemies. For a whole day and night the archives burnt. The cause of history lost immeasurably, yet a blow against the old order had been struck.

Caracciolo was a moderate anti-clerical, but the existence of the Apostolic Legateship had helped to keep ecclesiastics away from political power, and the Church hardly seemed a major obstacle to reform. He closed some more monasteries and reduced the number of feast days which required a public holiday. As representative of the Apostolic Legate he was ready to issue quite petty regulations about the number of candles on altars and expenditure by the clergy on sweetmeats. On a matter of more substance he forbade bishops and abbots to ask papal permission before paying tax, and prohibited the use of excommunication in cases which touched on politics. Though he kept the ecclesiastical censorship, the jurisdiction of Church courts was further restricted, and he encouraged the police to ignore rights of asylum in churches. None of this aroused much opposition: if he was criticised by Sicilians, it was rather for not reducing ecclesiastical tithes and not asserting even more forcefully the King's legatine powers over the Church.

A more serious objective in the hierarchy of privilege was the town of Palermo. The Viceroy had only disdain for the addiction to ceremonial of the Palermo senators, as he denied their claim to franchises which had little basis in law or history, and despised their inability to live within their means either as individuals or as custodians of the city budget. He tried to reduce the multiplication of jobs in the town administration and make the senators see that salaries were not just a mark of status. Much to their chagrin, he reduced from over a hundred to eighteen the annual parades which they claimed as a senatorial privilege. Like every strong Viceroy he tried to limit the carrying of weapons in the Palermo streets, though his notices to this effect were defaced by the guildsmen who realised that their privileges too were being attacked.

A conflict which broke out during a religious celebration then gave him an excuse to reform the statutes of the guilds. Processions at night were forbidden as a security measure. Some of these privileged corporations were even dissolved if it could be argued that they were concerned with essential services where public interest should be paramount. Those which survived were in future no longer to be closed monopolies; anyone was entitled to join them, and their subscriptions were to be voluntary; nor could they claim any separate right of *foro*. This was a most substantial defeat for the Palermo *maestranze*, and it explains why the more privileged shopkeepers and skilled workers shared with the aristocracy a fear of this Neapolitan reformer.

A special grievance, felt by even the *basso popolo* at Palermo, was over Caracciolo's attempt to interfere in the festival of St. Rosalia. In 1783 he ordered that these civic celebrations should continue for only three days instead of five: the money saved should go to provide dowries for poor girls and so enable them to get married. No other act of Caracciolo's aroused so much hostility, and the fact is a revealing comment on unreformed Sicily. Rich and poor alike were outraged. The Viceroy's life was threatened. In the end the King had to intervene and countermand this overbold attempt to alter popular custom.

Caracciolo's chief target, however, was the nobility, because two hundred people had "swallowed up one and a half million". He found that Sicily was "inhabited only by either oppressors or the oppressed", and its troubles could almost always be traced back to "the tyranny of the great proprietors". If agriculture was defective, it was largely because landowners took everything out of the land and put nothing back; if law and order were weak, this was partly because they placed themselves above the law; if industry and trade stagnated and tax revenue was small, it was the superior attitude of this small class which was again to blame. A country could not flourish if the ruling elite despised commerce and so successfully evaded tax; nor if debtors could retreat to the safety of some feudal jurisdiction; nor if the barons so terrified the peasantry by their relentless vendettas that no one dared appeal for government help. In Caracciolo's opinion, privilege could be justified only if there were a corresponding sense of public service; and of this the barons had very little. In his view they were merely *chevaux de parade* who had made everyone afraid of them but who could easily be deflated if their bluff was called.

The Viceroy first repudiated di Napoli's extreme feudal doctrines. Severe penalties were threatened against anyone who asserted that Sicilian fiefs were not held from the King and could not revert to him. Documentary proof could once again be demanded of baronial claims to jurisdiction, and baronial courts should remain under strict royal supervision: they could not, for example, be leased or transferred like real estate, since the King had only delegated and not renounced his rights of justice. No longer could a feudatory arrest his vassals without stated reason, but instead encouragement was given to any citizens who wished to buy their return into the royal demesne. Private armies and private military uniforms were declared illegal, and servants were forbidden to use swords even for purely decorative purposes.

Caracciolo also ordered the closure of the *dammusi*. He forbade the practice in baronial territories of substituting the barons' insignia for that of the King. He would have liked Ferdinand to come in person so that people could see him and realise that the barons had a master; but the King showed no sign of wanting to visit his remote, subsidiary kingdom.

Even though enforcement of these laws was difficult, the oppressed majority now occasionally took heart. Creditors were nerved to put pressure on defaulting aristocrats, and not only royal towns but feudal towns were emboldened to appeal against feudal impositions. Earlier laws were revived which forbade barons to interfere in town government. Magistrates occasionally felt strong enough to resist improper pressure in the courts, and the police were encouraged to enforce the law even inside baronial palaces. Nobles were arrested for protecting delinquents or for browbeating local authorities and suborning witnesses. No previous Viceroy had ever treated them so abruptly, and the public disgrace in front of their own subordinates was mortifying. They began to fear that the lower orders might take advantage of this discomfiture, and it needed only a sudden rumour of rioting for the town magnates in 1782 to fly into the countryside. Every means of influence was therefore used to make the King dismiss this terrible Viceroy before it was too late.

Caracciolo had been selected for his post because, as an economist, he might discover how Sicily could be made less poor and pay more tax. Some items of expenditure he was able to reduce. He lowered the official rate of interest on government borrowing; he repurchased the postal service and other regalian rights acquired by private families; and he tried to bring more German and English merchants back to Messina. For the first time a serious attempt was made by engineers to systematise Catania harbour. Collectors of taxes, superintendents of public works, civic officials and administrators of banks were all instructed to watch their accounts more carefully and have them ready for audit. Far more important than this, however, was the fundamental problem that those who could afford to pay tax still paid almost nothing. The tax on flour consumption, which produced most revenue, hardly affected rich people at all, but was "an open conspiracy of government and landowners against consumers". Caracciolo wanted to get rid of privileged exemptions and devise a tax system in which capacity to pay meant at least something. Without unduly burdening the country, taxes could be raised by a third, he thought, and Sicily in the process would be made more and not less productive.

As a tentative move towards progressive taxation he introduced an annual impost on carriages in order to pay for paving the streets of Palermo. There were some eight hundred horse-drawn carriages in Palermo, not counting numerous sedan chairs. The suggestion to make them pay an annual licence fee was hardly anything very substantial, yet the idea of taxing a luxury aroused the greatest indignation. When some of the nobles refused to pay, the Viceroy sent the bailiffs into their palaces to seize the best carriages and sell them.

Then he turned to the question of agricultural land and his favourite project for a land tax. Agricultural property carried only indirect taxes such as the *tratte* and the *macinato*, and these were regularly shifted either on to the poor, or, as Leckie said, on to "the middle ranks of society, who hold farms in copyhold, or perpetual quit-rent tenure, all noble and ecclesiastical fiefs being one way or another exempted". Military service was still given as the reason why feudal proprietors were exempt from thirteen of the eighteen parliamentary *donativi*; but, added Leckie again, "if you request their military service they tell you that they are commuted for the taxes, and thus they pay neither". In any case the voluntary declaration of property for purposes of the *donativi* was absurd, and in fact the true surface area of Sicily was perhaps twice that which appeared in the *riveli* of the census. Caracciolo told the King that the government possessed no list of baronial lands and could only guess at their income. He had no idea how much land was held outside Palermo by Palermitans and so escaped tax altogether; he had no idea how much allodial property existed, nor how much was held in mortmain. This was one of the main reasons why Sicily remained poor. A proper valuation of property was an indispensable prerequisite of tax reform. Yet both barons and ecclesiastics in the 1782 parliament formally objected to having one.

Caracciolo here came up against one of the chief pillars of the old regime. As a man who had seen enlightened authoritarianism in Paris and Naples, he regarded parliament as an institution which typified and protected waste, inefficiency and unfairness. The Sicilian parliament had nothing to do with liberty; on the contrary it was arbitrary and tyrannical. Only in the domanial House did he find, alongside its aristocratic leadership, enough lawyers who might hope for preferment at his hands and could therefore be won to his views. Against the wish of the two upper Houses, these representatives of the towns were now persuaded to petition that the privileged classes should at last have their lands properly surveyed and subjected to tax.

This parliamentary petition was the crucial confrontation on which depended the Viceroy's whole campaign. To the annoyance of the traditionalists, he in person read the King's speech to parliament; and behind courteous words they discerned an "ill-mannered and threatening tone". Some of his listeners walked out. Previous Viceroys had found little difficulty in packing parliament so that they could obtain their minimal requirements of tax, and in return used to turn a blind eye on its deficiences. Caracciolo, however, scorned any craven compromise: he wanted more efficiency in mobilising the resources of the kingdom, and knew that the upper two Houses would never voluntarily agree with him. Parliament would therefore have to be reformed. He believed that, just as the barons had invented unhistorical justifications for their own immunities, so parliament had been trying to invent a legislative authority it did not possess. In the process it had become the mouthpiece of a tiny minority who thought that they had everything to lose from change.

Caracciolo first learnt the size of this problem when in 1782 he had to go through the formalities of asking for the *donativi*. Again in 1783 another parliament had to be called for a grant to help repair earthquake damage at Messina. The parliamentary barons did not refuse to grant the money which he suggested: indeed that would have been unthinkable. But they did resist his revolutionary plan to change the type of tax and its method of assessment and collection. When he teased them with the suggestion that parliament should rather be called a 'congress', and the *donativi* called 'contributions', and above all when he tried to stop them claiming direct access to the King except through himself, they could see that the whole question of their social predominance was under attack. The public session of parliament in 1783 took only a few hours, but there must have been many meetings in private, and the opposition had the advantage that the King's chief minister at Naples was still the Sicilian aristocrat, Sambuca. The Prince of Trabia, who was head of the domanial House, wrote to Sambuca begging for "liberation from a slavery worse than that of the people of Israel in Babylon"; and, under pressure, the King decided not to push the matter to an immediate decision.

A somewhat easier target was economic protectionism, and here Caracciolo was aided by the fact that famine conditions after the Messina earthquake made emergency remedies acceptable. A profusion of corn laws had grown up over the centuries without any plan; yet they had not prevented starvation becoming more frequent, nor Sicilian bread being the worst he had ever tasted. In Naples and Paris he had observed that free trade might be a better remedy against famines than protection; he had learnt that monopolies, fixed prices, the innumerable excise offices, the refusal to allow people to sell their produce where they wished or to work where they pleased, all these might exacerbate the very same problem which they were designed to relieve, namely that of keeping people fed.

Profiting from Stigliano's experience, Caracciolo abolished the municipalised bakeries with their fixed prices for bread, because under cover of being in the consumers' interest they were open to much trickery and profiteering. Henceforward, at least in law, people could make what quality of bread and *pasta* they wanted, and could sell it for what price they could get. The Viceroy also insisted that it was against the public interest for a landowner to compel tenants to grind their corn at his mill or to crush their olives and grapes at his press; nor should they have to sell their produce to him at his own price. It was wrong for barons to impose taxes on their tenants capriciously and without appeal. Caracciolo was here laying down rules which were generally accepted in other countries, but the attempt did not ingratiate him with the Sicilian landlords.

His preference was also for free export; or, at least, he wanted to reverse existing practice and make free export the norm and impose controls only in an emergency. The complex system of *tratte* not only deterred foreign buyers, but had led to large-scale contraband and the systematic corruption of government officials; so doing, it had helped to mould patterns of behaviour and attitudes towards society that were becoming inveterate. At the same time the chief profits from agriculture were being diverted to a few merchants who specialised in buying and selling export licences. Prices could be manipulated artificially by these merchants, so that instead of controls keeping food cheap, the very reverse might be true. Caracciolo was determined to break the quasi-monopoly of this small ring of speculators, and he hoped that free trade would mean more export, more land under truly profitable cultivation, and so better agricultural wages. It would certainly make smuggling harder and the making of false declarations about wheat crops less remunerative.

The Viceroy was not so dogmatic a free-trader as some of his critics thought. At one moment of suspected food shortage he intervened to stop exports just like his predecessors, with the result that he made the shortage worse because people panicked and began hoarding. This taught him a lesson, for his original information had been false and probably derived from speculators who wanted to increase prices. A more beneficial experiment in government intervention was his convoy system against piracy, by which twice a year, in spring and autumn, merchant ships would congregate at Trapani to be escorted by frigates to Gibraltar.

Another well-intentioned scheme was to provide agrarian credit to help peasants own properties without having to capitulate to usurers and money-lending landowners. There existed at Palermo a *mont de piété* which originally had been created to lend money cheaply to small farmers; but, by a familiar process in this feudal world, the landowners had used their authority to pervert its functions. Schemes for cheap credit, they argued, would give their workers independence, for which reason landlords sometimes liked to include in tenancy contracts a stipulation that borrowing must be only from themselves. Landowners also wanted to borrow at cheap rates so as to be able to delay selling their wheat while prices were low. A public institution was therefore turned into something which was far more in the private than the public interest.

Caracciolo wanted smaller farms and knew that cheap credit was vital for this. Against the immobilism of the *latifondisti* he could argue that a growth of smaller copyhold tenures had in the previous century led to an improvement in Sicilian agriculture. Long leases and greater security of tenure would stimulate farmers to make agriculture more intensive and more highly capitalised. Perhaps villages could also be encouraged to let out part of their communal lands in *enfiteusi*. Some villages, in order to obtain money for their tax obligations and for other minor expenses over tithes and police, had been trying to turn these commons into profitable leaseholds, but local authorities were so much under baronial influence that the leases were generally offered to existing landowners, and the *latifondi* had thereby become all the more strongly entrenched. Caracciolo here touched on a fundamental problem, but it was more complex than he knew, and for the moment he could do little more than encourage the villagers to stand up for their rights.

Chapter 35

THE PARTIAL SUCCESS OF REFORM

Caracciolo's reforms were much less radical than some of those being carried out elsewhere in Europe, but hostility to them was immense. Up to a point his success was remarkable, especially in view of the fact that he had little force at his disposal. Nothing in Sicily was to be quite the same ever again; moreover the opposition which he provoked into life was going to be an important element in the country's political education. Yet his temperament was too abrasive and uncompromising. Believing in reason and progress, he was interested in the desirable rather than the possible. Perhaps he was at once too radical and insufficiently liberal to be a truly successful reformer, and he did not always stop to understand the historical roots of what he was attacking. He was excessively fond of a fight, as he also liked using sarcasm against people whose pride was easily wounded; and on occasion he was impulsive and angry where mere cunning and compromise might have succeeded. In his eagerness to magnify state authority he revived an old regulation against pasquinades, and even imprisoned one young noble for a satire which was no more than a boyish prank: this revealed an insufficiently light touch in meeting criticism.

Inevitably the Viceroy became unpopular with many different kinds of people. To the rest of Europe he was one of the most liked and admired of contemporary Italians, but in Sicily his charm, his intelligence and his sense of duty and service were unappreciated. High-born families remembered with nostalgia how Fogliani on occasion had graciously visited their houses, and how Stigliano made the fountains flow with wine in front of the Viceroy's palace. By comparison, Caracciolo was parsimonious, aloof and condescending. He banned the indecent masks and 'bacchanalian festivities' of carnival time, as he taxed playing cards and restricted gambling. He tried to stop bull-fighting in the streets and noisy nocturnal celebrations. Obviously he underestimated the difficulty of legislating about personal behaviour in a society where law and government were so discounted; yet simultaneously he went much too far himself in flouting accepted custom. It caused offence that he would not wear his hat in church as it was traditionally his duty to do as representative of the Apostolic Legate. His French manners were altogether too novel for this provincial backwater, and the social elite were indignant if they found themselves sitting at dinner next to a prima donna from the opera: actors and actresses, as everyone else knew, were not socially acceptable save in private.

Caracciolo found little active support inside Sicily, a fact which has variously been used to prove either the ineptitude of his reforms or the apathetic isolationism of the people he was trying to help. The traditions of the Enlightenment were too weak, and any changes therefore carried the extra disadvantage of having to be imposed from outside. Some of the intellectuals half-agreed with him, but a world which did not revolve around the aristocracy was unthinkable to most of them, and centralisation by Naples might well have seemed to portend fewer jobs and slower advancement for anyone who remained at Palermo. There was even a surprising unawareness of what Caracciolo was trying to do; the ground was unprepared, and there was no group of people or attitude of mind which he could employ.

He himself admitted that his most difficult task was to overcome the resistance of the very people whom he wished to deliver from oppression. "So degrading to the soul is servitude that it makes people unaware of their chains." Since the poor had no means of appealing to Naples, he construed it as his job "to rescue them from the claws of those wolves who call themselves the barons of Sicily". He found the peasants shackled to the world of feudalism by centuries of habit and servility. They had no political education, little knowledge of events outside their family and only a partial understanding of how the tax system was weighted against them. The Viceroy's order that civic officers should be elected was not something which ordinary townsmen could understand, nor in any case would their illiteracy and powerlessness have enabled them to obey him. If they had understood his treatment of the aristocracy they might well have been delighted, but they were as indignant as anyone when he tried to limit the gay life of Palermo, or when he insisted on all classes of citizens obeying the law.

Without doubt his reforms were sometimes seen as threatening not only aristocratic privileges but also the wider liberties of Sicily in general, and this feeling was assiduously encouraged by those who felt most threatened. There was an unwelcome sense of being treated as a conquered and even despised people; to some it seemed offensive that the King never visited the island, while Sicilians who travelled to Naples met with indifference or worse. Caracciolo could not avoid seeming disdainful of a people whom he thought degraded by tyranny. He referred to them as 'infamous', a word which was more insulting than he probably knew. Even many of the intellectuals were 'barbarians' and knew no Latin. One result of this condescending attitude was that a much more virulent antagonism to Naples now developed, which reinforced the traditional assumption that any government was an enemy; and hence, instead of encouraging the growth of social consciousness, Caracciolo's policy on this one material point had the very opposite effect. One visiting Englishman heard Sicilian nobles blame their troubles on governmental interference which, to their mind, prevented local resources being properly used; and this paradoxical argument without doubt won for the social elite some adventitious support in their struggle against reform.

Conservatism did not, of course, characterise only the upper classes. Peasants equally distrusted new methods of farming as something which would be bound to upset the precarious balance of agriculture. It was a common view, especially (but not only) in rural Sicily, that change must be for the worse, and this attitude reflected a deep pessimism about society which militated against any attempts at improvement. In an economy where everything was precarious, the ordinary farm labourer could never make plans even for the short-term future. Perhaps this unreadiness to think ahead was reflected in the absence from the Sicilian dialect of a future tense.

Caracciolo had a vision of building aqueducts and constructing roads to link up the centre of the island with the ports, but as soon as his own forward-looking stimulus had been removed, such schemes were forgotten. Most of his projects partially foundered on this rock. Appalled by conditions of marketing in Palermo, he bravely tackled the monopolies and racketeering in the wholesale food trade; but these rackets remained a byword for many generations to come. Appalled by the indescribable stink in churches, he built a new outdoor cemetery for Palermo, but the gravediggers (and the clergy who enjoyed fat fees from burial in church) were able to mobilise public opinion against this attack on a profitable perquisite. The senate of Palermo had already forbidden the practice by which the corpses of beggars were publicly exposed to beg alms for their burial; yet exposure of the dismembered bodies of criminals persisted long after the Viceroy tried to stop it. In almost every field the weight of tradition worked against change, just as it told against the notions of public service and social conscience. "Tradition", he confessed, "is the argument always brought up here by those who intend to feather their nest at the expense of the King and the poor."

Annoyance with some of Caracciolo's measures does not prove that his policy was generally unpopular. The rich were vocal and powerful; they were able to go to Naples and intrigue against him at court, whereas agricultural labourers had no contact with the government and no channel through which their views could be known. At Naples the Queen and her favourite minister, Sir John

Acton, were ready to support Caracciolo, realising that the Sicilian aristocracy were a threat to Naples and the monarchy; but King Ferdinand, though he often followed his wife's advice, was too busy with his minor pleasures to be bothered. Sambuca was not entirely averse to reform, yet he was lazy, corrupt and bound by many ties to his fellow Sicilian barons. The court of Spain itself was invoked to help oppose the Viceroy's attitude. Finally, he was honourably withdrawn by being promoted to succeed Sambuca at Naples.

Caracciolo himself chose as his successor the Prince of Caramanico, another Neapolitan and man of the Enlightenment who had lived in northern Europe; and another mainlander, Simonetti, who as *Consultore* had been second in charge at Palermo and an important inspiration of Caracciolo's reforms, remained in the administration to show that policy had not changed. Caramanico had less imagination and was less energetic than his predecessor, but in some ways was a more effective Viceroy. As well as being a convinced reformer, his more accommodating temperament won friends among the barons, and they went some way to meet him just because they now realised their vulnerability. He took care not to reveal any obvious signs of contempt or impatience towards them, but showed pleasure at entering the social round. Instead of a direct attack on the old regime, his own technique was to erode it gradually.

One of Caramanico's achievements was to make parliament agree to a new distribution of tax and the very survey of property which had earlier aroused such opposition. This census was delayed by the outbreak of the French revolutionary wars, but nevertheless the decision to have it was a useful threat. Parliament thus agreed to make taxes proportional to income in order "to lighten the load on the poorest classes of society". It was also agreed to change the inequitable system by which baronial towns paid less than their fair share of the *donativi*. Palermitans who owned property elsewhere in Sicily were no longer to be so favoured in tax matters. By accepting these changes, the nobles were publicly admitting the need for a new deal and the fact that their old privileges were not inviolable. Caramanico also established that the baronial monopolisation of the parliamentary Deputation was wrong in law as well as inexpedient.

Feudalism was further weakened when, by a pragmatic sanction in 1788, the King finally supported Caracciolo's view that the thirteenth-century laws, *Volentes* and *Si aliquem*, had made no fundamental change in feudal obligations. For this purpose the manuscript volumes on feudal services compiled by Barberi early in the sixteenth century were sought out in the archives and taken to Naples. Once again it was confirmed that fiefs were held in return for duties performed, and the King still kept lordship over them: they could not be bequeathed or alienated like allodial property, but royal confirmation and a special payment were needed before they could be inherited; and, failing a proper succession, or if a proper entitlement could not be proved, they should revert to the crown. Moreover peasants could not, except with compensation, be dispossessed of any rights of communal usage established by law or custom, not even on a baronial fief. Of course these were only legal decisions, and considerable efforts were made to mitigate their practical application, but ordinary people now received direct encouragement to assert their rights, and this was one ingredient in the gradual changing of public opinion.

The fief was a term in feudal law. In agricultural terms it largely corresponded to the semi-cultivated ranches where sparsely grown wheat alternated with nomadic cattle rearing. These *latifondi* covered most of Sicily. They were owned either by the barons and higher clergy, or sometimes communally by the villages. Sooner or later any reformer had to decide how this type of landownership and its concomitant methods of non-intensive agriculture could be bettered. A typical difficulty was that many villagers, by their immemorial rights of pasture on the *latifondi*, made intensive crop farming impossible even if landlords had been willing to allow it; indeed any change in farming techniques was rendered impossible without a group consent by all interested parties—which in this individualistic world was unattainable. These rights of common usage, helpful though they were to many individuals, were one reason why agricultural output was not keeping pace with a rising population. The *latifondisti* understandably wanted a more unfettered ownership over their property; and already, either by arbitrary enclosures or by buying out other parties, many landowners were moving in this direction. The government knew that any revocation of 'promiscuous rights' would deprive many shepherds and other farmers of a livelihood; they also believed, however, that if communal methods of extensive cultivation could only be replaced by small farms individually owned, this ought to mean increased production, and equally it would give landless labourers a beneficial stake in society.

An edict of 1789 therefore aimed at increasing smallholdings, by bringing new land into cultivation and old farms into more intensive use. Some of the common lands in village possession were to be divided into copyholds and given for preference to poor people in exchange for the surrender of their rights of pasture and wood collecting. A similar decision was made for the large areas of ecclesiastical land where the King was patron. The idea sounded promising. A peasant could hope to receive fifteen acres of land within four miles of his home, or as much as forty acres if further away; and in his own plot he would have security of tenure and a legal right to stop other people's animals grazing on his wheat.

In practice, however, these laws sometimes took an unexpected turn: either the peasants could not pay the ground rent and could not even acquire the basic capital needed for independent farming; or else the plots of land were too small and too distant; or else the laws were manipulated to their own profit by the local bosses in each village. There was a class of 'semi-gentlemen', as Sergio ominously called them, who were taking over from absentee landlords and had gunmen to enforce their will; and these men frustrated the reform by ensuring that the bosses and their friends gained the most from this division of land.

Economically desirable though it was to define rights of property, and though the number of peasant owners was in fact increased, socially the result of these laws was generally to enrich people who were already rich enough and in large part parasitic on society, at the same time as a rural proletariat was created which forfeited immemorial and valuable rights in the commons without receiving any compensation. Much the same effect was achieved, paradoxically, by another edict of 1789 which in theory abolished the last traces of villeinage and personal servitude. Peasants were being emancipated into casual wage earners, and Balsamo described how wages for the past twenty years had fallen behind the cost of living. The problem of seasonal unemployment often remained as bad as ever, for newly enclosed land was usually sown with wheat, and wheat needed no labour at all for most of the year. Instead of reducing revolutionary tensions as the government had hoped, there was a multiplication in the number of casual labourers who lived precariously and had little or nothing to fall back on in years of difficulty. Before long the rootlessness and desperate poverty of these largely unemployed labourers would make them a revolutionary force of real significance.

The Abbé Balsamo watched this process with some apprehension. He was one of a select body of intellectuals who had benefited from government patronage under two reforming Viceroys— indeed he became a pluralist with two abbeys as a sinecure. One or two of these intellectual reformers were of noble family, for instance Natale and di Blasi. The large majority were ecclesiastics who had a special interest in either education, science or economics. There existed only a tiny lay element in society which was educated and travelled, and a religious career was the most obvious means of preferment for any ambitious intellectual.

Among these ecclesiastics, apart from Balsamo, there was Giovanni Agostino de Cosmi the educationist, and Giovanni Evangelista di Blasi the historian. There was the economist, Saverio Scrofani, who had to leave Sicily for a time after some financial trouble and made good use of exile to improve his education; likewise there was Giovanni Gambini, canon of Catania cathedral, who transferred to Milan, where later he translated the *Code Napoléon* into Italian. Giuseppe Piazzi the celebrated astronomer was another, a man who had spent several years studying his subject in England. Giovanni Meli, the greatest dialect poet of modern Sicily, was in minor orders. Rosario Gregorio, appointed canon of Palermo cathedral by Caracciolo, was a distinguished legal historian, and it was he who first broke with the tradition of official chronicles; stimulated by the Scottish school of historical writing, Gregorio wrote about the Sicilian Middle Ages in a way which destroyed many mythological and stereotyped views about law and history. Feudalism and parliament were portrayed in his scholarly works very differently from the orthodoxy of fifty years earlier, and at last some sense was made out of the tangle of legislation which had grown up out of so many foreign conquests. Here was powerful intellectual support for the enlightened despotism of Caracciolo against those who looked to parliament for political salvation.

Education and agriculture were the subjects most in need of a new broom. Until 1767, the Jesuits were the dominant influence in education, and their work had hardly been an unqualified success. The intellectual world of Palermo, for example, was taken in by the impostures of the Abbé Vella until Gregorio taught himself Arabic. Meli, too, could become professor of chemistry at Palermo while knowing virtually nothing about the subject, and he had to reassure his students that he would keep a day ahead of them in the textbook. Meanwhile illiteracy was almost total. But slowly a new generation was appearing with very different standards. There was Domenico Scinà who in 1796, at the age of 31, became professor of experimental physics, and who also combined scientific interests with literary criticism and history. Caramanico wanted someone to organise teachers' training colleges, and his happy choice was Canon de Cosmi of Catania, a man who disbelieved in the formal traditions of Sicilian education, who deplored excessive antiquarianism and put practical concerns above abstract speculation. At last some thought was directed under his influence to primary education. Some of the barons, even those who were prepared to patronise the relatively innocuous world of *belles lettres*, called the training of teachers a waste of money, and there was an attempt to dismiss de Cosmi for being a dangerous radical. Perhaps others did not like his eagerness to insist on a correct knowledge of Italian, for this was a language which some professors at Palermo university still could not properly speak, let alone write.

Most thorough and thoughtful of all these reformers was Paolo Balsamo, for whom in 1787 was created a chair of agricultural science at Palermo and who later became professor of political economy. Balsamo used this appointment as a chance to spend three years touring northern Italy, France and England to examine the latest agricultural practices; but, unlike so many other Sicilian intellectuals in the past, he did not become a permanent expatriate, for government policies were now creating a more hopeful outlet for talent in Sicily itself. He returned with new agricultural methods and tools, and full of ideas learnt from Arthur Young and Adam Smith. He was then entrusted by Caramanico with the task of surveying the deficiencies of Sicilian agriculture.

Under Balsamo's influence, experiments now took place with irrigation, artificial leys, cattle sheds and the rotation of crops. He argued that Sicily could never become prosperous without more capital, and this could only be formed through agriculture; but it would need a wholly new attitude towards entails, mortmain, 'promiscuous rights', excises, the *tratte* and all the other restrictive practices which hindered rational development. Balsamo was remarkable chiefly because he rejected the pessimism which refused to see any possibility of improvement. Unfortunately he was much too excited about what he found in England, and too ready to believe that it could be adapted to the different physical and psychological conditions of Sicily. Yet nothing should have been so inducive to a break in the main psychological barrier as his expert conviction that there was nothing inherently wrong with the climate or the soil. Longer leases, less extortionate contracts of labour, more knowledge about the outside world, these alone might create a revolutionary improvement.

A few intellectuals, encouraged by two of the ablest Viceroys in all Sicilian history, were thus beginning to question some of the fundamental principles of the *ancien régime*. The idea of progress and notions about social obligation could now occasionally make their appearance. From the writings of Meli we can see that, already by the 1780s, Rousseau and Voltaire had become fashionable names to drop in the aristocratic salons of Palermo. The Prince of Aci and Prince Lanza di Trabia are examples of nobles who were interested in agricultural experiment. Especially in the much more open town of Catania there was even an infiltration of radically democratic ideas from France.

Ironically the French Revolution of 1789 then abruptly halted this process, for the King's more reactionary advisers persuaded him that further reforms might bring a demand for political liberty and so undermine both State and Church just as in France. The danger was real, for the influence of jacobinism was not negligible in Sicily, especially after Caramanico's death took away a moderating force. The new Viceroy, Archbishop Lopez, was soon confronted by the revolutionary army of the French republic which marched down through Italy until it was encamped over the straits within sight of Messina. Some individual Sicilians went into exile in France because of their advanced ideas. Others made one or two minuscule attempts at revolution. Francesco di Blasi, another reformer who had been employed by Caramanico, was spurred to translate Rousseau's ideas of social justice into action, and in 1795 planned a republican rebellion to take place during the Good Friday processions: a number of private denunciations, some of them apparently out of mere personal rancour, revealed his intentions to the police, and he was publicly tortured and beheaded.

Di Blasi's sympathisers seem to have been mainly among the artisan classes and more in eastern than western Sicily. They were not very clear in their ideas, nor convinced enough to risk prison and death, and they had no notion how to organise a conspiracy. Almost nothing bound them to the common labourers and peasants without whom there was no propulsive force for a genuine insurrection. They themselves were not for the most part men of violence, and at the first sign of a truly popular riot most of them were quick to line up behind their patrons, the aristocracy. Such riots took place fairly often now, whenever times were difficult. There were some, for example at Syracuse and Catania in 1798, and again in 1799 at Trapani and elsewhere. In 1801, another republican group, again in the progressive town of Catania, was once more betrayed to the police and ended in execution. But in general this kind of tumult seems to have had little to do with jacobinism or politics. Sometimes it was merely an excuse for private revenges, which merely provoked others to help the government imprison some private enemy. Nearly always it would begin as a hunger riot or as a spontaneous movement against a sudden rise in the food taxes. Sometimes it was instigated by the police, who were badly paid and hence uncontrollable; this was especially true in that the local police forces were largely proletarian organisations which enjoyed a virtual immunity for any offences committed and often had special interests of their own to promote.

The reformers of the Enlightenment had not succeeded in

prising Sicily loose from her history when a European war broke out which stopped change, provoked a counter revolution and temporarily restored the old balance in society. Sicily was, apart from Sardinia, the only region of Italy which Napoleon did not conquer and so escaped the message of the French Revolution. This fact, which helps to explain Napoleon's uncomplimentary opinion of Sicilians, was of the greatest consequence. Di Blasi bewailed the faint-heartedness of his fellow countrymen, but in fact there is no likelihood that any spontaneous political revolt could have succeeded. The middle class to whom he might have appealed was negligible, and even the songs of the common people were anti-jacobin. Balsamo became highly unpopular; twenty-five years later his teaching and even his name had been almost forgotten except by a very few. Only if French troops had landed would there have been a chance to break free from geographical isolation. Only if Napoleon had remembered to make provision for transports at Reggio di Calabria could the work of Caracciolo and Caramanico have been taken to what might seem its logical conclusion.

PART 10
Later Bourbon Sicily 1800–1837

Chapter 36

BRITISH INTERVENTION

If Sicily was saved for the old regime after 1789, this was in part because the King was frightened into abandoning a policy of reform and falling back on the barons and bishops as a defence against revolution. In the second place it was because Napoleon's victories resulted in occupation of the island becoming an urgent strategic necessity for Britain. At the same time, Napoleon's success made a close British alliance the one hope of survival for the Bourbons. When the French captured Malta, which was still nominally a Sicilian dependency, Neapolitan troops helped the British retake it; and though the latter at first claimed to rule in Ferdinand's name, Malta in fact found herself removed for ever from Sicilian sovereignty. Sicily, too, inevitably lost some independence as soon as it became a link in Britain's attempt to blockade Europe and keep open the Mediterranean sea routes. Though the British promised at first that they would "not on any account interfere in the civil administration of Sicily", they did not take long to change their mind.

When Napoleon's army invaded Naples in 1798, Ferdinand fled to Palermo on Nelson's flagship; it was his first visit in forty years as King. His personal papers show how rarely he had ever thought about Sicilian affairs until now, when he desperately needed a refuge. The main preoccupation of his government had been that enough Sicilian wheat should be sent to Naples, and this had sometimes amounted to as much as a million bushels a year. He had chosen excellent Viceroys to govern at Palermo, but their successes and failures evidently meant little to him.

The King's arrival was greeted with delight, because it seemed to signify independence once again from Naples and a profitable return of court life and court expenditure. In all outward respects, at any rate, the country gave Ferdinand unqualified support against revolutionary France; and the ferocity of the common people in this cause was such that some hundreds of sick French soldiers who landed at Augusta were murdered out of hand. The King, on the other hand, looked on Sicilians merely as a source of money for maintaining his court and as a base for recovering Naples. Deprived of his mainland provinces he was without five-sixths of his income, yet he could not bear to reduce his expenditure correspondingly. His Austrian Queen, who was his greatest extravagance, acquired what she confessed to the British to be a real hatred of Sicilians. Palermo seemed to her in every respect several generations behind Naples. "The priests are completely corrupted, the people savage, the nobility of questionable loyalty", so she wrote; and, true enough, some of the highest aristocracy were soon secretly in touch with the British and claiming that all classes would prefer annexation by Britain.

Sicily in some ways gained greatly by the arrival of these strangers. The King may have been uncouth and illiberal, but some of his entourage were, by comparison with what they encountered, sophisticated and progressive. Sicilians now learnt about new styles of architecture, new standards of personal living, and new ways of looking at politics and administration. But the debit side of the account was more in evidence, for inevitably it was very expensive to maintain the King and the hundreds of Neapolitans who came with him. Sir William and Lady Hamilton were showered with presents by the monarch; Nelson was given a huge feudal estate as Duke of Bronte, with all the perquisites of feudal jurisdiction and a large income which once had more usefully endowed the Palermo hospital. The "Anglo-Sicilian hero", as Meli addressed him in an ode, was delighted to stay near Lady Hamilton, and his blind eye began to improve with electrical treatment.

As for the King, "his Sicilian Majesty, accustomed to a life of continued dissipation, gives but little attention to the affairs of state, which are transacted chiefly by the Queen"—that was how Hamilton saw Ferdinand. Timid, bigoted and utterly lazy, with "no guide for his conduct but that of private considerations"— that was the view of Hamilton's successor. The King's main interest was a positive obsession with hunting, and he at once revived the forest laws and set up new game reserves. He was accustomed to publish an annual list of his hunting bag: it worked out at about a hundred head for each day of the year, and if possible he liked to have one or two thousand soldiers as beaters. The local aristocracy competed to offer him their hunting rights, realising that this would be an excellent excuse for enclosing open land and evicting shepherds and other farmers.

Ferdinand was not without amiable qualities, but the fact of being an absolute ruler since the age of eight had not improved his character. Though he himself made some attempt to speak Sicilian, his Queen conceded nothing to local sentiment and she it was who became the real brains and energy of the government. Maria Carolina was a great intriguer. Eventually she organised her own private espionage system and apparently encouraged a flotilla of privateers to prey on British and other commerce. Fra Diavolo, the arch-brigand, was in her employ. The key positions in the government preferably went to her Neapolitan favourites. Her need for money was insatiable. She tried to lay her hands on the road-building fund, and took deposits from charities and the Palermo bank; and once she even suggested that the British should buy Sicily from her for six million pounds.

The only regular source of revenue which conceivably could be quickly stretched was the *donativi*, though the King's failure to support some of Caracciolo's reforms meant that the privileged classes were strongly placed to fight any attempt to increase their contribution. Ferdinand, now that he saw Sicily at first hand, was belatedly convinced of the need to end the light taxation of the aristocracy which for so long had kept Sicily quiet, and this threat at long last brought a real constitutional opposition into being against the monarchy. Already in 1790 and 1794, the solidarity of the three Houses of parliament could be seen to be crumbling as the nobles became alarmed at the growth of egalitarian sentiment. Meanwhile Sicily was called upon to pay millions of *scudi* for yet another war from which she stood to gain nothing. These demands were met, until at last, in 1798, the two upper Houses asked for a prior assurance that Caracciolo's reforms would be annulled, that the King would visit Sicily, and that any new tax would not be spent just in the interests of Naples. The Viceroy in reply claimed that the vote of the hand-picked domanial House would be sufficient to authorise collection of the *donativi*, and he was supported in this novel doctrine by a few of the leading Sicilian princes. Others of the barons, however, unexpectedly attacked the royal prerogative by an equally revolutionary proposal to adjourn the session. Not since 1516 had opposition taken this positive form, and only a renewal of war saved Ferdinand from a difficult decision.

In 1802 the King presided in person over parliament; the last such occasion had been in 1714. The deputies met in the big hall of the palace, with ecclesiastics on the sovereign's right, barons on his left, and the domanial House and the senate of Palermo in front of him, with all the 'grandees of Spain first class' wearing their privileged hats, and with special boxes for select spectators. This had been intended as a purely formal occasion, but the meetings dragged out unusually; eventually a discreet offer of jobs and favours succeeded in neutralising some princely leaders of the opposition, and this enabled the King's friend, Prince Belmonte, to pilot an appropriate grant through the necessary stages; but Ferdinand had to promise that, if he returned to Naples, he would keep a permanent court at Palermo headed by a royal prince. Almost at once he broke this undertaking, for a treaty with Napoleon soon allowed him to return home taking the court and a good deal of Sicilian money with him.

When a recurrence of war compelled the royal family again to seek refuge at Palermo in 1806, this time they found much less of a welcome. The last four parliaments, coming on top of the challenge by Caracciolo, had given political experience and ambition to some barons, and made opposition almost an economic necessity. Instead of the nobles seeing the monarchy as their natural ally against the French revolution, heavy new taxes gave them an altogether new political outlook. They were now disinclined to accept that the kingdom was simply personal property given to the King by God. They could not accept his refusal to believe in the existence of a Sicilian nation. Sicilian history meant nothing to him. So unconcerned was he about the glories of the past that many twelfth-century mosaics were now removed just to give him a more convenient access to the palace chapel. Neapolitans again took over the main jobs, and this lack of employment (especially for younger sons of the nobility) was specially singled out by Scrofani as a serious motive of discontent. For the moment, however, British troops and subsidies made it seem unlikely that Ferdinand would need another confrontation with parliament.

As there was no Sicilian army or navy worth the name, in 1806 Ferdinand was reluctantly forced to invite a British force to take over the main responsibility for defence. He probably did not know that the British commander had orders to occupy Sicily by force if this invitation was not forthcoming. It was part of Napoleon's plan that the French should capture the island and so dominate the central Mediterranean. On the far side of the straits of Messina, Joseph Bonaparte, now calling himself King of the Two Sicilies, assembled an army of invasion much larger than the defenders could muster, and Napoleon wrote that Sicily was as good as captured. Several thousand French soldiers on one occasion made a landing near Messina, to be repelled by British troops aided by a few peasants armed with axes and sticks; but the decisive military fact was that British gunboats controlled the straits and the French lacked transports. Ferdinand was unable or unwilling to give any substantial help. He received a large British subsidy, but spent it on anything else rather than recruiting an army; he was certainly not going to waste money fighting for his kingdom if other people would do this for nothing; there was, moreover, always a chance that the French might win. His attitude forced some British officers to think that, for their own interests and in self-defence, they ought to intervene politically, perhaps in such strength that Bourbon absolutism could not survive.

The presence of a large foreign army brought a greater prosperity than Sicily had known for centuries; and the impact of prosperity was all the greater coming after thirty years of declining wage levels and deterioration in the balance of trade. Not only a direct British subsidy, but many loans, a fair amount of private investment capital from London, and large expenditure by the occupying forces all helped to create a minor boom for industry, commerce and agriculture. So considerable was Britain's commercial intervention that by 1812 she had thirty consuls or vice-consuls on the island. The salons of Palermo even developed a snobbish affectation of speaking Sicilian with an English accent. The resident population suffered relatively little from the war. Unlike some other Italians they were not conscripted, they did not have to endure exile and confiscation, nor was their property destroyed. Under British protection the pirates of North Africa were partially tamed, and British convoys escorted Sicilian ships as well as ensuring supplies of American grain if the local harvest failed. Farmers made huge profits from shortages caused by the continental blockade, and land values quickly rose by three or four times. Builders, shipwrights and craftsmen could rely on regular employment for the first time in their lives, and new asphalt and sulphur mines were brought into production. The Orlando family opened a small engineering shop which in later years—when it was transferred to north Italy—developed into the biggest industrial complex in the peninsula. Even farm labourers had money to spend and something like stable jobs; they wore good clothes, and some of them were said to be better off than their counterparts in England.

Continued war and inflation soon enough brought up again the question of finance and baronial tax immunities. Parliament therefore had to be summoned in 1810. Government officials explained to the three Houses that putting more taxation on the poor would be financially unproductive as well as a brake on the economy. The King knew that he could rely on the domanial House to vote any sum, especially now that the barons were the ones who looked as though they would have to pay; furthermore, Butera, Trabia and the Neapolitan Archbishop of Palermo were royal placemen who ought to be able to carry the two other Houses. Boldly the speech from the throne appealed to the "noble principle of equality", and the Deputation was instructed to act in accordance with this principle. Here was a direct challenge. Surprisingly it was accepted. Prince Belmonte, one of the few travelled and talented aristocrats, judged that the time was ripe for yet another drastic move; he therefore changed sides and made a fighting speech which persuaded the barons to reduce the government's request for money by half. Even more astonishing, he persuaded the ecclesiastics to turn against the Archbishop and join the barons in resistance.

Once the privileged classes realised that they would no longer be allowed to escape tax, there was no further reason for their usual subservience. A new menace of royal interference was threatening their income and social position. To dislodge the Neapolitan ministers, and as a bid for popularity, they therefore challenged the whole structure of monarchical absolutism by agreeing to a counter-plan which accepted some of the very reforms that the nobles had strenuously rejected in the 1780s. It was proposed to abolish the eighteen different *donativi* as being much too complex and expensive to collect. They also proposed giving up their feudal dues. Instead they were ready to pay a single tax of 5 per cent on the income of all real estate—with the significant exception of property in and around Palermo.

Coming from the barons, this offer was altogether unexpected. Possibly it was intended only as a tactical move without much intention of being taken seriously. Nevertheless, as well as being less than was required, it was a deliberate challenge to the royal prerogative. If the King wished to stand firm, he could fall back on British money; but this might mean some loss of independence and even acceptance of a more liberal policy, and he for one thought that too high a price to pay. Instead Ferdinand resorted to non-parliamentary taxation. In February 1811, supported by the advice of Trabia and other Sicilian princes on his council, he imposed a 1 per cent tax on all money payments. In addition he instituted a state lottery and even ordered the bishops to force tickets on their clergy. He also decided to nationalise a good deal of property owned by the Church and the villages, compensating the holders by government bonds and then selling the land for cash.

Ferdinand argued that the crown had always been allowed to impose emergency taxes in wartime, but this did not make his action the less provocative. Foreign merchants made the greatest fuss about the 1 per cent sales tax: the British merchants said it would force them to shut up shop, and to their surprise were told that in that case they were quite free to leave. Sicilians simply refused to pay; in order to make it unworkable, they even resorted to the desperate step of trying to abandon the use of written contracts. Very few lottery tickets were sold. But the most decisive fact was that forty barons, representing half the parliamentary votes and by no means just the liberals round Belmonte, presented a humble remonstrance which advised the Deputation to insist that any additional taxes should come through parliament. In reply, the Deputation, that vaunted guardian of Sicilian liberties, decided with only one abstention and no contrary vote that the King was perfectly within his rights. Belmonte now turned secretly to the British: he was ready to convoke a rival parliament at Messina, he said, and accept any King whom Britain might impose, even if necessary a Protestant. The King, whose baronial friends gave him ample warning of this somewhat half-hearted rebellion, waited for several months and then suddenly arrested the five chief protesting members of parliament; among these were Belmonte and his uncle the Prince of Castelnuovo; all five were deported to penal settlements in islands off the Sicilian shore.

This royal coup, strangely echoing the episode of the five members at Westminster in 1642, nearly succeeded, for the opposition crumbled without their leaders. The barons thronged again to the Queen's receptions and blamed the original remonstrance on the unfortunate five. One of the few notable exceptions was Louis-Philippe, one day to be King of France, who had recently married Ferdinand's daughter and become a parliamentary baron. But if the feudatories were unwilling to follow up their protest by action, it was otherwise with another foreigner, General William Bentinck, the British commander.

Britain had over 17,000 soldiers in Sicily and was providing most of the costs of government. Bentinck and his officers, over-bearing and meddlesome though they were, had some excuse for feeling alarm over the security of their forces and at the administrative chaos which made their task of defending Sicily so hard. They knew by now that they would have to control the spending of the subsidy if munitions and fortifications were to be provided. They also feared that local support might be forthcoming for a French invasion if there were not some lessening of the tension between King and barons and between barons and the rest of Sicily. It even came to their knowledge that the court, while taking Bentinck's money, was also in secret contact with the French. A number of urgent arguments therefore existed for political intervention. Sicilian pirates were harassing trade; British soldiers were being assassinated without the local police being of any avail; and all manner of taxes and other impediments were interfering even with the basic provisioning of the army. Furthermore, baronial privileges were, in British eyes, "vexatious and hurtful to the country", and ought to be lessened in the interests of national defence.

What Caracciolo had failed to do by enlightened absolutism, Bentinck now tried to do by a liberal parliamentarism which was quite exotic to Sicily. By threatening to withdraw his troops and suspend the subsidy, he made the government release the five barons and withdraw the extra-parliamentary taxes. Then, at his direction, the largely Neapolitan ministry was replaced by a more representative cabinet which included three of the five ex-prisoners. In the end he had to go further still and force the Queen into exile after using the secret service funds to pay off her enormous debts and get her jewels out of pawn. Without intending to become too closely embroiled in domestic politics, Bentinck manœuvred himself into a position where he was the virtual governor of Sicily, and under his influence a new parliament was summoned which abolished feudalism and planned a new liberal constitution.

Chapter 37

THE CONSTITUTION OF 1812

When parliament met in June 1812, the *ancien régime* suddenly appeared to collapse. The monarchy and the conservative feudatories accepted the most radical changes almost without a fight. The King desperately played for support by offering to revoke all the reforms of Caracciolo, but this came too late to win enough acceptance. He therefore temporarily handed over authority to his son, who was strongly under Bentinck's influence. Belmonte and Castelnuovo were now ministers and could use the block vote of the domanial House to support the cause of reform. They also controlled many of the proxy votes, and this gave them a majority among the ecclesiastics. The baronial chamber gave some cause for doubt; but Castelnuovo thought that the barons, if only out of fear, could be persuaded to make some sacrifice of their prerogatives. It might even be that some of the die-hards would for their own reasons support the liberals in limiting the power of Naples and an absolute monarchy.

Balsamo and his friends had meanwhile spent several months drafting an outline constitution, and during a single night session its main principles were now unanimously agreed. The excitement of the moment, the general readiness to accept authority, and no doubt a little panic, all contributed to this speed and unanimity. Among the chief features of the new constitution, the ecclesiastical House was merged with the House of Peers, and the baronial towns joined with the royal towns in a House of Commons. Parliaments were to meet each year. They were to have powers of taxing and legislating subject to royal assent, and could hold ministers responsible. Money bills had to originate in the Commons; the King, however, kept executive powers, together with a veto and the right to dissolve parliament. No peer would now have more than a single vote. A jury system was to be adopted, with everyone equal before the law and nobody to be imprisoned without due process. Torture was abolished, and so were all private jurisdictions and *fori* except those of the Church and the army. The press was free except where religion was concerned. Sicily was to be quite independent, and if the King ever returned to Naples, his eldest son should remain behind as an independent King. The sovereign was in any case forbidden, just as he had once been in 1296, to leave the island without parliamentary consent.

Quite as revolutionary was the abolition of feudalism to which the nobles agreed in a moment of mixed generosity and shrewd calculation. Some feudatories realised the necessity of change if they were to survive economically. If entails could only be mitigated somehow, that would encourage selling part of the big estates in order to pay off debts and make the remainder economically sound: this would put capital and land to better use. All younger sons of the aristocracy would gain from freer inheritance laws and no primogeniture. Other nobles simply wanted an excuse to rescind the 'promiscuous rights' in their fiefs which hitherto had given the peasantry a kind of co-proprietorship in the land. Others recognised that the war-time rise in cereal prices meant vast profits if the complicated edifice of restrictions on the wheat trade could be demolished.

At the same time, partly as a result of the war and the British occupation, a middle class was appearing with enough money to buy land if only feudal law could be modified to allow the fiefs to be broken up. This middle class had come into existence either by switching from wheat to more profitable crops on land held in *enfiteusi*, or by money-lending, or by managing the *latifondi* through the contract of *gabella*. The *gabelloti* wanted land for financial profit as well as just for prestige and power, and this gave their land hunger an extra force. Under the British occupation these middlemen had many chances to make money, and money for them meant land. Therefore they too, as well as the landowners, had an interest in opening up the feudal estates and destroying communal rights of grazing on private property.

The abolition of feudalism in July 1812 thus had a certain logic; and yet it was still a remarkable fact, and not all of the consequences were foreseen or given an unqualified welcome by many of its authors. Baronial jurisdiction, the *merum et mistum imperium*, feudal dues and privileges were all suddenly swept away, and the royal courts acquired an absolute jurisdiction. As the barons no longer gave military service to society, it was arguable that there was not the slightest reason for them to be lightly treated in taxation, nor should villagers any longer owe compensatory services which had been imposed on them in the heyday of feudalism. Castelnuovo and Balsamo even argued for the abolition of entails as a wonderful chance of transforming agriculture and appealing to the new middle class; but too many nobles, among them Belmonte, stood to inherit large estates by the existing laws of strict settlement, and they also feared that abrogation of entails might strike not only at the legal impedimenta of feudalism but at the whole edifice of aristocratic ascendancy. This vital point was therefore left in abeyance.

Some nobles thought, as did Castelnuovo, that in abolishing feudalism they were sacrificing class interests for the national good, but others knew that by destroying the power of the throne they were in fact increasing their own authority at the same time as they renounced very little which was not in process of disappearing anyway. There were solid advantages in losing the duties as well as the rights of feudalism. The surrender of feudal jurisdiction and private prisons was no great loss if in exchange they could rid themselves of other obligations to the King and their tenants. Fiefs had technically been held on condition of public service, but henceforward would be freehold: for example the sulphur mines, as part of the subsoil, had once been considered as still public property, but now they were simply given away to the landowners just when the industrial revolution made sulphur a product of fundamental importance in which Sicily had a near monopoly. Never again would a fief devolve to the crown for lack of an heir. Where a landowner surrendered local tolls and monopolies, he could claim indemnification by the beneficiaries at sometimes quite a high cost; yet, by abolishing 'promiscuous rights' on former feudal land, he was awarding himself an immense gain without offering any indemnity to those who were dispossessed.

In Naples, by comparison, when feudalism was legally abolished by the French in 1806, any feudal right over rivers ended and they became public property; but in Sicily many springs and stretches of river now tended to become more than ever a private monopoly, and in such an arid climate this one fact could mean all the difference between wealth and indigence. The freedoms invoked in 1812 had no connotation of freedom for the peasant to earn a livelihood as his father before him; they were more concerned with the freedom to convert encumbered estates into negotiable real estate, or the freedom to draw a veil over the usurpation of common property. In any case the ending of feudalism, in so far as it promised social and not just private benefits, turned out to be rather in general law than in practical fact; never was there any specification of precisely what was abolished, nor how the abolition should take place. All the really important decisions were left for the courts to determine, and the courts were rarely independent enough to decide against the landed interest. The *latifondi* went on being called 'fiefs', the landowners 'feudatories', and the peasantry 'villeins' right down to the twentieth century: and with reason.

This element of illusion was at first obscured in the general enthusiasm. Balsamo's constitution was hailed as a great victory for Sicilian liberties and was set alongside that of Britain. The small group of liberal barons were a strongly anglophile faction, and some of them had been brought up on Adam Smith, Hume and Blackstone's *Commentaries on the Laws of England*. They deliberately chose a bi-cameral legislature and referred to 'Peers' and 'Commons'. They spoke of bills and budgets and *habeas corpus*, of university representation and the division of powers. Peers under accusation could claim to be tried by their fellow nobles, and there was even a 'bar' of the House to which outsiders could be summoned. Some people had strong reasons to develop the myth of a close similarity between English and Sicilian parliamentary history. Adoption of British practice was even recommended in the belief that this would merely restore the true constitution of Sicily bereft of accretions and aberration introduced from Spain and Naples; but if the myth was false, like many myths it gave an impetus to political action.

Subsequently Bentinck was accused of imposing this British-style constitution on the country, but in fact he clearly warned Balsamo at the time that such an exotic transplant could hardly be expected to work very well, and other Englishmen were still more outspoken. The truth was rather that both monarch and aristocracy had a common wish to involve Britain, and it was thought that this kind of copy would compel the British to guarantee that no liberal or democratic practices would be introduced which went any further than current practice at Westminster. The King told parliament that he did not truly want a constitution, but that he would agree in the last resort to a British one. There was also a kind of fetishist assumption that any institutions which had made Britain successful would be an infallible specific for every evil. Bentinck eventually acquiesced in the decision, though his original doubts proved more than justified in the long run.

Once the main principles of the constitution had been agreed in parliament, the King and his son had little option but to give them general approval except in minor details. The pill was sweetened by the monarch being accorded a civil list income which, as Bentinck noted with disgust, was about half the national revenue. Bentinck helped to overcome any residual doubts at court by promising to use his influence to stop parliament from too direct an interference in the remaining royal prerogatives. Naturally he was anxious to play down any suggestion that the constitution was being forced on Sicily from outside, so he could not intervene to dissuade Belmonte when the latter allowed its details to be debated for the next eighteen months; but these debates gave the extreme democrats a public platform, and this in the end made the constitution unworkable. Quite unexpectedly a type of person was elected to the Commons who had played very little part hitherto in the country's political history. Discussion was sometimes protracted for weeks over a single clause. How to restrict the royal power, how far to lower the property qualification for members, and how far town councils could be freed from central control, these and many others quickly became issues of fundamental principle, and soon it was clear that the leaders of the constitutional party had few ideas in common.

When parliament met in 1813, it was during the St. Rosalia celebrations and against a background of popular riots in Palermo provoked by a bread shortage and the rising cost of living. Because of the riots, many civic authorities and members of parliament fled from the city. Belmonte had to invite British soldiers and artillery into the town to support the Neapolitan troops, and they arrived only just in time to stop the prison being forced. When sessions eventually began, the liberal government had to face not only a hostile reactionary majority of Peers but a hostile radical majority in the Commons. Most of the towns were genuinely electing their own members for the first time in centuries, and some of them wanted no part in the 'aristocratic' constitutional decisions of 1812. New middle-class elements, more from eastern but also some from western Sicily, and not only lawyers but merchants, landowners and intellectuals, also won control of some town councils. One of their leaders in parliament was Emanuele Rossi of Catania, the 'Mirabeau of Sicily', and a pupil of de Cosmi. Rossi had once been forced to leave Sicily as a result of certain alleged malpractices and then had lived in revolutionary France; he also nursed the additional grievance of having been subsequently imprisoned by Nelson when serving Napoleon in Egypt. Dr. Vaccaro, who became Speaker of the Commons, had also lived in France. To this 'French party' nothing was sacred any longer, certainly not Balsamo's constitution or the moderate reforms of Castelnuovo, and still less the interests of the British occupying force.

At once they raised many divisive points which the liberals would have liked to keep hidden. The democrats wanted cheaper food; they had serious ideas about agrarian reform; they aimed at the complete abolition of entails and a further division of Church property; they wanted a new land survey and a still fairer spread of taxation. Vaccaro told Bentinck that most Sicilians were dying of hunger, while the whole wealth of the country was owned by a few nobles who were interested only in personal ostentation instead of trying to encourage industry and commerce.

Vaccaro and his friends, however, lacked political experience. Often they seemed merely factious and irresponsible in the eyes of the liberal aristocracy. At one moment Balsamo thought that "we have here all the seeds and appearances of something like the

French revolution"; at the next moment these same people were allying themselves with the extreme Right to assist a restoration of royal despotism. They soon guessed, as the Queen had done from the first, that the constitution of 1812 was a baronial document which discriminated against the common people, and that parliament was an empty farce merely designed to turn people's attention away from serious subjects and to immunise them against the 'virus of 1789'. Until the constitution was reformed, therefore, they refused to grant a penny of tax, and this fact in the end made parliamentary government fail. The deputies from Messina and Catania in particular criticised the constitution for centralising government more than ever on Palermo and ending the jurisdiction which hitherto their towns had enjoyed over an extensive hinterland. In one or two places people went so far as to take arms against the new regime. Even inside Palermo itself there was considerable unrest, because abolition of the old tax system caused considerable unemployment, and the large class of lawyers found their perquisites threatened by proposals to set up new law courts elsewhere in the island.

Not only the Commons, but equally the Peers proved that a free constitution would not work in such a semi-feudal world. The nobles, said Balsamo, were quite as factious as the democrats, and more underhand; they automatically rejected any bill from the other House. The opposition was many-sided. It even included Natale, a man of the Enlightenment, who was offended that his title was not grand enough for a seat in the upper House. Many barons had supported the constitution only in the hope of obtaining still more power for themselves, and they were shaken by the appearance of a democratic middle class with ideas of its own. Almost all of them, said Bentinck's secretary in July 1813, were already repentant at having given up their feudal rights. They strongly resented the fact that Bentinck had put men "of little consequence in point of rank" at the head of all government departments. Another Englishman noted in his diary that "rather than yield to the people, they would yield to the crown again", in the hope of recovering "power to tyrannize over their feudal dependants". Mention of universal suffrage and land nationalisation was far more alarming than any indignity they had ever suffered from the crown in the worst days of Caracciolo, while riots in Palermo against the failure of price controls, to say nothing of illegal occupation of baronial land in the country, seemed to portend an imminent popular revolution. Moreover, since monarchical absolutism had been removed, only a foreign army was left to protect their social position, but the British presence was for other reasons undesirable, and in any case would not remain for long. Some nobles therefore set about forming a secret political organisation to bring back royal absolutism.

Even some reformers among the aristocracy, fearing a bloody revolution, were now ready to fall back on a much more conservative programme. The growing divisions among these reformers, especially between Belmonte and Castelnuovo, were an ominous sign. Belmonte, probably the ablest of the barons, was an immensely vain and somewhat slippery character; and in time he became obsessed by a jealousy of his uncle who was a man of much clearer liberal principle. Without agreement between these two men the constitution could hardly survive; yet Belmonte, while in public professing full support, at one stage encouraged his large personal clientele to support Vaccaro and Rossi in refusing to vote Castelnuovo's budget.

In the years 1813 and 1814, three parliaments were held which could agree on almost nothing, and the Peers reached a degree of anger and fear where they petitioned the King for the Commons to be dissolved. Too many people wanted the constitution not to work; or else, Bentinck commented, "they wanted liberty but no one would make any sacrifices for it". The British minister reported that "since the first establishment of the Constitution, there has hardly been one act performed in strict conformity with its regulations". Elections were held illegally, and Bentinck himself was hardly very scrupulous in his electioneering. Some towns elected no one at all. On one occasion a motion to impeach the whole cabinet was lost only by the Speaker's casting vote; on another there was an almost unanimous decision in the Commons that the financial deficit should be made good by the clergy.

As members persisted in their refusal to vote adequate supply, the British went on having to pay half the expenses of government and became increasingly impatient over doing so. Meanwhile the reformers were too confident that Britain for military reasons needed to preserve her position in Sicily, and hence that there was no hurry for them to agree among themselves. They plied the British representatives with requests for detailed information about how the British constitution worked, but had no idea how the answers could apply in such a different context. Nor could any such answer resolve the basic problem, which was that no likelihood existed of any elections producing an organised majority ready to approve the taxation which the liberal ministers wanted, nor indeed of producing a majority which could propose anything else. In other words, this kind of parliamentary system was unworkable.

Bentinck made one more attempt in 1814 to get Castelnuovo and Belmonte in harness together, but he failed. Belmonte at first thought that the only remaining hope was for a still more active British intervention in politics, but then concluded that the King must be brought back again. The English general, equally disillusioned, could not accept either alternative, though he had to admit that force alone was likely to work in a society where there was so little sense of patriotism and so little political courage. As early as 1812 an exciting scheme had been suggested to make Ferdinand the constitutional monarch of a united Italy, but any such development, close though it was to Bentinck's heart, was out of the question while Sicilians were so at odds. Impressed though he was with the potential future of Sicily, Bentinck was pessimistic about the chances of realising that potential without changes in the social system which were too big a project for his brief proconsulate. For a time he toyed with the idea that Britain should establish a formal protectorate over the island in order to impose radical reforms and perhaps go on to create a united Italy; but the ministers in London were utterly opposed to remaining in Sicily once French expansion had been contained. He, too, when he found himself threatening to use force against the 'enemies of the constitution', realised that he was in a false position.

Bentinck was the most energetic and yet the most moderate spirit behind liberal reform, and when he moved away to help liberate northern Italy, personal and sectional jealousies in Sicily became worse than ever. Belmonte gave up the cause as hopeless and retired to Paris. So did Louis-Philippe, regretful that the British had not used more terroristic methods. Castelnuovo, too, reluctantly agreed that his own government had "gone too far with liberty"; "we are not fit for the new constitution," he said; "nothing but fear and arbitrary proceedings will keep such people within any bounds". Among other architects of the constitution, the Abbé Balsamo now drew up a memorandum admitting that they had all been over-optimistic. There just did not exist enough enlightened and independent people to provide 154 deputies in the Commons. "Too much liberty", he told Bentinck, "is for the Sicilians, what would be a pistol, or a stiletto in the hands of a boy or a madman." As the war drew to a close it could be seen by everyone that the constitution depended more than ever on British money and troops, but any form of government needing the permanent presence of a foreign army was an absurdity, and in any case neither the British public nor the other European powers would allow such an occupation to continue in peacetime.

The next British minister at Palermo, A'Court, analysed the situation like this. Britain had never guaranteed the constitution, though "we are undoubtedly in some measure committed"; yet to keep constitutional government in being would need the permanent use of force, and that would make nonsense of any pretence to liberal government. "If we determine to uphold the constitution, we shall uphold what is very little adapted to the country"; for in a society where there was no education, no weight of public opinion, no impartial justice, any elected legislature was bound to depend on the armed might of either Britain or the King; at all events, no other source of power than these had yet revealed itself. "The Sicilians expect everything to be done for them", he added; "they have always been so accustomed to passive obedience." Some of them were still secretly asking him for annexation by Britain, but his own view was that his predecessor had already gone too far; instead of dabbling with a sophisticated constitutionalism in 1812, it would surely have been better simply to insist on more equality before the law and fairer taxes. If the peace settlement were to create a Sicily independent of Naples, that, in A'Court's opinion, desirable though it seemed at first sight, could only mean a revived feudalism just because the ex-feudatories were easily the strongest force in the island; and hence it would mean greater misery than ever for most Sicilians.

On the other hand, if the King and his Neapolitan ministers carried out a counter-revolution, A'Court thought that the future was even more dismal. Ferdinand, despite his promises, was evidently planning such a counter-revolution to coincide with the departure of British troops. The result of this would be "the most oppressive tyranny", something which would be against Sicilian but also against British interests. Yet outsiders could only act to stop it if Sicilians demonstrated unambiguously that they did not want it and were prepared to make sacrifices to prevent it happening; and three years of constitutional government showed that Sicilians were far too radically divided for this, as well as being unwilling to support a barren constitutionalism. Even the radical democrats disagreed among themselves. The nearest approach to agreement was the wish for a restoration of royal authority, because the radicals saw this as a return to enlightened absolutism, at the same time as the nobility hoped it might restore some of their own prerogatives.

Chapter 38

RESTORATION AND REVOLUTION
1816–1821

Before the end of 1813, royal agents were hard at work building up a party among the nobles and securing popular support among the mob and the workers' guilds. Eventually, when the King resumed government, the crowds cheered him and booed the liberal constitutionalists, while even the liberals realised that their experiment had failed. According to A'Court, some of those who had supported the constitution had done so merely to reduce central supervision over their managment of local affairs; and the same people had by now learnt from practical experience that they had more to fear from each other than from the monarchy. Elements of Left, Right and Centre thus conspired to bring Ferdinand back. Parliament itself, even before the constitution had been approved in detail, agreed to abandon it. Subsequently Sicilians blamed Ferdinand for destroying their liberal experiment, but in fact he seems to have had a fair general consensus of local support.

He still did not act precipitately. Only in 1815, after a succession of parliaments had produced no taxation, he dissolved the two Houses for the last time. He then left for the mainland, although this was illegal by the 1812 statute which he had undertaken to observe. Since the Austrian army had now reconquered Naples for him and relieved him from dependence on Britain, he had little further use for Sicilians; on the contrary he was delighted to be revenged on those 'cannibals' who had so humiliated him in many distressing years of exile. He had toyed with constitutional monarchy only so long as he needed British help, and now he secretly swore to the Austrians that he would break another solemn pledge and renounce for ever any compromise with constitutionalism.

For another year, no explicit statement was made, and during this period no serious resistance movement showed itself: on the contrary, 'the great proprietors,' according to A'Court, were delighted to see the parliamentary democrats deprived of their forum. Ferdinand therefore felt justified in giving the island less autonomy than even some of his Neapolitan ministers were recommending. In December 1816, with Austrian approval, he conceded to his very dear Sicilians an altogether new status. Hitherto he had been Ferdinand IV of Naples and Ferdinand III of Sicily; in other words he had been 'King of the Two Sicilies', to use a nomenclature dating back to King Alfonso in the 1440s who had called himself *Rex utriusque Siciliae*. Henceforward he was Ferdinand I of a new unitary state, the 'Kingdom of the Two Sicilies'. The British, realising that they had been outmanoeuvred, for a time refused to adjust to this subtle but significant change of title, but eventually they had to accept that, despite their wishes and some said despite their pledges, the King had discarded the last residual acknowledgement that there existed a separate kingdom in the island.

The Sicilian flag was now abolished; so was freedom of the press; and Ferdinand had no intention of ever calling another parliament. Laws and institutions were imported from the mainland, and this meant largely the Napoleonic code and system of administration which the French had imposed on Naples. Government was to be more centralised than before, and seven new provinces were created, to be administered by Intendants and non-elected town councils. A limited variety of conscription was imposed, and there were new registration and stamp duties which were almost equally unpopular.

The British had no option but to allow Austria a predominant influence at Naples, for the Austrians had borne the brunt of liberating the mainland provinces from Napoleon. Sicilians had shown almost no eagerness at all over Bentinck's appeals for help in freeing the rest of Italy, let alone over his vague ideas about a united Italian state. Britain had spent a great deal of effort trying to make parliament work, but thought that she could hardly be expected to fight against Austria in support of a constitution whose abrogation Sicilians had not resisted and for whose continuance there was apparently so little local enthusiasm. Some Italian historians have assumed that Britain had all the time been aiming to establish a permanent protectorate over Sicily, but contemporaries rather attacked British policy from the very opposite direction, namely for not establishing a greater protectorate in order to keep the constitution alive. According to Castlereagh, only the war had justified British intervention in Sicilian affairs. He was prepared to go on advising Ferdinand to recall parliament, and he made strong representations that individual Sicilian liberals should not suffer. The King did in fact assure him that some Sicilians liberals would be given office, and also that no new taxes would ever be imposed without a new parliament being summoned to approve them. The British were told that any concession beyond these would be vetoed by Austria.

Bentinck was as displeased as any Sicilian with this outcome. Many Sicilians, indeed, even seemed to be quite satisfied with it. Ferdinand's recently married second wife was a Sicilian, and a number of Sicilian aristocrats voluntarily followed him to Naples where they were given a large share—some Neapolitans thought it far too large a share—in court life. The Messinese made the King a special donation to signalise their pleasure at the restoration of Bourbon absolutism: they had gained nothing from the constitutional regime except a merely nominal freedom, and Messina's address of congratulation to Ferdinand was signed by nobles, as well as by merchants and representatives of the workers' guilds. Catania, Syracuse and the other new provincial capitals also registered some positive gains from the new system to offset against any loss of insular independence. Not only princes, but also liberals and democrats joined in the flood of application for jobs, and were glad to become Intendants or sub-Intendants in the King's 'unconstitutional' administration.

Palermo, on the other hand, lost heavily, both in pride and by ceasing to be the centre of court life. The lawyers, who were concentrated there, hated having to master a new code and a new hierarchy of courts. More generally, selective conscription was thought so oppressive that ordinary citizens sometimes mutilated themselves to escape it. As parliaments no longer met, the barons in practice discovered that they had lost one ingredient in their privileged world, and enlightened despotism was now reinforced by French-trained officials who since 1806 had been applying altogether new principles of equality and centralisation at Naples. Furthermore the land tax, which the aristocracy had approved in 1810, but which they had either not paid at all or else expected to collect from their tenants, became unexpectedly heavy as land values collapsed after 1815 and rents went unpaid.

These are some reasons why many of those who at first accepted the return of monarchical authoritarianism had second thoughts later. By defeating liberalism, the nobles had unwittingly restored the monarchy of Caracciolo which their fathers had so disliked. In time, therefore, separation from Naples became once again a political issue with the privileged classes. The lead was not taken by the liberals, nor by the small but vocal elements of democrats who had been so prominent in 1813–14. Neither jacobins nor liberals were any longer a significant and independent political force: either they were in exile, or they now supported centralisation and monarchical reform, or they again accepted dependence on the feudal aristocracy. It was the barons and their dependants who now unexpectedly needed to break out of the traditional political immobilism which had formerly been their safeguard. As the British minister wrote in 1820: "The only chance the Barons have of retaining any of their feudal privileges is by a separation from [Naples]. The only chance the Lawyers have of reverting to the ancient system of jurisprudence, so profitable

354

to themselves and so ruinous to all but the Barons, is by a separation."

Opposition was aided by the fact that a grave economic slump was blamed, somewhat unfairly, on the Neapolitan government. Sicily had profited from the war, and peace came as an economic disaster, all the more so because development had often been on credit, and war-time profits had not been used to bolster farming against the return of competition. Expenditure by the British of perhaps twelve million pounds a year stopped in 1815, and serious unemployment followed the departure of the army and the royal entourage. As a free international market developed once again in cereals, local wheat prices fell by three-quarters, and land (often bought at inflated prices) depreciated accordingly. Farmers sometimes could not afford to reap the fields, yet visitors saw people dying of hunger. Many private fortunes were ruined, capital went out of circulation, and unpaid debts accumulated once again.

Another grievance was that the restored Bourbons were not content with the legal termination of feudalism as effected in 1812. The barons had once been the King's chief enemy, and though monarch and baronage had momentarily come together against the principles of 1789, their old enmity quickly revived when the liberals gave up politics. Sicilian feudalism, unlike Neapolitan, had not been conquered; it had merely been changed voluntarily by an ill-phrased legal decision; and the barons who voted for the decision of 1812 were the very same who, once they had shaken off much of what they found burdensome in feudal relations, then tried to prevent further application of the law. The new generation of Neapolitan civil servants was irked by this fact, as also by the separatist feelings which grew in response to Neapolitan centralisation. For their part the nobles saw the Intendant as an unwelcome intrusion into the field of local affairs which had been their traditional perquisite, and the new provincial organisation cut across some of their intricate systems of patronage and clientelage. At the same time the suppression of the nominally distinct Kingdom of Sicily gave the aristocracy a chance to set themselves up again as leaders of the nation against oppressive foreign rule. It enabled them to associate the cause of anti-reform with that of local patriotism or regional autonomy.

Another provocation to them was governmental schemes of land redistribution. The Bourbons now went back to their pre-revolutionary projects for agrarian reform, because smallholders would obviously be a more stable element in society than landless labourers and would have more interest in agricultural improvements than either casual labour or absentee landlords. Recognising the value of the land reforms effected by the French in

Naples, Ferdinand's government in 1818 attacked the Sicilian entails which tied up most agricultural property and which Balsamo, Rossi and others had condemned as one of the main obstacles to prosperity. The law of 1818 aimed to facilitate splitting up some of the half-cultivated or uncultivated *latifondi* and transferring the land to farmers who could use it better. The laws of primogeniture were also changed so that property could be partly divided among younger sons. Obviously, however, this did not please those who looked on entails, primogeniture and the big estates as an essential element in aristocratic predominance.

Naples was soon hated in a way that Spain had never been; and when a minor insurrection in the Neapolitan provinces forced Ferdinand to make concessions to the liberal constitutionalists on the mainland, this suddenly released pent-up feelings in Sicily. The dramatic news of the grant of a constitution arrived just at that dangerous moment in the year when the Palermo streets were thronged with townsmen and strangers during the St. Rosalia celebrations in 1820. Tricolour emblems quickly appeared as a symbol of liberty. The governor promised that Sicily, as part of the new unitary state, would of course share in his political concessions, but the resultant applause was mixed with cries for independence, and some tricolour cockades were given an added yellow ribbon to symbolise Sicilian autonomy. It was clear that Messina was more than ready to accept the same liberal constitution as Naples; but at Palermo some interested parties regarded Naples and liberalism as the chief enemies, and they seized this occasion to invoke the much more conservative Sicilian constitution of 1812 with its non-elective House of Peers.

By all accounts the Palermo crowd was at first good humoured. Even the soldiers joined in the jubilation. But General Church, the Irish military commander, with excessive zeal tried to impose strict discipline and keep the demonstration within bounds. Some of the troops refused to obey, and some even helped to assault the tax offices. The sudden realisation of being able to escape the food taxes was, as always, enough to touch off a riot, and this in turn was the cue for an eruption of gang warfare and the breaking open of prisons. Probably it was no accident that most of the census returns of property (on which the Bourbons relied for the land tax) were also burnt. Some of the artisan guilds, after they had as usual been asked by the governor to organise squads to keep order, eventually clashed with the troops; and fighting broke out in the *Conceria* where eight hundred leather workers lived in a close, semi-independent colony.

Outside Palermo, landless labourers knew instinctively that this was the moment to occupy any areas of cultivable land from which they had been excluded by baronial enclosures of the commons and the ending of 'promiscuous rights'. Some escaped convicts returned to their villages to organise the forces of disorder, and some provincial towns were taken over by the gangs. Meanwhile armed bands of peasants from Monreale and Bagheria came into Palermo for their share of the pickings. Whether this was in any sense organised, whether any of the bands had political views, whether they were being paid and if so by whom, can only be conjectured. Among the first victims were several princes whose severed heads were carried around the city to the cry of "Long live St. Rosalia". Other nobles fled in panic, and General Church escaped to the imprisonment which awaited him in Naples.

Gradually some kind of order was restored by the consuls of the guilds who then formed a not very efficient administrative junta and tried to arrange for payment of the armed bands. One company of militia was formed by the masons and carpenters, another by the cobblers and rope makers, while the cab drivers made a troop of horse; but the leather workers remained the chief authority, and their guild was said to have received a very substantial sum for their pains. Good order was kept, reported one foreign representative, even though known murderers were openly being employed as policemen. The guilds, delighted as they were to rout the Neapolitan soldiery and regain the police powers which they had lost after 1773, did not want mob rule. They sent armed squads into the countryside to bring back the nobles; and then invited some of the latter to join their junta.

After two weeks the leading citizens were mostly back again in Palermo, and the Cardinal Archbishop and the Prince of Villafranca were managing to give the revolt a clearer and less haphazard direction. Villafranca had been one of the five arrested members of parliament in 1811, and in 1814 had actively promoted the monarch's counter-revolution; now he was again in the forefront of events and again playing what many people saw to be a highly ambiguous game. Ruggero Settimo, another minister in the years 1812–14, also joined the junta. Castelnuovo, on the other hand, though he was approached, refused to take part in this kind of revolt.

In many of its details the Palermo revolution of 1820 duplicated many earlier risings, as it also presaged a number of others in this century. On this occasion, as on others, it was to be seen that the peasants and the gangs were the main forces for disorder and revolution, but they lacked staying power, and their political ideas were elementary and undiscriminating. The guilds were another distinct force, but never so revolutionary that they wanted a clean sweep of the old regime. The political democrats hardly had much share in the events of 1820, and many of them would have found themselves out of place in such conditions of popular insurrection. Here and there were some groups of *carbonari*, secret confraternities vowed to a various admixture of political reforms, but these largely middle- and upper-class associations were far less important than the anarchic gangs of the countryside and the Palermo suburbs. The *carbonari*, apart from a generalised aversion to tyranny, had no clear or uniform political programme, and their most active elements almost certainly would be taking liberalism too far, and they were determined to extirpate the 'illegal' relics of feudalism.

The Two Sicilies had in 1820 been granted a joint parliament by Ferdinand, and consequently the Neapolitan liberals were extremely annoyed when rioting in Sicily upset their constitutional plans. They were determined not to recognise Sicily's right to secede. Representatives of the Palermo junta were unceremoniously arrested by parliament when they arrived at Naples to discuss Sicilian autonomy. In the eyes of the Neapolitan liberals, Sicilian autonomy would at best be taking liberalism too far, and at worst would spell reactionary feudalism.

Nor in Sicily itself was Palermo's political lead generally followed, and all the provincial capitals except Girgenti seem to have been against her. The news of the rising was sometimes taken in country districts as an excuse for social revolution, for instance in the Ragusa area where a considerable division of the land took place. At Trapani there was strong feeling in favour of the liberal Neapolitan constitution rather than renewed submission to aristocratic rule from Palermo; but Marsala then used the opportunity to break free from the provincial capital at Trapani, and destroyed crops and woodlands belonging to this rural city. Civic quarrels were thus far more in evidence than any common feelings of Sicilian allegiance; and when Messina turned against Palermo, it was almost automatic for some of the villages near Messina to take this occasion to favour the other side. In less feudal eastern Sicily there were strong feelings against Palermo for its aristocratic exclusiveness and its desire to monopolise political power. Messina and Catania stood to gain economically from closer connections with the mainland; they preferred to send representatives to the Naples parliament and opposed Palermo's appeal for them to fight on behalf of Sicilian independence. Four of the five newspapers in Messina were passionate supporters of Naples. So, among the eastern radicals, were Rossi and his friends.

But just as Neapolitan liberals would not allow self-determination to Sicily, so the Palermo junta would not allow that other parts of Sicily had a right to dispute Palermo's political direction.

To impose this view, Villafranca and the junta launched a terrible civil war, and did not hesitate to incite land-hungry peasants to social revolution. Boatloads of armed men commanded by leading officials of the Palermo fishermen and charcoal burners set off to attack Cefalù, and other bands went to subdue Syracuse and the east coast. The Prince of San Cataldo led an army of peasants and convicts to sack Caltanissetta, because this town was especially resented as one of the provincial capitals which in 1816 had inherited some of Palermo's authority. The Prince's men massacred many of its inhabitants, devastated the countryside and killed all the farm animals they could find. He was then publicly thanked by the authorities at Palermo for this act of liberation.

When the Neapolitan parliament decided to subdue Sicilian separatism by force, Palermo found herself with little support elsewhere. She had not been able to collect taxes or recruit an efficient army, and now had to watch Caltagirone and Termini welcome the Neapolitans as liberators from a reign of terror. The Palermo aristocracy had failed to impose their conservative constitution on the rest of Sicily, and now realised that the social revolution which they had partly encouraged might get out of hand; so the Prince of Villafranca, after a somewhat odd approach to Metternich to see if he could find Sicily an Austrian King, went with some of the guildsmen to meet the Neapolitan General Pepe at Termini and discuss surrender. On the other hand, some of the anarchic forces which had helped him to initiate the revolution were unwilling to accept peace and see an end to these months of independence and impunity for crime. A mob was soon in arms for the defence of Palermo; prisons were opened for the second time; and Villafranca's palace and his two country villas were sacked.

During several further weeks of fighting, the Neapolitans moved up with an army which now included armed Sicilian bands under contract and volunteers from Messina and Catania. After taking the grain mills, they were able to cut off food supplies. Palermo was bombarded from the sea, and the elderly Prince of Paternò made another more successful attempt to capitulate. Pepe was sensibly anxious to keep good will between Palermo and Naples, and (as his orders fully allowed him to do) obtained this surrender by agreeing to leave open the possibility that some degree of autonomy might be granted; but the constitutional government at Naples subsequently repudiated the terms he had made, and pretended that he had exceeded his instructions. As Palermo had been occupied by this time, they saw no further point in sticking too closely to the rules; and moreover the representatives of Catania and Messina in the Neapolitan parliament, claiming to speak on behalf of all Sicilians outside Palermo, welcomed the fierce treatment of this 'enemy town'.

Vast damage had been done at Palermo during these months of insurrection and rioting. Many nobles had lost their houses and property, and would not be so likely again to stir up a popular rebellion. They had also lost some of their local prestige. The Neapolitan liberals were interested only in putting down the rebellion and had few constructive ideas of how to bring reforms to Sicily. There was no great desire to satisfy any of the disparate forces of protest which had met haphazardly in this minor revolt. Palermo could be regarded as conquered territory, and the food taxes were now increased to meet the costs of a military occupation. As a reward for helping to defeat Palermo, Messina asked to be recognised as the leading city of the island, and Trapani wanted special tax exemptions: such requests were not granted, but along with Caltanissetta and Syracuse these other towns were freed from their dependence on the Palermo law courts. Another mild anti-feudal law was passed against the 'baronial hydra' and in favour of compensating those villagers who had enjoyed immemorial rights on baronial land. Rivers and springs were declared public property as in Naples, and private hunting rights were limited. Moreover redress was promised for any villages which had been hindered by permanent lawsuits and legal trickery from recovering common lands which everyone knew had been usurped by the barons.

The constitutional regime did not last long enough for such legislation to have any practical effect. Not much open opposition was encountered against Naples, but there was a good deal of sullen hatred and the usual difficulty in getting taxes or debts paid; and the result was that, when the Austrians invaded Naples in March 1821, the Neapolitan parliament found little active support in Sicily. The Austrian invasion was designed to restore the absolutist government of King Ferdinand, and Sicilians accepted this fairly passively. Soon there were ten thousand Austrian troops in the island. Whereas the British occupation had more than paid for itself, during the next five years Sicily had to bear heavy costs to pay for this foreign army.

Once again the most common political feelings in Sicily were shown to be those connected with passive opposition—opposition to autocratic and liberal regimes alike, and almost equally to government by foreigners or Sicilians. The initial enthusiasm generated for each revolution in turn was in part illusory: it rather reflected a negative desire for change, often also a desire by certain individuals for anarchy and the achievement of private non-political objectives. Attempts at reform by either constitutionalists or royalist autocrats at Naples had as little permanent effect on society as those of Caracciolo and Bentinck earlier, or those of the Piedmontese and Austrians a hundred years before; and the general reaction in Sicily to each of them differed remarkably little. At root there was still a deep political pessimism which shied away from any social action or from accepting any possibility of lasting gain as a result of political commitment.

But some forces were at last making for change. The spread of education, the growth of Italian sentiment, the dislike of Naples and Neapolitans, the desire for economic betterment and a realisation that life was better elsewhere, all these feelings were introducing new possibilities into a dangerously unbalanced world where the detonating force of social revolution was never far away.

Chapter 39

REFORM AND REACTION

Supported by Austrian bayonets, Ferdinand for the second time suspended a constitution which he had sworn to observe; and despite protests by England, even despite advice from Austria and France, he broke his own undertaking of 1816 to recall the Sicilian parliament before any increase in taxes. In fact the word 'parliament' was now expunged from official documents. Sicilian separatism had been doubly defeated by Neapolitan liberals and by Austria, yet some concessions were made to autonomist sentiment. The stamp and tobacco duties were not reimposed, and Sicily was left with one of the lowest general tax rates in Europe. Sicilians were to have a monopoly of jobs in Sicily. Conscription was stopped, partly because deserters were taking to brigandage, partly because Swiss mercenaries and even Protestant Irish were thought more trustworthy than local troops; and possibly there was a calculated desire to avoid training Sicilians in military discipline.

The King had learnt from the revolution that the privileged classes were still a danger. The guilds were therefore at long last abolished. Then a law of 1824, by allowing creditors to take land in settlement of debt, aimed at reducing another kind of restrictive privilege. Most of the large estates were mortgaged, sometimes over and over again to an amount greatly beyond their real value, and too much scarce capital was buried in these loans without agriculture being a whit improved. On the contrary, mortgages often acted as a kind of subsidy for inefficient landlordism. Furthermore, since the nobility possessed legal safeguards against being forced to pay their debts, creditors had in some cases been suing for fifty years without receiving any interest, or else had been glad to settle for 1 per cent or less.

The law of 1824, so Scinà hoped, would encourage new landowners to appear from among these creditors. The assumption was that they would be people who needed to make agriculture pay, who would put productivity above status and not become absentee landlords, but would take trouble to experiment with more rewarding types of crop; nor would they allow wheatlands to lie fallow and unused every other year. But Scinà was underestimating the psychological as well as the sheer practical difficulties of transforming the *latifondi*. In effect the main beneficiaries of the new law turned out to be existing landowners and ecclesiastical corporations, or else *gabelloti* who were little if any improvement on their predecessors.

Some division of properties was gradually taking place as the pressure of population grew, and no doubt two bouts of Bourbon legislation in 1789–92 and 1818–24 contributed towards this process. Especially near the towns, along the north and east coast, and in special areas such as near Modica and Marsala, there was a marked increase in the more intensive cultivation of vines, olives, oranges, almonds and sumac. The easier transferability of property enabled some of the more impecunious barons to sell property, and the succession laws of the *Code Napoléon* in favour of younger sons gradually had some result.

But legislation could not immediately effect the tradition which encouraged younger sons not to marry, and still there was a tendency for their portion of an inheritance to return at death so that the family holdings should not be dispersed. In the last resort, force could still be used to maintain feudal ascendancy, or else legal proceedings could as usual be dragged out by princely families who saw in the accumulation of *latifondi* an essential title to and justification of their sense of superiority. Social conditions thus strongly favoured the retention of the large ranch as a unit of agriculture; so did physical conditions of climate, soil and communications; and so did the fact that the ending of feudalism made enclosure easier. At Bronte, the heir of Lord Nelson more than doubled the extent of his huge domain during the century, and in the process he deprived many peasants of common rights which they had formerly enjoyed as serfs on the estates of the Palermo hospital. Nor was this by any means an isolated example.

These common rights were another field where legislation was always defeated by vested interests. The laws of Caracciolo and Caramanico on the subject had fallen into disuse during the war, and then the abolition of feudalism was too imprecise to bring any helpful result. Palmeri in the 1820s still knew "vast extensions of territory where one person owns the land, another the trees, a third has the right to cut down trees, and a fourth can pasture his animals". Every district had its own immemorial customs, and they had existed on both the village commons and the baronial fiefs. They varied from place to place, but usually they gave the right to obtain wood for making ploughs or charcoal, perhaps to glean in the stubble, or collect acorns and chestnuts for pigs; in one village the residents could cut peat, in another the roots of liquorice, in another wild asparagus and berries; more rarely they could sow wheat on the common lands, or they could burn limestone to make mortar, and at Bronte they could collect manure. Most common of all was the right to pasture animals. But naturally it was a grave restraint on agricultural development if flocks could damage standing crops and if every step in the farming cycle had to be regulated by tradition and the general sense of a whole neighbourhood.

Reformers and landowners had a common interest in wanting to change this relic of the past; and the Bourbon government, on the experience of Napoleonic practice in Naples, tried to transform 'promiscuous rights' wherever possible. In 1817 officials were required to work out a rate of compensation for any deprived beneficiaries. The lawyers then enjoyed decades of discussion over which precise rights were affected and the value of compensation. The peasants, even if they dared to ask, could understand little about the complicated legal proceedings involved, and so landowners were again able to round off their *latifondi* while giving little or nothing in return. Another law in 1825 tried to close some of the gaping loopholes, but the landowners had the advantage of occupying much of the land in question, and not only did they dominate the commissions set up to enforce the law, but their influence in the villages and in the courts could almost always demolish any residual opposition.

Some landlords put the change to good use and were encouraged by their new rights of ownership to invest more in the land. Others were more interested in extending their private hunting grounds. Typical, perhaps, was the attitude of the Butera family who had found it profitable to dam the outlet to the lake of Lentini, sterilising a large area of fertile land and turning tenants out just to increase the fish and game—in fact this was already a malarial swamp which proved a terrible curse to the countryside. Or there was the Prince of Villafranca who, when the village of Salaparuta in 1829 accused him of illegally enclosing communal woodland, burnt down the wood in defiance; and although the Intendant ruled against him, it took seventy-four years in the courts before he could be dispossessed of the land which he had ruined.

The administration in Naples was too far away and lacked an effective bureaucracy on the spot which could enforce legislation. In the absence of close surveillance, the artisan guilds, for example, though in theory suppressed, still maintained a close cohesion as each was grouped in a special corner of Palermo: they continued as quasi-religious or sometimes quasi-criminal associations which on occasion could keep the various trades tightly controlled in the old family networks. In the interior, moreover, the ex-feudatories with their *gabelloti* and *guardiani* often constituted the only effective local government; and there, as German and English visitors observed, the landlords had no direct connection at all with the agricultural labourers who did nearly all the work and paid such a large proportion of the taxes.

The Director of Roads, Waters and Forests, Afan de Rivera,

described how these administrative deficiencies made it easy for rich landowners to conceal their assets and escape the land tax. In some areas nearly half the *latifondi* were simply omitted from the tax registers. In others it was discovered how to avoid payment by adjusting one's mortgage. The old feudal monopoly on the purchase and sale of goods could be retained without much difficulty outside the towns, and the remoteness of landlords from government supervision allowed them to go on illegally exacting the feudal *banalités*; with the result that by 1820, according to the representatives of eastern Sicily in the Naples parliament, the ex-feudatories had gained and not lost from the so-called abolition of feudalism eight years before. Butera, Villafranca and Lord Bridport at Bronte possessed more resources and usually more knowledge of farming than the tenants they imposed upon or dispossessed, and hence they and their kind might have been able to lead the country in an agricultural revolution; but instead, out of miscalculated selfishness, they were precipitating a century of destructive peasant rebellion from which many people apart from themselves would suffer.

Ferdinand I died in 1825 after sixty-six years of reign. He had been up to a point well-meaning and a little less misguided than his opponents allowed. It should be remembered in his favour that he introduced the new educational methods pioneered by Bell and Lancaster as well as those of de Cosmi. It was also due to him that, within four years of Dr. Jenner publishing his researches on smallpox, an English doctor was invited to Sicily to demonstrate the new technique of immunisation; and though Sicilian doctors did their best to discredit it, the King was vaccinated himself—a *Te Deum* was sung in the cathedral when he survived—and he ordered clinics to be opened in every village and vaccination to be made compulsory. Doctors also had to treat poor people and prisoners without payment.

Ferdinand, nevertheless, could not be called either an able ruler or an intelligent man, and he had been scared into political reaction by experience of revolution and exile. Not long before his death he cut off his pigtail as a sign of moving with the times, but any subject so advanced as to wear whiskers was liable to punishment as a dangerous radical. "All the ingredients of a good and efficient government are wanting", wrote the British minister in 1822, and a few political trials and executions in Ferdinand's last years showed that opposition was growing.

Under his son, Francis I (1825-30), the government was no less inefficient and no less in the interest primarily of Naples. It was also more frivolous and corrupt. Francis was a weakling in mind and body, narrow-minded, intolerant and thoroughly inexpert in the arts of government. His ministers were almost as incompetent, though his valet and the Queen's chambermaid were shrewd enough to acquire considerable political importance and made a fortune out of bribes. Nothing was done to ingratiate the King with the thinking elements in society. This was a government essentially based on the threat of force; the army absorbed most of the revenue, and the late St. Ignatius Loyola was currently gazetted a field marshal on full pay.

Ferdinand II of the Two Sicilies (1830–59) began by making another effort at reform. He had been born in Sicily. His four visits there in the 1830s were something without precedent, and they showed him more of the island than many Sicilians knew. He appointed his brother Leopold governor of the island, and for a while this separate administration by a young royal prince who was also Sicilian by birth gave a welcome sensation of being the autonomous government which many people obviously would have liked. The continuance of job reservation for Sicilians was popular. An institute for encouraging industry and agriculture was set up in 1831, and in 1832 a Central Office of Statistics. A new census was decreed in 1833 in the hope that a more accurate land tax would make it possible to reduce the *macinato* tax on flour. Scientific journals began to be published and, as a sign of official interest, could be sent post free. The government also put out an agricultural manual commissioned from Ignazio Sanfilippo of Palermo university, which gave practical instructions on everything down to cheese making, compost heaps, the improvement of animal breeds and the building of irrigation canals.

These moderate essays in reform, however, did not reconcile Sicilians to being a Neapolitan possession. On the contrary, they can have only turned the *notabili* even more against Naples. Neither an increase in land tax, nor reducing the *macinato*, nor championing the rights of villagers on the ex-fiefs was likely to please the aristocracy. By now, moreover, some of the wealthier middle classes were more frequently buying themselves into a semi-feudal world where they would inherit and even reinforce the separatist and retrograde attitudes of the old peerage. Likewise the attempt to suspend the guilds, desirable though it was, must have aroused enormous resentment in Palermo. When the King arrived there in 1831, the nobility crowded to his receptions and he was received with applause; but what they really would have liked was a completely separate Sicilian government which would at once satisfy their sense of honour, create jobs for their children and in general give them the power to keep reform at bay.

When he visited Sicily again, in 1834, Ferdinand seriously meant to reduce the food taxes and try to tighten up the administration of justice; but, to frustrate his intention, very different rumours were circulated of his intentions, and the cool reception which he consequently received did not encourage him to propitiate local opinion any further. The King was by nature an idle man, and he knew that there were grave administrative difficulties in the way of making policy effective. After 1835 he lost interest in remedial legislation. Clubs were shut down and foreign books excluded by a harsher censorship. "Although the King and his ministers are fully sensible of the evils which exist in Sicily," wrote a foreign ambassador, "they do not possess sufficient talent or energy to meet them, and will leave things to take their chance." As a result the impoverishment of the peasants became more acute, and other foreign observers clearly expressed their fears that social revolution could not be far away.

One cause of poverty was the high crime rate and the diversion of so much talent and energy into underworld activities which crippled economic life. Here the Bourbons were as powerless as every previous regime. To Bentinck it had seemed that as many murders were committed in Palermo as in all the rest of Europe put together, and Bentinck's secretary had commented on the special difficulties of a social environment where personal revenge was regarded as a pleasure and a duty. The British army had reported the mysterious disappearance of many muleloads of guns on the trackless paths which served for roads; and indeed the presence of British and then Austrian troops, together with the experience of conscription and guerrilla warfare in 1820, all helped to make firearms readily available. Bands of brigands were again able to work right up to the walls of Palermo, and excellent cover was now afforded by the high walls put up by enclosing landlords to protect their orchards and hunting reserves near the city. Few people dared to go unarmed in the countryside, though Gladstone in 1838 noted that this was much less true in Eastern Sicily.

As usual, one of the most common crimes was the smuggling of food into towns past the excisemen. Much less common, but still serious, was the illicit control of water supplies, and we know from official reports that the drying out of the water table south of Palermo had made this quite rewarding by the 1840s. The most common crime of all was *abigeato*, the stealing of animals, which was made easy by the semi-nomadic system of husbandry in the roadless interior. The threat of stealing cattle, or of setting fire to sulphur at the mines, was commonly used to extort protection money from landowners, and strong pressure was then used to make the *latifondisti* employ criminals as *guardiani* on their estates. These early forms of protection racket did a great deal to establish the paramount force of the gangs in the interior. Kidnapping for ransom was frequent, and once again priests, since they were literate and could write the ransom letters, were sometimes employed as go-betweens. Once we hear of a whole village moving with guns and scythes to attack a near-by village over some local controversy. Terroristic activities of all kinds were deliberately used in order to inculcate fear: a surgeon in a scientific journal of 1831 described the terrible wounds created by the sawn-off shotgun, the *lupara*, and noted the extreme difficulty of making any victim give the name of his assailant.

All the ingredients of the mafia were present except the word itself. Early in the century, British troops had come up against secret brotherhoods with a reputation for courage, honour, cruelty and complete disrepect for the law. Many stories were told of landowners harbouring bandit groups, sometimes leading them, but more usually just employing them as field guards. Other such groups existed which seem to have been composed of peasants defending themselves against feudal usurpation, and we hear of one commanded by the local archpriest. Not all their activities were illegal. They could be active in politics either in favour of the Bourbons or against them. One way or another the more successful of them acquired resources to corrupt witnesses, to bribe functionaries, or, if need be, to secure the conviction of innocent victims. A leading theme in the countryside was the efforts of one gang to eliminate competitors and establish boss rule over a certain area, but sometimes they worked together so that a flock of sheep could disappear and be quickly sold in a distant town. Mediators existed who might obtain the return of stolen goods for a fee, and foreign visitors quickly learnt where to go to purchase protection. All that was lacking for this intricate, illegal sub-world was a name, and that would be forthcoming in the 1860s.

It was impossible to control crime of this nature and on this scale. Twenty-five Companies at Arms policed the countryside, but altogether there were usually fewer than 350 such policemen for the whole island. Two or three times a year a company of troops would arrive in each village and round up a token number of malefactors, but this would be followed by another few months of complete impunity. Honest and efficient policemen evoked universal detestation. Dislike of the police, indeed, was one of the most important elements in the growth of opposition to the Bourbons. The Companies at Arms were privately recruited groups which contracted with the government for a fee and could then be held to account for thefts: sometimes they were the feudal retainers of a landowner in whose interest they continued to work; sometimes they extorted protection money much like any other gang, and acted in collusion with criminals so as to be able to find stolen property in return for payment. At worst the police companies were brigand bands in their own right. Not unexpectedly, therefore, in this world of *omertà* there were proportionally far fewer arrests, let alone convictions, than in Naples, and the problem was rather how to live with crime than how to control it. The King promised that any brigand who brought another to book would be pardoned, and if he managed to kill the leader of a band he would be rewarded as well; but other remedies were generally wishful thinking. The government once arranged with Portugal to deport some Sicilian bandits to southern Africa, but it came to nothing.

The courts were still a weak point in the system. Some things had improved: for example, justice was public, and torture was in theory abolished; there were, again in theory, monthly visits to prisons to hear complaints; and nearly all the rival systems of courts and jurisdictions had been abolished. But there was still a quite disproportionate number of lawyers in Sicily, and to all appearance they were as much involved in evading justice as in enforcing it. The salary of all except the highest judges was still so low that the best lawyers would not take the office. Hence many magistrates remained grossly ignorant of the law. Sometimes, perhaps often, judges bought their posts; and it seems to have been not uncommon for them to recoup by accepting bribes or a retainer from some powerful clients who needed an occasional victory in the courts for his prestige and his pocket. Clerks of the court, too, were generally not paid but had to live on presents, and it could be thought disrespectful if a litigant did not call privately on court officials before a case.

Application of the law therefore depended on money and power. In subsequent history, the phrase 'Bourbon justice' was sometimes popularly used to mean honest and independent justice, but this is probably because so many Sicilians have always been tempted to look back on the past as better than the present. Although Ferdinand introduced some admirable Neapolitan judges into Sicily, they did not understand the language and could not easily make themselves understood. Nor did they like what they found. One Neapolitan magistrate at Trapani reported that "there is scarcely a single official here who does not prostrate himself before the aristocracy and who does not intend to profit from his post"; he also mentioned that the chief government prosecutor at Catania was a known smuggler, and the jailer at Trapani used to sell back to his prisoners the very arms he had confiscated from them.

PART 11

The Economy 1750–1850

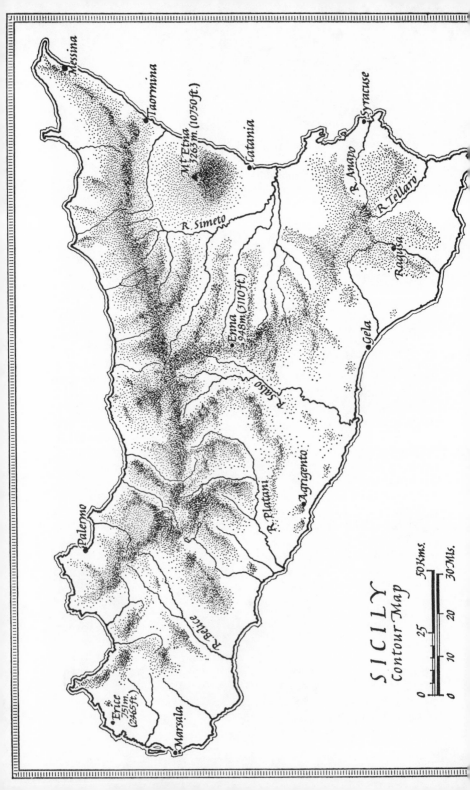

SICILY
Contour Map

Messina

Taormina

Mt Etna 3263m. (10750ft.)

Catania

Syracuse

R. Anapo

R. Tellaro

Ragusa

R. Simeto

Enna 948m (3110ft.)

Gela

R. Salso

Palermo

R. Platani

Agrigento

R. Belice

Erice 751m. (2465ft.)

Marsala

0   25   50 Kms.

0   10   20   30 Mls.

Chapter 40

COMMERCE

The slowness of Sicilian political development is in part explained by the slowness of the economy to expand or indeed to admit change of any kind. Until 1800, Sicily's overseas commerce was mostly carried by either the Genoese or the French, and the lack of any vigorous local competition to these foreign merchants contributed a static quality to social and economic life. The middle class, to the small extent that one existed, remained professional and bureaucratic rather than commercial or industrial, while the leaders of society lived off their rents and nourished a resolute prejudice against trade.

This genteel attitude towards commerce was a fundamental fact. Sometimes the Spanish were blamed for introducing it, though in fact many Spaniards had made fortunes out of Sicilian trade and had been despised by Palermo society for doing so. Alternatively blame was placed on the Bourbons for either too much or too little government intervention. More plausibly the courts were held at fault for not making debts easier to collect; or else the taxation of exported manufactures was said to be unfair; or the system of import duties was held responsible just because it did not encourage local enterprise, by taxing dyed cloth more than undyed, refined sugar more than unrefined. The unwillingness to engage in trade was ascribed by some merchants to the sheer expense of having to bribe everyone from the grandest minister down to customs officials and office porters. The fear of piracy, the social taboo against co-operative effort, the undue reliance on a single export commodity which was vulnerable to world changes —all these were explanations which rang partially true. So was the supersession of oared galleys by sailing ships which had less need to call at Sicilian ports for water and food.

Inevitably, in self-defence, blame was thrown on to Spain and other foreign governments; but obviously the matter was much more complicated. If the nobility sent their younger sons into the Church rather than commerce or practical agriculture, if they rarely considered moving their capital out of land, the prime cause can hardly have been government policy. Indeed it was protests by parliament and the Palermo city government which brought to an end several attempts by the Bourbons to stimulate commerce. The economist Scrofani, like others before him, was puzzled that the attitude of Sicilian landowners differed from that of aristocracies elsewhere: they seemed to accept without question that debts need not be paid and that productive work was undignified. Suspicion of each other made it almost unknown for rich men to form a limited company except on a family basis, and this meant that one indispensable ingredient of a flourishing economy was absent, for no Sicilian took readily to being a minority stockholder. The same lack of trust, explained the economist, Francesco Ferrara, was also responsible for the absence of Sicilian insurance firms, simply because Sicilians themselves always preferred to insure abroad with companies which had the reputation for paying up at once without going to court. Any insurance firm, incidentally, would expect a high premium from a Sicilian merchant, and this was another fact which contributed to make local businesses uncompetitive. Few people had such confidence in their neighbour that they were ready to pool resources, whether to concentrate capital in savings banks or to exploit mineral resources; and they would hardly even submit tenders for road building and other public works. When in 1828 an association was formed to take over under contract the collection of customs duty, this was said at the time to be the first commercial association ever formed in Sicily, and though this was incorrect, the fact that it could have been stated was not insignificant. Tax collection was evidently thought a more reliable investment than industry.

Lack of capital was a customary explanation given for the absence of joint stock enterprise, and certainly Sicily was no longer rich. Yet considerable amounts were spent in purchasing land, and there was a fairly considerable flight of money for investment in foreign luxuries and Neapolitan government bonds. One unhelpful factor remained constant, namely the sheer disparity of wealth; because too many of the leaders of society were not so much interested in increasing their income as in perpetuating a social system which was economically restrictive. Another hurdle was that, at a time when Naples was developing new and flourishing credit institutions, in Sicily it still needed an interest rate of 12 per cent or even as much as 20 per cent before money could be attracted into commerce. The government was occasionally begged to bring down interest rates by law, and to found the banks that private enterprise could not create; it was called upon to assist the formation of trading companies and to assure them by law of a monopoly; it had been asked to help industrialists by giving them cheap convict labour so as to reduce costs, and even by providing them with free factory space in the ex-Jesuit houses. But the government was not only ill-equipped to intervene in this way; it was also feared that such action would only make the disease even worse; and meanwhile commerce and industry were left to foreigners, who incidentally managed to do quite well out of them.

The spirit of association and mutual confidence could have been generated only in the towns, and part of the trouble was that town councils had for too long been an appendage of feudalism. Long after the Spanish had gone, the most coveted privilege for an urban councillor was still to be entitled a 'grandee of Spain first class', and there were outraged protests if any official called him 'Most illustrious' instead of 'Excellency'. In the big towns the office of senator was, for prestige and financial reasons, kept as an absolute monopoly of the nobles. The job was more honorific than onerous, but vast fortunes could sometimes be made out of it. Scrofani, like many visitors from overseas, observed that the ports, or in other words Sicily's more important towns and her chief point of contact with the outside world, were still poorly equipped for trade and empty most of the year. The rivalry of one port with another made it difficult to agree over allocating even the small sums set aside by the government for harbour works, while the towns themselves did precious little on their own account to foster trade.

Palermo, for example, despite its huge size, produced no exportable goods in any quantity even in 1850. Syracuse, which might have been one of the best harbours in the central Mediterranean, was usually deserted; its main jetty had been carried away and the sea walls were crumbling progressively. Augusta's splendid deep-water bay, ten miles in circumference, hardly ever saw a ship; and Licata scarcely possessed any harbour at all until after 1820. Pozzallo, the port of Modica, had no road and its population was only 1700 in 1831. At Sciacca, the major wheat port, there was no anchorage except way out to sea, no loading quay of any kind and not even a paved road down to the beach. Girgenti, the outlet for the sulphur mines, had been given money in the eighteenth century by its bishop to construct a breakwater out of the remains of the Greek Temple of Jupiter, but this was still only in part built by 1840: loading was extremely slow and expensive, and four hundred dockers were needed for even a small ship, while scores of convicts struggled continuously to keep the harbour clear of sandbanks.

Likewise at Mazara, where another bishop left money for a port, the citizens regarded an elegant marine drive along the seafront as a first priority on civic funds. As for Marsala, the once flourishing Lilybaeum, its harbour had never been cleared since the Spaniards blocked it for defence reasons in the sixteenth century; the Piedmontese had intended to equip Marsala as a naval port, but their few years in Sicily were too brief a period. At Catania, which was a rich centre of agriculture, a large breakwater had been under discussion since the first half of the fifteenth century, but, despite Caracciolo's interest, a familiar mixture of private jealousies and lethargy prevented proper harbour defences being built until the 1840s. In this great city, which foreign visitors more and more were to think of as the most agreeable and magnificent town in Sicily, which had more than tripled its population in the eighteenth century and where money had been forthcoming in plenty for baroque churches and palaces, there was no proper port, and anchorage was unsafe for most of the year.

It may be added that there were not even any adequate charts of territorial waters until the British admiralty, startled by the annual wastage through shipwreck (in twelve years, nine British vessels were lost on Cape Granitola alone), felt the need of one. In 1814–16, Lieutenant Smyth, R.N., aided by a British army engineer and the Abbé Piazzi, carried out a survey, though their findings still took a long long time to reach the charts. When a French ship was wrecked in 1835, the accepted explanation was that the maps had not yet taken into account the submergence in the first century A.D. of the Greek port of Tyndaris, and compensation had to be paid which might have sufficed to bring the port back into use.

Even Messina seemed apathetic and unenterprising to foreigners. Thirty years after the great earthquake of 1783, many of its streets were almost impassable; and Parkman, the American historian, found it crumbling to decay—"all was filth, and age, and ruin". Since the aqueducts at Messina were in disrepair, there was occasional flooding and a tainted water supply. Free port privileges existed, but importers generally found that bureaucratic difficulties made these customs-free facilities more trouble than they were worth, and the quarantine regulations were a law to themselves quite out of step with the health department at Palermo. There was barely more community spirit here than elsewhere: the Abbé Guerra, himself a Messinese, thought that the various classes were bent upon destroying each other's prosperity, and, just as in other towns, the nobles tenaciously held on to the civic administration because they relied on being able to allocate local taxes and local civic expenditure to their own advantage. Silk-weaving and leather-making continued, and there was a notable growth of cotton manufacture after 1815; otherwise, said a guidebook in 1840, Messina had no industries.

One fundamental fact in the sluggishness of the Sicilian economy was the smallness of the national merchant marine. The Austrians had been surprised to find only 4,820 sailors and fishermen in all the island of Sicily. The Bourbons had followed the Piedmontese in replacing the oared galleys of the navy by sailing vessels, and had offered inducements for private ship-building; but in the

1740s and again twenty years later we have information that, although about a hundred small Sicilian ships were engaged in overseas commerce to Naples or further, this seems to have been not much more than five thousand tons in all. Viceroys encountered the objection that sailors preferred not to face the open sea. Seldom did these tiny ships venture beyond Gibraltar, and it was recorded as a great event when in 1798 a Sicilian vessel at last reached the Baltic.

A larger fishing industry would have helped to keep the arts of navigation and ship-building more vigorously alive, but there was little if any deep-water fishing, and even the swordfish and tunny fisheries needed only rowing boats. Already in the mid-eighteenth century there was talk about fish catches declining: the fishermen blamed this on sharks and appealed to the Pope for his help against them, but there were also more material complaints against the thoughtless and indiscriminate use of poison by the fishermen, and against them employing nets with a fine mesh designed to catch the fry. Laws were published against this, but in vain. Another protest was against the rich owners of the tunny fisheries who tried to increase their privileged monopoly and so raised fish prices and put small fishermen out of work. At all events, by the end of the eighteenth century, salmon, herring and cod had to be imported from northern Europe and America to this Mediterranean island, and of course they came in foreign vessels.

When the British navy needed base facilities in the 1790s, no proper dockyard existed at Palermo, though subsequent experience during the Napoleonic wars gave the repair shops of Palermo and Messina a reputation of being as good as any in the world. At last in 1789, by the munificence of a private citizen Monsignor Gioeni, a nautical school was established. Encouraged by government bounties, larger ships began to be built, and after 1818 one or two began to cross the Atlantic to the United States and then Brazil. In the next twenty years the tonnage of Sicilian shipping doubled. The King was accused, a little unfairly, of holding up the development of steamships in Sicily by favouring Naples. Only in 1841 did the Scottish-built *Palermo*, of 150 horse-power, become the first steamboat registered in Sicily, but already in 1838–9 a sailing vessel built in Sicily rounded the Cape of Good Hope for a thirteen-month visit to the Orient, and its captain received a gold medal from the government. By then there were twenty small Sicilian ships on the transatlantic routes. Nevertheless nearly all Sicilian exports went on travelling under a foreign flag, and by now it was the British who carried nearly half of them.

One reason for the sudden spurt in maritime traffic after 1815 was safer conditions resulting from the decline in Mediterranean piracy. The pirates and privateers must have been responsible over the centuries for an enormous loss of shipping, and here there was a legitimate grievance against successive governments quite as much as against the reluctant Sicilian taxpayer. Perlongo in the 1720s had explained the empty ports by instancing the high insurance premiums against piracy which took the profit out of trade. Capture and enslavement was an ever-present fear. A parliamentary petition in the 1770s explained that piracy was the reason why Sicilian exporters preferred to use foreign ships; either Sicilian vessels were too slow, or else Sicilian-based pirates provoked a special degree of retaliation against Sicilian commerce by the North African pashaliks. The Sicilian coast was still "constantly a prey to incursions from the Barbary states", wrote a British merchant in 1801.

In 1797 the Prince of Paternò was captured at sea. He had just won a legal case which awarded him a large inheritance, and like others of the Sicilian aristocracy who could afford it he was transferring his large household to live in the more comfortable and less provincial world of Naples. They arrived not at Naples but at Tunis, and probably the captain of their ship had in effect sold them into slavery. Paternò was released on promise of 300,000 *scudi* ransom, but once safely home he refused to pay such a huge sum. The Bey of Tunis then sued him in the Commercial Court of Palermo, and after three years won the case; one explanation given for this is that Ferdinand needed good relations with the Bey; another is that the courts were influenced by important Sicilians interested in buccaneering and its ancillary trades.

Piracy was still a recognised business among Sicilians during the Napoleonic wars. An organisation at Messina, with affiliations at Catania and Palermo, used to specialise in capturing ships and if necessary killing the crews. To some extent this domestic variety of pirate could be brought under control, but against the Barbary states there were few methods of defence except regular monetary payments in return for their leaving Sicily alone. Sometimes shipowners were allowed to arm privateers and take what booty they could; but this was itself a kind of licensed piracy that only provoked further reprisals. After the expedition to North Africa by American and British squadrons in 1816, Sicily was given some respite, though an annual sum was still paid to Algiers, Tunis and Tripoli. Another expedition in 1823 by the navy of the Two Sicilies was disastrously unsuccessful, and an even larger tribute had to be paid. Not until French influence spread effectively along the coast of North Africa after 1830 was there a proper control of this scourge.

Chapter 41

INDUSTRY

Lack of commerce and of industry went hand in hand. At the beginning of the nineteenth century, native industry hardly existed except at a household level. Basic products such as shoes, nails, pins, buttons and knives were imported, and so even were bricks. Raw materials for making soap and glass abounded locally, for example soda, olive oil, castor oil and linseed; but they were generally exported for manufacture elsewhere and the finished products then brought back again. Cotton, wool, flax, hemp, silk, all these were grown in some quantity and were used by housewives as the basis of a domestic industry, and yet textile manufactures remained the most costly item in Sicilian imports. By 1825, Baron Turrisi had several small factories making enough paper for home consumption. The leather workers of Palermo were a numerous community, as were the silk workers of Messina and Catania, but export markets had shrunk and were still shrinking. Although hats, gloves, glue, starch and snuff were now being produced in or near Palermo, this was only in small workshops which generally seem to have had a short life; and still there was no quantity production of ceramics and household hardware.

Most Sicilian economists, and this included Balsamo, Scrofani, Palmeri, Ferrara and Busacca, were not enthusiastic about artificially encouraging manufactures if this required excessive protectionism and transferring scanty capital away from agriculture where they thought it could be more usefully employed. According to one French consul, Sicilians of rank were unenthusiastic about the establishment of local industry, and it was obvious that Turrisi's paper factories, needing high protective duties, meant high prices to the consumer. It was equally obvious that Sicily lacked the main pre-requirements of an industrial revolution. She had no iron that could be mined economically, no coal except a little bad quality lignite, no navigable canals and rivers at all, and very poor internal communications of any sort. Charcoal was expensive and, like timber, was now having to be imported in considerable amounts. The exhaustion of native fuel supplies was one reason why the glass, silk and sugar-refining industries of Sicily had declined. Water power was uncertain, since most rivers were now completely dry for much of the year, and some water-propelled machinery, for instance in the sugar industry, had thereby become useless. This left imported coal; but the pattern of demand shown in the British consular figures suggests that

379

Sicily in 1839 was spending five times as much on coffee imports as coal, and twenty-five times as much on imports of sugar: and smuggling probably made this a huge under-estimate of the true figures.

Lack of skilled labour was another factor. Ferrara mentioned a Stanhope printing machine brought to Palermo in the 1830s but which no one could operate, and this was probably not untypical. The *maestranze* had deliberately restricted industrial education in order to keep out newcomers and preserve each trade as much as possible a privileged monopoly for a few families. Because food taxes were high, ordinary labour was not all that cheap by international standards, but skilled labour was just not available at all, and this twin handicap was a permanent incubus on local industry. Most Sicilians were still absolutely without any formal education: in some villages the priest and the magistrate alone knew how to read. Ordinary citizens, furthermore, lacked the purchasing power to provide much of a market for manufactured goods. The great inequalities in wealth meant that money was used for buying sugar, coffee and fine clothes from overseas, not on fostering the basic industries and the infrastructure necessary for an industrial revolution.

The Neapolitan government after 1815 tried to encourage local industries by protecting them against imports from Naples, but the amount of protection was either insufficient as an incentive, or else was too high to be much inducement to increased efficiency; and British, French and Spanish merchants at first made things yet more difficult by insolently asserting an ancient right to be exempt from customs visitation. In 1824, some of the surviving taxes on exports were abolished and higher duties placed on imported manufactures; but the good effects of this were counteracted by the freeing of trade with Naples, and Sicily was thus exposed to imports from a country which over the previous century had outstripped the island in economic growth. Neapolitan, British and French manufactures continued to take the lion's share of the market after 1824, and certain local businesses collapsed. Some interested parties clamoured for still higher government protection and accused Naples of exploitation. Most local intellectuals, however, and among them Ferrara who was soon to be generally acknowledged the leading Italian economist of his day, concluded that free trade was best for the economy, especially as "the nation is not industrially minded".

An inevitable accompaniment of industrial protection was smuggling. The extent of contraband is still impossible to document, especially as even official statistics of trade were so unreliable, but some outsiders said that there was no country where the laws were more openly evaded: as one foreigner explained, "the import and export duties are so excessively high that it becomes not only profitable but absolutely necessary for the trader to evade them". The French consul in the 1830s estimated that six to eight times as much coffee and tobacco was imported into Sicily as the official figures recorded; and one confirmation of this was that tobacco—which was sometimes used even by women and children—could retail for less than the tax due on it. Yet conviction for smuggling was rare, "the offence being generally compounded before the trial comes on", commented the British consul, John Goodwin. Customs officers were paid too little, and they themselves engaged fairly openly in contraband, with the result that the amount of duty received was not large. The smuggling was mainly of imports. Exports were usually too bulky and too little in demand, though there seems to have been a substantial illicit trade to Malta. As for the network of illegal traffic between one part of Sicily and another, all one can say is that it must have been enormous.

Vicenzo Florio was one individual who showed by his example what could be done in both commerce and industry. Florio was a mainlander, born in Calabria, whose family had exiled itself to Sicily with the King. He began as a commercial traveller and, according to general belief, made his first money by smuggling. Then he set up a business in groceries. Later he took over the tunny fishery at Favignana; here he made a small industry out of conserving fish in oil, using the residue for fertiliser. At the same time he extended into sulphur mining and put up a spinning mill which employed steam power. Realising the importance of credit, for a time he seems to have had a virtual monopoly of banking in Palermo, and this may have been a very lucrative operation. In 1841, profiting from government support, he opened the Oretea machine shop and foundry, the only establishment of its kind in Sicily; here he made steam engines, pumps and mining machinery, and by 1860 was employing two hundred people.

As he was an agent for the Rothschilds, some of Florio's capital may have come from them. Foreign investors were certainly interested in Sicily. As soon as the Marsala wine industry was established by British merchants, Florio joined them; and when one of these, Benjamin Ingham, organised a shipping combine in 1838-9, Florio became the second largest shareholder—a number of Sicilian aristocrats joined foreign investors in supporting this company. His first steamship was launched in 1849. His variegated career shows that there were considerable profits to be made by people who did not accept the conventional disinclination for commerce and who were prepared to take risks with their money.

But few followed him along this unfashionable path. Two of the young Orlando brothers after 1840 were making engines to mill wheat and sumac leaves, but, for political as well as economic reasons, they eventually emigrated to the more favourable atmosphere of northern Italy like many other enterprising sons of Sicily. The Florio family itself married into the aristocracy and became part of the local establishment, though they never entirely overcame the snobbish aloofness of aristocratic Palermo society.

The one export industry of any note had traditionally been silk, but for some time it had been falling behindhand in quality and price. Mulberries were being planted more frequently in other parts of Italy, and foreigners were finding cheaper silks in France and as far away as China. The tax on manufactured exports from Sicily still placed a gratuitous premium on smuggling and on the export of raw silk rather than manufactures, while prohibitions against the import of manufactured silk cloth from abroad could never be properly enforced. The government introduced more silk weavers from the mainland, as well as new weaving machinery, but nearly all production remained in private houses where it was almost impossible to change traditional methods of manufacture.

The silk guild at Messina was at most periods reasonably successful in keeping up standards of quality, yet it was a narrow vested interest which, by discouraging competition and technical innovation, also kept the industry artificially small and backward. The wholesalers and guildsmen of Messina held a virtual monopoly of outlets for a large area of the countryside, and from a parliamentary protest in 1794 it can be seen that they could not restrain themselves from using their monopoly to exploit the farmers, with the result that mulberry growing sometimes became uneconomic and stopped entirely. The Messinese had tried hard to get the government to reinforce their position by forbidding all silk manufacture at Catania. They asked to be empowered to employ an army of inspectors to check how much silk was grown and exactly to record all sales and purchases at every stage of manufacture. Their guild had strict regulations against paying piecework rates, and insisted that permission must be sought before any changes in technique could be made. Supervisors had to be consulted before any dyeing operation of any kind could be undertaken. Even when the King put up the money for a technical school to teach poor people a trade, the guild was strong enough to remove weaving from the subjects included, and instruction was therefore limited to such innocuous arts as baking and cart making.

This attitude of mind helps to explain why the industry was not more dynamic and why the silk-cultivating areas of the north-east were not increasing their prosperity. Up to a certain point Catania managed to defy the restrictionism of Messina, and here the aristocratic houses of Paternò and Biscari had fewer misgivings about trade than their brethren at Palermo. A quarter of the Catania population in 1727 was said to be engaged in the silk industry, most of them no doubt being women working in their own homes. Catania itself, however, joined Messina and Palermo in trying to persuade the government to forbid silk weaving at Acireale, for in this small town the growers had been trying to break free from the mercantilist regulations favouring the three big cities.

The English commanding officer at Messina in 1810 reported that the single silk factory of any size at Catania had no water power but only "human beings acting on the great wheel like turnspits". The silk industry at Palermo, he found, was smaller; but, owing to the generosity of Monsignor Gioeni, the poor house had a factory run by two Frenchmen where a water wheel provided power and there was employment for four hundred orphan girls. Slightly better days for Sicilian silk came after the arrival of Jaeger from Hanover in 1818 and Hallam from England, who eventually set up mechanised Jacquard looms and in the 1850s introduced the much better white oriental mulberry. Evidently there was some scope for development, but in practice Sicily's important share of the European market was never recaptured. As for domestic sales, not only did rich people prefer imports from France, but poorer people (many of whom had still been wearing silk as late as the 1780s), ceased to be able to afford it as their standard of life went down.

More cotton was grown in Sicily than anywhere else in Italy, but again the system of taxes and protection helped to create a high-cost industry; again the same restrictive attitudes suggested incapacity for spontaneous growth, and most of the crop therefore went overseas as a raw material for foreign workers. Sergio and de Cosmi had complained at the end of the eighteenth century that, except for the very coarsest cloth, Sicily had to import all its manufactured cotton, wool and linen requirements; and sometimes even the woollen mantillas of the peasant women turned out to be of foreign make. Fine woollens were hardly possible until the King introduced merino sheep for breeding after 1820. By the early 1830s there were some Arkwright cotton mills in operation, and outside Palermo a Swiss industrialist, Albrecht, was using quite advanced techniques for printing fabrics. By 1840 the Ruggieri brothers and an English firm each had a large factory at Messina said to be employing about a thousand people, nearly all women and girls, and using flying shuttles. But there were still complaints at the lack of enterprise among manufacturers (foreign as well as Sicilian), at the lack of support among the public for home-made goods, and at the difficulty of instructing spinners and weavers in the basic skills required. It is probable, moreover, that female labour was a product of poverty, and that any increase in wealth, whether of a family or of an area, led not to an increase but to a reduction of those willing to take this kind of industrial employment.

Sicily's mineral deposits were well known, and at various times in the past there had been production on a commercial scale of iron, lead, silver, alum and antimony. But difficulties of internal transport and the lack of fuel were insuperable problems. About 1750, the government was still trying to work the mines which the Austrians had re-opened, but Saxon and Hungarian labour proved too expensive, and though Sicilians were sent to Germany to learn the art, in the end lack of skilled workers brought this experiment to an end. Apart from these mines, mineral oil and seepages of natural gas were found in many places, though the oil was used only for lanterns or medicinally.

Most promising of all were the large deposits of easily workable sulphur stretching over several thousand square miles of central and southern Sicily. For many centuries there had been a small trade in sulphur for gunpowder and medical use. Then, in 1794, the discovery of the Leblanc soda process opened up a whole new industry, and British capitalists began to interest themselves during the war in those areas near Sicilian ports where open-cast mining of sulphur was possible. Landowners near Girgenti and Caltanissetta suddenly discovered that they owned a near world monopoly in an essential commodity needed by the industrial revolution in Europe and America. When Ferdinand in 1808 waived his royal monopoly rights over mining in order to please the Sicilian aristocracy, a rosy future opened to many *latifondisti* and smallholders.

Soon after the restoration of peace in 1815, there was a rush into sulphur mining as England began to use the Leblanc process and a number of French firms also set up in Sicily. Thousands of new industrial uses for sulphuric acid were soon being developed. It seemed for a time as though the economy of Sicily might be about to change dramatically. Despite some casualties, output greatly expanded, and, by the peak year of 1834, exports of sulphur were almost three times the value of wine exports which came next on the list. About two ships a week were calling at Licata, one at Girgenti, and over two hundred mines were in operation. The bulk of these exports went to Britain, and over twenty British firms were actively engaged on the spot either in production or export. A fair amount of capital came with these foreign firms, as well as skilled labour from as far distant as Cornwall and Scotland. One British manager in 1837 replaced the dangerous hand pumps by steam pumps for keeping the mines free of water, and this must have been one of the first uses of steam in Sicilian industry.

Labour was cheap in the mines, because the workers were not townsmen but drawn largely from farms in the off season; steam power, on the other hand, would have been enormously expensive because coal had to come on muleback like everything else. Cheap labour and guaranteed exports meant that there was thus no great incentive to improve methods of production. Because of fuel costs, it was general practice for the mined ore to be ignited so that the sulphur could be melted out of the gypsum and limestone by the heat of its own combustion. This was dangerous as well as wasteful: mines used to catch fire, and the underground seams could go on burning for years over a wide area; also the gases released by this primitive method of smelting were injurious to health and ruined the surrounding vegetation, so that mining had by government order to stop near harvest time. Another danger was that, since pit props were too expensive, there were many accidents as soon as mine shafts were sunk underground.

The chief lack outside and inside the mines was wheeled transport. All the ore had to be brought to the surface on the backs of *carusi*, mostly small boys who were indentured to the trade by their families as what one can only call slave labour. Women, too, were employed as carriers, but the galleries were very low and hence boys or girls were preferred. Even on pittance wages this primitive method of transport could account for half the running expenses of a mine. As there were no proper roads, the sulphur was then taken on mules to the coast; and as there were no port establishments, stevedores waded deep into the sea to load lighters which then rowed out to ships lying beyond the dangerous inshore. This was slow and expensive. Already in the 1820s there was also evidence of restrictive practices among stevedores and muleteers which helped to keep these inefficient methods in being for the next century or more. Labour troubles were also encountered by a small French refinery at Girgenti and a British sulphuric acid plant at Messina, so that foreign firms found it cheaper to export the raw material.

The true profit and loss involved in these operations took some time to become known, just because open-cast mining was at first so easy; but by the middle 1830s, sulphur output was seen to be growing faster than the market, and a sudden fall in prices dramatically exposed the underlying weaknesses of this new industry. A number of people who had taken leases on mines went bankrupt. Attempts to get set voluntary limits on production were unthinkable in a world of such individualism and mutual distrust, and an urgent appeal therefore went up for government protection.

A French company, Taix & Aycard, who were caught with a great deal of unsold sulphur, eventually suggested that they should run a government-sponsored monopoly. The French and British governments, both of whom feared a price increase, tried to stop this project, and so did Busacca and other Sicilian economists, but the King was attracted to the idea. Not only did it promise to control output and reduce exploitation of Sicily by foreigners, but a very substantial revenue would accrue to the government at Naples, and Taix also undertook to set up a local industry for caustic soda and sulphuric acid, as well as to build twenty miles of road a year. In 1838, therefore, the French syndicate, with considerable local backing, was given a virtual monopoly, and other producers were obliged either to sell to it at a controlled price or else pay a royalty on their exports. The King himself proposed to become a shareholder in the enterprise.

Promising in theory, the idea worked badly, mainly because Taix was so anxious to clear his debts that he quickly tripled the price to the maximum permitted level and so aroused too much opposition too soon. Sulphur exports in 1839 dropped by three-quarters until they were less than half the value of exported sumac leaves. The new price stimulated the exploration of alternative sulphur deposits in Belgium and Iceland, and already people were beginning to investigate the vast quantities known to exist in the United States. Even worse, there was developed a substitute method of extracting sulphur cheaply from pyrites. In any case the monopoly proved unworkable, for extra export licences could be obtained by bribery, or else exporters sent their sulphur via Naples for which no licence was required. Palmerston, in his most bullying vein, accused Ferdinand of violating treaty and property rights and retaliated by sequestrating Sicilian ships; the King therefore ended the monopoly and made an empty promise to indemnify Taix. British merchants also put in preposterous claims for indemnification.

Sicily had to pay for this costly failure. Her extractive industry remained chaotic, and the promised chemical factories were not built, while she lost a valuable monopoly position when Germany and other countries switched to pyrites for their sulphur supplies. The mines went on working, and considerable profits continued to be made by Sicilian landowners; but the money did not go to research, or to develop new markets, or to buy the expensive excavating machinery which was already seen to be necessary, let alone to build the roads which alone could have made sulphur mining genuinely competitive.

The Neapolitan government had some hopes that landowners would co-operate in making the industry succeed. The King set an example by renouncing his legal right to 10 per cent of the sulphur produced, but this generous gift was taken very much as a matter of course and met no similar spirit among the landlords who, almost alone, gained from it. Hardly any of them mined their own land, and this was a serious handicap to the industry. Just as with their *latifondi*, they used the *gabella* system for the mines, and the great profits of the 1830s had taught them to keep leases short; but short leases only encouraged the manager or *gabelloto* to overproduce, to exploit both mines and labour uneconomically, and to resist any temptation to introduce any long-term improvements; towards the end of his lease he might even abandon the pumps and ruin the whole mine. The "immorality and greed of producers" was given by a government inspector in 1850 as one of his main problems. Landowners, it was repeatedly said, insisted on taking between 20 per cent and 40 per cent of the sulphur as their ground rent, and this royalty must have contributed more than anything else towards making Sicilian sulphur too expensive. Nor did they ever show any enthusiasm for using their profits to build up a local chemical industry which could use this precious raw material at home, and this despite the fact that yields were sometimes reported of up to 200 per cent p.a. net on invested capital.

"Another obstacle", wrote the British consul, "is the mutual distrust of the Sicilian capitalists. Suspicious of his countrymen, the Sicilian possessed of money shrinks from risking his capital by engaging in commercial associations or entering into partnership." The French consul in the 1830s agreed in singling out the complete lack of 'la bonne foi'. "Il n'y a point d'esprit d'association", he commented; "chacun veut gagner seul." Landowners could not agree among themselves, not even where, as so often happened, a mine could be properly worked only if it was extended into someone else's property. This was why there were so many hundreds of mines, so many tangled law suits between heirs, and why such a reliance had to be placed on government help.

Chapter 42

AGRICULTURE

The majority of Sicilians worked on the land, and agriculture was, as it always had been, the basis of most commerce and industry. The essential conservatism of rural Sicily coloured every other aspect of national life. When the nineteenth century began, cereal cultivation covered nearly all the huge area of the *latifondi* as it had done for centuries. Balsamo was ahead of his time in realising that Sicily was not going to be able to compete in cereals with Russia and America: his view was that, though yields could hopefully be improved and costs reduced, a diminution of the acreage under wheat was unavoidable. Current prices might have been expected to bring this about automatically, yet habits on the land died hard, especially as the boom years of 1807–14 left behind a memory of prosperity that few could forget.

This war-time bonus had enabled many landowners to triple their income. Louis-Philippe took advantage of such a windfall (and of his civil list pension from the Sicilian taxpayer) to pay off the accumulated debts on his estates; and Mr. Leckie near Syracuse used it to demonstrate that quite new agricultural projects were within reach of enterprising farmers—"but few of them", commented the tourist Galt, "attempted to imitate his example". Any landowner who took this kind of individual initiative invited the envy, but often also the hostility, of his neighbours. Most people therefore used wartime profits to buy up more land to grow wheat, and were less concerned to make existing cultivation efficient or more diversified.

The severe slump after 1815 came as an urgent pointer to the need for radical change. Much of the area brought into production during the previous decade had to be abandoned; land values tumbled by two-thirds, and rents fell by a similar amount. How much wheat went on being produced cannot be said, because, according to the Marquis Mortillaro, recorded figures for production still bore little relation to reality. Export statistics were no doubt more reliable, just because the profit had gone out of this brand of smuggling: wheat was still sent to Naples (some, too, was regularly imported by Messina from Naples), and, as late as the 1830s, cereals in a good year were exported to England, Portugal and France. Nevertheless, the pattern of trade had now changed, and other crops were generally much bigger earners of foreign currency.

Large areas of Sicily were well suited for wine production because of the mild winter climate and the infrequency of hailstorms. Fazello in the sixteenth century called the local wines as good as any in Italy, because of their durability and sugar content; and many Spaniards, too, thought them excellent. This particular industry received a great stimulus during the Napoleonic wars when Britain's other sources of supply were cut off; and Nelson left for the Nile with over forty thousand gallons of Sicilian wine aboard. John Woodhouse of Liverpool was ready to meet the demand. He had originally come as a dealer in vegetable potash, but in 1773 he had sent an experimental consignment of seventy pipes of wine to England. Twenty years later, profiting from the vogue for sherry and port and their high price, he opened a factory at Marsala for fortified wines of a similar strength and type. What he brought to Sicily was first of all capital and enterprise, but also ideas about overseas demand and marketing; within a few years he had made a large fortune and was even lending money to the King. Soon after 1806 another Englishman, Benjamin Ingham, set up a second establishment near by; and shortly there were four British firms at Marsala and several others at near-by Mazara.

Friendly rivalry between these foreign merchants had excellent results on quality and price. As one Frenchman acknowledged, they were the first to introduce scientific methods of vinification, and theirs were the first proper wine factories to exist anywhere in Sicily. Ingham went to Spain to study the solera system, and brought back information about clarifying wine and dosing it with spirit. He used to buy rough wine from all over the island, mature it for five years, and blend it to maintain a constant standard. Nor was he too discouraged by the slump after 1815, but at once began the slow process of developing a peace-time market. Ten years later, he and the others could claim that they had created what consumers in general regarded as an altogether new category of wine. At their own expense they built proper roads of access; at last the once famous port of Marsala was rehabilitated and re-opened to shipping. Before very long, the town had tripled in size—appropriately its patron saint was the Englishman, Thomas Becket. This enterprising group of foreigners encouraged the growth of small proprietorship and intensive, specialist cultivation, so that the area was eventually converted into one of the most prosperous in Sicily. After 1831, when Florio set up yet another winery there with a succession of British managers, Marsala wine became one of the most flourishing export businesses in the country. Other places followed this example, and by 1838 over two million gallons of wine were going to Brazil each year and nearly a million to Britain.

The growing of fruit and especially citrus fruit was eventually to cause a major advance in Sicilian agriculture. The Portuguese had brought the sweet orange to Europe somewhere about the 1540s; it was found to grow very well in the hot coastal plains of Sicily, where people liked to live yet where other kinds of agriculture did not flourish. In the 1750s, Leanti had found abundant citrus orchards along the coast. Exports began to grow when minor uses were discovered for citric acid in industry, and in the 1790s when lemon and citron juice became a standard specific against scurvy. As demand grew, vines were even cut down to make room for lemons and oranges. Then during the Napoleonic wars the citrus trees were themselves sometimes cut down to grow more cereals. Exports resumed after 1815, and by the 1830s their value sometimes rivalled that of wine, though as much as a quarter of this total was possibly made up of Calabrian fruit brought to Messina for re-export. Essential oils were also extracted with sponges from the rind and exported to overseas perfumeries. Citric acid could have been made locally as well, but the risk and expense were thought too great, and the fruit was merely salted in sea water for export to manufacturers elsewhere.

The limitations on such a potentially profitable kind of agriculture were, first of all, this lack of the added dimension which would have been given by industrial enterprise. Secondly, there was the fact that arboriculture needed longer leases and cheaper credit than landowners were ready to permit. Thirdly, there was the problem of transport by mule, which caused delays, spoilage and expense. Fourthly, there was the mafia which, by demanding protection money, by cutting trees as a reprisal or a warning, by monopolising water supplies and selling them expensively, and finally by taking its cut on transport and marketing, was probably the biggest handicap of all. When one adds to this the limited knowledge of farmers, who beat the trees to pick the fruit and often seemed to decapitate instead of pruning them, one understands why Sicily found prosperity elusive.

Raw silk, as an agricultural export, suffered from the fact that foreign merchants tended to find its quality inadequate. The cultivation of mulberries and silk worms were expert activities which elsewhere were receiving scientific study; but in Sicily, where absentee landlordism led to a neglect of agricultural education, techniques were generally primitive, and women still hatched the silkworms under their clothes as Fazello had observed them doing three centuries earlier. Foreigners would have liked to import more Sicilian cotton, and some adventurous farmers found it a rewarding crop, but again growers had the difficulty of obtaining enough capital, as well as of learning new skills and finding the most suitable varieties. Not only was there still a tax on exports, but unknown risks lay in switching from subsistence to export farming. The same risk applied to another valuable export, sumac, a shrub which grew wild even on slopes of 40 degrees or more and whose leaves produced a high concentration of tannin used in leather work. There were only a few Sicilian tanneries, but exports of powdered sumac leaves grew substantially in the first half of the century; the trade fell off only when heavy adulteration with myrtle and lentisk (this had been a problem as early as 1776) earned it a bad name and encouraged the development of substitutes.

Olive oil was a considerable export, and agronomists would have liked more olives planted instead of wheat. The Bourbons gave tax exemptions to encourage this, but rough and ready methods of pressing the oil, which allowed it to ferment and become rancid, proved impossible to change. Cultivation of olive trees was left very much to nature, and pruning, if it took place at all, was evidently designed to produce as much firewood as possible. Another export crop was manna, a resin from wild ash trees used in medicine and textile manufacture. Potash was made from the combustion of certain plants: this was in great demand overseas for bleaching, soap-making and for the glass factories of Venice, until more efficient artificial processes using Sicilian sulphur were developed after 1815. Liquorice was sent especially to England and Holland as a medicine and for dyeing. Cantharides, or Spanish fly, found a steady sale as an aphrodisiac in a number of specialised markets. Some indigo grew wild, and madder and saffron, but it was hard to persuade people to cultivate such rewarding but unusual crops.

Potatoes were being grown commercially at the end of the eighteenth century and the government encouraged this. They were even used experimentally for bread manufacture and animal fodder, but one inhibiting factor was a popular belief that the eating of potatoes was conducive to sexual immorality. The basic food of the ordinary people was often little more than beans and cactus fruit. Wheat bread was, after 1815, too expensive for the really poor except as an occasional luxury food, though maize became more common and could sometimes even be referred to as the 'Sicilian grain'. The prickly pear cactus, that most durable relic of Spanish rule, was said to be what kept the common people alive and healthy. It was a hardy plant in stony soil and conditions of great dryness. Its fruit was available for most of the year, and custom in many villages allowed that anyone could pick it anywhere.

Cattle and sheep farming of a kind was undertaken on the sparse vegetation of the inland hills. This was the typical *latifondo* country where, if water was not properly used, ten acres would barely support a single emaciated cow. Animals were therefore in continual daily movement, quite apart from the long annual journeys between coast and mountains to escape the extremes of climate. The frequent journeying was bad for meat and milk production. It also meant that animal husbandry had to be largely divorced from the rest of agriculture. The ordinary farm labourer, living as he did in a village remote from the *latifondo*, was not equipped to bring sheep and cattle into his regular routine.

Balsamo said that this was one of Sicily's main problems. Evidence was available—or so he hopefully thought—that in many areas artificial leys could be created from which half a dozen crops of hay and lucerne could be taken in a single year, to say nothing of turnips and other root vegetables; but this kind of farming was in practice unknown. Balsamo travelled carefully over most of Sicily and found almost no cattle sheds and hardly any crops grown specially for stall-feeding. Everywhere the animals wandered almost wild to browse as they could, and this could be a disaster in winter time or if the rains failed and there was no grass, to say nothing of the damage done to crops and trees. They were always prone to disease. He was sure that intensive meat production could be made profitable, but few farmers would face the hazards involved. On the contrary, as more land was put under the plough, the number of animals continued to decline; sometimes they had to be imported from Tunis. Sicilians had once been renowned meat eaters, but were now becoming known as vegetarians. Ploughing, too, regularly had to be done by hand. The British army quartermasters, when they found provisioning extremely difficult, worked out a scheme to set up special cattle ranches; Balsamo was consulted and approved of their project, but he doubted if there could be found enough farmers who possessed the 'uncommon qualifications' of uprightness, energy and skill needed to make it succeed. In the 1820s the government placed large export duties on meat and livestock in order to keep up the number of animals and so maintain a better balanced agriculture, but this only made cattle-raising more unprofitable than ever.

By the early nineteenth century, destruction of the forests was rapidly accelerating. Until now there had been wild boar, roebuck and wolves to be hunted, and some writers could describe the island as fairly wooded; but by the second half of the nineteenth century there were very few boar, and deer existed only in a few private hunting reserves. The chief forestry inspector in western Sicily made a rough estimate that, during the thirty years to 1847, the remaining woodlands had been reduced by over half. A shortage of charcoal had been noted a century earlier, and of course this became worse as the population went on growing. Apparently even oak, olive and cork trees were regularly cut for fuel, and there were soon no trees at all left near the sulphur mines. But domestic fuel requirements were perhaps the most destructive of all, especially as the simple open stove generally employed for cooking was extremely uneconomical.

Much of this was simple improvidence. For example, instead of merely stripping off bark for the tanneries, the trees were felled wholesale. The burning of the stubble each August was also a way in which destructive forest fires were sometimes started inadvertently; or else they could be a deliberate act of vendetta, as for instance in 1813 when five hundred men from Bagheria set fire to a forest which the local aristocracy had turned into a private hunting reserve. Fires were also becoming more common than ever as a means of clearing scrub and woodland for the plough, and in this way enormous damage was done for what was often a very temporary return. As existing wheatlands became progressively exhausted by the absence of crop rotation, new virgin territory was always being sought, and few people except the government ever thought of the future or of whether this practice was in the interests of the community as a whole. It was hard to think of the future when hunger was a permanent problem and when employment of any kind was so precarious.

In 1819 and 1826 the Bourbons made laws which were aimed at preserving what was left of the forests; but such legislation needed more community sense and less avarice than could be expected from the *latifondisti* or their shepherds. The forest guards were not paid nearly enough, and used to supplement their wages by illegally cutting trees and helping criminal gangs to manage the clandestine traffic in timber and firewood. Where 'promiscuous rights' continued to exist, the custom of the manor generally allowed any villager to cut firewood; where they were suppressed, the new landowners or *gabelloti* found it easy and profitable to sell what timber was left. Either way the results could be serious. This kind of de-afforestation had been going on for years; and yet the ending of feudalism in 1812 and of entails in 1818 initiated a much more damaging phase in the story. The new landowners often did not have the same income as the old, and so were more tempted to consume capital; they thought themselves less obliged to consider common rights in the land; nor would a *gabelloto* on a short lease obtain any advantage by replanting. The courts were easily persuaded to connive at the kind of legal fiction by which grafting a crab apple or a wild olive would turn officially registered forest into 'cultivated land', and the Marquis di Rudinì and others used this method to justify large-scale sales of timber from their estates.

Some incidental effects of this process were studied by one of the Paternò family among others. At Catania there were average annual rainfall figures of 785 mm. for 1808–12, but only 453 mm. for 1866–79. The river Simeto was later shown to carry twice as much sediment as the infinitely larger river Po in northern Italy which had sixteen times as extensive a watershed. A considerable falling off was also noticed in its flow after 1824. Springs regularly dried up and did not reappear unless trees were planted again. On somewhat flimsier evidence it was said that the climate was becoming more severe, both hotter and colder and in general dryer than before. The government did something to use the rivers Simeto and Dittaino for irrigation, but on a very small scale. Prince Biscari built an aqueduct to his rice fields, but few private people had the resources or interest to follow such an example.

Probably the most ominous sign of forest destruction was soil erosion on the hillsides, and though the Intendants had instructions to stop any ploughing on the steeper slopes, this had little effect. Cereals would grow in Sicily as high as a thousand metres or more above sea level; and since a third of the whole land surface was over five hundred metres above sea level (and, worse still, on a slope greater than one in five), land hunger, where uncontrolled, had ruinous effects. Little was known of contour ploughing. According to the forest inspector, Schirò, ploughs were still used on slopes of up to 25 degrees; and on steeper inclines up to 60 degrees one could see peasants digging while hitched by ropes to a rock. He commented that "all the land cultivated on slopes becomes sterile after a few years". The civil servant and historian, Bianchini, pointed out that by 1840 almost every hill-top was bare and eroded. Particularly one could see this to the south of Palermo, where there was almost total aridity on the hillsides leading down to the city; though on their far side, where this land hunger had still not arrived, the slopes were fertile, moist and tree-covered.

Meanwhile the silting up of rivers, itself a direct result of these agricultural practices, caused regular floods and crumbling of river banks. The spread of malaria seems to have altogether ended the existence of some villages. As earth was washed off the slopes, mountain streams became more and more torrential in the rainy season, doing great damage among the vineyards and orange groves. Erosion produced five torrents which threatened the town of Messina itself; they were responsible for a terrible destruction of houses in 1819, 1823, 1831 and 1839. Elsewhere landslides sterilised large areas of fertile ground. One village was destroyed by a landfall in 1838, and other similar examples were noted in 1851 and 1853.

Chapter 43

RESTRAINTS ON ECONOMIC DEVELOPMENT

Deliberate de-afforestation, with its widespread effects, was one example of how certain attitudes of mind burdened trade and agriculture. Another damaging attitude was the conviction that only short-term gains were worth considering. Another was the individualistic unwillingness of people to co-operate with each other, let alone to assist governmental projects for reform. Cockburn was surprised to discover almost no one interested in tree planting, even where tree crops would have paid better than pasture and would have brought unused and sterile land into production to the great benefit of the community.

Another harmful attitude was the dislike of appearing to work hard and the snobbish preference for living off unearned income. Accumulation of wealth was less admired in this society than the acquisition of 'respect'. Indeed Ferrara pessimistically concluded that the 'character' of Palermitans would always prevent their town becoming a commercial centre. The old families would not sully their hands with new methods of estate management so successful elsewhere. A similar contempt of the country way of life could also be seen in the filth with which the townspeople of Palermo pelted the rustic 'villani' at carnival time. Humbler citizens, in order to keep their self-respect, would try to acquire a non-manual job. The humblest office porter was thus marked out as in a sense a *galantuomo*, as a 'hat' instead of a 'beret', and even successful merchants seem to have preferred a professional rather than a mercantile status for their children. This kind of job carried social esteem. It also carried an element of stability and permanence in a world where everything else was precarious and long months of unemployment were the rule in town and country alike.

Another pervasive attitude of mind was the instinctive, protective preference for monopoly and restriction, a preference which governments as well as governed had inherited from the high summer of mercantilism. An assumption that the amount of trade was strictly limited was what led Messina to seek government help in restricting the commerce of Catania, and Catania that of Acireale. Messina tried to insist on a civic monopoly of baking, and a by-law compelled peasants to come from afar to purchase bread in the town. Palermo, too, in 1813 was still insisting on its right to fix both the purchase and selling price of flour, despite

Balsamo's demonstration that this was bound to defeat its own object and reduce available supplies of food. Since smaller villages received most of their revenue from food taxes, they followed suit and imposed stringent controls of their own. Villages had powers to prevent their own produce going elsewhere and to forbid that of another district entering theirs; they could compel growers to sell one-third of the harvest to the local authority, and at a price fixed not by the market but by the magistrates. Privileged contractors might have a monopoly of providing the towns with certain foods, and foreign merchants would find that someone had bought up monopoly rights on the manufacture or sale of a certain commodity so that they would have to operate through him alone and pay whatever he demanded. To set up a soap factory might thus cost 5,000 *scudi*. Below this level, moreover, the guilds had their own local monopolies in the retail trade.

Price controls, permits, sales restriction and often an outright prohibition of export, all these had contributed to the decline of the wheat trade, and a host of public officials had grown up to enforce a system of corn laws which was as restrictive as it was expensive to apply. One foreigner early in the century found that export licences "are seldom granted on fair and legitimate grounds or with the view of promoting national industry. They are in general attained by corruption and bribery, and they are granted to the favourites or dependants of ministers as a means of amassing wealth." As the British minister was informed, price-fixing was one more "cover for collusions and frauds of every kind". Some traders and most consumers, therefore, were more than ready to accept a new attempt by the Neapolitan government to end what was left of this protectionist system. Many vested interests had to be bought out, and still some restrictions had to be reimposed in any very bad year, but compulsory deposits in the *caricatoi* were no longer demanded after 1819.

Another deadweight on economic life was the diversity of weights and measures. Each area still kept individual measures of its own, the very names of which often went back to Greek or Arab times, and the difficulty of internal communication helped to perpetuate them. There were said to be a hundred different dry measures, many more for liquid, and as many for length and surface area. Neighbouring villages might have completely different systems, and some of these individual systems could themselves be irritatingly imprecise. When the issue arose in the parliament of 1741, the baronial and domanial Houses of parliament had not been anxious to have this muddle reformed, but the Bourbons, like the Spanish Viceroys before them, recognised the advantages of uniformity. The *latifondi* could hardly be divided if there was no agreed measure of length; nor were exports easy if a *salma* as a measure of wheat not only varied from Messina to Palermo and in between, but even in the same village could be a quite different capacity when used for barley, lime, or charcoal. Foreign wine merchants were hardly encouraged to buy Sicilian wines when the *caffiso* could vary by a factor of 50 per cent, and customs and excise taxes were rendered very hard to collect. Accordingly, in 1809, Ferdinand tried to bring in a version of the metric system. His intentions were good, but it was not easy to enforce them, and Balsamo and others warned him that some people would dislike a uniform system of weights and measures; quite apart from natural conservatism, some may have clung to the old system for the profits which could be made out of the confusion.

Abolition of the *donativi* made no difference to the fact that governmental and local taxes both continued to fall most heavily on agriculture. Flour, cheese and wine were still taxed at the gates of every town and village, and the *macinato* tax on flour was still farmed out at a discount to what a British official called "needy adventurers". These food taxes were said to be almost twice what they were in Naples. Palmeri in the 1820s thought that they made up over a third of the basic cost of food; Nassau Senior about 1850 estimated that, whereas the land tax produced rather less than a third of the revenue, the food excises produced more than a third (the French consul said over a half). This meant a high cost of living and was another handicap to economic development. At the same time it explains a dangerous insubordination in the country-side which made this the most revolutionary century in Sicilian history. The need to evade the food taxes was the strongest and most widespread motive in successive 'political' rebellions; and it was an important factor in building up the mafia-like organisations which in their turn were such a burden on the economy.

Balsamo had noted a decline in the wage-earners' standard of living over the last thirty years of the eighteeenth century, and this same trend seems once again to have affected Sicily after 1815. Population, by official reckoning, increased from 1.9 millions in 1798 to 2.3 millions in 1861, and then to 3.5 millions in 1901, but without any major changes in agriculture to provide the necessary increase in food supply. Many Sicilian villages continued to be more or less self-sufficient, and even in the twentieth century some were still using barter as a means of exchange. All too often, the peasants remained bound to the soil by fetters of debt, without any money to spend. On the wheatlands there was work for them during only two months in the year, at harvest and sowing time, so that long periods of unemployment continued to be a normal condition of life. They were still expected to call their landlord 'Excellency' and kiss his hand in deference.

To escape malaria, brigandage and solitude, these agricultural labourers lived in large villages remote from their work, too far away for efficient agriculture, too far for the women to help in the fields even if work had been available for them; and there they existed in conditions of squalor and brutality which frightened the occasional visitors from the towns. Balsamo saw some of them dwelling in caves like "wild beasts". Meli, once a village doctor, described how they lived largely on wild plants and roots, with bread only a rare treat; according to him, they often could not afford to get married, or, if married, could not produce large families. Sanfilippo, the agronomist, wrote in 1833 that conditions on the land had grown steadily worse since 1815, and death by starvation was once again far from unknown. As Ferrara wrote to the British consul in 1847, "three fourths of the peasants, sallow, sickly and deformed, vegetate rather than live. Born to no other end than to moisten the clods with the sweat of their brow, they feed upon herbs, clothe themselves in rags, and sleep huddled up together in smoky huts amidst the stench of a dunghill."

Meanwhile landlord absenteeism was still very much the rule. Social pressures prevented landlords putting their estates on a proper economic footing, and beneath them there was a sometimes equally parasitic class of provincial gentry who whiled away their time in the *caffè dei nobili*. If only these *galantuomini* had spent more time in the countryside, or had been more observant and public-spirited, they would have realised the importance of roads, bridges, farm cottages and outbuildings; they would have recognised the need to drain malarial marshes and lay on water supplies, to plant trees and in general plan long-term improvements. Gino Capponi when he toured Sicily in 1817 reported, just as Scinà did at the same time and de Tocqueville later, that the handful of landowners who owned most of Sicily were opposed to improvements. "While the barons were thus enjoying the empty parade of unprofitable power", wrote one Englishman to A'Court, "they were depriving themselves of the solid advantage of wealth." Great areas of their estates were quite unnecessarily going to waste, and other people unfortunately suffered from this fact more than they did.

Some landowners stood out from the rest. Notably there was the Duke of Monteleone who, helped by the profits of his Mexican mines, maintained the river embankments above Terranova and so kept this area under partial irrigation. On another estate, at Avola, he maintained the last commercial sugar plantation in Sicily, where excellent rum was now made. There was the Prince of Raffadali, a German who succeeded by marriage to many of the Butera estates: by the 1840s, he had made high profits from following the market and planting almonds and sumac, though communications were a problem and the conservatism of his tenants was intractable. He built houses for his labourers, only to find that they were unwilling to leave their villages and live in the isolation of the *latifondi*. Following Balsamo's example he bought English ploughs and offered extra wages for their use, but suspected that they were deliberately broken; his workmen preferred the primitive plough without wheels or coulter, a tool which they constructed for themselves and which for thousands of years had merely scratched the top soil. Raffadali also imported a threshing machine, but there was no one who could keep it in repair, and he had to fall back on the wasteful method of using horses' hooves like everyone else. Another progressive landowner, Prince Castelnuovo, set up a teaching institute for his peasants and printed an agricultural calendar for free distribution; but he was an isolated eccentric, an anachronistic liberal who refused to accept the Bourbon counter-revolution of 1816 or to pay any taxes which had not been granted by parliament. Such a person was not an object of general admiration.

Compared with these men, most landowners possessed neither the courage, nor the will, nor in many cases the money to carry out changes; they preferred to work through a *gabelloto* who in turn hired share croppers to do all the hard work in return for a small fraction of the harvest. But no one on a yearly or three-yearly contract would plant trees or build cattle sheds or even manure the land if this would merely profit whoever succeeded him, while vines and citrus would bring no income until after four or five years. It was said that, in some areas, irrigation would have increased land values by ten or twenty times, but this would have needed enterprise and confidence in the future, as it would also have required security of tenure for tenants. There was still a markedly primitive knowledge about the rotation of crops, and hence half the available land was left uncultivated and fallow each year. Sowing had to be done broadcast. Animal manure was regularly burnt. And those who worked on saints' days were liable to a prison sentence—so important was the Church as a regulator of morals. Landlords in northern Italy were now organising their farms on a capitalist basis and expecting a fair rate of growth, but in Sicily most landlords and tenants looked no further than survival.

One possibility of improvement was that the *gabelloti* might change into an enterprising class of middling landowners, but in practice they had no wish to overthrow the old system of feudal relations. To most of them, as to the aristocracy they copied, public life meant the enjoyment of a privileged situation without any corresponding responsibility. These were the men who often became the real bosses in each locality, enclosing the common lands, as a rule not farming actively, but imposing their authority on local government just like their aristocratic predecessors and with an equally cynical contempt for the law. The Prince of Lercara's *gabelloto* had a son who became the local magistrate, and between them, because of their influential friends, these two men could even use the regular soldiers against villages which dared to resist their tyranny. This kind of man was becoming the main influence in Sicilian agriculture. Often he was a person of great shrewdness and ambition; sometimes he was a good farmer; but usually it seems to have been his interest to depress rather than to stimulate the economy.

Contemporary books and journals show that in the years after 1815 a few individuals were beginning to have a real exchange of views about how agriculture could be improved, and this was an important sign of change. It was generally accepted that smaller or middle-sized farms and above all longer leases were needed, and that a much higher proportion of the national income should be diverted back into the land. Balsamo ideally would have liked the *latifondi* to remain but to make their owners more interested in active farming; as this was impossible, the alternative was to give those who actually worked the land a greater share in ownership and an interest in increasing productivity. This too, however, was proving difficult to bring about.

One government agricultural expert, the Lombard economist de Welz, observed in 1822 that Sicilians had too high an opinion of their own capabilities to be anxious to learn or to change. Balsamo could lecture on deep ploughing and manuring; he could bring in long-handled Lombard scythes and Norfolk ploughs which would do four times the work done by the prehistoric implements still in use; but the real problem was to persuade the more enlightened farmers and landowners to set a good example by using these new methods and granting improvement leases. As Scinà complained, foreign students were coming to Sicily and discovering more than Sicilians knew about their own island and its natural resources. Popular apathy and governmental inefficiency were such that, already in the 1830s, it was possible to think that Sicilian agriculture was being overtaken by that of North Africa.

The absence of state authority or community sense was nowhere more visible than in the continued lack of roads. The example of Naples and Malta was quoted to show that road construction, far from being too expensive, would pay for itself and electrify the economy; but in Sicily this lesson went unregarded. In the 1820s we hear of grapes unharvested and lemons left to rot on the tree because of transport costs. Wheat might double in price because of carriage to the coast, and Busacca confirmed that it might cost more to send goods from a farm into Palermo than from Palermo to London. If a proper rotation of crops was almost unknown, one reason was that root crops and beans were bulky and so expensive to carry on the universal muleback. According to the Intendants, moreover, where roads were built the number of crimes fell by half, while elsewhere theft and intimidation contributed to make farming quite unprofitable.

By the 1820s there existed about 250 miles of carriageable road, not all of it paved, some of it very steep and sometimes knee-deep in either dust or mud. The journey by *lettiga* from Palermo to Messina now took only four days in good weather, owing to the activity of the British army engineers during the war; but a guidebook of 1826 warned foreigners that stretches of the main road from Messina to Catania were practicable only by mule. There were some toll gates along this road, but the dues were either insufficient or not properly spent. The government had once opposed toll barriers on the grounds that, if dues were high enough to obtain enough revenue, either traffic would cease, or else people would merely learn how to evade them; and experience after 1815 was to show that these first thoughts may well have been right. The 175-mile road from Palermo to Catania was being built slowly, but a third of the distance was unpaved by 1850, and wheeled traffic could be held up for days in bad weather—and this when, in Naples, the railway age was beginning. The river Salso on the path from Girgenti to Catania was still unbridged in 1842, and many accidents continued to happen at this dangerous crossing; nor was there a bridge over the Simeto between Catania and Syracuse, and mules and baggage had to cross by raft.

A really resolute and enlightened government would have done more than the Bourbons to deal with this problem. Unfortunately, since no central authority had ever possessed effective means of coercion outside the big towns, reliance had to be placed on the local authorities in each province. This worked tolerably well at Syracuse where money from charities was used and a building programme undertaken as a means of unemployment relief. It also worked at Marsala, where there developed a fair sense of civic responsibility. But many examples were to be found elsewhere of the same obstructionism which had met Count Persichelli in the 1780s. Proprietors resisted the passage of roads through their land; and one official reported that, by 1850, large areas of the *trazzere* had been usurped by neighbouring landlords, so that the King's highway had become private property from which ordinary citizens were excluded. Prince Lanza agreed with Palmeri that the routes chosen for new construction were sometimes absurdly circuitous and over-expensive just to please some grandee, and apparently in some instances they made travel no faster. There were stories of contractors whose roads fell to pieces in less than a year, of insufficient inspectors to check their work, of municipal rivalries holding up construction, of villages so impoverished by lawsuits arising out of the end of feudalism that they had nothing left over for public works.

In 1808, and again in 1824, the Bourbon government drew up new schemes for completing the network of roads. After finding that tolls as a form of revenue did not provide even for the cost of repairs, it was decided to finance them by a substantial loan. It was also sensibly decided to use McAdam's new techniques of construction, especially since this would greatly save money on repairs. By 1838, however, it was evident that leaving the main responsibility to local authorities had not worked, so the decision was taken to centralise this branch of the administration at Naples and bring road engineers into Sicily from the mainland. This was strongly disliked in Sicily, and dependence on a remote bureaucracy at Naples had undeniable drawbacks. Great feeling was also aroused against de Welz, a non-Sicilian, when he had McAdam's treatise translated into Italian for use in the Island. But Neapolitan engineers possessed more technical experience and were less involved in the Sicilian environment.

For a short while some local authorities were encouraged to bestir themselves; the Intendants' annual reports began to be full of reports about road building, and the mileage noticeably increased. But taxpayers were still unwilling to pay for public amenities. Sometimes they were positively against reform of any kind, especially any reform coming from Naples, while the government for its part was too inefficient as well as too reluctant to impose its will. Sicily was condemned in this vital respect of public communications to fall progressively behind the other provinces of Italy. Her various provinces, and even neighbouring villages, still knew little of each other, and movement from one town to another continued to be something of a rarity.

PART 12
The Risorgimento 1837–1860

Chapter 44

DISLIKE OF NAPLES

The last years of Bourbon Sicily were troubled by more than merely the slowness of economic growth. A brief revolt in 1837 indicated that tremendous social forces were waiting to erupt. This rising was touched off by an epidemic of cholera, a disease which struck terror because it had never been seen before in western Europe. Even university professors and the Archbishop of Palermo believed that the infection was a poison deliberately spread by the government. Many thousands died, including two prominent intellectuals, Palmeri, and Scinà who was the Chancellor of Palermo university. In the general panic, cities suddenly emptied; villages sealed off all paths of access, something which was not hard in a world where towns could still close their gates at night and not let people out until dawn. Soon governmental authority scarcely extended beyond the walls of Palermo. The ordinary channels of food supply were cut. Villages fought each other, and many innocent victims were lynched in the general hysteria, while peasants invaded the towns in search of loot.

Palermo on this occasion remained fairly quiet. Only at Catania and Syracuse was there any serious political motivation behind the disorders. At Syracuse the rioting began in the fishermen's quarter and seems to have been directed against foreigners in general, as the rumour about poisoning suddenly spread. Some leading citizens tried to calm the crowds, but nearly all the civic authorities and even the doctors fled into the countryside to escape the horrors of a popular rising. Soon there were corpses everywhere and the gangs had free play. Peasants also turned savagely against the *gabelloti* and then invaded the town.

At Catania the yellow flag of Sicilian independence was raised and a revolutionary committee formed. Rich and poor were seen embracing each other in the streets. Messengers were sent to stir up a patriotic revolt in other cities, but the replies were depressingly negative, and any dissidents elsewhere showed little sense of solidarity with those of Catania. No doubt the *cordon sanitaire* prevented news spreading. Three days after publicly swearing allegiance to the revolt, the leading members of the patrician classes realised their isolation and decided to change sides. To such people, the town mob and the radicals were dangerous, not to say terrifying, allies; and as soon as a Bourbonist counter-revolution seemed imminent, the nobility acted quickly so as not to be caught on the losing side and not to run the risk of a social

405

rebellion. They arrested some of their more liberal fellow revolutionaries. They even collected money to commission another statue of the King to replace one that had been inadvertently destroyed. The Swiss troops were welcomed back, and a few executions then concluded this melancholy episode.

In 1838, King Ferdinand II toured Sicily and was persuaded that popular unrest chiefly arose because existing laws were not enforced. He was told of feudal dues and *corvées* still unlawfully being claimed, and of innumerable lawsuits deliberately used to frustrate or delay his projects of agrarian reform. Large areas of apparently fertile land remained undercultivated for this reason, and meanwhile banditry was paralysing commerce and agriculture. Even the land survey which had been decreed twenty-five years before was still incomplete in nine villages out of ten. One cause of all this was the lack of enough able public servants, but another was the determination of the local *notabili* to disobey the law and the unwillingness of the government to rule with sufficient firmness.

One of Ferdinand's first reactions was to re-establish Messina university in order to speed up the provision of administrators and an educated class: this was to be largely at government expense, and the decision naturally met with a welcome at Messina. The reservation of jobs for Sicilians was withdrawn, because practice had convincingly shown that locally born officials were exposed to family networks of clientelage and to intimidation by the local bosses. The King wanted more Neapolitans appointed as Intendants, and would have liked the entire police force replaced by men less tied to local interest. Other jobs, too, were to be opened to talent by public examination in the hope of replacing the graft and nepotism which was at the root of bureaucratic inefficiency. Naturally not everyone was pleased by this, nor by the decision to take roads and public works away from local direction. Ferdinand also intended to reintroduce conscription and the taxes on salt and tobacco, but on second thoughts agreed to allow Sicily preferential treatment over Naples in these two important respects. Instead he decided that the tax most resented by the poor, the *macinato*, should be lowered, and the deficit made up from an increased land tax and a levy on the mine owners. The majority of Sicilians, so the French consul reported, saw much to approve in these proposals, because fairer taxation and a more detached and impartial administration were bound to be of general benefit. The setting up of public banks at Messina and Palermo, and the negotiation of numerous commercial treaties with foreign countries, were also welcome.

Land reform, however, was not so easily accepted. The government wanted it as a means of achieving both social peace and agricultural betterment. Palmeri, for example, had been convinced that a farm of several hundred acres would in general be much more economic than the large ranches which covered most of Sicily. Yet on the one hand there were too many landowners who wanted larger and larger farms and who used their money not to develop agriculture but to buy more land; while, at the other end of the scale, land hunger among the really poor was one of the most ominous factors behind the social unrest manifested so tragically in 1820 and 1837. What the government would have liked was more property holders and more security of tenure as a means of obtaining a greater 'affection towards the soil'. At the same time, from information supplied by Neapolitan civil servants such as Ulloa at Trapani, they realised the paramount need to reduce the influence of the feudal aristocracy; not only were there obvious social and economic reasons for this, but from the time of Caracciolo onwards the aristocracy had been becoming more and more the champions of Sicilian autonomy against Naples.

Accordingly another order was made in 1838 for further action over dividing the ecclesiastical *latifondi* in royal patronage. This, if only it had been properly applied, would have affected a large area, since the King was patron of all the major benefices and many minor ones. Intendants were also enjoined to open up any usurped rights of way and stop interference with rights of access to water and woodland. At the same time they should hurry up the commutation of 'promiscuous rights'.

A remarkable law of 1841 then prescribed that landlords must compensate the villages by giving them at the very least one-fifth of any ex-feudal territories where common rights had once been enjoyed. According to the plan, the land allocated to each village would subsequently be distributed to the poor, and this should be done by lot and not by sale. Each allotment should be free from any action by creditors for twenty years. The Neapolitans on the Royal Council, acting on the experience of the mainland provinces, had proposed a much stronger law than this, and would have liked to prosecute landowners who had arbitrarily enclosed common land. But the Sicilian aristocracy just in time managed to persuade the King to admit actual possession of land as evidence to title, with the result that local populations had the impossible burden of producing documents to prove illegal usurpation. Antifeudal laws were thus once again being twisted to favour the rich, and the King accepted the fact in a mistaken bid to win the support of the local elites.

The *latifondisti* recognised this to be a vital struggle. Their chief strength was that most villages were run by a narrow oligarchy which was accountable to them quite as much as to Naples. In the absence of strict government supervision, these villages now were persuaded to sacrifice yet more of their old communal inheritance: their ruling cliques would be the chief gainers if enclosures were sanctioned, if legal compensation was not applied for, and if they did not distribute quotas to the poor as the law of 1841 prescribed. Officials estimated that the peasants were thus deprived of millions of *scudi* worth of land, so that property which for centuries had been partially owned by more than a million people now passed into absolute possession of several thousand. Some villagers, encouraged by the royal Intendants, did put up a fight, and the township of Butera even pursued the Prince of Butera to the court of appeal at Naples. But most villages were governed by people who had a strong interest in frustrating the law. In any case most local authorities were in debt, and legal expenses now made them more so. As baronial enclosure of the commons left them addition- ally short of revenue, they increased the food taxes to make up for it, so that government policy was doubly frustrated. If ever ordi- nary citizens succeeded, it was only by defying the law and allowing the 'promiscuous rights' to continue, and this could only result in large areas being left under primitive cultivation or none at all.

The government went on trying to apply its reform policy until the revolution of 1848 brought a period of more or less enlightened despotism to a close. This maligned phase of Bourbon administra- tion provided the last occasion for almost a century when any Sicilian government supported a serious and even-handed pro- gramme of agrarian reform. This was the last time for decades that a comprehensive plan was drawn up for draining and irri- gating the fertile plain of Catania, and the failure of this plan meant that hundreds of square miles remained uninhabited. Experience now proved the impossibility of carrying out such projects given the existing balance of society and the existing machinery of local government. The central authorities as well, far from being too authoritarian and intrusive as their enemies later complained, were too half-hearted and inefficient. There was not even any official record kept of what land had been transferred to full baronial ownership by the law of 1812, let alone of what changes were brought about in practice as a result of legislation between 1818 and 1841. There was even some doubt about whether tithes had been abolished or not.

In any case the lesson had yet to be learnt that this kind of land reform would have to go much further if it were to be successful. In a world where credit could rarely be obtained except on exorbitant terms from the landlord or *gabelloto*, and where charitable credit organisations and the 'corn banks' were generally being taken over by landowners for their own use, few peasants possessed the resources for efficient cultivation on their own. Even when lucky enough to receive an allotment, often it was not large enough to be economically cultivable, or it was poor land, or too far away, and the new owners were tempted just to get a few quick crops and then sell out. Without credit they often could not afford seed, or farm implements, or even the food to keep their families alive until the harvest. Without technical assistance they were sometimes equally helpless. The failure to provide this assistance meant that, again and again, the policy of distributing smallholdings to the poor had the reverse effect of that intended, and there gradually developed the powerful myth that agrarian reform was unworkable.

This attempt at reform by legislation was inadequately administered and in some respects misconceived, but the main reason it failed was that agrarian reform was anathema to the only people who counted. Young radicals such as Filippo Cordova might support it, but they were powerless. The Intendants' reports repeatedly refer to the opposition encountered, and in fact this was what seems to have occupied most of their time. No doubt it was simple-minded of Ferdinand to think that provincial Sicily was governable by 'foreigners' who did not understand the language. He had hoped that, since they would be outside the existing systems of patronage and clientelage, they would be more difficult to corrupt or intimidate than their predecessors; and up to a point he was correct. The Intendant of Palermo, for example, dared to expose the fact that the city government kept no proper accounts and was vastly overspending its income on a plethora of purely nominal jobs for the richer citizenry and their friends. To the local clienteles themselves, however, it was clear that the Neapolitan government did not understand the traditional art of the Spanish Viceroys, to leave well alone and indulge the aristocracy. The *latifondisti* and *gabelloti* therefore acted to neutralise Ferdinand's attempt at reform. By mustering their retainers and *bravi*, by playing on local patriotism, xenophobia and the prevalent dislike of all laws and regulations, they tried to convince people that it was not they themselves but rather the hated Bourbons who prevented improvement and kept Sicily poor.

In one respect the landowners were creating future difficulties for themselves, because proletarianisation made the peasantry into a more revolutionary force than anything ever known before. The small herdsman, who even in normal times might be a danger to society, could lose his job when the pastures and the sheep runs were enclosed, and then might become quite ungovernable. The ordinary agricultural labourers, in other words the majority of

Sicilians, were being converted into serfs by the abolition of feudalism, and this was less paradoxical than it seemed since they were now more than ever dependent on the landlords and possessed hardly a single free right in the land. Normally they were conservative and the greatest enemies of change; but as population increased they became more exposed to the threat of famine, and the confiscation of 'promiscuous rights' not only diminished their lives but affronted their sense of justice and made any retaliation seem fair. In every village a memory was retained of which land had been wrongfully usurped, and these were the areas which in revolutionary years such as 1820, 1837 and 1848 were an object of invasion. On top of all this, moreover, the *macinato* and the other food taxes condemned Sicily to a permanent state of class warfare from which everyone suffered.

The two chief potential revolutionary forces in Sicily were peasant unrest and a dislike of Naples. Both were growing fast, though the first was much stronger than the second. There was also a third force of a very different kind, very weak at first though subtler and more sophisticated, by which there was gradually being generated the idea that Sicily might change her whole political alignment and join a federation of Italian states. Her links with northern Italy had not hitherto been particularly close, and her commerce with England in the 1840s was ten times as large as that with all the other Italian states. Culturally the influence of Spain had been replaced by that of France and England as much as that of Italy. Nor did north Italians show much awareness of any common heritage with Sicily, but rather spoke of it as somewhere remote and deserted, where brigandage made travelling unwise. Nearly all the strangers who travelled in Sicily and wrote about it came from other countries altogether. The occasional Italian who penetrated off the beaten track was liable to be taken for an Englishman, and his language was often not much help to him.

Yet cultural contacts with Italy had never disappeared in the centuries of Spanish rule, and political reasons now made them more and more important. Even though all Sicilians continued to speak dialect at home, Italian was used by the literate few as a written language; in the courts and in parliament it had long been employed as the most intelligible means of communication between educated Sicilians from different regions, who could not always have been familiar with each other's local speech; and under the Bourbons, of course, it became the language of government. The exaltation of Rome was already familiar to those with a classical education. Dante and Foscolo were eagerly read by a few intellectuals, and one English visitor in 1809 found that Alfieri's tragedies were acted frequently and well at Palermo.

In the other direction, Giovanni Meli, who himself was brought up on Ariosto, was translated into Italian as well as into German and English. The composer Vincenzo Bellini, like Scarlatti before him, achieved a far greater success outside than inside his own native Sicily: he studied music in Naples and lived most of his active musical life at Milan until his tragically early death at Paris in 1835. Here was one more instance of the fact that the most outstandingly able Sicilians had to go abroad for their education and their careers. Hitherto this had been an incalculable source of weakness to the country; henceforward it was to be in one sense a strength, since the small middle class of intellectuals thereby produced a number of leading figures who possessed an international experience and an accumulated frustration which turned their minds to the possibility of radical change.

The desire to break free from Naples was soon found among a few Sicilians of widely different outlook. Some simply disliked foreign rule; some opposed absolutism and political censorship; some were against centralisation as a threat to boss rule in local government; some simply disliked reform of any kind. There were those who looked on Taix's sulphur monopoly as an attempt by Neapolitan speculators to ruin the Sicilian mine owners. Others thought that Sicily, while providing a quarter of the joint tax revenue, received less than a quarter of governmental expenditure. Before long there would also be some sympathisers with those north Italians who were aspiring to a national *risorgimento* which would unite the various Italian states in one kingdom. The idea of Italian unification could rarely if ever be mentioned in print except to be rejected as pernicious or utopian; but a few Sicilians, realising their own political powerlessness, gradually began to wonder whether joining an Italian federation might not provide their best hope of defeating Naples and recovering more local autonomy.

One who came to believe this was a scholar and minor government official named Michele Amari. This man possessed a much wider European education than most other young Sicilians. Among his early volumes was a translation of Scott's *Marmion*, a fact which serves as a reminder that Scott as well as Byron was a strong political and literary influence on this generation. In the 1840s, Amari published a history of the Sicilian Vespers, a book which escaped censorship only because the deliverance of Sicily from the French in the thirteenth century was not immediately recognised by officialdom as an allegorical reference to winning freedom from Naples. This volume acted as a catalyst of opinion

as well as a positive act of political education. After a long monopoly by the royal historiographers, Fazello, Maurolico, Mongitore,
di Blasi, at last a revisionist and non-official interpretation of
Sicilian history became a stimulus to political revolt.

Amari himself had to escape to Paris, and it was in exile that he
and others became conscious of more sophisticated political ideas
and wider loyalties. The mere fact of arriving in Paris, wrote
Cordova to his father, "is like coming to a new world". A lawyer,
Francesco Crispi, a journalist, Giuseppe La Farina, a doctor,
Raffaele, an industrialist, Luigi Orlando, these middle-class
radicals in exile taught themselves to be a kind of political leader
which Sicily had never known before. Often they were out of touch
with public opinion back home, but in return they were infected
by the romanticism and patriotic idealism current in northern
Europe. They were able to recognise that Sicily must seek outside
help. Economists such as Busacca and Ferrara could also see from
the vantage point of Tuscany or Turin that freer trade with Italy
and a more unified 'national' market would be natural and
advantageous. Particularly among a few members of the legal
profession, among the small class of liberal aristocrats and among
an amorphous but important class of university students, discussion now took place of subjects which had a revolutionary
potential.

These new ideas hardly took much hold until 1848, nor were
the exiles at all sure about what they wanted, let alone in agreement; nor could they rely on much support inside Sicily itself.
Some clandestine pamphlets appeared protesting at Neapolitan
rule, but hardly enough to worry the authorities very seriously.
A number of newspapers—especially at Catania and Messina,
which were near to the mainland and indeed which saw an Italian
connection as a partial deliverance from Palermo—took advantage
of a relaxed administration of the press laws to try to educate
public opinion. Mazzini, the great prophet of Italian patriotism,
had little influence so far south. Some Sicilians came to admire
Mazzini, but very few became disciples, and Mazzini himself
learnt by experience to see these islanders as too much attached
to their own independence to be relied on as a strong initiating
force for Italian patriotism.

Quite apart from ideology, the social system inhibited the
growth in Sicily itself of a literate middle class which might accept
revolutionary ideas of liberty and economic progress. Not only
were the lawyers as a class still thoroughly obsequious, but historical accident had left Sicily with very few of the professional
soldiers upon whom other countries relied for their revolution:
and those few were loyal to the Bourbons almost to a man. The

three universities were feeble institutions which contributed little to either the conservative or the liberal cause, except in so far as their narrow outlook helped to make the students a sometimes ungovernable force. The British admiral exaggerated who in 1810 thought that there could hardly be more than 1500 literate people in Sicily; nevertheless Neapolitan and other visitors were surprised by the ignorance they encountered.

It is hardly surprising that few people were prepared to begin an actual revolt. The early 1840s saw the growth of a generalised feeling of opposition, but often this reflected merely the kind of anarchic protest with which all governments of Sicily sooner or later became familiar. It became more political only when a demand for Sicilian autonomism acted as the focus of many different animosities against Naples. Among a small group of the politically conscious, Neapolitans were blamed for corrupt justice even when the judges were Sicilian; they were blamed for bad laws when the real culprits were powerful Sicilians who frustrated application of the law; they were condemned for police severity when the true villains were often Sicilian policemen and the large number of police informers. This mainly arose from a widespread feeling of wounded pride at being ruled by foreigners, a pride which grew in proportion as national self-consciousness became more articulate and as government after 1838 became increasingly centralised on Naples.

What proved very hard was to find leaders inside Sicily itself who could convert these various discontents into political action. The police could not prevent demonstrations in honour of the new 'liberal' Pope, Pius IX, nor could they stop clandestine pamphlets from circulating, but without leadership these could only create unfulfilled hopes. There was an abortive outbreak by a handful of people at Messina in September 1847, and once again the peasants were ready to take advantage of this rift among the governing classes; but a few soldiers easily restored order, and the overwhelming majority of citizens, sympathetic though they may possibly have been, remained silent. No more than in 1837 was there any inclination by other towns to take concerted action, because planned co-operation was as difficult in politics as in commerce. Even the few leaders of this minor rising in 1847 were divided over their aims; nor could they see much chance of starting any political revolt except by stirring up primitive instincts for rapine and vendetta among people who would not stop to count the cost and for whom an agreed programme was unnecessary.

This posed a further problem: for a long succession of proletarian risings in Sicily had created a kind of ancestral memory of terror, and among respectable citizens the first reaction to such a movement was either to load their goods hurriedly on some neutral ship, or to flee into the hills, or at the least to board up their shops and warehouses. If the government then restored order, property owners were usually more than happy. Only after the insurrection succeeded or failed would they return, hoping to save what they could and either to support authoritarianism or to canalise the revolt into another direction which favoured their own interests. The Bourbons knew this, as they also knew the divisions inside Sicily and the lack of opposition leadership. Experience had taught them that, even in an emergency, quite a small garrison of troops could usually keep the island in check. But in 1848 their calculation was proved entirely wrong, and they were suddenly faced by a broader and more powerful Sicilian revolution than history had ever known.

Chapter 45

THE REVOLUTION OF 1848–1849

The first days of 1848 were a time of exceptional unrest in Palermo. Rumours of a new constitution were in the air. Student riots provoked the dangerous decision to close the university, and the arrest was decreed of eleven eminent citizens known for liberal views, several of whom were nobles. One of the younger radicals circulated an unsigned manifesto which, claiming to speak for a probably non-existent revolutionary committee, announced that a revolt for Sicilian freedom would start under cover of the King's birthday festivities on 12 January. The ruse succeeded, for though the authorities could not take seriously such a public announcement of intent, the news was just such as would become a general topic of conversation and create suspense.

When the day arrived, the usual holiday crowds vainly waited for the mysterious committee to manifest itself. Some cheers greeted the troops, but it was noted that, to avoid provocation, police and soldiers kept out of the Fieravecchia and Palermo's other poorer districts. Taking courage from their absence, a popular preacher in the Fieravecchia began an incendiary harangue which was met with even more cheers; it was here that a riot now developed, fanned by the bolder or more rash of the patriots. The streets in the richer residential districts quickly emptied, doors were barricaded, and the shutting of shops added to the general alarm by raising fears of a food shortage. By the evening, barricades were going up, and the British consul saw people leaving to stir up trouble in the near-by villages. Early on the 13th, squads of peasants and 'mountaineers' had already arrived in Palermo, greatly excited at being able to destroy the excise barriers and disobey the law with impunity. Money had been seized from a government courier returning from the interior. The revolt was off to a flying start.

The small class of liberals suddenly discovered that political reforms might now be within their reach, whether it was Sicilian autonomy, or a liberal constitution, or possibly a federal Italy; nevertheless a parallel and far stronger social revolution was unexpectedly confusing the issue. Many of the insurgents, even those waving tricolour flags, can only have had the haziest notion, if any, of what Italy was, or a constitution; but the inarticulate desire for social betterment, for more regular work, for land to cultivate, for the commons of which they and their forebears had been deprived, all this made the peasants by far the most

415

revolutionary element in an aggrieved but usually submissive society. Especially in a year of bad harvest, their need for cheaper food and to abolish the *macinato* gave them the frightening power possessed by those with little to lose from insurrection and just possibly a great deal to gain. They had a grudge-war against the *gabelloto*, the tax collector and the local money-lender, and this made them a force which, whenever the government was caught off guard as in January 1848, could bring all ordinary life to a stop. The mountain shepherds had a permanent sense of injustice against the landowners of the plain who had burnt down the brushwood and stolen their pastures, just as the plainsmen reciprocated by treating the wandering goatherds (with even more reason) as a mortal enemy of settled agriculture; and meanwhile countrymen in general kept up an endemic vendetta against urban society, a vendetta which they could properly resolve only in a moment like this.

Revolutionaries of such a kind had no recognisable political views except the crudest; nor did they have much staying power, for life itself depended on their returning home infallibly at harvest and sowing time. Yet the news from Palermo on 12 January was a signal for all who had a grievance to rise and remedy it, and this gave the revolt an immense and unexpected force. In the villages and towns there were bread riots and attacks on the 'clubs' where the *galantuomini* used to meet. Whole flocks of sheep were killed, crops and hay ricks burnt. Over the next few weeks an enormous destruction took place in many of the surviving woodlands, as land was seized and cleared for cultivation. Often the Town Hall was attacked and there was a bonfire of the title deeds to property which symbolised centuries of social persecution. Government ceased as officials fled for their lives. The tribal morality of a subject population was evidenced in a general assassination of policemen and suspected informers, sometimes with unbelievable cruelty. It was noticed that the soldiers, who were mostly foreigners, provoked far less hostility than the police, who were generally Sicilians, and this fact tells us something about the nature of the revolution.

Another element in the rising was what later would have been called the mafia. The most prominent of the armed squads which appeared at once out of nowhere were brigand bands under a local boss of the underworld. Some of these bosses had probably been, and went on being, Bourbon employees. Some were hired by the ex-barons as a private police force, and some apparently by the liberals, while some were independent and anarchic elements who simply used the riots as an occasion to divide up parts of the *latifondi*. The village *squadre* had close contacts inside

Palermo, contacts which must have grown up out of joint activity for excise evasion and the marketing of stolen cattle. This enabled some of the squads to appear on the Palermo scene almost at once, and the significant fact was noted that they were well provided with arms and money. A breakdown of government was an ideal situation for them, especially when they could expect payment from one side or both. Di Miceli in Monreale, Scordato in Bagheria, men who like the initiators of revolution in 1647 were notorious delinquents, at once seized effective authority in their villages and marched their men into Palermo where for several months they remained near the centre of power. La Farina, who was a close eye-witness, did not dare say as much in his history of the revolution, but privately acknowledged that these brave, frightening and disreputable elements were the natural leaders of this revolt which brought the Bourbon government to its knees.

Officials in Palermo were baffled by such a resistance movement, and the army was untrained to fight it. There were no contingency plans in existence, because nothing quite like this had been contemplated, and the absence of popular support for law and order was thoroughly demoralising. The six or seven thousand Bourbon troops in Palermo were joined by reinforcements, but leadership was poor and provisioning difficult. After some initial reverses, they decided to bombard the city. This aroused the most tremendous indignation, especially when a shell set fire to the municipal pawnshop on which so many plebeian but also aristocratic families depended. In a wave of retaliatory vandalism the royal palace was sacked, though the Palatine chapel was again spared; hundreds of prisoners were released from jail, the police archives were set alight and the fire spread to do irreparable damage to the records of the royal chancery. After only about three dozen people had been killed, the soldiers acknowledged defeat and left the town just as they had done on similar occasions in the past.

Initially, many citizens must have had mixed feelings over the dramatic events of these few days, and even some of the liberals were momentarily confused. But as soon as the Neapolitans retreated, it was as important to tame the fury of the *popolani* as it was to steer the rising into a fruitful political channel, and therefore the only group of people who had a political programme now came to the fore. Committees were hastily improvised to provide munitions, to keep order, collect money and arrange food supplies. These committees were largely composed of the more liberal and anti-Neapolitan among the patrician classes. As the danger of counter-revolution receded, and as the revolt became more political and less social, other citizens increasingly declared their support. Messages were sent round the island, and Catania, Messina and a hundred villages had joined the revolution by the end of January. Civic rivalries had diminished ever since Palermo lost her much-disliked authority over the island after 1820, and everywhere a tremendous pride was felt that a large foreign army had been defeated by this popular movement.

Meanwhile on the mainland the King yielded to events and granted a liberal constitution. To Sicilians he offered local self-government on condition that they would accept Bourbon sovereignty. But the emergent revolutionary leaders were too excited to see the weakness of their position: their brave reply was that Sicilian opinion demanded complete separation from Naples. This impelled them to revive the Sicilian parliament, and procedure was hastily improvised by the committees to make this possible. A literacy test excluded all the peasants and nearly all townsmen from the vote. There was to be a property qualification for deputies, and the 1812 House of Peers was taken over substantially unchanged. The result was a moderately conservative parliament in which both Chambers included a large number of representatives of the old aristocracy, but the lower House also included the returned exiles and the leading intellectuals of the day.

When parliament opened on 25 March, conservatives and radicals joined in a coalition government of which the leading figure was Ruggero Settimo. The King's offer was formally and proudly rejected: "Sicily does not demand new institutions, but the restoration of rights which have been hers for centuries." Ferdinand's deposition was then proclaimed, and all the deputies leapt to their feet and shouted enthusiastically for half an hour: no one could have spoken against such a proposition even if they had wished to. Everyone assumed that the revolution was over and Sicily was independent—truly independent for the first time since the fourteenth century. The white flag of the Bourbons was replaced by the tricolour, the Bourbon lilies by the three-legged figure which was the ancient emblem of Trinacria. Sicily was declared to form part of a notional federation of Italy, and a token force of a hundred Sicilians was sent north to help liberate Lombardy from the Austrians. A few flags and cannon were also offered to Rome and Tuscany as a sign of brotherhood. This strong feeling towards the rest of Italy was genuine enough, even though it never had time to be translated into truly effective action. Nevertheless, other Italians were still able to reproach Sicily for her 'civil war' against Naples and for being so preoccupied with her own separatist nationhood that she was more hindrance than help at this moment to the formation of an Italian union.

Soon the revolution had serious problems of its own to bother about as its social and political elements became increasingly out of phase with each other. The armed squads aroused considerable hostility among some revolutionary leaders. Some of the gang leaders were already the heroes of popular ballads. They had been made honorary colonels, and in order to placate their followers they had even been given special charge of public security where they had ample chance to use their familiarity with the underworld. Scordato and di Miceli were both involved in serious disturbances. The 'berets' and the 'hats' were soon openly at odds. The squads were said to be expensive and disorderly: they kidnapped people and took money by threats from all classes of the population; and sometimes they fought each other in order to stake out rival zones of interest. So long as they were in receipt of pay they had no wish to go home; yet not only did their usefulness disappear once the Bourbon army had withdrawn, they even became a dangerous source of division when their more hooligan elements tried to perpetuate disorder and put social above political objectives.

The conservatives therefore decided to recruit a National Guard to protect property and, if need be, oppose the squads. This was exactly what had happened in 1820. The National Guard was designed as a class militia; it was unpaid, and manual labourers were specifically excluded; eventually there were eighteen princes and a hundred other assorted nobles among its officers. More than once it was to intervene in politics against the radicals and so contributed to the divisions opening up inside the coalition government. Armed militiamen were occasionally deployed in the galleries of parliament during an important vote. One indication of the general scale of priorities was that the National Guardsmen succeeded in getting weapons even when there were not enough to equip the army, and it was they who were given charge of the fortresses. They represented one side of the social war which was now cutting across the political fight for freedom. While, on the one hand, proletarian agitation was making the rich less enthusiastic about winning national independence unless it could be done very quickly, on the other hand the poor, who had risen to obtain bread, work and lower food taxes, lost interest when they were side-tracked and then disarmed by other interests who had a completely different purpose.

Fighting broke out at the end of April between the National Guard and an armed band in the Fieravecchia led by a formidable woman known as Testa Di Lana. This lady was a goatherd who wore trousers and carried pistols; because of a family vendetta against the law, she proved a bloodthirsty and successful butcher of the police, but was less at home after the initial phase of destruction. Her gang claimed wages for a payroll of 1200, though possibly it numbered no more than 200. The liberal politicians and the National Guard resented this kind of expense as being a direct subsidy to the underworld. They also saw that the success of the revolution might depend on disarming the *squadre* before she and others could make a bid for power by raising the issue of land reform. The peasantry in January 1848 had in fact been incited to rise against the Bourbons by being promised gifts of land, and some leading parliamentarians thought this a promise which it was both expedient and right to fulfil. Most politicians, however, strongly disagreed; and since neither the peasants nor the squads were directly represented in parliament, the former could be simply ignored, while the latter were first requested to go back to their villages, and then ordered to dissolve. In this way the revolution was split right down the centre and its main propulsive force was alienated.

Other signs of malaise soon helped to diminish the great initial enthusiasm aroused by this remarkable revolution. A decline in trade hit many people. The disorganisation of the legal system bore hardly on the class of professional advocates, and a proposal to set up courts elsewhere than in Palermo provoked a demonstration by 600 lawyers shouting for parliament to be dissolved. Holders of government securities received no dividends, and a great number of excise and *macinato* officials were put out of work. In Messina as well as Palermo there was an unedifying scramble by would-be job holders and pensioners: the pressure was such that many more new appointments were made than could be afforded, and of people who had absolutely no experience in administration. Conditions of public security were disastrous. In some areas the gangs, edged out of Palermo, took over control of whole villages, pillaging wherever they went, killing all the *galantuomini* or 'hats' that they could find, or else forcing the peasants to abandon the fields unless they paid for protection. For some people the great patriotic year 1848 in retrospect simply recalled a moment when brigandage had gone unpunished. Many citizens must have longed for a speedy return of efficient government, even if necessary of Bourbon government.

The practice of elections and parliamentary rule was not easily learnt after so many years of political authoritarianism. By early May, some of the radicals were forced out of the government coalition, and thereafter personal rancours and rivalries increasingly clouded the consideration of urgent political problems. While abduction and robbery continued unhampered in the villages, the deputies allowed themselves rhetorical displays over whether to celebrate St. Rosalia's Day, or how to rename the streets of Palermo, and what kind of commemorative medal to issue. While Ferdinand restored his despotic position at Naples, they bickered over whether the Jesuits—who, remarkably, supported the revolution—should be expelled; they debated abolition of the decimal system as a tyrannical Neapolitan importation, and how much lip service to popular sovereignty they should pay. It was in keeping with their earlier history that Sicilians were overwhelmingly preoccupied with questions of liberties and local autonomy, despite the fact that an indispensable prerequisite of these liberties would have been to create a strong revolutionary administration. Seven different ministries therefore succeeded each other without a single one being able to establish a firm authority. Meanwhile lack of leadership and ever-widening disagreements made it impossible to concentrate resources on winning the war.

Finance, for example, was a question which was as controversial as it was vital. People had stopped paying taxes in January, and the destruction of the tax records and assessments had been a prime and successful objective of many revolutionaries. Collection of adequate revenue was therefore impossible, and no ministry was ready to risk its own popularity and that of the revolution by trying to put the finances in proper order. Amari was hopelessly inefficient as Minister of Finance. He was succeeded by Cordova who was brave enough to challenge the richer classes by reintroducing the window tax and confirming abolition of the *macinato*; but many wealthier citizens became very angry when a forced loan was imposed and paper money depreciated their savings. A month of valuable debating time was spent on Cordova's project to nationalise and divide up some of the *latifondi* into smaller holdings, and the very suggestion turned some would-be liberals into conservatives. Members of the Upper House of parliament did all they could to hamper his attempt to balance the accounts, yet they suggested no alternative method of finding the money, and finally they forced his resignation. The most they would do was to agitate for a restoration of the *macinato* so as to obviate the need for any taxation of luxuries; yet this was to repudiate what for most people must have been the main objective of the January rebellion.

An even more serious weakness was that so little was done to enlist soldiers and arm them, for the revolutionaries discovered that the factories and the skilled labour were lacking, as also was the taste for fighting in any public cause. A few troops were sent on a wildcat scheme to aid a non-existent revolt in Calabria, but this expeditionary force did not distinguish itself. The gesture was made of melting down convent bells and bronze statues of the King to make cannon; but when some deputies asked for a debate on national defence, this was said to be inopportune and indeed unnecessary. Nor was any discussion permitted of Crispi's proposal for conscription, since the very idea of compulsory service was repudiated as intolerable to a free people. Eventually nearly 20,000 volunteers were said to have enlisted, but against them was ranged a much better equipped and larger Neapolitan army, and in practice barely a quarter of these volunteers can ever have been effective. In eight months, said one French observer, only two battalions had been properly organised, and officers to all appearance were as numerous as the rank and file. Some turned up just to collect their pay. The Minister of War explained apologetically that recruitment had in part been a method of indoor relief for poor people who were unable or disinclined to fight.

Evidently most ordinary Sicilians were not eager to make the sacrifices implicit in the refusal by the revolutionary leaders to consider Ferdinand's offer of a separate Sicilian parliament. They had been assured by these leaders that Ferdinand was beaten and could not fight back; so when Britain strongly recommended a compromise solution, this was curtly rejected. There was a blithe assumption that Britain and France would in the last resort be obliged to defend Sicilian independence. Help was also expected from other Italian states, though none was forthcoming. Parliament even elected a Piedmontese prince as King of Sicily, but without first asking his consent and without recognising that the kind of kingship they envisaged did not make a very attractive offer: he showed a notable lack of enthusiasm over the news of his election, and indeed northern Italy had little enough reason to add to her other troubles a war against Naples.

Suddenly, in September 1848, a large Bourbon army landed and attacked Messina. Repeated requests by Messina for arms and money had run into many obstacles at Palermo, and the Palermo National Guard, realising the defencelessness of their own city, once even threatened to use force to stop help being sent: in the end some of the squads were allowed to go as a means of getting them out of the way. The defenders of Messina had internal divisions of their own, but for a few days made a heroic resistance. Owing to the fierce hatred now generated between Neapolitans and Sicilians, there were brutalities on both sides; when the rumour spread that prisoners had been mutilated, the attackers could not be restrained from looting. Fires swept through the town. The British and French admirals stationed at Messina were shocked by this, as they were perhaps equally shocked by the destruction of foreigners' property, and they therefore brought pressure on Ferdinand to allow a six months' armistice. This was entirely to the advantage of the Sicilians because it was now fairly clear that they had no hope of successful resistance. Nevertheless the revolutionary government did very little to use such a fortuitous period of grace.

Somewhat late in the day, it was now suggested that a foreign legion be enrolled. That romantic guerrilla leader, Garibaldi, promised he would try to come, but was side-tracked at Florence. Instead the government chose a Piedmontese officer to command the Sicilian army. This man reported well on the fighting spirit he found at Palermo, but could hardly find words to describe his feelings for a government which after a year still did not have a single soldier properly armed. When he was refused permission to produce an overall plan of resistance—La Farina, the minister in charge, decided that a unified command would be "unconstitutional and a danger to liberty"—he resigned. For a few days he was succeeded by a Frenchman; who in turn gave way to a young Pole, Mieroslawski, who was ready to accept a more limited authority. Mieroslawski's inexperience and his inability to speak Italian made him something less than an optimum choice, and anyway he was hamstrung by the amateur soldiers in power at Palermo and by the lack of soldiers and arms. Most of the cavalry still had no horses though plenty could easily have been found.

When the Bourbons in February 1849 again offered Sicily a separate parliament and viceroy, the offer was again refused, and it seems that some of the revolutionary authorities deliberately encouraged a popular hysteria which made impossible any rational discussion of the alternatives to this offer and the probable consequences of its rejection. When some deputies cried out boldly for war, no one dared voice the obvious difficulties. The excitement was enormous, according to La Farina, even the mafia called a temporary halt to crime. Meanwhile the Bourbon army, since war was what public opinion was said to want, renewed its advance as soon as the armistice ended. Mieroslawski found the Sicilian levies disorganised, untrained and mutinous. He tried to defend Catania, but this merely showed other towns the inadvisability of resistance: for columns of smoke were soon rising over Catania and its surrounding villages; and neither side showed much inclination to take prisoners. Syracuse, rather than risk a similar catastrophe, surrendered without a fight; and indeed, apart from at Messina and Catania, there was no serious resistance anywhere in the island.

As the Bourbon troops marched almost unopposed on Palermo, it was at last realised that other countries were scarcely keen to defend a country which was so little ready to defend itself. Hurriedly trenches were dug round the capital, and ministers, priests, titled ladies and peasants from twenty miles around all lent a hand. But the political structure of the revolution was crumbling. One by one the ministers resigned, and no one was left who would take responsibility for decisions. Many citizens fled the town. Others began to parley with the enemy. Baron Riso of the National Guard, supported by Florio and other merchants, suddenly became a convinced supporter of peace. Inflation, forced loans, social revolution, the destruction of property and the ruin of trade, all helped to separate these conservatives from La Farina, Crispi and the radical die-hards. Crispi, who in time was to be revealed as the greatest Sicilian politician of the century, wrote that "the moderates feared the victory of the people more than that of the Bourbon troops". Perhaps he was right; and perhaps the moderates were equally right.

Here and there the squads of 'mountaineers' with their distinctive dress began to be seen again in the city streets. Sometimes they took to looting, but a British naval officer reported that some gang bosses were once again the principal upholders of law and order so long as they were given money to go on paying their men. La Farina tried to employ di Miceli and Scordato in fighting the Bourbons, only to find that he had been forestalled and they were being paid by Riso to do the very reverse. The division was clear: on the one hand were the National Guards, who announced that they would not resist the Bourbons but would merely defend property against attack by the populace; on the other hand were the radical leaders, some of whom momentarily considered the desperate step of opening the prisons and handing over Palermo to the 'mountaineers'.

When the red flag was raised and a leaderless crowd began manning the barricades, most of the National Guardsmen quickly disappeared and the civic authorities took refuge on a French vessel. Baron Riso hurriedly made contact with the Bourbon troops, playing exactly the same part which Prince Paternò had done at a similar moment in 1820. He was helped by the fact that the gang leaders needed to be on the winning side if they were to go on being paid and were to retain enough authority over their men. Di Miceli and Scordato accompanied Riso when he met General Filangieri, and then in person guided the Bourbon soldiers into Palermo. The squads from Bagheria, Parco and Partinico patrolled the streets, urging citizens to lay down their arms and replace the red flag with the white ensign of the Bourbons. Riso, too, courageously remained at his post to assist the entry of the Bourbon army into Palermo and help the more compromised among the revolutionary leaders to escape.

The Sicilian army, apart from an experienced unit of French volunteers, had not the morale or the training needed in such a situation. Some hundreds of Sicilian volunteers had joined the enemy troops attacking Palermo. Addresses of congratulation from titled Sicilian gentry and city administrations were soon thanking Ferdinand for delivering them from 'the Palermitan yoke', and the revolution thus ended a good deal less gloriously and hopefully than it had begun. Many people quickly tried to forget the part they had played in it. To many, indeed, the restoration of monarchy came as their salvation. The revolution had been an interesting experience as political education, but the one genuine insurrectionary force had proved to be the chronic rebelliousness of the plebs, and this made a true political revolution unattainable. Sicily was unlikely to win either autonomy or constitutional government in the foreseeable future without a good deal more co-operation among Sicilians and without considerable help from some outside power.

Chapter 46

THE END OF THE BOURBONS

The victorious general, Filangieri, became Governor of Sicily in 1849. An amnesty was granted, from which forty-three Sicilians were excluded, and the few who now went into exile included all the potential opposition leaders. Most of the ex-deputies and peers of the revolutionary parliament begged the King's forgiveness and assured him that they had been coerced by physical threats into supporting a revolution which they truly detested. Filangieri had to govern under considerable difficulties, though on the whole he ruled with sense and humanity. Parliament was abolished, but once again some degree of local autonomy was permitted in matters of justice, finance, police and ecclesiastical affairs. All officials in the island except the most senior were to be local men. The tax system remained in some respects unexpectedly favourable to Sicilians, and they were again excused compulsory service in the army.

Filangieri's chief problem was how to control the country districts. Thousands of convicts had escaped from prison, and a succession of weak revolutionary governments had resulted in extending the authority of the 'Little Shepherds', the 'Cut Throats', and dozens of other gangs which were the one flourishing form of association in Sicily. The head of police, who was an able and loyal Sicilian named Maniscalco, replaced Neapolitan security officers with Sicilians who understood the country and its ways. On a slender budget, there were sometimes only two hundred policemen for the whole of Sicily; Maniscalco therefore chose to co-operate with some of the armed bands, and perhaps he had little option if any government authority were to be restored. Scordato, the illiterate peasant boss of Bagheria, and di Miceli of Monreale were among those of the gang leaders now employed in the strange role of tax collectors and coast-guards, and they became rich in the process. Law enforcement at Misilmeri was handed over to the famous bandit Chinnici, who luckily found a common denominator between lucrative kidnapping and a rigorous suppression of liberalism. Such people could obtain very considerable power outside the main towns, and the government, by ignoring their offences, was able to establish some kind of loose supervision over other forms of crime. The less successful bands went on posing for too long as liberals, and by misreading the signs of the times lost their place in the local conflict for power.

Ferdinand II had been soured and frightened by the revolution.

As a result he now lost his interest in Sicily and his enthusiasm for reform; and this was a major achievement by the revolutionaries. Ferdinand and Francis II, who became King in 1859, were inadequate as rulers and increasingly out of touch with a new age of liberalism and nationalism. They were not interested in competing with Piedmont to make the Two Sicilies into the leading monarchy of the peninsula, just as they quite failed to develop a kind of government which might have mitigated the absurdities of hereditary absolutism. Theirs was a despotic state, based on a tiresome if ineffective censorship, with penal settlements in Lampedusa and other islands. Citizens could be imprisoned on mere suspicion, and freedom of movement was greatly restricted. Police methods were sometimes cruel, and the unwillingness to allow a safety valve for public opinion added a special element of instability to public life.

Nevertheless, Sicily suffered not merely from the failure of a discredited regime and dynasty; there was also a larger failure of southern society as a whole, and not least that of the lazy, absentee nobles who were now at last losing their exclusive claim to be the Sicilian political elite. Quite as harmful as foreign oppression was the fact that a growing middle class of *galantuomini* took over the same irresponsible attitudes as the aristocracy whose social position on the land they were inheriting. If most Sicilian villages possessed no school, if the leading families preferred to spend their money on other things than teaching their own children to read and write, the explanation was only in small part to seek at Naples. Maniscalco admitted that his fellow Sicilians were "uncivilised and without either education or ideas of morality"; he also acknowledged a degree of official responsibility for the fact; but it was equally true that many important Sicilians liked things as they were.

Any country town of about 10,000 people would by now have contained perhaps a hundred families of these *galantuomini* who had emerged over the previous half-century as property owners and now constituted the resident upper class. These were the *cappelli*, the men who wore hats; they met daily in their own exclusive café, and their names carried the honorific prefix of 'don'—this title was now taken automatically as a sign of status. No one who had reached this position in society could ever completely sink back again into the undifferentiated mass, and it was the primary activity of all of them to maintain or increase the differential which was their claim to respectability. This middling class of landowner had often made money during the British occupation, and had then profited from successive laws between 1812 and 1841 to take over small portions of the feudal estates.

By purchase, fraud or intimidation they had also annexed a significant portion of the village commons. Large areas of communal land had been arbitrarily enclosed during the lack of government in 1848–9, and the same process continued as a dominant theme of the 1850s.

Reformers had long looked forward to the day when middle-sized farms would appear in Sicily alongside the large ranches and the one-acre plots of land which were for the most part so uneconomic. But the chief interest of these new landowners was in acquiring power and respect; they were not concerned with direct farming to improve the land. Wherever the Intendant was weak, they sometimes wielded considerable influence, because the absentee nobility did not often stoop to dispute with mere country gentry the conduct of mundane local matters. As the numbers of these small-town gentry grew, their solidarity could break, and a conflict for power between different groups of families was another theme running through this period. Some of the *cappelli* were thus ready to encourage revolution and even to incite the *berretti* to mob violence if this offered them a chance to edge their rivals out of some local point of vantage. Others played along with the Bourbon authorities out of the same desire for power, and acted as police informers in return for official connivance at private illegalities of their own.

Neapolitan attempts to reform this society, though they continued in the 1850s, were less strong than before. The King not only lacked the requisite ability, but experience had taught him that administrative reforms might merely hasten political revolution. Social changes also presented him with a new and baffling political problem. If he applied the law strictly and tried to reconstitute the communal domains, this would infuriate the *galantuomini* who were now an essential element in local government; while if he left the usurpers in possession, that would keep the peasants permanently at boiling point. In other words he had no alternative but to stir up feelings of either political or social revolution; and either way he lost, especially as political revolution would at once precipitate social revolution, and vice versa. This was a built-in tension with no obvious way of escape; and ultimately it meant that a repetition of 1848 could not be long delayed.

The Bourbon administrators, even in the 1850s, were far from being the black reactionaries painted by patriotic propaganda, especially when compared to these provincial gentry. Bourbon prisons may have been as bad as Gladstone said, but some other foreigners who saw them thought he had exaggerated the facts for political purposes, and we now know that the prisons in enlightened Piedmont were not all that much better. Bourbon justice, though it was harsh on political offences, was sometimes regretted after 1860. The lack of railways, though it too was in part justifiably ascribed to Ferdinand putting his own convenience before that of his subjects, was due even more to the fact that Sicily was too poor to build railways or use them. Even between Palermo and Messina, said the liberal economist Ferrara, a railway would be quite uneconomic, and the boats which plied between these two main ports of Sicily still carried few passengers and little merchandise. Sicilian capitalists had other uses for their money, and, when railway building was aired in the newspapers, the opposition came from private citizens rather than from the government. To judge from the public controversies, many Sicilian towns would rather not have had railways at all if it meant that neighbouring towns were preferred in the choice of routes.

Similar considerations affected the much more important matter of road building. Messina still did not think it worth while to construct roads into its hinterland, and the main highway from the east coast to Palermo could still be described as for part of its length an almost pathless track. Road construction was in fact remarkably good in the 1850s when judged by previous standards; but the government was still not authoritarian enough to impose its will, and few Sicilians liked the increase in local taxes and borrowing which this essential public service made necessary. Nor is it irrelevant that landowners continued to enclose large stretches of public path and shoreland. Although the administration continued to resist this anti-social behaviour, the offenders were so well established in local positions of authority that they often got away with it.

Likewise with other public works, it was useful to be able to blame Naples for any deficiencies, but not entirely fair. Maniscalco pointed out that, although 300,000 *scudi* a year were now being allocated to public works of one kind or another, the machinery of local government was simply not adequate for using this money effectively. Naples was far away from Palermo, and in bad weather could sometimes be cut off for a month at a time. The *notabili* of each village therefore found it fairly easy to assert themselves. Decisions taken at Naples could result in engineers planning quite extensive schemes for irrigation in Sicily. It was nevertheless more difficult to get these schemes applied in practice than to plan them. About seven hundred miles of electric telegraph and several undersea cables to the mainland were installed by the government in the 1850s; yet this aroused what was probably some kind of mafia opposition, and Calabrian labour had to be imported to complete the job. As modern methods of communication brought government interference nearer and nearer, so passive and eventually active resistance was bound to grow.

The years after 1848 were a period of relative economic well-being. The increase in steam navigation helped trade in general, and the Sicilian mercantile marine in 1859 was 2½ times what it had been in 1825. Exports of sulphur doubled in the 1850s, helped by the Crimean war and the discovery that sulphur was the only remedy against a destructive vine fungus. The government set up a commission to discover more economic methods of smelting sulphur, and this eventually helped a little to reduce production costs. Meanwhile quite large areas were being planted with citrus fruit. The port of Messina was dredged, and that of Catania was at last made safer by a breakwater; while in western Sicily there were Florio and Ingham to show that, on certain terms, capitalists could continue to operate on quite a large scale even in this semi-feudal world.

High protective duties were nevertheless a symptom and sometimes a cause of stagnating domestic industry. Sicily lacked the raw materials and the enterprise needed for a real industrial take-off, and what capital she possessed was ineffectively employed. An attempt to start a savings bank movement proved abortive, and the reason given was that gambling had too strong a hold—the Bourbons did try to abolish the state lottery, but an outburst of popular feeling forced them to give way. With a little more success they attacked the setting up of monopolies in restraint of trade, for example among the millers who supplied Palermo. But thoroughly unhelpful was the crippling slowness of their administrative machinery and the fact that so large a part of the not very substantial tax revenue was allocated to the army and the police.

It was Bourbon taxation which the generality of Sicilians chiefly resented at the time, rather than any presumed lack of reforms. The *macinato* was far more disliked than any suggestion that the Bourbons might be insufficiently 'Italian' in their outlook. Here was another dilemma for Naples, because genuine economic progress would have needed much more governmental expenditure and hence even higher taxes, whereas that would have produced a still further increase in both political and social opposition. The food taxes had been perhaps the most important ingredient in the outbreak of 1848; then their abolition by the revolutionaries had helped to bring the revolution to a halt by depriving it of cash; and in 1849 the Bourbon King had been urgently requested to restore them by none other than the village administrations and the men of property. The *macinato* normally produced three times as much revenue as the land tax and had the advantage of being much harder to avoid, so Ferdinand agreed that it would have to be restored. Yet this gave enormous leverage to any future revolutionary; because anyone, sincere or insincere, who ever promised to remove it and could make the news widely enough known, could at any moment reactivate a ferocious peasants' revolt; and here in fact the government was to find its most vulnerable point.

Many Sicilians continued to serve the Bourbon regime with loyalty. Yet there also existed an extensive feeling of opposition, even though with little enough leadership or consensus of view. The desire to belong to a federal Italy affected a few people strongly—one can thus see from Amari's letters how he developed towards federal views from his earlier belief in a separate Sicily— but was never anything remotely resembling a widespread motive for discontent. Among most Sicilians, Italy was still unknown territory: sailors could travel hundreds of times from Palermo to Tunis or Malta without ever going to Naples, let alone Genoa; and perhaps many had not been even to Messina. What little they knew of Italy might be a cause of offence, since Neapolitans were disliked because they were the government and because they were outsiders who spoke a different language. Opposition against Naples was a far stronger and more widespread sentiment than attraction to the rest of Italy. It was as morally offensive to the population as it was costly that so many foreign soldiers were stationed in Sicily, and it was especially undignified for the local *notabili* to be crossed in running local affairs. Such people would not be particularly friendly towards Maniscalco and his police. They hated any royal Intendant who tried to stop them blocking rights of way and enclosing communal land. The *latifondisti* strongly disliked the law which said that they should give at least a fifth of their ex-fiefs to a new class of smallholders; nor were they pleased when, overcoming half a century of obstructionism, the government finally completed its census of land as a new basis for the land tax.

Any estimates about 'public opinion' in Sicily are bound to be based on inference from a limited range of information. One is on surer ground when concentrating on the few score of expatriates— in Genoa, Turin, Marseilles, Malta, even in North Africa—to see how they developed a wider political horizon. Among these exiles, there were about a dozen liberal aristocrats, but like Belmonte and Castelnuovo from whom their ideas generally derived, they were easily discouraged to the point of abjuring active politics. The democratic radicals were more active, though in attempting to explain their own failure in 1848–9 Calvi, La Farina and La Masa wrote many wounding things which opened up gratuitous divisions among themselves. Knowing how little talent they possessed for co-operation with each other, they were now the first to recognise that Sicilians were not sufficiently agreed or politically conscious to win independence on their own. They had given up their earlier belief that England would fight on their behalf, but the growth of Italian patriotism showed that help might possibly be found in northern Italy.

Just as the moderate liberals were hampered by their aversion to violence and social revolution, the radicals were mostly infected with a doctrinaire republicanism which prevented them looking for salvation to monarchist Piedmont. Both groups, furthermore, moderates and radicals, were moved by separatist feelings about Sicily, which made any idea of a full union with other Italian states unthinkable. Only when they could begin to cross this kind of barrier would their sort of revolution become possible once again. In the meantime these exiles contributed a real service of political education; not only did they keep Sicily talked about in London, Turin and Paris, but by arguing with each other, by maintaining contact with their friends in Sicily and smuggling books into the country, they greatly contributed to the sense of frustration and the awareness of greater liberties elsewhere. By 1859, some areas of Sicily which ten years earlier had been slow to support political revolution, now showed a noticeable development of political maturity. Suddenly it began to seem possible that Naples might not be able to hold on to the island much longer without a greater expenditure of effort than the cause was worth.

Meanwhile, in northern Italy, Garibaldi, a freelance soldier and Italian patriot, took up what had once been Mazzini's idea of starting a Sicilian rebellion to create a base for the unification of all Italy. Even if Italian patriotism was not strong in the south, a special situation was created there by peasant unrest, the tradition of armed squads, and the fact that insular patriotism against Naples could be made into a splendid temporary leveller of classes and factions. Some of the more active exiles secretly returned home for brief visits in 1859 to propagate the programme of Garibaldi. Among these was Crispi who, more than any other Sicilian, was a disciple of Garibaldi and Mazzini. Crispi was a lawyer and so belonged to a democratic bourgeoisie much less tied than the liberal aristocracy to sentiments of regional autonomy and memories of 1812. Once back in Sicily he established contact with some of the gang leaders, and instructed his friends how to make bombs and how to co-ordinate and synchronise a revolt. This was an ideal country for guerrilla warfare, and intelligent leadership might make the squads into a force which not even a large army could hold in check.

At the same time the more conservative Sicilian exiles, alarmed by hairbrained schemes which threatened to repeat the tragedy of 1849, directly approached the government of Piedmont to sound out the possibility of diplomatic and military intervention. Count Cavour, the liberal Prime Minister of Piedmont, had occasionally wondered about annexing Sicily from the Bourbons as one step towards creating a larger Italian state; but he decided that any positive step would be premature, and he was not ready to promise any support until Sicilians had shown that they could effectively defy the Bourbons on their own. To give them some encouragement, however, he held out the expectation that Sicily would be given a large measure of self-government if ever she agreed to accept annexation by Piedmont.

Cavour's policy was more subtle but not more practical than that of the radicals. He would have preferred no action at all in Sicily. Garibaldi's adherents, on the other hand, had positive actions in mind; they could appeal to a much wider audience and to people who would do more than merely talk about rebellion.

When minor disturbances by students and other radical elements in Sicily became more frequent early in 1860, the rumour began to spread that another revolution was imminent, and this kind of rumour was a highly effective revolutionary weapon. As the government knew through its informers, clandestine groups in Palermo were beginning to discuss both the possibility of annexation by Piedmont and Garibaldi's plan to land in Sicily with a force of irregulars. Quite as important as this kind of discussion, moreover, was the fact—as Bourbon officials also noted—that the common people were again beginning to bestir themselves in their search for justice and jobs; nor were the mafia groups slow to sense further possibilities for acquiring profit and power. Evidently a social revolution of enormous force was ready to be touched off by anyone who had enough courage and popular appeal. A grass-roots movement among the common people was essential if the large Bourbon army in Sicily was to be defeated: this was something which Garibaldi understood but Cavour did not; and this it was which eventually enabled Garibaldi to cut through all the differences between the various groups of Sicilians and to unite Sicily to the rest of Italy.

Chapter 47

GARIBALDI

Unrest was converted into insurrection after an armed clash occurred with the police in a Palermo suburb on 4 April 1860. As in 1848, some kind of concerted arrangement existed between a handful of insurgents in the town and the peasantry of the surrounding villages, but the timing was imperfectly synchronised, and apparently the police had once again been tipped off. The rising was clearly a movement over which the patrician classes and moderate liberals had little if any influence; even those of them who were ready to contemplate rebellion were unwilling to rebel before they had promises of outside help; at least they needed convincing that the right type of revolution would break out and that it had a fair chance of success. The radicals, on the other hand, had no doubts at all. Some of the liberal aristocracy left the country as soon as serious fighting broke out, for they feared that the insurrection would fail, or else they were apprehensive that it might succeed. Others, however, remained behind to follow up and make what could be made of this brave attempt to defy the government.

Although the authorities succeeded in putting down the first outbreak of disorder, within twenty-four hours most of the military outposts around Palermo had been attacked by popular insurgents. Telegraph lines were cut, and the sudden stoppage of information caused panic among government officials who remembered the kind of ferocity which had accompanied similar outbreaks in the past. Among ordinary people the news travelled secretly and fast across the island. To control Palermo was not too hard for the troops, but they were still not trained to fight in the countryside against "an enemy who never shows himself". Even the feeding of Palermo became a problem when the mills had their water cut off—the mills which symbolised the *macinato* tax and the private monopolisation of public water supplies. Food shortages and a sudden increase in prices made law enforcement additionally hard, and as there was now an excellent excuse for citizens to stop paying taxes, officials often could not be paid their wages. Within four days another minor insurrection occurred in Messina; the police had to fire, and many families abandoned the town. In a number of other places policemen became a favourite target of attack, and with such atrocities that they deserted wholesale and left the field wide open to revolution.

Any political motives among the revolutionaries were now almost entirely swamped by another peasants' revolt, a rising for food, land and social justice. In many villages the poorer clergy supported this social revolution, a fact which may have had considerable importance in helping it to succeed. More important still was that the break-down in law and order gave full play to mafia-type gangs which were always ready to use such a moment to extend their authority. Di Miceli and Scordato, who after supporting the revolution in 1848 had switched to backing the victorious Bourbons in 1849, at some point again became active revolutionaries, for they flourished on disorder and sensed a threat to their own private empires if they allowed these popular forces to escape their control. It is not impossible that some gang leaders possessed genuinely political aims, but it is safe to assume that their main motives were the prospect of pay and loot, the chance to destroy a rival group, to burn police files, to release their friends from prison, and make their name a word of terror and 'respect' over as wide an area as possible. These *mafiosi* were not mere criminals. Crime was for them just one method of obtaining money and power. Political revolution was another method; and this strange fact now helped Sicily to contribute a decisive and partly unwitting leverage to the cause of Italian unification.

Throughout April the fortunes of the insurrection were in continual doubt. Until there was more likelihood of success, the upper classes would not commit themselves and accept leadership of the movement; on the contrary, many landowners and others tried to put it down. The government encouraged the formation of a middle-class volunteer militia among Sicilians of good will; and the Intendant of Messina was able to report that these militiamen quickly restored government authority. Other Intendants accelerated road building so as to provide work and clear the vagabonds off the streets. Local contractors, mine owners and merchants took similar action, supported by government subsidies; and landowners also used their private armies of *guardiani* to help the Bourbon cause. Officialdom thus found a good deal of local support, since, even among those who did not like the Bourbons, many liked a peasants' revolt much less. Dozens of reports soon came in to say that order was being restored, and many congratulations were received on the victory of this 'counter-revolution'.

But the congratulations were premature. The interior was impossible to control; the peasants, the brigands, the Italian patriots and Sicilian separatists all continued to act here and there with varying degrees of independence and success. As weeks went by without the Bourbons proving that they could protect property, the unpolitically minded middle classes began to lose confidence in them. Hostility against Naples grew when the troops requisitioned food and fed their horses on the ripening crops, and above all where whole villages were left unprotected and at the mercy of the armed bands. In Palermo and Messina the shops were frequently shut, businesses suspended, and respectable citizens reduced to destitution. Often there was shooting at night. Because of the general fear, Palermo looked like a 'city of the dead', and at Messina half the population was reported to be in the hills. Even though active rebellion in the main cities may have been held in check, it was impossible to prevent crowds suddenly assembling in the city streets as rumours started, and government officials lacked enough ruthlessness in their attempts to control them.

Among the more radical exiles, some were ready for just such an emergency. One or two landed secretly and got in touch with their former contacts among the armed bands and the political dissidents in Palermo; soon their story that Garibaldi was about to invade had become common property, and this caused a dramatic release of tension and energy. When the government circulated a photograph of Garibaldi to the port authorities, clearly defeatism was spreading. The fact that Garibaldi had not yet decided to come was quite irrelevant: the mere expectation was enough to keep the revolution alive and give him time and incentive to make up his mind; in this respect it was like the Sicilian Vespers and Peter of Aragon all over again.

On 11 May, five weeks after the initial rising, Garibaldi arrived at the recently re-opened port of Marsala with two small paddle steamers that he had stolen. With him were just over a thousand ill-armed but eager volunteers. Against him were some twenty-five battalions of infantry as well as several artillery and cavalry regiments. Yet Garibaldi defiantly and irresponsibly proclaimed himself a dictator, ruling on behalf of King Victor Emanuel of Piedmont. The local inhabitants of Marsala were at first bewildered and terrified, but Garibaldi's mesmeric personal charm and his frank appeal to the common people quickly won support. This notorious anti-clerical and anti-Catholic was soon being venerated as a saint, even as a reincarnation of Christ himself, come to redeem Sicilians from centuries of ill-treatment; and shrewdly he did not discourage this charismatic image. Deliberately appealing to a peasants' war, he abolished the *macinato* and promised eventual grants of land to the poor and those who took arms. Many who had never heard the words 'Piedmont' or 'Italy' could easily comprehend this programme, and gladly took a chance to resolve many accumulated personal grudges and many vendettas against authority. With savage fanaticism they swept away the last relics of Bourbon government. Farm labourers did not generally make good fighters. Their only weapon might be a nail driven through a stick, and sometimes their chief object was to strip the fallen soldiers of either side; but the terror they inspired had a galvanic effect. Garibaldi obtained from them most of the information he wanted, as well as lodging and food for his troops, whereas the Bourbon soldiers met with sullen opposition.

Most prominent of all were the armed bands, in particular the *montanari* from the hill villages, who were a legend and often a fearful legend in the towns. Some seem to have remained faithful to the Bourbons; some were out for what they could get without any political commitment; and others were hired by rich men to protect their property and probably to act for one side or the other as occasion demanded; but most of them were more than ready to assist a revolution which promised so much chaos and liberty, all the more so when the days went by without Garibaldi suffering any reverse. Some of the forty Sicilians among his thousand volunteers were sent into the interior to organise as many irregulars as possible to help his attack on Palermo. In little over a fortnight there were said to be about five dozen squads drawing rations and pay, each between 10 and 200 men in size, and La Masa eventually claimed to have enlisted on his own over six thousand men.

Sometimes these local irregulars proved a liability. They might dissolve into the hills at any moment of danger. They lacked discipline and sometimes fought each other. Their objectives were often dubious, and they used to go off at weekends to see their wives and get a clean shirt. But it was of the greatest advantage for Garibaldi to find auxiliaries already organised and armed. They knew the countryside. They created diversions and cut off stragglers. One perceptive Venetian among Garibaldi's officials wrote home that "the Sicilian revolution turns out to be little more than these country bands which here they call squads, composed for the most part of emeritus brigands who fight the government just as an excuse to fight the landowners". Faced with such a ruthless and sinister force (which the Papal Nuncio thought "more abominable than the Arab and barbarian invaders"), the Bourbon troops withdrew into the towns. Even in Palermo some of the main offices had to be closed when civil servants decided to abandon their work. The Bourbon generals, especially Lanza and other Sicilian officers who knew what they were up against, lost heart and brought out their only plan for such an emergency, which was to fall back on Messina as they had done in 1848.

This happened at the end of May after a few hundred insurgents had infiltrated into Palermo. Garibaldi's policy had been to avoid an open battle wherever possible, especially as Cavour's friends had managed to confiscate most of his firearms before he left northern Italy. Street fighting and guerrilla warfare suited his resources much better, and these were arts at which he had no peer in Europe, for he had learnt them during ten years of professional fighting in South America. His favourite stratagem was by quick marches and accurate dispersion to create the illusion that his men were part of a larger army; for he had at all costs to keep up a fast pace and the impression of constant success. By this means the enemy was demoralised and the squads emboldened. Completely deceiving Lanza about his movements, he eventually brought some of his advance units into Palermo, and after this convincing sign of success the townsmen enthusiastically erected barricades in his support. Prisoners were released from the jails to add to the confusion. His Sicilian opponent, the Bourbon general, began shelling the town, but Ferdinand's defeatism and no doubt also his humane feelings brought the order to withdraw in order to avoid further destruction and bloodshed. The revolution had won against what, in purely military terms, must have seemed overwhelming odds.

Garibaldi had little time to reorganise the island, for his main pre-occupation was to pursue the conquest of Naples and Rome in order to fulfil his lifeong dream of a united Italy. He ruled as a dictator in Sicily for five months, and his enormous moral authority allowed him to outdo in reforming zeal any of the half-dozen reformist governors of the previous century and a half. Plans were drawn up to nationalise Church property and carry out land redistribution. His government had paper schemes for building new villages, damming rivers, re-afforesting mountainsides, draining marshes and bringing waste land into cultivation. A contract was at last signed to build the first Sicilian railway. Other planned reforms ranged from introducing freer trade to building nursery schools. One new law provided for three technical high schools, and in these five months the number of university chairs was almost doubled.

Garibaldi's programme of reforms was ridiculed by many of the moderate liberals for its optimism, its idealism, and what was held to be its excessive concern with the common people. Clearly he lacked the experience and political skill to carry through this policy, especially once the local *notabili* recovered from the immediate shock of such a challenge. His political views were too simple, too radical and too hastily compounded. He naively tried to stop peasants addressing their landlord as 'Excellency', as he tried to stop the servile hand-kissing which still survived in this feudal society; trying to legislate against fashions of personal behaviour was the same mistake as Victor Amadeus and Caracciolo had made. These few months were too short a time, especially for a professional soldier who had to improvise wholly new machinery for law-making and administration at the same time as he built up a large army out of nothing and conducted a major war.

The revolutionary government quickly ran into the same difficulties as that of 1848. The armed bands, once their initial and essential job was over, proved a divisive force threatening social war; they also showed that they could be hostile to Italian as well as to Bourbon government if they were not cosseted. Garibaldi tried to replace them and devised an alternative plan to conscript 2 per cent of Sicilians as a local militia, but his conscription order was quite unenforceable; the gangs resented the attempt to supersede them, and there was mention of possible civil war. The Sicilian irregulars had probably all been raised on a traditional basis of clientelage; they were the personal following of either a landlord or some other 'man of respect', and not even Garibaldi could enforce a different method of recruitment. Nor could he stop thousands of Sicilian volunteers deserting rather when the alternative was to continue fighting on the Italian mainland for a cause which they found largely unintelligible. One of Garibaldi's lieutenants complained that "Sicilians will neither provide soldiers nor pay taxes, though they deluge us with applications for salaried jobs". There were other complaints that contraband was rife, and arms and ammunition were being stolen for sale on the black market. After a few weeks of euphoria, many ordinary citizens seemingly felt that the course taken by the revolution was irrelevant to their real needs, and hence began to treat Garibaldi's government much like any other.

Worse still, different towns and villages were in bitter and sometimes armed conflict, while rival families and clienteles used the prevalent disorder as a chance to suppress any local opposition to themselves. When the dismissed squads returned home, anarchy returned to the countryside. The English wine merchants at Marsala, like other landlords, could not get rents paid; their crops and cattle were stolen, their agents attacked, and they had to pay protection money to the armed bands. Landlords had to fall back on hiring private gangs of their own, so adding to the horrors of class war. This was perhaps the most burning issue of all, and it had little to do with defeating the Bourbons or the making of Italy. Thousands of country folk had been deprived by both big and middling landlords of any rights in the land, and when Garibaldi promised to redress this kind of wrong there took place a spontaneous movement to occupy portions of the old *latifondi*. "Like wolves driven by hunger", wild men in goatskins came down from the hills, and any of the gentry who failed to escape ran the risk of being assassinated to the cry of *"Viva l'Italia"*: in extreme cases they were burnt alive and their livers roasted and eaten.

One such outbreak, at Bronte, was put down with exemplary severity by Garibaldi; for, social reformer though he was, he was no anarchist, and he had come to carry out a political revolution for which he needed the support of the landowners. While he undertook to divide the ecclesiastical estates and recover village property which had been privately enclosed, he could not approve of this brutal and extra-legal action. Garibaldi in fact never took as firm a line against the ex-baronial *latifondi* as the Bourbons had done; and hence some landowners who had hitherto been neutral or hostile began to see that co-operation with Garibaldi and Piedmont might be their best hope of restoring order and re-taining as much as possible of the past. By showing that he was ready to check one of the strongest forces in the Sicilian revolution, Garibaldi thus succeeded unexpectedly and decisively in associa-ting many of the conservative aristocracy, the *galantuomini* and the local elites with the cause of united Italy.

The dictator, much to Cavour's annoyance, delayed handing over full sovereignty to Piedmont until he no longer needed a base for further operations on the mainland, and ambitiously began to conceive that he might persuade King Victor Emanuel to get rid of Cavour and accept a more radical programme; but in the meantime he gradually introduced Piedmontese laws and institu-tions. The *lira*, the Piedmontese decimal system and the north-Italian flag were all officially imposed on Sicily by Garibaldi's personal fiat. Instead of reviving the centuries-old Sicilian parlia-ment, he proclaimed the very different Piedmontese parliamen-tary system. Some Sicilians were surprised and offended that they were not consulted by this northern dictator and that no provision was made for local self-government: suddenly it was beginning to seem as though there was to be no Sicilian autonomy but simply an annexation of Sicily by Piedmont, and their own passive accep-tance of this fact was apparently deemed to be self-evident.

Other Sicilians, on the contrary, now realised that they wanted annexation to Piedmont even more quickly than Garibaldi was ready to go. They feared that genuine social and agrarian reforms would be introduced if he were left much longer in sole control. Some of them probably disliked his further plans to conquer Naples and make a united Italy. It caused particular offence when he set up a 'Dictatorship of the Two Sicilies' which recalled the very same connection with the mainland against which they thought they had been rebelling. Count Cavour looked like a far safer politician; for one thing he was further away; moreover they already had been given reason to believe that he would allow Sicilian autonomy, and it was a fair assumption that he would reinforce the existing balance of social classes. Some of the Sicilian princes, a category of people who—unlike previous revolts in 1820 and 1848—had taken noticeably little share in the events of 1860, now hurried to Turin to beg for Piedmontese intervention. Cavour knew so little about Sicily that his first proposal, no doubt at the instigation of the grandees, had been to restore the separate Sicilian parliament and the aristocratic constitution of 1812; but he quickly realised that he was in a strong enough position to dictate his own terms to people who were so anxious for his help. What he really wanted was outright annexation of Sicily with no strings attached; incidentally he also wanted his personal and political enemy, Garibaldi, ejected from power as soon as possible, and so he acted to undermine the latter's position.

One of the few generalisations that can be hazarded about politically conscious opinion in Sicily by the autumn of 1860 is that nearly everyone wanted and expected some kind of regional self-government. Most people, too, had come to welcome as inevitable and desirable some fairly close political link with the rest of Italy. The number of dogmatic and unqualified Italian patriots can still not have been large, but many who knew little about Italy also knew that only north Italian help would insure them against a Bourbon counter-revolution or further instalments of radical reform.

Minor differences of motive were reflected in the sometimes conflicting ideas about what kind of link with Italy was needed, and yet the possibility of an unqualified union with the north was scarcely envisaged by more than a handful of people until they found that it had already happened. Sicilians had been used to a fair degree of autonomy even under the Bourbons, and few considered that this might now completely stop. Few bothered to think what it would mean to have not only new money and new weights and measures, but a completely different system of administration and justice, let alone what to ordinary people was an altogether new language. Even at this late stage, perhaps most Sicilians had never heard of Cavour; for some his name was rather connected with cigars; and *l'Italia*, or rather *la Talia*, was for years thought by some to be the name of the King's wife. Whether Sicily was rich enough to assume northern rates of taxation and tariffs, or sufficiently advanced to operate a system of juries and elections, these were questions which Cavour had no time to ask.

PART 13

Italian Sicily 1860–1890

Chapter 48

UNION WITH ITALY

In October 1860, Garibaldi held a plebiscite in Sicily which by a 99.5 per cent majority favoured the formation of a united Italian nation under King Victor Emanuel. This plebiscite was meant as a political demonstration to regularise something which had already happened. North Italians, however, read it rather as a test of opinion and so misunderstood what was happening. Few voters had more than a superficial awareness of what was at issue, for there was neither time nor machinery to instruct them, and opposition voices were discouraged from stating their case. Votes were accepted from anyone, even from non-Sicilians. Some peasants fled into the hills fearing a plot to press them for military service, while others were simply told that they were voting their appreciation of Garibaldi. Many areas produced no negative votes at all. The ballot was entirely public, and most voters, being illiterate, were at the mercy of presiding officials who wanted a political demonstration that was really convincing.

Some of the ambiguities concealed in this almost unanimous vote soon became explicit. Its immediate effect was to end Garibaldi's dictatorship and hand over power to the parliamentary leader at Turin, Count Cavour; this offended those Sicilians for whom Garibaldi was a hero and deliverer. Even more offence was caused when Cavour reneged on the vital point of regional self-government. Suddenly he had realised that Garibaldi's conquests made possible a centralised state which would be far more manageable as well as more acceptable to northern public opinion, and probably he misread this overwhelming majority as support for the Sicilian aristocrats who had begged him to lend Piedmontese troops and impose strong government. He therefore interpreted the vote as meaning acceptance by Sicilians of unconditional 'annexation'. There was to be no Sicilian autonomy after all. Arguing that there was insufficient time to plan a new constitution, Cavour preferred to outdo Garibaldi in imposing Piedmontese institutions on Sicily before anyone had time to object: his own snap judgement was that southern Italy was corrupt and needed a good dose of efficient and moral rule from the north.

In the prevalent conditions of emergency, Cavour had to take this fateful decision in the dark. He knew nothing of Sicilian laws and institutions, but simply assumed that they should be changed; and as he did not want to leave his central post of command in

Turin, he had to rely for information either on those of the local aristocracy who wanted to use him to defeat Garibaldi and the democrats, or else on expatriate Sicilians who deceived him for not always very estimable reasons of their own. On their advice he chose personal enemies of Garibaldi to administer the island, deliberately playing the partisan from the very start, ignoring the ex-dictator's popularity, and so provoking a bitterness which was as ruinous as it was unnecessary.

Garibaldi had appointed a committee to report on the special needs of the region—a committee of the most eminent Sicilians he could find, if anything with a conservative bias and certainly not packed with his own sympathisers: they recommended establishing a regional assembly with considerable powers, and no doubt this was the overwhelming wish of most politically conscious Sicilians. Eighty-five years had to pass before an Italian government accepted this advice. Cavour continued to promise Sicilians that one day he would give them self-government, but in private he instructed officials to ignore local opinion. Piedmontese laws had to be introduced at once, without discussion, and if necessary by using armed force. Before parliament met at Turin a few weeks later, the deed was mostly done, and a Sicilian deputy who questioned the propriety of this method of procedure found himself ruled out of order by the chair.

It was perhaps unfortunate for Cavour that emergency conditions did not leave more time for debate and preparation, and inevitably some people thought that the emergency was being used as an excuse to justify a partisan policy which was ungenerous and even dangerous. The unexpected result was to strengthen rather than weaken autonomist sentiment, and the legend was allowed to develop that Sicily had initiated a patriotic revolution only to be tricked into a false vote and then annexed as a conquered colony. Within a few weeks, therefore, the enthusiasm of the plebiscite dwindled into disillusionment, and observers remarked on a tremendous feeling against everything which smacked of Piedmontese.

The administrators who now arrived from the north were equally disillusioned. They had not been prepared to find a society so completely different to their own and a language so unintelligible. In their most pessimistic moments some of them reported back that the southern provinces of Italy were "a bottomless well of filth", that her people were 'bedouin', indolent and indifferent to free institutions, and that habits of clientelage made Piedmontese traditions of government unworkable. To find a world so exclusively built on kinship and patronage was a novel experience to northern politicians. Nepotism here, far from being in any sense immoral, was recognised as a primary duty of every good family man, and almost every Sicilian belonged to a network of client-patron connections designed to defend him against other networks and even against the government. There was thus an immediate failure of understanding. Victor Emanuel's common sense deserted him when Palermitans joyfully unharnessed the horses of his carriage and drew it themselves: this was their kind of welcome and well meant, but he roundly told them to desist as he preferred men to be men and not beasts. The King soon yearned for the orderly, sophisticated world of Turin. He and his fellow Piedmontese saw themselves as coming to deliver Sicily from bondage, whereas local opinion was rather of the view that Sicilians on 4 April 1860 had launched the liberation of Italy. Northerners assumed that they were conferring great benefits on Sicily by annexation; they were surprised when the word 'annexation' aroused anger and when their superior knowledge and experience were not received with gratitude.

The same anti-governmental feeling which originally made possible Garibaldi's success against Naples was soon directed against Italy itself, and the first anniversary of the rebellion was celebrated with a riot. After the tax-free holiday of the interregnum, annexation by Italy was to many people a new enslavement. It thus seemed a breach of faith when Garibaldi's promise of land distribution was shelved. Tax collectors and policemen were as unpopular under parliamentary government as under a despotism, all the more so when they proved more intrusive and efficient. Even though the government hesitated for a few years to restore the *macinato*, the tax burden was heavier than ever; some village authorities announced that they would not pay tax until their legitimate Bourbon sovereign returned.

Particularly hated was conscription. The Bourbons had found this same aversion in 1820, as the revolutionaries had also done in 1848 and 1860; and the imposition of Piedmontese laws about compulsory service took place too fast for any adjustment which local conditions might have made advisable. To escape conscription, some families did not send their children to school, or else they even accepted the indignity of registering boys as girls. Some villages resorted to lynch law against the recruiting officers, and often over half the recruits simply disappeared. There was particular resentment that people with money could buy exemption, as, for example, did the young Sicilian writer Giovanni Verga; whereas poor people could be compelled to fight though they could not vote, and this seemed a double and contradictory injustice. Conscription was a special hardship in an agricultural society where women did not work the fields—indeed in which rigid social customs even prevented women shopping or walking freely in the streets. It was also disliked because identified with the state, in other words with something which ancestral memory taught that it was a virtue to disobey: being compelled to fight for a cause beyond the family or the village was too big a jump for the level of social awareness of the ordinary Sicilian peasant.

Shirkers and deserters therefore went to swell the criminal underworld. Brigandage, so northerners tended to assume, should have disappeared as soon as honest, liberal, northern government had replaced Bourbon corruption and Garibaldian latitudinarianism; but instead, banditry and the mafia were to grow out of all recognition, just because liberal government surprisingly proved more corrupting and more easily manipulated, as well as being more limited in its means of repression. Instead of one police organisation as under the Bourbons, there were to be four, without common information services, and occasionally with a strong dislike of each other. Fearful of encouraging insular patriotism, the Piedmontese stressed a division of the island into smaller provincial units, and usually allowed the Prefect of Palermo no authority over the other six provinces, so that it was as easy as ever for outlaws to escape from one jurisdiction into another.

Within a few months, gang warfare was clearly becoming worse, and it continued without respite for ten years. The sulphur miners were tyrannised into giving up part of their wages. On the rich agricultural land round Palermo, secret organisations levied a toll on herdsmen and farmers and obviously had a helpful arrangement with the police. In Palermo itself a dozen people were stabbed to death in a single night; and when the British consul was kidnapped just outside the walls, a popular ballad extolling the heroism of his captor sold for a halfpenny. Arms were found even inside the prisons; contraband activities continued to involve customs officers; respected aristocratic names were among the known patrons of brigand bands; and ordinary Sicilians generally refused to give evidence for a prosecution.

In 1863 a dialect play describing life in the main Palermo prison achieved a tremendous success: it was called *I mafiusi della Vicaria*, and this title popularised a word from the criminal jargon of a suburb of Palermo. The mafia had existed long before the name gained general currency, but it flourished after 1860 as never before. It was used by landowners who needed strong-arm men to collect rents and intimidate labour; and by the *gabelloti* who, as well as coercing their workers, had to intimidate the owners in order to rent the *latifondi* on easy terms. There were *mafiosi* in every class, and their operations ranged from the most trivial manifestations of licit or illicit influence, up to fraud on a huge scale and armed gang warfare. Many of their non-criminal activities, if idiosyncratic, were not particularly dangerous. Nevertheless crime was the ultimate sanction on which they relied to widen the circle of patronage and fear on which they depended, and it was essentially as criminals that they infiltrated local government, the big urban markets, the orange groves and any area of life where crime could be made to pay.

The mafia was no single organisation. The various *cosche* spent much and perhaps most of their energies fighting each other to extend their sphere of influence and their right of pre-emption on local crime. Frequently they needed political help, and this is one reason why they were so strong in and near Palermo. But even in eastern Sicily there was a dangerous development of gang life in the decade after 1860. Assassination was sometimes as frequent in Messina as Palermo, and criminal syndicates on the east coast were involved in commerce, industry, gambling, public works and even the theatres. Taking Sicily as a whole, the number of assassinations was ten times as high as in Lombardy or Piedmont.

If the landed classes emerged from the revolution of 1860 stronger than ever, this was in part because they as well as the mafia had an interest in exploiting the new dispensation, and in particular because elections offered a better field for bribery and intimidation than autocratic government had ever done. Whereas the Bourbons had been paternalistic to the poor and suspicious of the gentry, now parliamentarians of both Right and Left found it advantageous to leave local affairs to the *notabili* in return for electoral support. The novel of Federico de Roberto, *I vicerè*, described in detail how elements of the old ruling elite cynically adopted the techniques of liberal government and became stronger than ever; and, much later, Giuseppe Tomasi di Lampedusa's novel, *The Leopard*, showed in a different way how former attitudes of mind persisted unchanged despite alterations of circumstance.

With an electorate of little more than 1 per cent, the landlords and their friends and employees were often the only voters. Rarely was any non-Sicilian elected in Sicily except at Messina, and this fact was publicly defended as proper and inevitable; without it, indeed, the system would not have worked. If there were any doubt about the result of an election, intimidation was usually effective. As early as January 1861, when the very first parliamentary elections were held, the whole paraphernalia of mafia influence was employed, and henceforward it became habitual in many constituencies. Any Prefect who honestly tried to preserve free elections could be quickly brought to heel, or else would be tactfully removed by the government after complaints had been received—in seven years after 1861 a dozen Prefects quickly followed one another at Palermo. If anyone were brave enough to challenge this kind of conspiracy, it was not difficult to make life unpleasant for him: the attempt to arrest Crispi in January 1861, the brutal assassination of General Corrao in 1863 in which the government was almost certainly implicated, the imprisonment of Giuseppe Badia in 1865, these were the kind of methods chosen for dealing with Garibaldi's main Sicilian lieutenants.

The new local government law in 1861 gave considerable authority to the village notables. Some of the local bosses may have been honest men, but official reports suggest that these may have been a tiny exception, just because the ceaseless struggle for influence and prestige favoured mafia methods. The *galantuomini* had learnt in two revolutions and under Bourbon reforming governors the necessity of controlling the localities, as they had also learnt how simultaneously to use both the underworld and the police for this purpose. If they failed to rig the elections, they might lose control over municipal revenues and communal lands; so a new Prefect might find that a delegation of notables would come to see him to help him draw up the voting registers for the provincial and communal elections. If opponents then protested against being disenfranchised, the documents could easily be lost until the election was over. Much more than the Bourbon Intendants, who had been responsible to an absolutist King, the Prefects in course of time became partly responsible to the 'Grand Elector' who was the local boss and often a leading *mafioso* in his own right: a Prefect's main task thus became not administrative but political; he had to try hard to win elections for the government, and in return reward the Grand Electors for their help.

Some government officials have described how justice and the control of charity and credit institutions were gradually taken over by families who had a hereditary monopoly of local power. Hospitals often did not present proper accounts, nor did village and town administrations, let alone the many thousands of local charities which now tended to be engulfed by various kinds of malversation. A legacy to found a poor house would disappear and turn up later as a loan to a local councillor; a fund to provide dowries for poor girls was easily converted into one providing for daughters of the rich; contracts for road building would go to friends of the mayor as he built up the patronage which made him a man of influence. The new Bank of Sicily was obviously in at least some departments another mafia perquisite, and credit was thereby channeled to political allies instead of being used to galvanise agriculture and industry. Gun licenses somehow went to criminals friendly to the administration—"first a gun, then a wife" ran the proverb; and possession of weapons was an indispensable mark of status for 'a man of respect'. Licences to open shops for gambling or selling salt and tobacco were dealt with in the same way.

Local taxation continued to be controlled by the village oligarchies, and especially in western Sicily this power was much abused. Friends of the mayor could be entirely exempt, just as they also escaped conscription. A tax was due for the mules which were so necessary to the peasant, but not for cows and horses owned by the landlord. Nearly all local revenue continued to come from excises chiefly paid by the peasants, while some villages had no direct land tax at all: there was little point in direct taxes where, as in Monreale, no one would admit to having income from property; in the same way as a land tax had little appeal where landowners decided everything and the peasant had no vote.

If liberal government in many ways proved a misnomer, it was because an exciting and potentially fruitful revolution was in this way veneered on to a traditionalist society which was quick to adapt and exploit liberal institutions. There was no parallel social revolution except in so far as the *risorgimento* brought increased power to a narrow class whose liberalism was much less genuine than that of Cavour. The jury system in their hands meant impunity for the mafia: it was not unknown for jurymen to protest formally if they were not bribed, but in any case conviction might invite a vendetta. The local elite was not interested in popular education and often refused to build schools despite the law on compulsory education: moreover the staff in existing schools was sometimes unpaid, since the bosses had more profitable uses for public money unless (as fairly often happened) the teachers were their own kin. At Monreale, in 1875, almost all the municipal employees were said to be relatives of the mayor.

Naturally this kind of society had little to say about land reform, and landlords could hardly be taken to court over the enclosure of communal property since this would have meant the ruling clienteles suing themselves. Although the law of 1841 which said that villagers had to receive grants of land from the ex-fiefs was not repealed, its application was handed over to the very people from whom these grants of land would have to come, with results which might have been expected. It can be argued that agrarian reform, quite apart from considerations of political expediency and social justice, would have been an indispensable prerequisite for making the revolution of 1860–1 into the real turning-point of Sicilian history which many people had hoped. Without it the mixture continued much as before, despite all the promise conveyed by a liberal, parliamentary regime and a unified Italy. Though the moral effects on Sicily of Italian unification were in the long run to be considerable and beneficial, its material effects at first were therefore surprisingly negative and unhelpful.

Chapter 49

REPRESSION AND REVOLT

Northern officials found Sicily hard to understand, and her incidence of crime as well as of radical and autonomist opposition was inexplicable as well as frightening. Faced with the huge task of welding together a new nation, they suddenly realised that Italy seemed about to dissolve within months of its creation. Desperately there was an attempt to inculpate Garibaldi and the Bourbons in order to escape a more painful appraisal which might have undermined self-confidence still further; for ministers could not afford to assume anything else than that this was a problem which mere repression would solve. Martial law was declared, and the generals had to be given civil authority: the excuse was said to be 'brigandage', but, barely concealed by this word, there raged a fierce and debilitating civil war.

It took a long time before repression could be seen as a stultifying, expensive and irrelevant non-solution to the problem. Meanwhile parliament heard from Sicilian deputies that the Italian government was coming to be hated as much as the Bourbons had been. When one deputy suggested that Sicily's chief problem might be economic and social rather than one of public security, his remarks were held to be unpatriotic and indeed insulting: too many people stood to lose from a fundamental debate on such a suggestive and perilous theme. Parliament in 1863 preferred to give General Govone full powers, allowing him to hold military tribunals and shoot people on the spot. The army found that many farmers did not dare leave the security of their villages to cultivate the fields—this was a fact which had been noted dozens of times in previous centuries. Thousands of young men were in the hills escaping from justice or military service, and travel inside Sicily was once again undertaken in armed caravans for safety.

Govone gradually restored order, but by methods which made Italian rule less popular than ever. In a world of *omertà* he had no option but to arrest people without trial, and some remained untried in prison for years; he took hostages from the more recalcitrant villages to coerce them into obedience; torture was sometimes used, as was the threat to cut off water supplies in the summer heat. Some Sicilians even appealed for foreign intervention against treatment so reminiscent of that from which the Piedmontese claimed to have delivered them in 1860. Govone made things worse by unguardedly telling parliament that no other methods would succeed in a country which "has not yet completed the cycle which leads from barbarism to civilisation". There was an outburst of indignation at this phrase, though some Sicilians in private were prepared to admit that it might be true.

By a strange and unlucky misunderstanding there was a common belief in northern Italy that Sicily was one of the most fertile countries in Europe. This was because Cavour and his associates knew the island not at first hand but by report and from reading ancient history or modern poetry. One consequence, and it was convenient for many northerners, was the assumption that the Sicilian economy was robust enough to need no special treatment. Whereas Spanish and Bourbon governments had regarded cheap food as a primary object of policy, the new free-trade economy sponsored by Cavour, while it could be a boon to landowners, took little account of labourers who were regularly unemployed for over half the year and unable to demand higher wages to keep up with the cost of living: any benefits were quickly counteracted by increasing prices and a growth in population which left unemployment as bad as ever.

Unification with the mainland of Italy was eventually to give Sicilians the advantage of joining a larger and more active market; but for the moment it brought new problems and removed a cushion insulating them from a fierce and competitive world. Diseases were introduced which caused havoc among the mulberry, orange and lemon plantations. As subsistence agriculture gave way to dependence on outside market conditions, cereal farmers switched to cotton growing to take advantage of a shortage created by the American Civil War; but there was little official guidance to help them adjust to this kind of change, and many bankruptcies occurred when the end of the war brought lower prices again. As for industry, northerners had no interest in continuing the pre-1860 protection of southern domestic industries which might prove competitive with their own. Far from Sicily being dragged into a modern world of industrialisation, standards of living therefore diminished for many people as her handicrafts began to collapse, and over the next forty years the traditional Sicilian industries continued to decline at the same time as those of northern Italy leapt forward.

The Italian centre of gravity, political as well as economic, was firmly located inside the triangle of Turin, Milan, Genoa, and the interests of the new Italy were therefore largely equated with those of the north. Northern industry had all the already-existing advantages of better communications, more skilled labour, nearer markets, cheaper power, greater social flexibility; and it was a plausible argument that available resources should go rather to the north where they could make the most of the infrastructure already in existence. Yet one corollary was clear: the north was not only more advanced economically, but these built-in advantages would enable it to go on progressing far more rapidly; and this big differential between Italian regions was to continue widening for the next hundred years, with official encouragement—and not without many harmful side-effects.

Few Sicilians quite realised what was happening, because there was no explicit statement of policy. The decision was made almost casually that theirs should remain a region which imported manufactures and exported raw materials, just as it was assumed without any debate that the northern legal and administrative systems should be imposed on the whole kingdom. Cavour's doctrine of free trade helped Sicilian olive oil and wine exports to increase substantially for a few years, and sulphur exports also greatly improved; but little attention was given to discussing the balance of the economy or to the discontents and frustrations which had underlain the revolt of April 1860. Though some degree of social reform and regional levelling out was accorded theoretical approval, in practice a much higher priority went to stringent taxes to balance the budget and an austerity programme which kept the south backward.

All this followed naturally enough from the way the national revolution had been completed in 1860. The elimination of the Sicilian silk and other textile industries was in part a simple calculation of efficiency; in part it was an attempt to make more palatable to northern industrialists the annexation of the south; in part it came from an assumption that Italy had at all costs to be made industrially strong, and hence that an industrial (or even an agrarian) revolution in the south should be avoided as something which might hold up the accumulation of capital in the northern triangle. This policy was applied with stringency and some clumsiness. There was no time to debate the underlying moral considerations, nor the possibility that higher living standards in the south might have created a healthier nation and helped northern industry to expand still faster. The backwardness of Sicily was to remain as a deadweight on the national economy and the development of national consciousness: it was even to impair the growth of liberal institutions.

Tax policy was equally inconsiderate. Sicily came into the union with some assets: unlike the rest of Italy she had a favourable balance of trade; she also had a smaller national debt than other Italian states, and the amalgamation of regional debts after 1860 thus appeared a net loss to her. The servicing of this collective indebtedness required much higher taxes than Sicily was accustomed to, and so did the policy of developing a big military and industrial potential. In other words, an economic pace was chosen which suited the north, and to help pay for it Sicily was expected to increase her tax contributions suddenly by about a third. One helpful fact, for which Sicilians were not sufficiently grateful, was that Italy took over some responsibility for the existing debts of individual towns and villages; but this benefit was then cancelled by placing a great burden on local authorities for roads, schools, doctors and cemeteries, a burden which was tolerable in the north but intolerable in Sicily. Increased taxes resulted in bankruptcies and in smallholders having to give up their land. Tax policy was changed after 1878, but only to favour the wheatlands of the *latifondi* at the expense of more specialised crops, which for every social and economic reason needed encouragement. More serious still, taxes had the overall effect of taking money away from southern agriculture for investment in the north, deliberately increasing a regional disparity which was already dangerous.

A similar effect was obtained when tariffs were reduced by sometimes as much as 80 per cent in order to bring Sicily into line with the north. Southerners were thereby given another excuse to suspect that Turin and Milan wanted to ruin southern industry and to do this under emergency regulations without hearing what Sicilians might have to say. Certainly a more gradual application of the tariff would have given time for adjustment; but the Sicilian deputies in parliament advanced surprisingly few objections to what was happening, since the landed gentry were far the strongest pressure group, and their sectional interest stood to gain as much from lowered tariffs as industry stood to lose. It was convenient for them to be able to grumble against the government, but sometimes it was convenient not to begin grumbling until too late for remedial action; in other words, the bigger landowners needed a scapegoat for the fact that they were condemning the rest of Sicily to a low level of economic growth.

Another element of disorientation was the sudden introduction of Piedmontese anti-clerical laws. Many of the lower clergy in Sicily had actively helped Garibaldi's national revolution, for their interests and family ties were closely bound up with the peasants; moreover the Apostolic Legateship, until it was finally given up in 1871, partly insulated the local clergy from the current vogue of Catholic illiberalism, so that even the Sicilian Jesuits were less rigid than those at Rome. But the politicians felt that Italy should impose a degree of liberalisation on the Church. Cavour's advisers in Sicily recommended caution, on the grounds that the clergy were more popular there than in Piedmont, that they were more patriotic and possessed an influence which it would be foolish to challenge unnecessarily. Moreover the charitable activities of the monasteries could hardly be replaced. Yet successive governments overruled such advice and decided to make Sicily conform to northern practice by dissolving some monasteries and confiscating ecclesiastical property. They stood to gain more than a tenth of the surface area of Sicily, and this would be a magnificent windfall.

Sicilian landowners were equally enthusiastic about this nationalisation of Church property. In a world where land meant status, the moneyed classes welcomed half a million acres or more being suddenly thrown on to a buyer's market. It was a plausible argument, and one shared by the radicals of the Left, that the Church owned too much property in mortmain, and indeed that there were too many clergy—Caccamo, with about 6,000 inhabitants, had thirty churches and nine monasteries. It was said that this represented a dangerously reactionary element in society. The radicals, in any case, were still hoping for enforcement of Ferdinand's and Garibaldi's laws about dividing the ecclesiastical *latifondi*, arguing that if the distribution of Church land were linked with the compensation of propertyless families for their loss of pasture on the commons, it might create a new class of smallholders and give the patriotic movement deeper social roots among ordinary people.

These radical ideas were held only by an eccentric few in Sicily. The victors in the political revolution were moderate anticlericals who were not enthusiasts for social reform; and they realised that Church lands could be auctioned to cover part of the cost of the *risorgimento*. They therefore vetoed any suggestion of distributing small holdings by ballot to landless families who had no money to invest in agriculture, and instead argued that both government and landowners would gain if this ecclesiastical land were sold by auction and in much bigger units than Garibaldi had conceived. Parliament accepted this view, and so did most Sicilian deputies. They made some attempt to curtail possible abuses by prescribing that no one should buy more than one unit of land; but in practice many buyers illegally bought a hundred units or more. With the aid of the mafia, peasants were excluded, the auctioneers were intimidated, and a few powerful buyers formed secret rings which eliminated competition and kept prices minimal. The government thus lost in some cases nine-tenths of the value of the land, and this huge amount was simply presented to a class of rich people who were not notable for their sense of public responsibility or their economic enterprise.

An enormous area was by these procedures transferred from the Church to the *latifondisti*. Only a small fraction went to altogether new landowners or to those who actively farmed their own land. Many areas of Sicily were undoubtedly made more productive as a result; but *latifondisti* not only were content with a 2 per cent return on their money; they often seem to have made it a point of class pride to leave their estates derelict and barren. Capital which would have been far better spent in agricultural improvements was immobilised in these purchases. The government did not even redeem its pledge to pay a good proportion of the purchase money to individual Sicilian villages, but the proceeds were once again funneled off to northern Italy.

Among other disadvantages, many speculators bought this land on credit and realised the money by cutting timber and killing cattle, or else got their arithmetic wrong and went bankrupt. The new landlords were more grasping than the Church had been. The dissolution of the monasteries meant not only great hardship for the religious themselves, but caused unemployment for what was estimated at 15,000 laymen in Palermo alone, and the government had no substitute for the charitable functions which had been so important to the urban poor. Politically, as Prefects were quick to report, the shallowly rooted gratitude of the landlords had to be weighed against the hostile reaction of many others: of the autonomists, for example, who thought that this land should be regionalised and not nationalised; of the peasantry who had to watch helplessly as existing legislation in their favour was simply abrogated by the bosses. Above all there was opposition from the Church itself. From now onwards, hostility towards Italy and disrespect for law and order were given ecclesiastical support; so, sometimes, was the mafia itself; and not for nothing did the Benedictine abbey of Monreale, its archbishop, and many other secular and regular clergy now fall foul of the police. Worse still, the sight of nuns forcibly ejected by soldiers from their convents outraged popular religious feelings and ties of kinship.

This kind of opposition had not been foreseen by the politicians. Its result was merely to make them yet more authoritarian so as to convince Europe that Italy was strong and indissoluble. Garibaldi and his friends continued to be treated with notable ungenerosity, and Mazzini too, who was several times elected to parliament at Messina, was not permitted to take his seat. The two greatest Italian patriots were thus in a sense politically excommunicated. Even more dangerous, at the other extreme, were conservatives with nostalgic memories of the Bourbons: some Sicilian parliamentary representatives were already in 1862 hedging their loyalty by secret negotiations with the Bourbon ex-King; and some of the gang leaders—di Miceli, for instance, whose variegated career of criminal and police activity had by now made him a rich landowner in his own right—sensed another profitable revolution and changed sides for the third or fourth time. Much more considerable still were the various groups, especially in Palermo, who wanted a partially self-governing Sicily: those, for instance, who believed that centralisation was illiberal; those who thought that Sicily was being exploited economically; the traditionalists who refused to speak Italian and for whom only mainlanders were 'Italians'; the liberals who had doubts about making Italy a strong military state; and, not least, those who wanted autonomy because it might mean power for themselves and jobs for their friends.

The refusal to allow adequate parliamentary expression to these various minority views drove them underground and forced them into a strange alliance with each other; and the result was major rebellion at Palermo in 1866. Fundamentally this was another social revolt by working people whose standard of life was threatened, and who were near enough to starvation to be ready for any violence. As a foreign journalist put it, the cultivators of the soil were "taxed above their means and their patriotism". They were not represented in parliament, and the radical deputies of the Left did not speak for them: Crispi, for example, was by now a man of influence; he had managed to buy some ecclesiastical land, and he was already showing that his ambitions for power depended on a fairly sophisticated system of political alignments. Some of the Prefects had urgently requested aid for the poor in order to forestall a revolt, but the replies from remote northern Italy were slow and unhelpful. When a dry spring brought a food shortage, basic prices rose by up to 50 per cent and made trouble inevitable.

A number of minor factors helped to precipitate rebellion, among them the abolition of the St. Rosalia festivities. In May the introduction of paper money caused a panic and led to a fall in the value of money and of real wages: naturally it was thought to be a piece of governmental fraudulence. In June the tobacco monopoly was introduced and the free cultivation of tobacco forbidden. Conscription, new kinds of stamp tax, unemployment caused by the new tariffs, higher rents and food prices, all this aroused indignation, and so did dismissals among the inflated bureaucracy. Each successive municipal administration tended to create patronage by duplicating jobs: that is why the poorest village might have more than one musical band, and why the official gazette in Palermo had ten times the staff of that in Turin. Yet dismissing supernumerary employees added to the white-collared unemployed at the same time as it threatened many entrenched systems of patronage.

Gradually an ideal situation built up for those of the armed bands who wanted another excuse to extend their power; and when the large garrison in Sicily had to be withdrawn for a war against Austria, above all when the national forces received several resounding defeats, the way was clear for these bands to revolt, along with all those who wanted social reform or a Bourbonist counter-revolution. Thousands of deserters reinforced the *squadre*. The British consul described a situation where "secret societies are all-powerful. *Camorre* and *maffie*, self-elected *juntas* share the earnings of the workmen, keep up intercourse with outcasts, and take malefactors under their wing and protection." Many of the revolutionaries were the very same men who had initiated the patriotic revolts of 1848 and 1860; some were paid to revolt by richer citizens who, just as in May 1860, preferred not to act openly themselves; others, with government encouragement, had been recruited by landowners as a private militia.

The revolt of 1866 was the fourth such outbreak in half a century, and the series was accelerating with a shorter gap between them each time. As with the others, there existed some kind of plan, but, just as in any mafia-style operation, the leadership remained unknown and nothing was committed to paper. The rising was once again announced in advance, and the message spread that people should act as soon as they heard shooting. After several false starts the first effective spark was ignited at Monreale, and a dozen armed bands quickly began moving down towards Palermo under the high walls of the private orchards. Behind them, cartloads of food were waiting to be brought into town once the excise offices were destroyed. Later the same carts returned home loaded with stolen goods. Criminal elements were far the most prominent of all, and di Miceli met his death trying to release prisoners from the Ucciardone jail. Many legal and police documents in the archives were destroyed on this occasion. A fiercely cruel grudge-war against the police was an important ingredient of the rising, yet church bells also called people to arms, and so did a printed notice signed by six princes. Another summons came from groups bearing a red flag and demanding a republic. Mazzinians, Bourbonists, the mafia and the clericals were all hoping to exploit the occasion in their own way.

Not many Palermo citizens emerged to take part in the revolt, but very few actively opposed it. The Marquis di Rudinì courageously remained at his post as Mayor, and indeed his support of the government made it difficult for him (and for some others who stood with him) to go on living at Palermo in future years. People in general had learnt to be cynical about revolution and to put a proper value on silence until they saw how things developed: the National Guard, for instance, mostly refused to obey orders.

Palermo remained in a state of anarchy for a week. After several days an organising committee announced its existence, including Baron Riso and three princes of the front rank: these men later said that they had been intimidated into this action, the very same excuse that they had made to the Bourbons when their revolutionary actions in 1848–9 failed. Unlike 1860, no Garibaldi arrived to support the revolt, and the Italian navy shelled Palermo into submission. As soon as 40,000 troops succeeded in restoring order, the city council unanimously disclaimed responsibility for the revolt and demanded exemplary punishment by military tribunals for anyone who threatened social order and property; but it is safe to assume that many of the chief culprits knew how to survive this change of fortune.

Chapter 50

THE 'SOUTHERN PROBLEM'

The revolt of 1866 was treated as mainly a police matter, its deeper social causes being left undisturbed and indeed largely unknown; but one clear conclusion was that Sicily could not easily be governed by the ordinary methods of liberal parliamentary government which had succeeded elsewhere. For another decade a large part of the Italian army had to be stationed there, and many Sicilians continued to feel that they were living under foreign occupation or as participants in a submerged civil war. General Medici, who combined military and civil power in his own hand, would still not travel without a large escort of soldiers when he went five miles away to dinner in Monreale.

Official reports confirm that the mafia continued to have widespread support from rich and poor alike, and some lawyers obviously made large profits out of helping it. Landowners were using it to control elections and ensure their local preponderance, although they too could be the victims of mafia outrage if they failed to pay the price of protection. One official was astonished to find a private system of vassalage in being, a kind of revived feudalism under which people commended themselves to one or other local boss: yet the probable truth was that there had never been a time in the whole of Sicilian history when this kind of relationship was not more significant than that between ruler and subject. Every Sicilian habitually disregarded official channels. His first recourse if he needed help was to kinsmen; but, in dealing with the threatening world of non-kin, he needed friends or 'friends of friends' whose patronage and system of contacts would help advance his family's fortune. These friends were people whose assistance he could claim either in virtue of future allegiance, or else through some past service by himself or a relative.

Those who took part in such a reciprocal system of patronage had the excuse, now as always, that the government was at once oppressive and yet weak, so that self-defence was doubly necessary. Crispi said that Sicily was more of a police state than in Bourbon times, though others simultaneously found less individual security than under Maniscalco. For both reasons the government was disliked, disregarded and disobeyed: so much so indeed that, according to Giacomo Pagano, any foreign country which might have tried to take Sicily from Italy would now have received the same enthusiastic support which Garibaldi had encountered against the Bourbons.

In order to keep some control over the situation, officials sometimes supported one gang against others and allowed certain illegalities in return for help in controlling petty theft. When Antonio di Rudinì became a Prefect in 1867, he as a Sicilian understood these matters: on one occasion he came to terms at a private meeting with an escaped bandit who was under sentence of death, and he quoted this publicly as a not abnormal procedure. As he reminded parliament, force had only a limited usefulness where *mafioso* behaviour was the norm. Albanese, who was Medici's chief criminal investigator, employed notorious delinquents as policemen; he did not dismiss them when they were implicated in further crimes, nor even when they were accused of using their office for large-scale criminal operations. This became known when Diego Tajani, the senior member of the Palermo judiciary and a non-Sicilian unfamiliar with such methods, issued a warrant for Albanese's arrest in 1871. To Tajani's surprise, the government ordered his warrant to be disregarded; and, almost as ominous, a number of witnesses for his case disappeared by assassination.

The government could not dismiss judges, but its power to transfer them was regularly used to punish an enemy and reward a friend. Tajani's judicial career was ruined. He stood for parliament at Palermo, but, as an outsider and a trouble-maker, he had no chance of being elected. He was successful at Amalfi, and once he was in parliament he made these facts public. Parliament did not like discussing the mafia, because the Sicilian deputies were either too involved, too timid, or too proud to welcome such a discussion, and they alone knew the details; moreover their defection on a crucial vote might upset the government's majority and inflame regional sentiment. Sicilian parliamentarians used to meet in private to concert a common policy and protect local affairs from too probing a scrutiny. When Tajani, an outsider, dared to break silence, they tried to minimise the matter. Crispi, who led the Sicilian Left, was strangely reticent in his comments; and another Sicilian deputy, a much respected man but from a notoriously *mafioso* area, insisted that the mafia did not exist but was an invention by northern policemen who needed a scapegoat for their own corruption and incapacity.

Tajani, however, unlike Crispi's political friends, was not responsible to the Grand Electors of western Sicily, and his later career as Minister of Justice shows that he was a man of some responsibility and judgement. From his considerable legal experience in Palermo, he was able to tell parliament that the mafia was allowed to flourish for political reasons and was strong only in so far as it remained under official protection. He explained that magistrates in Sicily were sometimes ordered by the government to connive at gross police irregularities. How, he asked, could one expect citizens to come forward to give honest evidence in open court when it was common knowledge that the police and the courts were involved with the 'Honourable Society'? If Medici, di Rudinì and other senior and highly respectable officials felt that they had to act in collusion with members of the underworld, ordinary Sicilians could be excused for doing the same.

The parliamentary discussion which followed, though it infuriated Sicilians with its implications of moral disapproval, alerted Italy to the defectiveness of government policy. If there was evidence that crime in Sicily was connected with political corruption, there was also evidence that northerners had made this worse and not better. Another sensitive point was that foreign newspapers were beginning to criticise northern Italians for showing so little interest in their southern provinces and knowing so little about them. The years 1874–6 were therefore marked by a growing sense of guilt in the north and a growing resentment among the 48,000 voters of Sicily. When an election suddenly gave 44 out of 48 Sicilian seats in parliament to opposition candidates, the alliance between governments of the Right and the local political machines had obviously collapsed. The main forces of the mafia had changed their allegiance.

Minghetti, the Prime Minister, reacted to this secession of the Sicilian political elite by proposing further emergency regulations, and for one year his government at last seems to have made a genuine effort to break the mafia and brigandage. After defeat in the elections he had nothing left to lose; on the contrary, crushing the existing electoral cliques was urgently needed in order to reinforce his failing majority. Sicilian deputies tried to make his task as difficult as possible, and though they grumbled against brigandage, they grumbled much more against attempts to repress it. It was left-wing newspapers and parliamentarians who in self-defence now denied that the mafia existed, who opposed emergency regulations and tried to preserve their enclaves of boss rule; but they also received a surprising amount of support from conservative landowners; and together this coalition of Sicilian deputies helped bring to an end a fifteen-year period of rule by the Right. Before resigning, Minghetti appointed a special committee of parliament to examine conditions in Sicily and find out what had been going wrong. But he already knew the main answer. Sicilian politicians would fight hard against any attempt at forcible suppression of boss politics and the mafia; and as they had now shown themselves strong enough to bring a government down, future administrations would think twice before challenging them again on such a sensitive issue.

The Bonfadini committee (Romualdo Bonfadini was the *rapporteur*) gave themselves time only for a hurried and superficial study based either on official information or on evidence from the local notables who had every interest in putting up a smoke screen. They seem to have been determined to see things in the best light and to restore the good will of the landowning class. Political reasons ruled out any fundamental analysis. In their report they noted the great complexity of the mafia and its connection with politics; they confirmed that rich men were involved in it and that, either from fear or favour, vast numbers of other people gave it support. Nevertheless they concluded that Sicily needed no special treatment. Standards of living were not worse than in some other parts of Italy, and they assumed that crime was much the same elsewhere.

Far more thorough was a private report made by Baron Sonnino and Baron Franchetti, two of the most distinguished Italians of their generation. These two men were both from Tuscany, and as outsiders, quite apart from being landowners and conservatives, what they said carried weight. They visited many more places in Sicily and sampled a far wider range of opinion than the parliamentary committee. Far more than Bonfadini they took trouble to check evidence by personal observation, and had no political reason for telling less or more than the truth. Where the committee exaggerated the number of smallholdings created out of the ecclesiastical estates, they stressed on the contrary that away from the immediate vicinity of the cities the *latifondo* was almost invariably the basic unit of land; and the *latifondo* was a barren waste where agriculture was as miserable as could be. So far as they could judge, union with the north had on balance done little for the economy. There was still an almost total illiteracy in the villages, and despite many laws and promises the great majority of the population had not been given a stake in society by a better distribution of land. Until this was done, there would be a continual danger on the one hand of revolutionary violence, and on the other of the counter-violence needed by the rich to subdue the poor—"violence which is the only prosperous industry in Sicily".

The report by Leopoldo Franchetti and Sidney Sonnino in 1876 was the first serious study of the effects of Italian unification, and its depressing conclusion was that things had changed remarkably little since Bourbon times. The old elites had been glad to accept a united nation provided they could go on dominating the localities, but liberal government was vitiated by this proviso. The most talented and independent-minded Sicilians still preferred to leave Sicily. Local government was utterly corrupt, and it was a deeply ingrained assumption that everyone in public office must be feathering some private nest; while, in the bitter struggle for power, the winning family group in each village took all. Tax money was spent very little on roads or medical centres, and far too much went on theatres and political corruption. Palermo, for instance, had several of the most splendid theatres in Europe before it had a good hospital, and the Prefects had to beg help from the central authorities to counter the typhus and cholera which periodically ravaged its multiplying slums. Even a village of six thousand inhabitants could maintain a theatre for the use of the leading citizens.

This analysis enabled Franchetti to come nearer than anyone to penetrating the myths surrounding the mafia. The 'Honourable Society' was a legend, for the mafia was not an organisation any more than it was a merely casual phenomenon; and though it might have some chivalrous elements, for the most part its so-called code of honour was merely a device to conceal every kind of cowardice and treachery. It could hardly derive from a popular desire for personal independence if Sicilians submitted so supinely to terrorism and boss rule. Another familiar theory, that the mafia evolved from opposition to foreign governments over the centuries, was equally implausible, because its greatest successes came through infiltrating successive governments and co-operating with the police. Far from representing hostility to government, it rather filled the gap left by the absence of any effective government, and its main function was to impose some rudimentary organisation on the anarchy of Sicilian life. Crime was a means only; the chief object, as always, was to win respect, power and hence money.

Crime was profitable, and many had known how to use this fact to profit from the making of Italy. The most ferocious murderers were admired and protected by members of upper Palermo society, whose standing was said to be the higher the more criminal their protégé. Hence the leading aristocrats would boast of their friendship for assassins and secretly house them in Palermo during winter months. If the landowners truly wished it, said Franchetti, brigandage could be stopped at once; but unfortunately, either from fear or because of mutual advantage, "there is not a single proprietor living on his estates who does not deal directly with them". Sicily was organised for the exclusive advantage of the landowners. "While the government quickly stamps out popular disorders, it is miserably impotent against brigandage and the mafia which depend on the possessing classes"; and one explanation of this terrifying fact was that the profits were distributed all the way up to the central government in a complicated series of relations which tied up petty criminals with some of the most important names in the land.

Sonnino and Franchetti found western Sicily a place where brigandage was an accepted institution and where the effective rulers were criminals. Sicilians might pretend that the mafia did not exist, and Sicilian newspapers kept astonishingly silent about it, yet in fact it crippled agriculture and industry. Its agents were often recruited in prison, for even there the mafia's word was law. No jury and few judges would convict a man who had powerful friends. Illicit associations of this kind grew up naturally where there was little faith in public authority and no sense of social obligation, for "the great majority of Sicilians have no idea of any such thing as a social advantage distinct from individual interests and superior to them". Admiration was reserved for those who knew how to defend and enrich themselves by their own strength and influence. Even killing innocent people was a justifiable means of inculcating fear and so obtaining respect.

Both authors agreed that fundamental changes in Sicily were urgently needed; but whereas Sonnino thought that Sicilians might find their own remedy if left to fight it out among themselves, Franchetti believed that leaving power in the hands of Sicilian police and magistrates could only make things worse. This difference of opinion reflected a basic dilemma of many successive governments: if Sicilian officials were appointed, they would be exposed to intimidation, nepotism and clientelage; on the other hand outsiders could never penetrate the mysteries of this arcane world or succeed in making themselves obeyed. According to Franchetti's analysis, the government had incurred a clear responsibility by acquiescing in local corruption. Yet he also stated explicitly that the Sicilian ruling class was the chief villain. Naturally, therefore, they tried to bury his report. Too much was at stake for them. With enormous indignation his book was labelled a typical piece of anti-southern prejudice, and clear warning was given to northerners against translating its conclusions into action.

Possibly most landowners and *galantuomini* would have been glad to escape from the way of life described in these volumes, but, if so, they kept quiet about it. So long as the government feared to act, they preferred to resign themselves to the mafia, even to follow official example and co-operate actively with it for their own safety. And because of their real or feigned indignation over any attempt at reform, this substantial study by Franchetti, perhaps the most penetrating there has ever been of Sicilian society, bore no fruit. Local pride and the interest of the Grand Electors thus kept the *ancien régime* alive. Northern Italy went on being blamed by Sicilians for taking no interest in the south, but this charge was at best an exaggeration, and at worst was deliberately designed to divert attention from the local veto on remedial action.

Meanwhile at Rome, which by now had become the capital of Italy, the Left won political power in 1876. They were backed by the great majority of Sicilian deputies, and so the general attitude towards the 'southern problem' changed little. The new Prime Minister, Agostino Depretis, knew Sicily from his experiences there as Garibaldi's administrator in 1860. He now held elections in which every kind of illicit influence was employed, even more than the already scandalous frauds used under Minghetti two years before. The new Sicilian deputies reflected this fact: at Caccamo, for example, the election of Raffaele Palizzolo launched the political career of a notorious *mafioso*—though he sustained a momentary set-back when it was discovered that in one area he had the suffrage of more than 100 per cent of the eligible voters. Other gentlemen who were only a little less shameless could become Mayor of Palermo and Director of the Bank of Sicily.

Some Sicilian deputies never spoke in parliament. Nevertheless, except on rare occasions such as in 1874–6 when their compact with the government broke down, most of them would vote automatically for any official measure; and in return they had the assurance that Sicily would be left unreformed and the facts revealed by Tajani and Franchetti would be forgotten or at least forgiven. When the time came to debate the Bonfadini report, the Chamber of Deputies was almost empty. Some northern conservatives who recognised the need for land reform—Luigi Luzzatti for example—were surprised to find the Left against it: indeed, the agricultural minister of the Left was Baron Majorana, a *latifondista* and banker of Catania whose constituency was his own fief of Militello, and who had led the Sicilian deputies in frustrating Minghetti's last-minute struggle against the mafia. Such a man was a guarantee that social and economic relations on the land would remain as they always had been. Far from Rome being able to reform and improve the south, it was rather southern methods of clientelage and political sharp practice which would soon be seeking further areas of profitable employment in the national capital itself.

Chapter 51

SOCIETY AND THE ECONOMY

An immensely detailed report on Italian agriculture by a commission under Senator Jacini was published in 1886. The volumes on Sicily show that union with Italy had brought some improvements but had done little for the farm labourers and share croppers who were the bulk of the population. Of the benefits received, freedom of speech and the press meant little to such people. They had no vote, since they were illiterate; hence no one courted their favour, and hence the schools were not built which would have equipped them to vote. Some villages continued to lack either school or doctor: apart from the priest, there was only the local witch or magician to take their place. The rich, on the other hand, even when illiterate, were always a power and could extract plenty of concessions from Rome; yet they were not interested in improving the condition of the poor; if anything, they understood their interest to lie in depressing it.

Sonnino, who was an experienced landowner, told parliament that agricultural labourers in Sicily were worse off than any in Europe; and though official figures incline one to think this an exaggeration, perhaps he, like Jacini's collaborators, saw some things which escaped the official records. He added that in twenty years the government had not introduced a single effective measure to improve the lot of poor people and make them see any material advantage in Italian rule. Instead of remedying the social malaise revealed by the revolt of 1866, the *macinato* had been reimposed in 1868, the very tax which for centuries had been the chief ingredient in Sicilian rebelliousness. New alcohol taxes then ruined one prosperous branch of agricultural industry, and the extension of the tobacco monopoly to Sicily ruined another. Hundreds of small factories shut down in the early 1870s, and thousands of workers lost their jobs. Alfred Marshall the economist, when he spent the winter of 1881 at Palermo, noted that even industrial artisans had a semi-feudal dependence on their patrons and were regularly unemployed for much of the year. Most Sicilians lived under such precarious conditions of employment that any thought for the future was impossible. They had no stable labour contracts. The peasants had so little bargaining power that three-quarters of what they produced generally went to the *gabelloto* for the privilege of working casually on his land. If a peasant family had a pig living with them in their single room, that was a sign of wealth. Hundreds of thousands, probably, were afflicted with malaria, especially in the south-east. Sugar and meat were almost unknown in their diet, while even bread was still often a luxury.

This kind of fact was not generally known until the time of Verga and the school of 'true-to-life' Sicilian novelists at the end of the century. Few people can have read the vast bulk of Jacini's report, and no government used it as the basis for any remedial policy. Social relations in this patriarchal society remained static. Evidently the *droit de seigneur* had not disappeared entirely, though seigneurial feudalism had long been abolished by law. Incest was common in many country districts. Abject deference was shown to every 'don' and man of property. Sons had to call their father 'Excellency', and wives, even ladies of rank, were kept in what one princess called "almost *oriental* seclusion". Fear of female emancipation was one important brake on change. The women who once wove textiles at home would hardly have been allowed by local custom to take factory jobs without losing face and honour, and hence the number of Sicilians gainfully employed went on declining. Even the dramatist Pirandello, though he lived a good deal outside Sicily, thought it quite natural to come home to Girgenti to marry someone selected by his father and whom he had never seen.

The chief problem of the Sicilian economy was the inability to keep food production in pace with a rapid rise in population; and this once again brought up the question of the *latifondi*. These large estates hardly seemed to have diminished in size, because any land transformed by intensive cultivation had been matched by more waste areas being brought under extensive cereal farming. Perhaps three-quarters of Sicily was owned by *latifondisti*. According to Jacini, the labourers on the big estates were commonly treated as slaves or even as animals, with contempt, cruelty and absolute possessiveness. Even the relatively enlightened di Rudinì spoke of his employees as "complete savages". No wonder, therefore, that this persecuted majority regarded the law as imposed upon them for the benefit of others; and, where the law seemed at variance with natural justice, lawlessness easily became a virtue.

Despite the splitting up of Church estates, the number of property owners went on decreasing, largely because of forfeiture for non-payment of taxes during a period of agricultural depression. The gap between rich and poor was becoming wider than ever, just like the gap between north Italy and the south. The laws about dividing and sharing out the communal village lands, after decades of non-enforcement, were finally abrogated, and retrospective legal sanction was given to an enormous extent of illegal enclosure by the village oligarchies. The results of this were made worse by the fact that, while rich families had powerful social reasons for trying to keep their estates intact, poor families generally divided land between their children because of population pressure and the absence of alternative kinds of employment. There was thus a tendency for smallholdings to become smaller (and less economically viable) while large ones remained the same or even grew. Even the richer peasant families could thus end up owning half a dozen tiny particles of land, perhaps in widely distant areas.

These facts, and their results for agricultural production, reinforced some economists in their view that only large estates were adapted to the unchangeable social relations of Sicily and to the impervious clay soil and lack of water which characterised so much of the island. Other experts, on the other hand, pointed out that vast areas of the big estates were anyway cultivated in tiny units by share croppers, so that Sicilian farming in fact had all the disadvantages of smallness and none of the advantages of peasant proprietorship or long leases. Baer and Damiani, both of them authoritative students of this problem, suggested that, when given credit and secure tenure, peasant proprietors whose holdings were not too microscopic did better than most *latifondisti*, and Sonnino was optimistic enough to think that three-quarters of the *latifondi* could be profitably divided. Smaller-scale farming would present problems, especially on poor land; nevertheless it would create more employment, and it would diminish a fierce element of wasteful strife which for centuries had helped to keep Sicily divided and impoverished. Introduced judiciously, it would also result in much better land utilisation.

The alternative was to persuade the *latifondisti* to give up absenteeism and their preference for a low-yield and low-cost type of agriculture; or at least to persuade them, if they would not themselves improve their farms, to put up the capital and encourage their tenants to do so. This was an attractive possibility, just because smallholdings were in practice often too fragmented and undercapitalised, whereas a well-planned ranch could offer genuine economies in production. Against it, however, was the simple and decisive fact that social pressures made most existing landowners unwilling to change their habits, and political reasons prevented them being forced to do so.

Smallholdings, on the other hand, were easier to create; and, once created, there were the most pressing reasons why their owners should want to make them more productive. The chief problem was to avoid pulverisation into tiny patches of land in places where improvements were not easy. In some areas even a farm of ten acres would be insufficient for subsistence, let alone able to provide a surplus for investment in increased production. Any land converted into smallholdings would therefore have to be selected with this in mind. Technical help and credit would also be needed. Until 1860 there had been scores of local charities which offered agricultural credit at 4 per cent or less; by 1877 it was thought that only about half a dozen of these were left, since they had been taken over by the village bosses for their own use, and the money lent out sometimes at 100 per cent.

Here was a field wide open for government intervention, but unfortunately no one was either brave enough to risk his political career or knowledgeable enough to stoop to such lowly details. No one at Rome took the decision to work out basic statistics about how much money was available or needed for agrarian credit, or even about how much land in Sicily was uncultivated or under-cultivated. There was no question of taking another land survey which would show the extent of the *latifondi*. Even Jacini did not hazard any detailed statement about remedial measures, What was needed was a political decision; but, under the Italian practice of multiple-party coalition governments, no politician had anything to gain from raising this sort of issue; there were few votes to be won in it, and many to lose. Hence Sicily was left with the worst of both worlds. On the one hand there were too many fragmented smallholdings. On the other hand the growth of population and food consumption made the *latifondi* increasingly and dangerously uneconomic, while yields per acre remained so low that large amounts of imported cereals were now often required.

A few enlightened *latifondisti* encouraged their tenants to try new crops and methods. Di Rudinì, when he left the less mobile environment of western Sicily, succeeded near Syracuse in converting unhealthy marshes into smallholdings on long leases for the cultivation of vines, nuts, olives and carobs. Vines were the quickest of these intensive shrub and tree crops to come into production and so the most easily encouraged. Apart from Marsala, Sicilian wine had by now lost its former reputation for quality, because even the smallest farms insisted on making their own and no concession could be made to modern techniques or equipment; but its cheapness and alcoholic strength made it suitable for 'stretching' and blending elsewhere. After the phylloxera began to devastate the French vineyards in the late 1860s, large areas of Sicily were planted with vines, even to the point where olives and orange trees were uprooted. Scoglitti, the port of Vittoria, trebled in size over a period of five years. Then in the late 1870s the phylloxera reached Sicily, and since an emergency

472

regulation obliging growers to destroy non-resistant vines could not be enforced, the disease proved extremely damaging. Unfortunately it was the more enterprising farmers who had switched to vines, and it was they who suffered most.

Other specialist crops also ran into trouble. The silk mulberries, which were expensive in labour, continued to attract high taxation even though competition from oriental silks now made this uneconomic. Likewise olives were taxed at a rate fixed before mineral oils and gas supplanted olive oil as a form of lighting. On the other hand the orange and lemon groves still paid relatively little in tax, and although they needed a good deal of capital, the rewards were very large once steam navigation revolutionised transport. For a time, Sicilian citrus developed a good market across the Atlantic, until American competition began to be felt after 1884.

A special problem for the fruit growers was mafia intimidation. It was observed that the 'black hand' was trying to monopolise water supply and marketing, and this was inflating prices and damaging exports. Especially in the *conca d'oro* round Palermo, where citrus trees now took up more land than any other crop, some growers had to use a third of their turnover to pay for irrigation. There were many murders in this area, reported the *Annali di Agricoltura* in 1873–4; every night there was shooting, just as in time of war, and the absolute lack of security was such that people were too frightened to trade freely or work on the land. Professor Inzenga, the agronomist, thought this the main obstacle to the development of Sicilian agriculture. According to another official statement in 1886, the various activities of the mafia were causing starvation prices in Palermo.

The national tariff policy continued to work against the south but now in a very different way than before. The reduction of protective duties after 1861 had overwhelmed Sicilian textile manufacture, and this policy was changed only when there were no southern industries left to benefit from it. Protective tariffs after 1878, and especially after 1887, were then introduced to aid the already industrialised parts of Italy. If Sicilian politicians were among the architects of this discriminatory policy, the reason no doubt is that the *latifondisti* and their dependents were simultaneously given a duty on imported cereals. This protection of grain was a concealed subsidy for wheat as against cattle breeding; it helped the feudal Sicily of the interior at the expense of the more intensively cultivated vineyards and orchards of the coast. It delayed the splitting up of the *latifondi* and encouraged the already excessive cultivation of cereals on altogether unsuitable land. The tariff of 1887, strongly supported as it was by Crispi, thus condemned large areas of Sicily to a low level of productivity. Because of industrial protection, the price of manufactures rose for Sicilian consumers, and the cost of living also rose when the compensatory duty on imported cereals enabled domestic growers to increase the cost of bread. On the other hand, exports of Sicilian wine and citrus fell by over a half when foreign countries retaliated by restricting imports from Italy; many farmers were ruined, wages were sometimes halved, and the more progressive areas of Sicilian agriculture suffered severely.

Where the central government might have compensated for this tariff was in the provision of essential public services, but Sicily with 10 per cent of Italy's population received less than 3 per cent of government expenditure on such a fundamental matter as irrigation and water control. Nor was road building greatly accelerated despite all the resources of the new government, and the main road across difficult country in the centre of the island still took thirty years to complete. Because Piedmontese laws were extended to the south, all except main roads became a charge on local authorities; but this was to apply northern experience to areas where utterly different conditions applied, and the poverty and tax policy of Sicilian villages (to say nothing of the greater cost of road-building in mountainous country) meant that few local roads were built. In the thirty years after the law on provincial highways, Messina did not complete even one of the routes prescribed. Furthermore local authorities, which were dominated by the landowners, took no action to recover the sheepruns from illegal enclosure. Half a dozen proprietors constructed private roads; a few thought of clubbing together to build routes of common access, only to find that mutual distrust was an insuperable obstacle; some, on the other hand, misused their power not only to enclose existing public highways but to hinder the building of new ones, perhaps fearing that faster travel would mean the end of feudal Sicily.

The results were crippling, because half the villages remained with no access by road, and some could not even be approached on horseback, while dried-out river beds often remained the chief means of communication. Bonfadini and his committee in 1876 were prevented by rainy weather from reaching the sizable town of Sciacca by land, and yet there was not even a proper harbour or quay for those who arrived by sea. Travel from Palermo to Girgenti still involved fording a river, and Catania was still two days' journey away. The interior of the island was so remote that news of the King's death in 1878 took several weeks to penetrate; and to go from Bivona to Ribera twenty-five kilometres away meant following a sometimes precipitous track for five times the distance, fording a river a dozen times. Wheeled transport was thus impossible, and the Lorenzoni report of 1910 said that many Sicilians had never seen a wheeled cart. Lack of roads was therefore still a primary fact in keeping Sicily backward and much of it uninhabited. The price of wheat, the main crop in the interior, still rose to being twice as high by the time it reached the coast. For the same reason, mechanisation on the farm and artificial fertilisers were too expensive.

Railroad construction began after 1861. Within five years there were twenty-five miles of track, and after fifteen years there were fifty miles completed. This, despite many grumbles, was a considerable achievement. Finance was the main problem, and it is unlikely that the Sicilian railways were financially profitable on any reasonable method of computation. Relatively little money was subscribed locally. The various towns quarrelled all the way up to the level of debates in parliament about which routes should be chosen; it was therefore almost impossible to plan an integrated regional network, and sometimes the choice was taken for electoral rather than economic reasons. Sicilian workmen, because of superstition or mafia threats, were sometimes unwilling to work on railroad construction, just as they had boycotted the electric telegraph earlier, and again labour had to be imported from the mainland despite high local unemployment. At last, in 1881, goods could travel by train from Palermo to Rome, albeit circuitously; the direct line from Palermo to Messina was opened in 1895. This was of great importance for Sicily. Several projects were considered for building a railway bridge or tunnel across the straits of Messina, but these after some discussion were put aside: there was not enough traffic to justify the expense—though perhaps the traffic could not be increased sufficiently until the money for a bridge could be found.

The sulphur industry, above all, needed better communications, for most of the mines were in the undeveloped provinces of Caltanissetta and Girgenti. Sulphur prices began to decline about 1875, but output went on increasing till the end of the century. By that time about five hundred mines were being worked and it was said that nearly a quarter of a million people were dependent on them. But a new steam process then opened up the huge deposits in Louisiana, and soon American sulphur began to reach Europe at under the cost price of all Sicilian produce except that from about a dozen mines. This was a tremendous blow, yet for many reasons little could be done about it, and mutual distrust among owners and managers made it very hard for them to take collective action. Demand was increasing for pesticides, as also for sulphate of ammonia and superphosphates, but insufficient was done to develop ancillary sulphuric acid or fertiliser plants, and production techniques were so imperfect that a third of the sulphur was still burnt as a fuel to smelt the rest. The new Gill method made the process much cheaper, but its foreign inventor could not secure payment of royalties, and this was typical of a general attitude which hindered the introduction of technical improvements.

Seventy-five families, the *latifondisti* of the area, owned most of the sulphur industry, and such was their political pressure that the Piedmontese mining law, quite exceptionally, was not extended to Sicily in 1861. In northern Italy the government controlled subsoil rights, and property could if necessary be expropriated for mining, just as neighbouring mines could also be forced to run as one unit. In Sicily, however, the landowners kept their rights of property, lamentable though this seemed to those who wanted large mines, rationally developed, and efficiently costed and financed. Small-holders, moreover, proved as restrictive and unenterprising as anyone. The mines were mostly let to *gabelloti*, and the fact that leases were generally for only nine years, or less, discouraged the introduction of machines and encouraged wasteful overproduction. According to official figures the landlords continued to take between 20 and 40 per cent of the profits in return for no work and no monetary investment, and one instance was mentioned in parliament of 67 per cent. This alone would explain why Sicilian sulphur became uncompetitive. Quite apart from the additional percentage due to the *gabelloto*, ground rent for a mine could be more than the wages of all the miners put together.

Inside the mines, most of the ore was still carried to the surface on the backs of children whose daily stint might be thirty journeys to the surface and who worked anything from six to twelve hours a day. A government commission in 1875 recommended a total prohibition against using women, or children under 14, as carriers; but a first tentative law in 1879 merely forbade the employment of girls and allowed that of boys only if they were over ten years old. Even this could not be enforced, and any further attempt to reduce child labour encountered dozens of well-organised representations from mine owners, municipalities and Chambers of Commerce. These representatives claimed to speak in the interests of the *carusi* themselves and their parents, but it was also stated specifically that, without child labour, most mines would be unprofitable. Few people made it their business to consider whether this cheap labour, by preventing mechanisation and keeping inefficient mines productive, was not a major economic as well as a moral disaster. The *contratto di carusato* was unknown elsewhere in Italy, even in the equally poor mining region of

Sardinia; though in the pumice caves of the Sicilian Lipari islands, according to a private report by Norman Douglas in 1895, children were given some of the more strenuous jobs and could be employed as early as the age of five.

The effects were appalling. The mining areas of Sicily had more homicides than anywhere in Italy, and much of their male population was totally unfit for military service. Many miners lived in underground grottos; others, and many of the children, lived permanently inside the mines. Labour was regularly organised by *mafiosi* to whom payments were due from both sides of the industry, and a *caruso* who fled from a mine without redeeming his indenture did so at his peril. Other criminal organisations existed at the ports and took a cut on exports. Pirandello's father, the manager of a sulphur mine, reported five attempts on his life by the local mafia, and probably violence was used to prevent price cuts or labour economies. Road and rail construction were forcibly opposed by the mule owners, because the wheeled transport which might have saved the industry would have forced them to change their job. Likewise at Ragusa, the muleteers refused to carry asphalt from the local mines to the railway station, because they obtained much more money for going all the way to the coastal ports; and they, too, were quite ready to back their monopoly by violence.

Government policy was therefore only one factor, and not the most important, in delaying economic development. Some Sicilians had irrationally imagined that the *risorgimento* would mean lower taxes and greater prosperity, and were disappointed when the reality proved more complicated and upsetting. The change from paternalism was no doubt harsher than it need have been; but in order to make Italy industrially strong, Sicily had to make some sacrifices. The exposure of her industry and agriculture to northern competition, however harsh, was a prerequisite of economic progress. It may be added that Sicily sometimes suffered when exceptions were made to the general rule: for instance, Florio was strong enough to extract a large official bounty for Sicilian shipping, but this eliminated some of the competition which might have reduced freight charges, and still did not prevent a catastrophic bankruptcy of one of his rivals in 1876. To take another exception, tax differentials favoured the *latifondi*, just as mining laws favoured the sulphur mine owners, but in both cases this was money wasted and ultimately a depressant to the Sicilian economy.

Government investment continued to be far heavier in the north, and there was bound to be some chafing by Sicilians against such apparently unfair treatment; but grumbling was also an excuse for not having to examine their own shortcomings.

There was an ingenuous expectation that politicians at Rome should be finding an answer to Sicily's problems without much help from Sicily itself. The two main government enquiries into the local economy, those of Jacini and Lorenzoni, both complained of lack of local assistance: three out of seven Chambers of Commerce refused to give any evidence to Lorenzoni, and the others gave very little, while most *latifondisti* refused to answer his questionnaire. Northerners would hardly want to invest much more time and money in Sicily until Sicilians were themselves confident in their own future, more prepared to help, and less eager to protect their private areas of privilege from the threat of change.

This was an old problem which had still not found a solution. As a parliamentary report of 1867 noted, the richest Sicilians distrusted trade or industry and were still too frightened to associate readily in business enterprises. A spirit of genuine co-operation would have been needed in order to make good wine on a commercial scale, or to embank rivers and drain marshes where this was beyond a single individual's capacity. The fact that group agreement could not be obtained over constructing a single mile of drainage gallery resulted in many mines at Lercara remaining inactive even after the arrival of the railway. The government commissioner, Bruzzo, therefore bewailed "the stupidity which thinks only of today, never of tomorrow, and the lack of common services which can be obtained only by association". Even in Messina there was said to be "an absolute lack of any spirit of association". Evidence given to a government commission in 1882 showed that Messina was in full decline, quite outstripped by Malta as a port for the greatly expanded trade brought to the Mediterranean by the Suez Canal. Sulphur was sold but hardly any sulphuric acid, lemons but little citric acid, sumac but not tannin, wine but almost no tartaric acid; linseed was exported but not linseed oil, and fermented grape juice was exported in vast quantities to be properly remade into wine and vermouth elsewhere. In 1889 it could be said that most of the managers of the big wineries were Frenchmen, and the four companies mining asphalt were all British.

Poverty was still given as an excuse for inaction even though plenty of cash had been forthcoming to buy up the ecclesiastical estates. A much more important reason was restrictive attitudes of mind and a standard of values unlike that of northern Italy. Prestige was still accorded not to the businessman but to the 'man of respect' and the rentier. One of the most widespread ambitions was to become a bureaucrat, an employee with even a poorly paid job in the administration. Savings went into the post office or into state bonds, which meant that they continued to leave the island; or else they were used for buying degrees and diplomas to qualify for an administrative post. Not for nothing did people say that the only prosperous industries in Sicily were the mafia, the acquisition of university degrees, and litigation at the Palermo bar.

The one exceptional family was still that of Florio, whose economic empire included most basic types of industry and was a standing proof that the acquisition of great wealth was not impossible. After Vincenzo Florio died in 1868, his son Ignazio doubled the family fortunes. His Oretea iron foundry and machine shop at Palermo employed 800 workers in 1876, using British coal and imported scrap, but it was inevitably a high-cost operation and produced only a few thousand tons of metal a year. Florio's shipping company flourished on government subsidies, though his predominant position in the cargo business from Palermo was more an advantage to himself than to the competitiveness of Sicilian exports. As soon as French competition became serious, he merged his shipping interests with the much bigger industry of the north. Likewise his textile and glass industries, despite some tax exemption, could not hold out against lower-cost products from the mainland. His ceramic firm, his Marsala wine interests and his fish canneries, all eventually fell into the hands of northern businesses which had little interest in Sicily except for what they could make out of it.

Ignazio Florio was almost certainly one of the richest men in Italy, though perhaps he absorbed some of the feudal mentality of Palermo as he tried to win acceptance in local society The fact that he failed to win full acceptance is important, and the local aristocracy boycotted the unveiling of his father's statue by the Hereditary Prince in 1874. One day when his career has been traced in greater detail, when we know more about his relations with the successive governments and his reasons for finally selling out of Sicily, we shall understand more about politics and society in this elusive environment.

PART 14

The Failure of Parliamentarism
1880–1922

Chapter 52

CRISPI AND THE *FASCI* REBELLION

The governments of the Left at Rome after 1876 did little more for Sicily than their predecessors; and even under two Sicilians, Crispi and di Rudinì, who between them held the office of Prime Minister for almost ten years in succession, conditions worsened. Crispi was more interested in colonies than in benefiting his native island. To make Italy militarily strong he needed high taxes and a severely controlled expenditure on public works, and this fell with special severity on the south. His government deferred some road building and brought railway construction to a halt, while his neurotic feelings of hostility towards France precipitated a tariff war which lost Sicily her chief foreign market. The French in North Africa had given material help to Sicily by facilitating immigration and putting down piracy, but in 1881, when they occupied Tunis across the narrow straits, Crispi boiled with patriotic indignation and truculently called for a second Sicilian Vespers against them.

To Crispi, as to other Sicilian ministers, the welfare of the island receded in importance as he became more involved in national affairs and began to climb the rungs of preferment at Rome. So long as submissive deputies were returned to parliament, he too, like his predecessors, allowed corrupt local clienteles to retain the substance of power, to violate the law at their pleasure, and keep Sicily unreformed. He once had been, as in part he remained, a radical reformer, but he was first an Italian patriot and secondly an ambitious man who liked power. From humble origins, he had become one of the chief *notabili* of Sicily, and his mere presence as an advocate in court could be enough to silence the opposition counsel. His electoral machine, moreover, depended on the backing of Florio and certain dubious factions for whom the government seems to have been a source of personal favours rather than of remedial legislation.

This is one reason why the reports of Bonfadini and Jacini were treated not as a basis for action but as a conscience-satisfying excuse to do nothing. As di Rudinì once said in private, "Our parliamentary system has resulted in abandoning Sicilians to exploitation by local factions." Di Rudinì was honest enough to admit from his own experience that a social question did exist, and he suspected that one day it would have to be tackled by a reform of local government. The sociologist, Vilfredo Pareto, went much further: like Tajani and Franchetti he stood sufficiently outside the system to be outright in his condemnation, and spoke of "groups of criminals who flourish under government protection". Pareto saw Crispi as inescapably dependent on such people; this was why Sicily still had few schools, hospitals or roads; this is why the government did nothing about the massive misappropriation of communal property by the local oligarchies. Pareto favourably compared the British government of Malta, and thought it explained why the Maltese were more loyal to Britain than Sicilians to Italy. "The government does nothing to suppress these abuses, because the same persons who dominate the communal councils are the chief electors of the deputies, who, in their turn, employ their influence with the government to screen the misdeeds of their friends and partisans."

Crispi had moved so far away from home that he underestimated the danger to public order in leaving the peasants at the mercy of their employers. He himself in 1860 had encouraged these same peasants to make an indispensable contribution to the welding of an Italian nation, promising them in return a new deal; but subsequently a bitter sense of injustice had grown up over the way ecclesiastical and village property had been dissipated. Crispi's friends warned him in the 1880s that a social war was building up, and that local authorities were continuing to place the main burden of taxation on people who were already too near to starvation. This was a time when agricultural prices were sharply falling, as railways and steamships brought competition from American grain. A depression was then intensified by Crispi's trade war with France, by the arrival of vine disease and a reduction in mining wages. A British consul could write in 1891 that "the price of labour has not risen in Sicily during the last 20 years, while the cost of living has doubled".

The common people were not quick to rebel against these worsening circumstances. We hear of a group of peasants electing one of themselves to be a King, but such utopian opposition was not dangerous. Only after a year of really bad harvest did they become less docile: the flagellants then processed the streets as they had done in 1647 and 1773; images of the saints again had their ornaments confiscated and were put in irons amid general derision. Just as in 1860 and 1866, religious enthusiasm could then be harnessed by popular preachers who called people to abandon the priests for a new religion of Christ. Economic distress, when overlaid with this kind of chiliastic religious excitement, easily led to acts of violence.

By 1890 there were certain changes in society which made the sense of dissatisfaction more articulate. A few farm labourers could now read and write, and as conscripts elsewhere in Italy they had learnt of altogether new needs and possibilities. In a number of villages, minority groups among the gentry, excluded from influence and jobbery, had a casual interest in stirring up agitation; and a growing class of doctors, lawyers and other university-educated men were ready to formulate and canalise a widespread feeling of frustration. There were also a few outright revolutionaries who advocated socialisation of the land and the mines: one socialist, de Felice Giuffrida, won the municipal elections at Catania in 1889 and formed a popularist administration, though a few months later the outraged Crispi had him dismissed. Crispi told parliament of his regret that workers were striking for better pay in the sulphur mines and were beginning to show an inclination towards violence.

Sicilian villages were, on average, three times as large as those in Piedmont; and this fact, together with the concentration of workers in the mines, made it possible for agitation to spread easily, especially when groups or *fasci* began to form an embryonic trade union movement. Some of the early *fasci* were much like the old guilds, interested in sickness benefits, funeral insurance and the establishment of co-operative shops. Some were run by socialists though others were dominated by elements of the mafia, and some were simply part of the faction fight which went on in each village to control municipal government. Occasionally, therefore, the *fasci* were merely the old clienteles in a different guise; but usually they were vocal champions of lower-class unrest, and this was a novel and offensive phenomenon which required a firm government response.

For the first time in history, villagers were discovering how they could organise against illegal enclosures of land, and occasionally agricultural strikes succeeded in obtaining more generous contracts. It was not usually the absentee aristocratic landlord who was the target of such pressure, and the Nelson estates at Bronte suffered little at this critical moment. It was rather the middle-class landowners, the provincial *galantuomini*, who were the object of popular violence. The half-Spanish Duke of Ferrandina had at long last agreed to give the villagers of Caltavuturo about six hundred acres as compensation for their loss of 'promiscuous rights', but the village oligarchy filched this land for themselves; so, early in 1893, the peasants occupied it illegally. The municipal authorities opened fire and there were fifty casualties. The radical deputy, Colajanni, warned parliament that the same terrible story was waiting to be repeated elsewhere and a civil war might develop if justice were not done quickly.

Some of the landowners, on the other hand, asked the government to dissolve the *fasci* and bring in the army, promising that once this was done they would increase wages; but Giovanni Giolitti, the Prime Minister, did not believe them. While he deplored violence by either side, he argued that strikes were no crime and the peasants had every right to agitate against manifest illegality. In the eyes of many proprietors, Giolitti's neutral attitude threatened to undermine the control of elections and local taxation which underpinned their power and wealth. They saw with alarm that the old *mafioso* methods of subduing the peasantry seemed to be breaking down, as a new and unwelcome element inserted itself into local politics. In May 1893 this threat reached the point where a regional socialist congress met in Sicily; then in July some of the peasants met to discuss common problems; and several months later there was a congress of sulphur miners. All this seemed to many landowners like deliberate provocation. More repressive means were therefore adopted by the village authorities, and this led to yet more violence: soon it was the old story of tax offices being attacked, prisons opened and land registers in the town halls being burnt. Some demonstrators cried "Long live the King", for they hoped that the central government was on their side; some were led by the clergy; others raised the red flag.

At this point Crispi was urgently brought back as Prime Minister, with a policy of martial law. Crispi believed, or said he believed, that the *fasci* were trying to sever Sicily from Italy with help from Russia and France: this was his remarkable excuse for sending the fleet and thirty thousand soldiers to quell the revolt. He was helped by the fact that Sicilian deputies and the local notables had their own reasons for welcoming military repression. One Sicilian senator privately explained that Sicily was an oriental country which could be governed only by force, and hence it would be useless to have an enquiry into the revolt or to pay much attention to the qualms of public opinion. It was even asserted in parliament that Sicily had no particular economic hardship, no special weaknesses in local government, no discriminatory taxes which needed reform; and an unfortunately publicised meeting of Sicilian landowners called on the government to go to the root of the trouble and abolish compulsory education. These men thought that the army alone could restore their authority. It did not matter that most *fasci* had not rebelled, nor that some had tried to stop violence; for it was politically desirable to suppress them all and to ensure that military tribunals gave savage sentences to de Felice and other left-wing leaders.

Crispi was determined to reimpose a national unity which he thought in danger. He was equally determined to use the emergency to stage new elections in which he could displace his predecessor's parliamentary majority, even though in doing so he was bound to antagonise many of the *latifondisti*. Tens of thousands of electors were struck off the roll, many of them no doubt quite properly for in some districts half the registered electors seem to have been men of straw; but even university professors were disenfranchised on the grounds of illiteracy, and many electors were arrested to keep them away from the polls. Convicts were given provisional release from prison in return for using their influence on behalf of government candidates. Not for nothing did de Felice call Crispi the worst *mafioso* of them all.

The Prime Minister was not, however, deceived by landlords who said that there existed no social problem in the island; and some of his friends were prepared to admit in private that the rebels had a reasonable case. Soon he had still other reasons for changing tack. The socialist scare may or may not have been widely believed at first, but in time it came to look very unsubstantial, and the publicity attached to the trial of the deputies de Felice and Garibaldi Bosco persuaded moderate opinion that Crispi's repressive policy had been miscalculated. As these cases dragged out, northerners were made aware by the newspapers of the other side of the story, and of how the selfishness of a few people could keep one part of Italy in permanent semi-rebellion. They learnt that the food taxes produced twice as much revenue in Sicily as in the infinitely richer provinces of Lombardy or Piedmont. Fully a third of the income of Palermo came from taxes on flour paid largely by the poor; and whereas landowners were strong enough to bring the property taxes down, the food taxes were always the point of least resistance whenever revenue had to be augmented.

Suddenly Crispi proposed a thorough reform of the *latifondi*. Since his African policy had completely unbalanced the budget, he thought he could disarm the reformers by tackling the land question. Prosperity and social order evidently depended on making agriculture more productive, yet Sicilian landlords would not voluntarily carry out the improvements which the experts said were possible. On the assumption that land and labour were both under-utilised, he therefore proposed that all uncultivated properties should be liable to conversion into smallholdings; so should all private estates over 250 acres in size and any *latifondi* still owned by the villages. Learning from previous mistakes, the new units were to be between twelve and fifty acres in size, and held on leases of not less than fifteen years' duration. Auctions would not be used, nor could lots be accumulated in one hand, but tax concessions would be granted to encourage intensive methods of agriculture, and cheap credit would be provided so that even poor leaseholders could make a success of the scheme. Most drastic of all, recalcitrant proprietors might be expropriated.

Crispi made this revolutionary proposal apparently without so much as informing his cabinet, and clearly it was a hurried and insufficiently considered move. It aroused the most tremendous opposition: not so much from north Italians, who were surprisingly unmoved, but from the Sicilian deputies. In hoping that the landowners and their political cliques would trust him as they had done in 1893, Crispi was overestimating their intelligence and unselfishness and underestimating their power; but as soon as he saw his parliamentary majority disappearing, he thought it prudent to drop his bill before it could be discussed in the Chamber.

The Marquis di Rudinì, who himself as a wealthy Sicilian landowner led this opposition, again became Prime Minister in 1896. He knew that the socialist scare in Sicily had been a complete fraud. His first aim was to reduce taxes by withdrawing from Crispi's ambitious African commitments. His land policy was also quite sensible, to keep the *latifondi* intact but made more efficient by giving tenants better credit and longer leases. In order to destroy Crispi's electoral machine he tried to ally his own conservatives with the extreme Left; he also courted the Sicilian autonomists and appointed a special regional commissioner in the island with some independence of Rome.

The idea of returning to the status of a semi-autonomous region might have been expected to attract many Sicilians, but the experiment did not prove a success. Giovanni Codronchi, the commissioner, was full of good intentions, but as a northerner he found the cards stacked against him, and since he based his administration on Palermo, there was a strong sectional opposition from Messina and elsewhere. He planned to reform local government and see that local revenues were spent properly. He intended to introduce rural banks, carry out some division of the land and undercut the usurious rates of interest which kept the peasants in bondage. But he found Sicily a world where the ordinary rules of politics did not apply and where local cliques could easily frustrate his programme of tax reliefs and credit for the poor. Codronchi quickly discovered that mafia-type networks were in existence all over the island, organised on very businesslike lines, with their capitalists and technical directors, their political contact men, right down to the common criminals who did the hatchet work; and any politician who did not work in with at least some of these networks evidently had small chance of success.

Regretfully the commissioner had to admit that nine-tenths of the Sicilian deputies were opposed to his experiment in Sicilian autonomy. Desperately, even blatantly, he tried to rig the elections, using all the devices which Crispi had used before him, but with less success. De Felice, though a member of parliament, was declared under age and incapable of even voting; and in rejoinder this socialist leader accused the government of using the mafia for political purposes. Crispi was too strongly entrenched at Palermo to be ousted, and many other Sicilians deserted Codronchi when he attacked their private electoral enclaves. Clearly the local clienteles were not going to accept reform from di Rudinì any more than from Giolitti or Crispi, and they could easily play one politician off against another to ensure that things remained much as before.

Chapter 53

THE MAFIA AND POLITICAL
CORRUPTION

Some of the sinister background to this political rivalry was revealed through the unexpected publicity given to the murder in 1893 of a distinguished public servant, the Marquis Notarbartolo. This man had seen at first hand how the higher echelons of the mafia infiltrated municipal administration. He had seen them in Palermo's medical services when he was on the hospital board. After several notorious bankruptcies had revealed financial irregularities in the Bank of Sicily, he was made a Director of the Bank to put things to rights, and he found that a number of private fortunes had been created by the manipulation of credit and then protected through 'political contributions'. Many people must have been anxious to secure his removal before he had time to unravel this embezzlement and political corruption; at all events he was soon dismissed. As an additional warning, in traditional mafia fashion, he was kidnapped and made to pay a large ransom.

For years Notarbartolo for some reason remained silent, but eventually he dared to pass certain incriminating information to the government. Within hours, his confidential letter to a minister was known and in detail to those he was accusing: the obvious explanation was that someone in the government had obligations towards certain Grand Electors, notably to Palizzolo, one of the Bank's governors. Palizzolo, the boss of Caccamo and a manager of various Palermo civic charities, had been excluded from parliament for corrupt practices in his inexperienced youth, but had since become an outwardly respectable deputy who from the time of Depretis onwards voted unobtrusively and fairly consistently for whichever party was in power. He and his friends were using the Bank's money for improper purposes, and these probably included paying some of Crispi's political expenses; so that when Crispi's corrupt relation with other Roman banks became known, there was a sudden fear in Palermo that di Rudinì might manage to have his old friend Notarbartolo reappointed as Director of the Bank of Sicily and so uncover yet further malversations. At this point Notarbartolo was brutally murdered, with every sign of it being a mafia crime.

For years an inquiry to discover who paid the assassins dragged on, but one suspect, Palizzolo, was not even interrogated while Crispi was in power. When di Rudinì again became Prime

Minister in 1896, Codronchi asked permission to bring up Palizzolo's name; but on reflection the matter was allowed to rest and once more he was elected to parliament. After another change of government he was brought to trial in 1899. But the police lied in court to secure his acquittal, and documents implicating him disappeared from the Palermo police station. At long last, in 1902, a non-Sicilian jury convicted him, but their judgement was set aside; and, ten years after the murder, another trial resulted in an open verdict after many witnesses had unaccountably changed their stories.

Many people no doubt welcomed this reversal, for mafia help and 'the Sicilian vote' were as important as ever to politicians of many different colours. A dangerously hysterical local patriotism had also been aroused among Sicilians of both Right and Left who, even while resenting Palizzolo for giving away the worst side of Palermo's barbarous machine politics, resented still more the supercilious and sometimes contemptuous reaction of northerners. Some Italians were at this point writing about the south in terms of a racial inferiority which would explain Sicilian delinquency as incorrigible; and Sicilians, outraged by this attitude, lionised Palizzolo after his acquittal. A special ship was chartered to escort him home in triumph and he found himself a local hero. Sicilian pride once again was protecting the mafia and condemning Sicily to further damage.

The profound political corruption underlying this episode was described by a foreign observer, Bolton King, just after 1900.

> Where the Mafia is strong, it is impossible for a candidate to win a parliamentary or local election unless he promises it his protection. Thus it has its patrons in the Senate and Chamber, who use it for political and worse ends; and the government has its well-understood relations with the *mafiosi* grand electors. The gangs are allowed free rein; they have licenses to carry arms, while honester citizens are denied them; they know that there will be no interference with a discreet blackmailing, provided that they terrorize the opposition voters at election time.

Nothing in the whole peninsula, thought Bolton King, was more sinister than this.

The system was taken over by Giolitti and used on occasion to support his paramount position in Italian politics between 1900 and the outbreak of war in 1914. Giolitti had the reputation of a left-of-centre liberal, but his liberalism was more in evidence elsewhere, and he was said to think of Sicily just as a group of deputies to conciliate. In four general elections he perfected the art of winning a majority: at the lowest level the price of votes was quoted openly in the newspapers, and private armies were allowed to intimidate voters by every means up to and including assassination. In certain areas the blandishments and bullying of Giolitti's party agents were successfully resisted, and some Sicilian radicals, notably Colajanni, denounced these procedures and their terrible effect on local politics; but in general such conduct was thought nothing exceptional. Hence the quality of Sicilian deputies remained poor. Their job in Rome was not so much to champion Sicilian or national interests; it was rather to seek patronage for the local bosses and to act as an intermediary in negotiating with government departments.

In return for support in the constituencies and in parliament, Giolitti and the liberal politicians were prepared to turn a blind eye. He liked to recall with cynical amusement how one Sicilian town, in order to avoid tax, persuaded the authorities to list it as missing and untraceable. Sicilian politics were to him as unintelligible as they were unchangeable, and he was too shrewd a politician to support reforms which could only cause offence. Boss rule could not be stopped, so it should be accepted with a good grace. Under his auspices the word 'liberal', like the word '*galantuomo*', hence developed a pejorative connotation which eventually made fascism seem the lesser evil.

Each area of Sicily had its particularities, but everywhere parties tended to grow up around a person rather than a policy. Wanting to obtain influence with the police, needing a gun license, a lower tax assessment, a personal recommendation, or a road-building contract, the more unscrupulous seekers after power had a common interest. Sometimes their first step would be to perpetrate some atrocious crime so as to create a quick and incontrovertible impression of fear and respect. Once impunity from the law had been established, they had to make themselves indispensable to the Prefect as a controller of votes and a curb on petty crime. It was also important to multiply jobs so as to place relatives in positions of authority and establish a network of unrequited obligations. From such a position of strength it was easy to become rich, to own land and ultimately to influence policy. This in time would place a man in a position where he would determine the local taxes and control their allocation. The audit of local finances would be relaxed; voting registers and the selection of juries would be carefully supervised; water supply would not be laid on to villages where rich landowners already had enough water of their own; and, above all, land owned collectively by the villages would be purloined.

Boss rule of this kind became an unqualified disaster, and its effects were soon visible everywhere. Popular education continued to be resisted as a waste of money, with the plausible argument that in any case poor families preferred their children to remain at home and look after the goats. Bad roads, the lack of good ports, the spread of malaria as rivers became more and more prone to flooding each year, all this was conveniently blamed on the government, but in fact it followed naturally from these peculiarities of Sicily's political system. Worst of all were the effects on popular morality and the prevalent attitude towards politics.

The best-known Sicilian politician in the early twentieth century was not the independent-minded Colajanni, nor was it the radical priest Don Sturzo, who was another critic of this system; it was Nunzio Nasi, leading citizen of the pre-eminently *mafioso* city of Trapani. Nasi was another deputy who judiciously supported Crispi and Giolitti in turn, and by so doing built up an enormously powerful clientele which included both conservatives and leftists. For forty years his careful attention to parish-pump interests enabled him to continue as Trapani's representative in parliament. An inflated municipal pay roll provided plenty of jobs for his friends, and a well-placed vote in parliament earned him a fairly free hand from the government. No outside body was allocated to disturb his control of the electoral lists. But eventually he made the mistake of becoming a minister; for at Rome different standards of behaviour were required, the press was less easily muzzled, and there existed an opposition waiting for a chance to criticise. Instinctively, and without realising the dangers, Nasi went on using the only techniques of government with which he was familiar, inflating his entertainment and travelling expenses, and occasionally misappropriating minor sums of public money to reward himself and to increase his powers of patronage.

None of this amounted to very much, and perhaps Nasi was genuinely surprised when rival politicians—some of them Sicilians—took the excuse to promote a criminal action against him. Trapani, which had done particularly well out of the minister's benefactions, then made him into a martyr: portraits of the King and Queen were burned; Victor Emanuel Street was renamed Nunzio Nasi Street; and for a short while the French flag even flew over the Town Hall. This sealed his fate. Nasi prudently disappeared abroad for three years, but when he returned he was impeached before the Senate and found guilty of peculation. Even on the eastern seaboard of Sicily there were riots against this verdict and against the supposed slight thrown on the island by prudish, hypocritical northerners. Luigi Pirandello and his distinguished fellow-writer, Luigi Capuana (who had personally benefited from Nasi's patronage), fully shared the sense of outrage.

A fierce press campaign broke out against the Italian 'foreigners', with extravagant appeals to memories of the Sicilian Vespers against "a slavery worse than that of the Bourbons". A large subscription was raised, and Nasi was brought home to a triumphal reception as great as Palizzolo had received. Though barred from parliament, he went on being elected again and again by over-whelming majorities.

Catania on the east coast was different from Trapani, yet not unrecognisably different. With one of the fastest population growths in all Italy, with (unlike Messina) a productive agricultural hinterland, and with reputedly no mafia at all, Catania was becoming the richest industrial Sicilian city. On several occasions it was administered by a coalition under the socialist de Felice. Crispi's harsh repression of the *fasci* had, by reaction, helped the spread of socialism, and the Sicilian socialists eventually took on a local colouring when they found that they fitted not too awkwardly into the general scheme of Sicilian politics. De Felice was a decorative and extremely combative anarchist-socialist. His views were not always consistent, but his drive and personality made him, like Nasi, the object of enthusiastic municipal pride. He readily collaborated on occasion with his close friend the Archbishop, or with the *latifondista* di Rudinì, or with the big businessman Florio. At one point Giolitti was supporting the socialists in Catania at the same time as he backed the anti-socialists at Palermo, and this was quite proper in an environment where personalities counted for more than policies.

De Felice's reform programme promised a general attack on corruption and inefficiency, and it attracted many of a remarkable new generation of intellectuals centred at Catania; yet his own coalition seems to have become only a little less inefficient and corrupted than the rest. By 1911 there was not a great deal to show for his reforms, and the town was heavily in debt. The familiar criticisms were made that he had employed favouritism in contracts, misappropriated charitable funds and multiplied salaried posts for the benefit of his followers. It was said that he had an arrangement with some of the most reactionary barons, and his electoral machine recruited the 'mountaineers' and goatherds to come down with their ugly weapons at election time.

The Catania of Verga, Capuana, Mario Rapisardi and de Roberto was no mean city as a cultural centre; but the impact of these men on the rest of the island was not large, and most creative artists and writers preferred to live in Rome or Milan if they could. Pirandello wrote some dialect plays, and both he and Verga had an enormous nostalgia for Sicily and a guilt about leaving it. Verga's themes were obsessively Sicilian, and it comes as a shock to find him writing from Milan for his friends to send him a collection of Sicilian phrases to make his work sound yet more authentic. Likewise Pirandello preferred to return home every few years to obtain fresh plots and local atmosphere; but he never stayed for long.

If the intellectuals failed to change Sicily, one relevant fact was the defectiveness of Sicilian education. Not only was there a general 58 per cent illiteracy in 1911, but the three local universities were still geared to producing lawyers and bureaucrats, and had a built-in prejudice against the practical agricultural and engineering studies of which there was so much more need. Local families who could afford it preferred to send their children to universities elsewhere. The urge to leave Sicily, coupled with the strong predilection for white-collar employment, had the result that educated Sicilians obtained a disproportionate number of the administrative posts at Rome, which northerners affected to despise. Some people called this a grave loss for Sicily, and there was no reciprocal immigration of other Italians to compensate for it. Unfortunately the 'continental' Prefects and professors who were posted to Sicily regarded this as a novitiate or a punishment from which they should escape as soon as possible. The letters of the poet Pascoli, when he taught Latin at Messina after 1898, show how cut off such a man could feel from the mainstream of national life.

Sicilians and non-Sicilians alike evidently found the local atmosphere unhelpful and even sinister. The presence of the mafia, the relics of feudalism, the lack of a large literate class, all this was unattractive. It was easy to be bored by a world which was so closed and provincial. Sicilian deputies were called to order in parliament for speaking of 'Sicily' and 'Italy' as though these were two different places; northerners spoke in exactly the same way, only no one noticed. Indeed, though great numbers of Sicilians crossed the straits of Messina on military service, very few Italians knew Sicily at first hand, and this helped to accentuate the sense of isolation and inferiority.

Strong efforts were, of course, made by both sides to bridge this gap and make Sicily more obviously Italian. Military service was very important, and so was literature. Verga, in many spectacular short stories about his home environment, tried to make his characters speak with a sufficiently orthodox Italian syntax to be generally understood, even though this made them implausible to Sicilian readers. Partly for this reason, he was surprisingly unappreciated in his native Catania, just as he was sometimes positively disliked there for publicising the shabbier side of local life; and yet Verga himself spoke Italian badly and was not free from a distinct provincialism of outlook. A contributory factor in delaying the cultural fusion of Sicily was that some schools continued to use dialect in instruction. Gradually this changed, and by 1917 the Sicilian philosopher, Giovanni Gentile, hazarded the opinion that there no longer existed a Sicilian cultural world distinct from Italian; others strongly disputed his reasoning, and indeed it was all too easy to argue that a number of distinct sub-cultures existed even inside Sicily itself.

The differences between western and eastern Sicily were without doubt growing wider. Soon after 1900, for example, Palermo was overtaken by Catania as a port for overseas trade, and this signified a great reversal of fortunes. Palermitans went on referring disdainfully to other Sicilians as *regnicoli* or *villani*, but this vanity now had a hollow ring. Over much of western Sicily the ex-feudatories and their hangers-on were still the arbiters of taste and conduct. Habits of behaviour learnt on the *latifondi*, including the employment of retinues of armed *bravi*, were applied in Palermo to city politics and the practice of boss rule. *Spagnolismo* or 'Spanishness' was one generic word used elsewhere in Sicily to describe what was thought wrong with this Palermitan environment; others preferred to blame the Arab rebels who in the thirteenth century had been driven into the hill fastnesses behind Palermo and had there learnt to live by the law of the tribe and the jungle; while still others pointed out that the separatist aristocracy of Palermo had for centuries profited from the subsidisation of gangsterism and could hardly grumble if the sorcerer's apprentice proved disobedient. In any case, Palermo had lost its political hegemony over the rest of Sicily, and this had as depressive an effect in the west as it provided a release of energies elsewhere.

In eastern Sicily, however, a more open society and a more forward-looking attitude helped to create conditions where it was harder for criminals to win economic and political power. The currently fashionable racialism of Lombroso's school of anthropology was drawn upon to stress that eastern Sicily had been more Greek while western Sicily had been more Arabic; but even those who disliked this explanation could see that the traders and artisans of Messina and Catania were more aware of the damage which mafia-type behaviour could do and so were more on guard against it. These eastern towns were physically closer to the rest of Italy, and this was important for them. Their handicraft industry had succumbed to north-Italian competition much more quickly than that of western Sicily, with the result that they were also quicker to enter the factory age. Commercial investment was here as important as landed property, and enterprise was more likely to be admired and rewarded. Moreover socialism, just like jacobinism a century before, was stronger on the eastern coast and frequently acted as an idealistic and purifying force.

Even agriculture was different here. Over large areas of the east, tenancies were longer, there was a greater diversification of crops, more intensive production and more irrigation. On the fertile slopes of Mount Etna, smallholdings could be truly small and yet truly efficient, while the rivers Simeto and Alcantara were partially fed from snowfields and so retained some flow in the drought of summer. Round Modica and Ragusa, the *latifondi* were disappearing, rich people managed their own estates in person, and both rich and poor sometimes lived on their farms. At Acireale, citrus farms on average were to be nearer ten acres in size then the one-acre holdings which were common round Palermo, and growers were therefore strong enough to hold out against mafia control of marketing and water supplies. The province of Syracuse had the least crime in all Sicily, as it also had the best roads, more wells and windmills, and the best relations between owners and labour. Jacini and Damiani in the 1880s found that only four villages in Syracuse province were exposed to mafia activity, and only five in that of Catania; this was negligible compared to the west, and moreover the influence of the gangs was growing less. According to the British consul ten years later, in eastern Sicily people "rarely go armed", whereas in the west it was "universal"; and he was also impressed to find that, far from co-operating with brigandage, individuals in the east would act to put it down. This was a remarkable and hopeful fact.

One reason for the strength of the mafia at Palermo was that this town had for so long been the centre of government. Palermo had therefore been a fountain-head for the patronage needed by every boss and politician. In this town was the one really large sub-proletariat of unemployed, and here lived most of the rich landowners, as well as the lawyers and fixers who had always battened upon this aristocratic world. In the hill villages surrounding Palermo the gangs learnt their trade. Once they were established in the relatively prosperous *conca d'oro*, they dominated the routes into Palermo and the main food markets of the town.

The provinces of Trapani, Caltanissetta and Girgenti in western Sicily were almost as bad, and evidence from the magistrates' courts—unless this should just be interpreted as meaning that statistics were now more comprehensive—confirms that mafia crimes here were much more numerous in 1910 than forty years previously. The murder rate in Caltanissetta province was nearly ten times as high as in Messina, twenty times that of Venice, and here the statistics cannot have been entirely wrong. Some areas, wrote Bruccoleri about 1910, were completely under the control of brigands, who could even use the columns of leading newspapers to demand protection money from their victims. Here, just as Franchetti had once found, every landowner still paid dues to the underworld or else he would infallibly lose his crops; and these dues could be as high as the taxes paid to the government. In return he obtained a useful control over his peasants and much greater security than was provided by the police.

Already by 1910, mafia elements who had once emigrated to America were returning with more refined techniques of crime. One such was Vito Cascio Ferro, a friend of powerful Sicilian politicians, a man who seems to have come nearer than anyone else to organising the various racketeering groups into a syndicate of crime. In 1909, when Lieutenant Petrosino of the New York police came to Palermo to study the background of the American 'Black Hand', he was immediately assassinated on arrival, and Don Vito boasted of being the assassin. This so-called 'head of the mafia' perfected a system by which he imposed a levy on every commercial or industrial enterprise in his area of influence. He also controlled a fishing fleet which exported stolen cattle. The effect of these returned *americani* on every department of Sicilian life— and not least on the language—still awaits a full study, but it was undoubtedly important, for good and bad.

Most contemporary students of the subject—Giuseppe Alongi, Sonnino, King, Napoleone Colajanni, Mercadante, Bruccoleri— agreed that the mafia was the most distressing problem in Sicily. They also agreed that politicians and government, just because they needed local support, deliberately chose to allow criminals a wide freedom of action. When Giolitti was taxed with government permissiveness, he said that he was powerless where so many ordinary Sicilians were in collusion with the *malavita*: the fact may have been true, though it was hardly an excuse for his inaction. Possibly, like many northerners, Giolitti believed or half-believed the outraged indignation of most Sicilian politicians when they protested that the mafia either did not exist at all or that it was an essentially honourable society. Certainly this would have been a comforting reason for not challenging the various sub-affiliations of the political machine on which his majority depended.

Chapter 54

GIOLITTI AND THE ECONOMY

While the period of Giolitti brought prosperity to the rest of Italy, Sicilians were slow off the mark. At a time when Italy was experiencing a great expansion in industry, the numbers of industrially employed in Sicily declined between the censuses of 1901 and 1911. Sicilians' grumble was that more money left the country in taxation than the island's economy would stand, but northerners rather preferred to blame Sicily's social system and lack of commercial-mindedness for the slowness to develop her natural resources. Sulphur and citrus fruit, which were now Sicily's most valuable products and among Italy's principal exports, were each an example of resources inadequately exploited. When the lemon growers of Syracuse formed a sales and research organisation, mutual jealousies soon broke it up, for not enough people even in progressive eastern Sicily would acknowledge a common interest in pest control or keeping up standards of quality. Lack of any spirit of association also explains why the first electricity-generating plants in eastern Sicily apparently owed little to local investment. Few people were prepared to make short-term sacrifices for future gain or for the benefit of the community. Producers wanted immediate profits, even where, as in essential oils for perfumery, or in sumac exports for leather work, this led to adulteration and so to the undermining of an important trade.

In 1896, owing largely to foreign initiative but also with the backing of Florio and a small amount of local capital, an Anglo-Sicilian company was formed to rationalise the sulphur industry on a voluntary basis, before it succumbed to American competition. In ten years of life this company showed that Sicilian sulphur might still be profitable so long as output could be controlled and bi-lateral arrangements made with the rival American producers. Yet though the mine owners had agitated for just such an organisation, half of them thought that they stood to gain even more by remaining independent: they were delighted when it succeeded in raising prices, but only so that they could undersell and make its achievement temporary. The result was that the company, after making a good profit for its foreign shareholders and bringing the Sicilian sulphur trade to its maximum point of efficiency, ceased operations in 1906.

This suddenly threatened the industry with ruin. Obviously so many inefficient mines could not exist in free market conditions without radical reform. In a series of parliamentary debates, some speakers said that the only hope was expropriation, or at least to limit the royalties paid to mine owners; others suggested that proper enforcement of existing laws against night work and child labour would eliminate higher-cost mines; but since neither of these solutions was politically acceptable, the government set up a compulsory sales organisation guaranteeing minimum prices. This proved a complete disaster, but unfortunately many land-owners stood to gain by it, and their powerful lobby was repre-sented inside the cabinet by another of the Majorana family, who now advocated straight government subsidisation. The counter-argument was put by another Sicilian, the political philosopher Gaetano Mosca, who objected that feather-bedding would en-courage more uneconomic production and merely protect the industry from a thorough overhaul. Mosca adventurously sug-gested, with Keynesian prevision, that it might be cheaper to pay miners to remain idle than pay them to go on mining; but the lobby was too strong, and the economy suffered accordingly. By 1910 the cost of American sulphur was less than half that of Sicilian, and Spanish sulphur was even being imported into Sicily itself. Moreover a new and more efficient mining industry was growing up on the mainland of Italy which eventually almost excluded Sicilian sulphur from mainland Italian markets.

This was one way in which Sicily proved her own worst enemy. The landed interest acted to delay industrial progress, and even in go-ahead Catania there was strong support for just this policy of protected and uncompetitive monopoly which was so demoralis-ing. When Florio sold his industrial and commercial interests to northerners, this removed what some people had hoped would become a fruitful element of challenge and innovation in the Sicilian economy. Meanwhile most Sicilian parliamentary depu-ties, though angry about government neglect when talking to their electors, needed too many favours to cause the government much embarrassment at Rome. The result was lack of criticism and economic stagnation. Luigi Einaudi could complain that it took three months for Sicilian wine to reach north Italy by rail, with the result that the wine not only lost its virtue of cheapness but was undrinkable without adulteration. Citrus fruit similarly spoiled in transit. Road building continued to be drearily slow, and the fine harbours of Syracuse and Augusta still remained deserted for most of the year. At Palermo itself the lightermen were able to resist the building of sufficient quays, and many passengers went on having to disembark in rowing boats.

The great city of Messina was largely destroyed in 1908 by an earthquake, the worst of a long series of eruptions and earthquakes in eastern Sicily; and a great wave of water carried away whole farms and villages. No one ever knew quite how many were killed, but over the whole area it was not far short of 100,000, and communications were so shattered that it took several days before government help was forthcoming. People buried alive were still being released over a week later, and fires burnt for a fortnight. None of Messina's many earlier disasters caused so much havoc, and some of the ruins were still unrepaired when war brought yet another disaster in 1943. The remarkable thing was that the inhabitants each time continued hopefully to build up life anew. Messina was the nearest point of contact with the mainland, and the damage to its port was the more consequential for the island as a whole. The simple fact that so many of the town archives were destroyed goes far to explain why Sicilian history has to be told largely from the one-sided point of view of Palermo.

In the years 1907–10, a detailed socio-economic investigation into Sicily was made on behalf of parliament by Professor Lorenzoni. His report described what was still a feudal world. The old aristocracy still owned most of the large estates, and all too often they still conceived it their interest to retard economic development. Conditions of soil and climate were very difficult, but a dozen *latifondisti* gave positive evidence that some large estates could be greatly improved. The other few hundred, however, who made up less than a tenth of 1 per cent of the population but owned half of Sicily, had little intention of building farm houses or undertaking land reclamation. Things were changing for the better, but only exceptionally were leases longer than six years even though this had been denounced for a century as a principal cause of Sicilian poverty. Only exceptionally were leasehold contracts framed to encourage long-term improvements, and the result was overcropping for quick profits and the uneconomic growing of cereals on barren land which sometimes produced as little as two or three times the quantity of seed sown.

Lorenzoni referred to a number of expert studies which showed that Sicilian agriculture could be radically bettered. Italian hydraulic engineers had demonstrated that there were large untapped supplies of water; but although wells, steam pumps and windmills caused greatly improved production in some areas, they were completely unheard of in many other places where they could have been cheaply installed. Canevari and Travaglia in the 1870s had recommended building a number of dams, but nothing had been done; and though the government allocated money for the upkeep of embanked rivers, this was more useful to northern Italy than to provinces where such rivers hardly existed. Only about 2.5 per cent of the money allocated by the government to 'bonification' between 1861 and 1920 was in fact spent in Sicily. Eucalyptus trees had been introduced from Australia via Algeria in the 1860s, and by 1880 were showing good results in diminishing erosion and marshland, but few private individuals had the patience or public spirit to replant trees and obey the existing forest laws. When the government tried to drain marshes or carry out irrigation works, sometimes it encountered opposition from landowners, because they thought water supplies too valuable to be left in public ownership. Yet this traditional resistance to change was becoming more and more anachronistic, and low-production *latifondismo* was far too expensive an impediment for a fast-growing population of three and a half million.

Some changes for the better were certainly visible by 1910. For one thing northern attitudes were changing. There was still an occasional tendency to excuse government failings by arguing that Sicily must be in some way incorrigibly inferior; but now that northern industrialisation was far advanced, other Italians could afford to admit that a rise in southern standards of living was possible and would help everyone. It is doubtful if many deputies read Lorenzoni's volumes, but parliament did give more attention to the 'southern problem' than when former debates had taken place in an almost empty Chamber. In 1911 the government went so far as to accept in principle that the *latifondi* were the chief cause of Sicilian poverty, even though tariff policy continued to discourage the transformation of these ranches towards more specialist kinds of production. The next year a widening of the suffrage dented the oligarchic monopoly of local power.

Another change was that the *fasci siciliani* had taught the peasants their strength. Agricultural strikes sometimes succeeded in securing better contracts, and although proprietors frequently asked for troops against the strikers, Giolitti usually preferred not to intervene. Not only were better contracts of labour and land tenure gradually coming into favour, but there was a welcome appearance of agricultural co-operatives. These co-operatives were only moderately successful at first, for strong vested interests against them did not shrink from intimidation or even murder, and in any case Sicilian peasants were too individualistic to take kindly to co-operation; but it was at least proved that altogether new types of landownership were feasible. Co-operatives sometimes took over and effectively administered an entire *latifondo*, completely cutting out the intermediary *gabelloto*. They did more for agricultural education than anyone had ever done before, and it was particularly under their auspices that farmers learnt about phosphates and crop rotation.

Co-operatives, notably the pioneer organisation of Don Sturzo the Mayor of Caltagirone, above all recognised the need for adequate agrarian credit. The Bank of Sicily had been notoriously ineffective in this important field, preferring to lend outside Sicily and in quite other fields than agriculture. The Bank also went through another bad patch when its council was dismissed again for grave irregularities. The only credit normally available to small farmers came from either the landowners or the *gabelloti*, and here Lorenzoni discovered rates of interest up to 400 per cent, even in one village 1,000 per cent. On the other hand, co-operatives, where they managed to exist, could lend at 7 per cent to their members, and this was a kind of service which was indispensable if smallholdings were not to perpetuate the under-capitalisation which had typified the *latifondi*.

Even more important as a cause of change was the rapidly increasing rate of emigration. Many landlords had always liked living overseas, but now the peasants, too, began desperately to leave in search of food and work; and for a people so attached to their families, this was a remarkable fact. Seasonal migration inside Sicily, and the remoteness of the *latifondi*, had already done a great deal of damage to family life. Already, by 1900, thousands of Sicilians had achieved in Tunisia under French rule the peasant proprietorship which was so elusive at home; and incidentally they had exploded a whole series of myths by proving that they would take easily to radical agricultural innovations and could create flourishing farms out of conditions not unlike those on the *latifondi* at home. By 1900, Sicily was becoming one of the chief emigration regions in the world. Emigrants were going chiefly to the United States, but also to the Argentine and Brazil. Altogether one and a half million Sicilians found it necessary to leave the country before the world war put a stop to this way of escape. Here was one of the most prodigious facts in all Sicilian history. Some villages lost most of their male population, and were even reduced by as much as one-fifth in a single year.

This huge exodus was a terrible exposure of Sicilian poverty and the growing imbalance which the government had encouraged between north and south Italy. Yet it had some beneficial effects. The report of large fortunes made overseas was a great stimulus to education and literacy, as was also the wish to correspond with relatives overseas. More obvious was the fact that labour shortages were created, and this in turn meant that, in 1905–11, wages went up by a third for those who stayed behind. Already by 1906 some landowners were complaining of the indignity of having to go cap in hand and beg workers to help in the fields.

Marginal land under wheat was no longer so profitable in these conditions: hence some was allowed to revert back to pasture and woodland, and cereals now took up less than 70 per cent of the agricultural surface. Many landowners discovered that they could no longer afford a type of agriculture which flourished on unemployment and led necessarily to soil impoverishment and erosion. Some proprietors who did not want to reduce their standard of life decided to reside on their estates and take over management from the *gabelloti*; in the last resort they would sell land to more practical farmers, and quite generally they were ready to grant better leases. In other words, agricultural practices which many people had thought incorrigible were beginning to disappear without any of the drastic legislation which Crispi had thought necessary. By 1910, farmers had quite widely given up the habit of leaving land idle every second or third year; beans, tomatoes and artichokes were all being produced on some *latifondi* with good results, and Lorenzoni thought that the multiplication of smaller farms was gradually changing the whole aspect of some of the traditionally poorest regions of Sicily.

Emigration caused enormous suffering, and the loss to Sicily was in one sense irremediable; yet by 1907 the economy was gaining in return the huge sum of a hundred million *lire* a year in remittances by émigrés to their families at home—and this was only the official figure. Never before had there been such an injection of capital into Sicilian agriculture. By 1907, moreover, many of the *americani* were also coming back home to retire, with savings to invest in buying the social position which only land could confer. They brought with them the expectation of a higher standard of life. Some had learnt frightful habits of gangsterism, but others brought back a practical experience of democratic government, and especially a self-respect which prevented them treating the *notabili* with the deference that custom required. All this helped to weaken the tradition of supine resignation and the refusal to look ahead which characterised the agrarian society to which they were returning.

Land erosion beneath a Greek temple at Agrigento

Latifondo in the interior

Fosco Marain

A hill village in the interior

Chapter 55

LIBERALISM IN CRISIS

Where the politicians had failed, Sicilians were thus beginning on their own to redress the balance, but at this critical moment politics intervened to halt progress. Giolitti's conquest of Libya in 1911–12 devoured the scanty resources which might otherwise have been applied to solving the questions which Lorenzoni had begun to define; and this colonial war was enthusiastically supported by many Sicilians, for instance by de Felice the socialist as well as by di San Giuliano the conservative landowner, who was Giolitti's foreign minister. A close connection with North Africa had accompanied many of the island's most prosperous periods of history, and great hopes were aroused here by the prospect of a new Italian empire.

The Libyan deserts, however, proved to be an expensive mirage, and then came the First World War. Sicily's export markets were largely cut off until 1919, and this was a grave blow to an economy which depended on exports. Moreover few war industries were allocated to a region where skilled workmen and efficient transport were lacking, while job reservation as an alternative to military service applied to northern industrial workers rather than Sicilian agricultural labour. The government needed cheap food and so fixed artificially low prices for flour, with the result that officially declared wheat production declined by about 30 per cent between 1914 and 1917. Black market prices soared. Prefects had powers to compel people to plough their land, but were easily disobeyed, and fuel shortages led to further cutting of trees despite all the law could do to stop it. Meanwhile inflation helped to displace wealth from agriculture to industry—in particular away from agricultural Sicily, where savings were traditionally kept in depreciating bank deposits and government securities, to the north where they were invested rather in plant and stocks.

The mafia seems to have made great strides during the grim years of war. That notorious character Don Calogero Vizzini, ex-*gabelloto*, master criminal and boss of Villalba, somehow managed to secure his own release from the army and made a fortune out of wartime shortages. Deserters and fugitives from conscription again reinforced the underworld, and an official circular singled out Sicily and 'the traditions of the island' for particular mention in this respect. A law against animal stealing in Sicily had to be passed in 1917, because high prices and government controls were leading to the wholesale disappearance

505

of flocks. A special police organisation was set up which proved that mafia activity was more easily put down than previous governments had liked to pretend; but strong measures were not appreciated by everyone. When Battioni's police unit was dissolved after the war, cattle stealing again became common, and dozens of unsolved murders again accumulated in the files.

These two wars inevitably speeded up many processes of social change. Those who went to fight returned with new skills, new aspirations, new grievances; those who stayed behind sometimes dramatically altered their economic circumstances. Meanwhile Giolitti's broad liberal grouping in parliament was losing its hold and its coherence. Liberalism had been discredited, and not least by its encouragement of the political clientelage and economic disparities of Sicily. Until the 1913 election, Sicily had nearly always returned a solid majority of 'ministerialists' to Rome, whoever the chief minister happened to be; but in 1913 the number of Sicilian liberals in parliament was cut from 43 to 21, and seven socialists were elected instead of one. The old formula was ceasing to work.

The Prime Minister in 1919 was one of Giolitti's disciples, Vittorio Emanuele Orlando, a Sicilian who had piloted Italy to victory in the war. Orlando had built his political career in one of the most mafia-ridden and clientelistic areas of all western Sicily. As a direct result of the war, manhood suffrage had to be introduced in 1919 and elections were held before the political machines had time to adjust to this undermining of their authority: the result was that only half a dozen liberals were returned out of fifty-two Sicilian deputies. The new voters were asserting themselves against boss rule of the old variety, and a new type of politician suddenly appeared who appealed directly to them with revolutionary schemes for Sicilian autonomy and agrarian reform. Nationalisation of the mines and the *latifondi* was suggested yet again, and this was a frontal challenge to the 'ruling class' which Orlando said that he represented.

Dangerous moment though this was, the political climate in Sicily was notably different from that in other parts of Italy. No fascists were elected there until after Mussolini's conquest of power in 1922. The socialists also were much weaker than on the mainland and there was less militant labour unrest. This was largely because an industrial proletariat was still lacking, but it was partly due to the fact that, whereas the landowners of northern Italy needed Mussolini's help against trade unionism, Sicily possessed more traditional methods of intimidation. A number of union leaders and peasant agitators were assassinated, and of course the culprits ran little risk of conviction.

A renewed demand for land reform was the chief threat to the existing order in this period of social disturbance. During the war the soldiers had been promised land distribution in order to encourage them to fight, but they returned home to find unemployment, inflation, and a fierce resistance to their claims. Other countries now made emigration difficult, and this added to the tension. Some farmers were able to use war-time profits to buy land, and proprietors were sometimes persuaded to sell under-utilised properties which brought in no rent; still more common was that villagers arbitrarily staked out their claim on uncultivated territory and another bitter social war broke out in which many peasants and some policemen lost their lives.

This occupation of the land was on such a large scale that it significantly altered the pattern of landownership. Sometimes it was a concerted action by ex-combatants carrying the Italian flag and singing patriotic hymns, sometimes by people who carried the red flag and sang the communist *International*; and still other groups were led by their priests, since the catholic popular party of Don Sturzo strongly favoured land reform. Hundreds of thousands of acres were transferred in this way to smallholders, and dozens of new co-operatives were formed to assist the process of cultivation. For a few vital months most landowners were too frightened to resist; and in any case it was not all loss to be forced to put profit before prestige, since they often gained new rents even if they lost control of the land.

Such a vast movement of land distribution, though it reduced the *latifondi*, could not by itself destroy the old methods of extensive agriculture which characterised the practice of *latifondismo*. There were now other Italian regions with a greater number of large estates than Sicily, while at the other extreme Sicily possessed proportionally more smallholdings of up to two acres in extent than existed on the mainland; but these tiny plots did not necessarily mean a change for the better. Some of the new tenants were just out to draw a quick profit, and often did not possess enough land to give a balance of crops and maintain regular employment for their families. Sometimes they sold out. Sometimes, out of ignorance or miscalculated greed, they continued to overcrop with repeated plantings of wheat in a kind of 'peasant *latifondismo*' which mimicked and even aggravated previous practice.

Nevertheless, the gain seemed to outbalance the loss. Dangerous social tensions were diminished; some land was brought into more profitable cultivation; and most farmers who actually worked the land now had a greater interest in improving than in impoverishing their farms. Few areas where division took place did not end up showing better crop production in the aggregate wherever tenants were backed by co-operatives which could help with finance and technical advice. Professor Lorenzoni, when he returned to Sicily, remarked that, where methods of landholding had changed in this way, it seemed that a pent-up elemental force had been released. Better drainage and irrigation, better rotation with beans and clover replacing fields under fallow, less absenteeism, a further elimination of the purely parasitic kind of *gabelloto*, and a much greater pride in the land, all these advantages were evident and "went far beyond what the experts had thought possible".

Government action played relatively little part in this process except to sanction what could not be prevented. Three successive ministers of agriculture in 1919–20 had to legitimise retrospectively the spontaneous movement to occupy the land, preference being given by law to co-operatives. Government decrees on the subject left much to be desired: they were applied differently in different areas; local committees for land apportionment were subject to political and other pressures; and often the co-operatives lacked the requisite technical capacity or even the willingness to co-operate. But one result was that the scale of these arbitrary land occupations diminished in 1921, that is to say well before Mussolini's 'march on Rome'. The agrarian communism which was later adduced as justifying the fascist counter-revolution was under control long before that counter-revolution took place.

The most serious threat to the *latifondisti* was the Micheli law voted by the lower house of parliament in the summer of 1922, for this confirmed the right of the state to expropriate uncultivated portions of any large estates where improvements were possible. This menacing decision served clear notice on Sicilian landowners of what they could expect from a parliament dominated by the socialists and the reformist catholic party; and no doubt it caused a big swing towards Mussolini and his tiny minority of fascists. Mussolini's aid was not required against communism or peasant violence; it was rather needed because the liberals, the *latifondisti* and the village *notabili* had in two successive elections lost control of parliament. Giuseppe Micheli, a Christian Democrat, was later brutally assaulted by fascist thugs, and the parliamentary vote for his land reform was simply ignored.

Sicily has been called the least fascist region in Italy, and at all events there was little resemblance here to the violent conquest of power by the fascist squads which northern Italy experienced in 1921–2. A handful of Sicilians living in Milan were on the fringe of Mussolini's entourage as early as 1919, and in 1921 they had enough followers to form a congress of Sicilian fascists. They also registered one minor but practical achievement when they displaced the socialist Mayor of Ragusa. Nevertheless, until the summer of 1922 fascism hardly made much headway in Sicily.

After 1922, however, many of the vested interests which had worked with Giolitti and Orlando were quick to adjust to Mussolini's regime, for they had always liked a close understanding with whoever was in power at Rome. The *latifondisti* required Mussolini's help in vetoing the Micheli law and damming the flood tide of agrarian reform; local businessmen, such as Vincenzo Florio, were soon helping fascism in the elections. The mine owners not only had to stop nationalisation, but in the critical post-war period of adjustment they needed to overcome trade union opposition to lower wages, and they had to revoke a decree advocating a reduction in their royalties. Among the intellectuals too, as one can see from the outspoken views of both Verga and Pirandello, there was plenty of contempt for a parliamentary system which was so obviously corrupt in its operation and which had signally failed to help Sicily in sixty years. Pirandello liked the fascist doctrine which put national strength above liberty or legality, and he ostentatiously chose to apply for party membership in 1924, just at the moment when Mussolini's involvement in political assassination had been placed beyond doubt. Fascism promised to the educated and the half-educated a multiplicity of jobs in the party hierarchy and an inflated state administration: this was especially appreciated in Sicily where unemployment was severe and an official post was so often the acme of ambition.

The fascists had won no Sicilian seats in the 1921 elections, but in 1924, aided now by Orlando and his liberals, they elected 38 out of the 57 deputies for Sicily, as against only two socialist deputies and a single communist. Here was another electoral revolution on the same scale as that of 1874, and no doubt it reflected a similar realignment of the local clienteles. Once they had won effective power, the fascists proceeded to alter the rules of the parliamentary game and guarantee themselves by law a permanent majority. This came as a considerable surprise to some of the surviving liberals. Orlando, bewildered to discover in the local elections of 1925 that Mussolini would no longer collaborate with the existing system of political machines, resigned from parliament and returned to his legal practice. He and his friends in what he called the Sicilian ruling class had hoped to find in fascism an instrument for the perpetuation of their own power. Their narrow oligarchy had succeeded in dominating successive governments of both Right and Left since 1860, but now their bluff was called, and although most of them were quick to jump on the new bandwagon, it was no longer so easy for them to fend off outside intrusion into local affairs.

PART 15
Sicily Since 1922

Chapter 56

MUSSOLINI

The history of Sicily under twenty-one years of fascism is surprisingly empty. The philosopher Giovanni Gentile was almost the only Sicilian in the party to reach the highest ranks, where policy-making could be influenced; and he was soon in disgrace. Mussolini, to judge from his writings and speeches, gave less thought to the island than most Prime Ministers before him. Much more money was allocated to public works than before, though a good deal of it was inefficiently and corruptly spent. The local oligarchies had to submit to much more central surveillance over local taxation and expenditure, one beneficial result of this being that roads, bridges and schools were built faster than before. Fascism succeeded up to a point in arousing a new sense of social concern and national consciousness. A good deal was done for agricultural education and to work out the statistics on which economic policy could be based. But although the pace of change became more noticeable, it was less than elsewhere in Italy and much less than promised by fascist propaganda.

Mussolini's success as a politician was chiefly based on his skill as a propagandist, and his journalist's instinct told him that in Sicily there were only a few things he could afford to do which were big or showy enough to be truly worth doing. By comparison the economic development of the Italian overseas empire was much better calculated to make headlines and capture world attention. Fine phrases were cheaper and not infrequently more effective than practical achievements: one such phrase simply asserted that he had solved all Sicilian problems, and a magazine entitled *The Problems of Sicily* therefore had to change its name.

It followed that no special help was needed for the south. Surprisingly little was done for tourism. On the mainland the principal railroads were electrified and given a double track, but not in Sicily; few railway connections existed apart from the main coastal line, so that hundreds of thousands of people still had little contact with the rest of the nation. Splendid roads were constructed in Africa at a time when some Sicilian villages were linked only by the dried bed of a river. Aqueducts were built; though, as Mussolini accidentally discovered, they did not always work. Somewhat pettily he changed certain town names to make them sound more Italianate or Roman: Girgenti became Agrigento, Castrogiovanni again became Enna, Terranova was changed back to Gela, and for esoteric political reasons Piana dei

Greci became Piana degli Albanesi. His chief interest, however, was making a strong military nation, and this meant industrialisation, which meant investment in northern Italy; whereas Sicily's task was to provide cheap raw materials. The quest for national grandeur left little money to spare for the backward areas of the fatherland.

Fascism did not at once oppose the mafia, and the help given to Mussolini by the local bosses and the liberals in 1921–4 may have made such a confrontation seem unnecessary. Yet Mussolini was not someone who could endure the independent existence of so secret and formidable a force, whereas to defeat it would be good publicity. After the liberal political machines had helped him into power their usefulness came to an end, so he abolished the electoral system on which they and the mafia had flourished. Mussolini made three lightning visits to Sicily, which was perhaps more than most other parliamentary deputies, and on one of them, in May 1924, he realised that local problems were more urgent and much more easily solved than the liberals had liked to pretend. Some of the local bosses on that occasion presumptuously treated him as though he were another liberal premier like Giolitti or Orlando, and he found that he was expected to leave a "few hundred criminals" with the substance of political and economic power. On top of this he suffered a grave loss of face in a public encounter with Don Ciccio Cuccia, the boss of Piana dei Greci.

Mussolini therefore gave emergency powers to an efficient law officer who during the war had proved that, with sufficient ruthlessness and above all with a genuine will to succeed, the police could control the mafia. Inspector Mori was also a veteran of the post-war campaign against peasant agitations, and so knew a great deal about conditions in Sicily and the techniques of police action. He realised the importance of scoring an immediate and resounding success, for it was necessary to destroy the legends about romantic bandits and mafia courage and honour. Above all he had to establish that this time the government meant business, so that no longer need anyone fear to give evidence in the courts.

Mori concentrated his efforts and made an example of a few select places. One of the first of these was the hill town of Gangi, where for decades various mafia groups had ruled more or less as they liked. By exploiting their rivalries and the inarticulate desire of an intimidated population to be rid of them, a hundred *mafiosi* were captured and convicted after a regular siege operation: among them was the 'Queen of Gangi', a lady who dressed as a man and was accustomed to execute her own highly personal system of justice. Other mass trials followed elsewhere. A number of innocent people almost certainly suffered and some novel police methods were used, but for the first time in fifty years this major criminal industry came under full attack, and some guilty men discovered that corruption and official connivance no longer sufficed to protect them. Don Ciccio Cuccia was soon imprisoned, Dons Calogero Vizzini of Villalba and Genco Russo of Mussomeli also found themselves treated like ordinary criminals. Don Vito Cascio Ferro, of an older generation, died in prison. The number of firearm licenses was drastically reduced, cattle were more effectively branded, and citizens had to carry proper identification. Walls and hedges were also removed from the roadsides. Mori even offered a prize for the best essay by a schoolboy on how to destroy the mafia, and was surprised to receive no entries.

The results of this police action have been variously interpreted. If the mafia had been a society rather than a way of living, perhaps Mori could have killed it for all time, but in fact its complicated social and economic causes could not be removed in this brief period or by these methods alone. Perhaps there was insufficient wish among certain people for more than a surface victory of prestige; and Vizzini and Russo were later released for 'lack of proof', which suggests that popular attitudes and official complicity may not have entirely changed. Some people have accused Mori of collaborating with one part of the mafia against another, and a number of dubious characters found it expedient and easy to join the fascist party. Mussolini of course claimed a complete victory, but the fact that there were further batches of arrests after 1935 was something which even totalitarianism could not conceal.

Nevertheless, on any computation, the mafia had suffered the biggest defeat of its history. Mussolini claimed that the murder rate fell from about ten a day to three a week, and other more reliable figures suggest that it fell by about three-quarters. Robberies with violence also decreased. The worst outward manifestations of the mafia were thus brought under control, and the task was not even particularly difficult. The tithe on commercial activities, the organised sheep and cattle rustling, the intragang warfare, all of these were greatly reduced so far as we can tell. Agriculture gained from the fact that landowners and labourers could now move around the countryside with less fear. Landowners who had once needed the mafia to protect their property and keep the peasants in fear were glad to have this done less expensively by the government: they were relieved from paying protection money, and their rents sometimes went up astonishingly when they escaped from the mafia pressure of their *gabelloti*.

Mussolini's need to produce cheap food was bound to fasten

attention again on the *latifondi*. Official statistics left a great deal untold, but the study published by Professor Molè in 1927 shows that the large estates went on gradually changing by force of circumstance. Molè found flourishing co-operatives and small-holdings in areas where it had been customary to say that they could not possibly exist. Those who wanted an excuse for conservatism had always argued that the interior of Sicily was too dry for intensive agriculture, but now that statistics were available it was coming to be appreciated that the barren interior had a higher rainfall than the fertile coastal plain. Many more of the large ranches were being transformed by olives, almonds, vines, even by cotton and citrus.

Yet these changes did not come easily, and the revaluation of the *lira* in 1926–9, followed by the great depression, forced many new smallholders into bankruptcy. Not only did the *latifondi* once again begin to increase in size, but the psychological and physical obstacles to their improvement still remained as formidable as ever. It is likely that most *latifondisti* in the 1930s were still absentees. One current proverb said that the man who sells land falls in general repute, while another added that the man who works on his own never loses. Half the major landholders had still not taken some of the most elementary steps to improve their estates, even where it had now been proved that more intensive cultivation was possible and many more jobs could be provided. Rarely did they do much to educate their tenants, though simple changes in ploughing techniques might by themselves have caused a dramatic improvement. While in some places they allowed vast amounts of water to go to waste, in others, where water was badly needed, they made no use of government subsidies available for the sinking of wells.

The fascists had no consistent policy about these large estates. In their early socialist phase they advocated introducing powers for legal expropriation, but subsequently they supported the *latifondisti* against any reform of private ownership. Mussolini encouraged the grant of smallholdings to army veterans, but discouraged the co-operative and trade union movement which would have helped such smallholdings to survive. More and more he realised the importance of increased wheat production, especially when foreign politics led him to isolationism and a programme of national self-sufficiency. This meant subsidising the *latifondi*. As he coveted the propaganda-value of being able to say that he had made Italy self-sufficient in cereals, he was glad to find that Sicily had a large area which could grow wheat provided that expense was no object. Helped by heavy protective duties, marginal lands were therefore brought back into cultivation, and the use of fertilisers sometimes resulted in notably improved yields for a few years.

Judged as an exercise in publicity, this was good politics. It was not so good as economics. Government subsidies and price supports proved of great benefit to the *latifondisti*, who therefore had less reason than ever to change the traditional methods of tenure, management and production, which were at the root of the Sicilian problem. Few agricultural experts were consulted about the *battaglia del grano*: for the expert agronomists knew that Sicily needed fewer not more acres under wheat; she needed variety instead of monoculture, more intensive instead of more extensive cultivation. In practice, the result of subsidies was that the same fields were regularly sown with wheat for many successive years, and fertility decreased as the dust bowl spread; while crops were more and more easily washed away. The number of farm animals sharply decreased as pasture was ploughed up, with results that were bad even for cereal production: one expert in 1934 said that cattle had almost disappeared from Sicily, with grave loss of manure and of traction power on the farm, not to speak of lack of protein in the general diet. Sicily in 1938 had little more than 2 per cent of the cows and pigs in Italy, but she had nearly 20 per cent of the goats, an animal which did more harm than good. If she also had over 20 per cent of the horses and mules, this was another index of poverty, for it represented the many wasted hours travelling to work and back in the deserted Sicilian countryside.

More specialised crops also suffered from clumsy attempts at state interference. Olive-oil production, for example, decreased as more land was cleared for wheat. There were special reasons for trying to encourage cotton growing, but production in Sicily went on using methods and varieties which dated from Arab times, and it proved impossible to emulate other countries which were successfully adjusting to lower world prices. Citrus fruit made up half the value of Sicily's exports and were a useful earner of foreign exchange at a time when the rest of Italy was in deficit; but they did not recover their pre-war level, and indeed fruit exports fell by half in the difficult years of 1930–4. Autarky was bound to damage these export crops just because it provoked retaliation, yet price supports on the home market made it less urgent for fruit growers to reduce costs or find new markets, and citrus growing in Spain and Israel was thereby greatly encouraged. Sicilian produce was soon meeting severe competition, and this was aggravated when artificial means were found elsewhere for making citric acid and the essential oils of the perfume industry. Political interference sometimes left the situation even worse.

It was specified that sales representatives overseas had to be politically sound rather than technically expert; and artificially low prices were also fixed for oranges sent to Nazi Germany. Typically fascist explanations were given of how puritan squeamishness made Englishmen unable to stomach Sicilian blood oranges, when in fact Mussolini's anti-Jewish laws had simply provoked a spontaneous boycott of Sicilian produce in the London markets.

The increase in government power under fascism made possible much more stringent laws on re-afforestation and land reclamation. More money was available for this than before, and private property owners could now be coerced into giving assistance; but not until about 1933 was the government genuinely converted to the same idea of expropriating private land which they had once dismissed as 'unfascist'. Some beneficial results were achieved, but, despite plans and promises, few schemes of land reclamation and improvement were completed. By official reckoning, over three times as much money was spent in Apulia as in Sicily; fifteen times as much was spent in Emilia, where Mussolini had a much greater interest; and later figures suggest that Sicily now received only 1.59 per cent of the total allocated funds for drainage and irrigation, in other words a much smaller percentage even than before 1922. There was no single dramatic project in Sicily which could catch the public eye to the same extent as draining the Pontine marshes or the Volturno valley. New village settlements were designed, and given grandiose names such as *Mussolinia* and *Dux*, yet it was easier to plan than to build them, let alone make people live there; and though landowners were forced into setting up co-operative planning committees, the government itself was surprised to find how ineffective these committees were unless there was a clear private gain to be had at public expense. Much of the money spent by fascism on this kind of programme went to the considerable bureaucracy which was required to operate it.

On what was perhaps the most urgent problem of all, that of water control for irrigation and electricity, there were far more promises than action. Even the plain of Catania continued to lack proper irrigation. Railways and orange groves were regularly washed away by rivers breaking their banks, while whole villages occasionally disappeared in landslides caused by erosion, and the continuing spread of malaria ensured that large areas of the *latifondi* were uninhabitable in the summer months. It is likely, indeed, that land erosion and malaria became worse and not better as a result of Mussolini's presumed totalitarianism.

For some time there had been optimistic talk of building about forty artificial lakes to irrigate perhaps as much as a quarter of the island. One of these reservoirs, at Piana dei Greci, had been begun before the fascists achieved power, but the authorities continued to talk only vaguely about most of the others. Meanwhile the problem was becoming acute, and sometimes the supply of drinking water in large towns had to be rationed to a few hours a day. Although Mussolini ordered the old dam which had been built centuries earlier on the river Gela to be reactivated and extended, eighteen months later little had been done about it. Agronomists continued to say that land reclamation would not be uneconomically expensive, yet by 1937 official plans still affected less than 3 per cent of the total surface area. It was publicly stated that in four years only one aqueduct had been built by the government in Sicily as compared with four hundred in the rest of Italy; and it was less than two miles long.

The policy of national self-sufficiency created many more problems than it solved. The forced increase in grain production, for example, probably ruined more land than was being currently reclaimed. Sicilian wine was turned into alcohol which was used as a petrol substitute and for electricity manufacture, but this was an expensive way of buying inefficiency, and the necessary controls over wine production proved enormously unpopular. Straw was, of course, used to make paper. Sicilian castor oil was employed not only for punishing political dissenters but as a fuel, though belatedly castor beans were found to be an unsuitable crop. The same policy of economic nationalism caused a drying up of foreign capital, and yet this was bound to damage a region where foreign enterprise was so involved. Sicilian manufactures still remained largely at the stage of artisan industry based on the single family, and complaints continued to be made in the 1930s that business associations were rarely found. Even such a basic manufacture as cement was on a very small scale. The total number of industrial workers was little greater than it had been fifty years before, and the increase was mainly in the building industry. One positive achievement was that Augusta came into its own as a naval harbour, but the commercial tonnage handled in Sicilian ports fell to half of what it had been fifty years earlier, and was still apparently falling in the 1930s.

The sulphur industry at first gained from a government prepared to eliminate some of the really high-cost mines and reduce by half the royalties paid to mine owners. A law of 1927 virtually nationalised the mines, something which till now had seemed the very extreme of revolutionary impracticality. Yet though Mussolini boasted that he had a magic solution to this major problem, in practice the lack of cheap power and good communications continued to place Sicilian sulphur progressively at a disadvantage. Subsidised by the taxpayer, the mines went on producing above world costs by primitive methods; and loading a 6,000-ton ship with sulphur still took a week in 1931. Investment in chemical engineering had little appeal to most of those who organised the industry. Few of them concerned themselves with the possibilities for fertiliser manufacture offered by the utilisation of sulphur along with phosphates from near-by North Africa, let alone the potash known to exist in Sicily itself. Mussolini's policy of national aggrandisement might have been expected to help a department of the armament industry, but in fact production of sulphur continued to decrease even in the war years after 1940, because the need for cheapness and efficiency exposed the unsoundness of this fundamental ingredient of the Sicilian economy.

When Mussolini in 1937 again visited Sicily, rumour said he intended to set up a special kind of regional government for this depressed area. In fact he came only because suddenly the island had acquired a new importance with the Spanish war and the development of an African empire on the other side of *mare nostrum*. "Sicily is the geographic centre of the empire", he announced, and it was therefore going to be made into an impregnable fortress. Carried away by a Sicilian audience, he unguardedly promised to make their country "one of the most fertile in the world . . . and to inaugurate one of the happiest epochs in your 4,000 years of history"; the *latifondo* would simply be 'liquidated' along with the whole practice of extensive agriculture which kept Sicilian life at such a primitive level. The cavedwellers, whom he had been surprised to find living in the interior, were to be properly housed, and the shanty-town outside Messina resulting from the earthquake of 1908 would be removed at once. Sicilians may have wondered why it had taken fifteen years of totalitarian government to reach decisions which could be taken with such ease and finality; perhaps some of them remembered that the *Duce* had promised urgent action against these 'horrors' in 1923, and guessed that his latest remarks were not aimed much further than the newspaper headlines.

Even if intended mainly as propaganda, Mussolini's threats in 1937 about the *latifondo* nevertheless reflect a change of mind. He was suddenly captivated by the popular appeal of such a simple and sweeping programme. It was equally clear that the growing aggressiveness of Italian foreign policy made it needful to utilise domestic resources more efficiently. Moreover his own political ideas were moving into another anti-bourgeois phase as he was angered by the recalcitrance of the landowners and their failure to co-operate in making fascism a resounding success. He

'endor of oranges, Palermo

inari

Alinari

Vendor of ricotta, Agrigento

Publifoto, Mil

The straits of Messina, seen from Calabria, with the pylons that
carry electricity from the mainland to Sicily

concluded that "the mafia suited the Sicilian barons far more than did any restitution of law and order". Some of his colleagues went on championing the rights of private property in the late 1930s even though official policy was already heading in the opposite direction.

Two years after his visit, Mussolini decided to translate his words into some kind of action. A group of top fascist leaders was sent to Sicily, where they arrived with banners and spades to inaugurate what was announced as the greatest event in Sicilian history. This was the liquidation of the big estates, and the first ceremonial furrow was ploughed by the national party secretary in person. Ambitious targets were fixed, and an undertaking was given that production of wheat would be further doubled by skilful government action. Finally, in 1940, a law was passed reviving much of the 1922 project against the *latifondo* which Mussolini had once found it expedient to reject.

By this time it was too late for any serious action, because the Second World War had begun. In any case this belated plan for the re-invigoration of Sicily was misconceived, since it was all made to hinge on building new villages in the countryside, and this was dogmatically placed above all the complementary requirements associated with water provision, social education, agricultural research and encouragement of co-operatives which would have been necessary if these new townships were to succeed. Many officials knew by experience the difficulty of making either the Sicilian peasant or landowner change his traditional way of life, but this was too political a matter to be left to the experts. One new hamlet had recently been built by an enterprising landowner near Acireale, and Tuscan peasants had had to be imported to populate it because Sicilians would not leave their existing villages even when they were offered much better accommodation. Ignoring this free lesson, eight more villages were hurriedly constructed, with churches, schools and fascist party headquarters; but the results were absolutely negative except on the morale of politicians and the newspaper-reading public.

Mussolini had fallen victim to his own illusion of omnipotence and to his instinct for putting propaganda before practical reforms. People complained that meetings were held to choose the names of these new villages but not to discuss the complex agricultural and sociological problems involved: in this topsy-turvy world it could be plausibly argued that the names were more important. Anyway insufficient money was allocated, and available resources were diffused in too many places. Landowners were easily able to delay matters. The proper development of the Sicilian economy would have required elaborate research followed by some fundamental changes in agriculture and society; and such a painstaking and unspectacular programme would have been little to Mussolini's taste.

Professor Lorenzoni in 1940, thirty years after his original researches, reported little change in most areas where the large estates continued to exist. Agriculture was still in great part nomadic. Most country roads could not be used even by a rough cart. Short leases were still common. The *latifondi* were still called 'fiefs' and seemed a feudal world remote from the twentieth century; for evidently not even fascism had penetrated deeply into the Sicilian interior. Perhaps nearly half the peasants lived in one-roomed huts along with their animals, just as their ancestors had always done, and their economy was one of subsistence and little more.

From other official reports we can discover a further corrective to the picture of unrelieved progress put out by fascist propaganda. Unemployment was bad and was made worse by Mussolini's strong prejudice against allowing internal migration. Economic growth can hardly have been much above 1 per cent a year. In thirty years there had apparently been little if any rise in the standard of living. A share cropper would normally surrender at least half his produce in lieu of rent, and he still owed personal services to his master as under feudalism. Perhaps most Sicilians now ate bread, but rarely meat. Public assistance was a good deal less well organised than officials believed, and the indebtedness of Sicilian towns and villages made it impossible to supply what the state left undone.

An equally depressing record was true for other areas of the economy. In the provision of power, for instance, there is a certain irony in the fact that all Mussolini's ambition and authority could not harness the latent natural resources which after his death were to cause a minor industrial revolution. He justifiably claimed to have increased electricity supply, but by surprisingly little, and in 1939 it was only one-tenth of the average for Italy as a whole. The telephone had reached only half the Sicilian villages. It was officially admitted that there was a considerable potential for hydro-electricity which lay unexploited. Investment was rather in thermal electricity which, though cheaper, required imported coal and so made nonsense of national self-sufficiency.

Mineral oil and methane gas had for centuries been known to exist in dozens of places, and it had long been a local practice to take up oil in sponges from inland pools, and the sea, for use in lamps and as a remedy against worms and rheumatism. Ragusa in particular, near the asphalt mines, was known to be one of the most likely places in all Italy for oil prospecting. Yet Sicilians were reluctant to invest in such a speculative area of the economy, while the government and the big national combines preferred to concentrate their search for oil and gas in northern Italy, nearer the main industrial complexes. Early in the twentieth century, French, British and German companies had been drilling in Sicily, but Mussolini's policy of economic nationalism after 1922 did not offer much encouragement to prospecting by outsiders. Several bore holes were sunk by the national A.G.I.P. company after 1926, but this was a half-hearted procedure, and apparently reliance still had to be placed on a fifty-year-old geological map that was full of errors.

Only in the crisis years after 1937 was there a sudden burst of enthusiasm when circumstances forced upon Mussolini a realisation of what fascist dogmas implied in practice. The vulnerability of his system was exposed by international sanctions and the huge increase in oil imports arising out of his war policy in Abyssinia and Albania. By this time, far from being self-sufficient as he had promised, Italy was more dependent on overseas supplies of raw materials than ever before in her history. At almost the eleventh hour, in 1939, Mussolini decided to put more resources into reactivating the mining of lignite and the old iron mines near Messina; but when World War II began, it was too late for further exploration, and the discovery of the Sicilian gas and oil fields had to wait for quieter times and a more realistic and more liberal government.

Mussolini's new interest in the 'geographic centre of the empire' came at a moment when imperialism left little money to spare. When one minister, not a Sicilian, bravely asked for more money to be spent on Sicily and less on Africa, he was dismissed. Foreign qualms over Italian policy were soon reflected in a sharp decrease of tourist earnings and remittances from emigrants, and this was especially damaging to Sicily. As prestige became more expensive, taxes and the cost of living rose; and as export markets became more difficult, this too hurt Sicily more than other regions which had a better diversified economy and were less dependent on a few exported commodities. On the other hand, the compensating increase in munitions industries was scarcely felt at all in this remote, vulnerable, and in the last resort expendable, province.

Chapter 57

WORLD WAR AND ITS AFTERMATH

As Mussolini became more extremist, there were signs of latent opposition in Sicily. At first many people had gained or thought they gained from fascism: only 116 Sicilians, for what little the figures are worth, voted negatively in the plebiscite of 1934, and the total population was now almost four millions—of course there were no alternative candidates and voting was not secret. Gradually the confidence trick became apparent. Sicilians had always been notorious for their opposition to every government in turn, and their traditions of individualism did not take kindly to fascist discipline; nor was the enduring undercurrent of Sicilian autonomism appeased by the most consistent imposition of outside authority that the island had ever known.

The government, indeed, was at once too interfering and insufficiently helpful; it was also ineffective, and this can be read in part as a symptom of local opposition. Despite rigid fascist dogma and a plethora of regulations, the drift of people to the cities continued. Despite all Mussolini's instructions, the birth rate began to fall. All the resources of fascism could not dissuade Sicilian children from their massive evasion of school, and 40 per cent of Sicilians were still illiterate in the 1931 census after seventy years of 'compulsory' education. Even the mafia seems to have begun to assert itself again, reinforced by top-level gangsters from the United States searching for that mixture of central controls, rationing and corruption which was an optimum milieu for their work.

With a succession of wars after 1935, the natural logic of fascism led Mussolini increasingly to challenge traditional methods of behaviour in Sicily. Orders about the compulsory surrender of agricultural produce encountered widespread disobedience, and the *latifondisti* must have lost many illusions when fascist policy demanded their liquidation. The official introduction of adulterated bread in 1937 provoked much the same hostility as similar attempts by Spanish and Bourbon Viceroys; yet low purchasing prices antagonised producers as well, and the attempt to depress wages encouraged labour to abandon the land. Complicated form-filling was simply disregarded by illiterate peasant cultivators. The attempt in 1938-9 to make officials work fixed hours with no coffee breaks and no long lunch period with the family, the attempt to make ordinary professional people wear uniforms, the increasing interference with everyday life, with dress, language, gestures and behaviour, all these were as annoying as they were unenforceable.

The worst legacy of fascism to Italy was the world war which it advocated so tirelessly and which it finally helped to bring about, but for which so few preparations had been made. Sicily, because of her insular position, was bound to suffer special hardships from any war, and particularly from one which had a major front in the Mediterranean. The ferry boats from Sicily to the mainland had to give priority to military traffic. Export markets were largely closed, and the difficulty of importing food meant that at some moments Sicilians had almost nothing to eat except a glut of oranges. Local frustration and discontent were reflected in the fact that, in August 1941, the government made the astonishing decision to transfer all Sicilian-born officials to the mainland because of suspected disloyalty: this included everyone from appeal judges downwards. Former rulers of Sicily—for instance Charles of Anjou, the Duke of Medinaceli, or King Ferdinand II—had thought along these lines but had never gone as far as this. Like other fascist laws in Sicily, the order was disobeyed, but it tells us something about both Sicilian rebelliousness and the incompetence and essential triviality of the regime. From fascist sources we know that the rationing system broke down completely; that everyone including officials had to break the law to survive; and the courts were so choked with cases about black marketeering that justice ground to a halt.

Strategic reasons once again made Sicily of crucial importance during the war, and the Allies chose it for their first full-scale landing in Europe against the forces of Hitler. Mussolini promised the fascist leaders that no Allied invasion could possibly succeed in Sicily, and he confirmed this a few days after his generals had given him overwhelming written evidence to the contrary. He did not dare mobilise the population for defence, because arming the people would have been highly dangerous; moreover it would have been a sign of failure and so might have risked exposure of the bluff upon which he depended. Though he said that he could blacken the sky with his aircraft, in fact there were not even any proper coastal defences, let alone adequate air cover against an invasion, and the generals complained that most of the artillery was horse-drawn and some of it quite unusable. Another of Mussolini's self-delusions was that his land reclamation policy had eliminated the disease-carrying anopheles mosquito, and subordinates feared to tell him that in some areas of Sicily over half his soldiers were incapacitated with malaria.

Landing near Gela in July 1943, the Americans swept through western Sicily, while to the east the British and Canadians met the brunt of German resistance. In a moment of panic, the strongly fortified port of Augusta fell to the invaders without a shot, but there followed a protracted battle on the plain of Catania. Sicilians could do little but hope for a quick decision. Sometimes they were able to inflict minor damage on the German army as it retreated, and it was not unknown for hostility to be shown to Italian units, for the war had accentuated the feeling of distrust towards Italians of the mainland. Sicily eventually fell after five weeks of fighting. The Allies, despite their complete air and naval superiority, allowed the Germans to escape across the straits with most of their equipment. The Italians too, though largely abandoned by the German higher command and poorly provided with vehicles and ferry boats, were able to evacuate many of their troops. Once again the island was severed from the rest of Italy and ruled by an alien conqueror.

The war had been a disaster. In its last stages there was a great deal of physical destruction, especially at Palermo and Messina; some villages were almost obliterated, and damage to power supplies had a very injurious effect on post-war Sicily. At no time was there any sign of a revolution against Mussolini, but defeat was followed by the sudden disappearance of every fascist official. The Allies brought food and so were welcome. They brought new drugs which at last made it possible to control malaria, that scourge of the Sicilian countryside. Their victory also meant the restoration of free government and new possibilities of self-determination. Of the new forces which freedom allowed to emerge, the most obtrusive at first was a strong separatist movement, and the separatist question now dominated Sicilian politics for three years: there was even question of a plebiscite to decide whether Sicily should become an independent republic; a petition in this sense was addressed to the San Francisco conference, and wild talk was heard about annexation to the United States.

At the same time the mafia was restored to its old position of power. The accusation has been frequently made, and not convincingly denied, that this was done deliberately by the Allies in order to facilitate the conquest of Sicily. Certainly there were very close relations between gangsters in America and Sicily, and mafia help would have been very useful for obtaining information if nothing else. Certain details in the careers of Lucky Luciano, Vito Genovese and other celebrated Sicilian-American criminals give some credibility to the story. Genovese, for example, although still wanted by the United States police in connection with many crimes including murder, and though he had served fascism in Italy during the war, strangely turned up as a liaison official in an American unit; he used his position and kinship with the local mafia to help restore their authority and so undo some of the little good that Mussolini had ever done.

An important fact was that foreign administrators, who suddenly had to find Sicilians to fill thousands of jobs vacated by fascists, often had to rely either on local men of influence, or else on the not always disinterested advice of Sicilian-American interpreters who were part of the local kinship networks. Vizzini, the best-known of the surviving mafia leaders, who had been imprisoned and bankrupted under Mussolini, was immediately appointed to a position of trust and influence, and one may assume that it was his handiwork when Russo and other *mafiosi* acquired public office in other influential departments of local government. The ordinary kind of normal professional politician was unavailable for these jobs, since he had invariably been a fascist and as such had aroused too many jealousies which now had full play. There had been no organised partisan movement in Sicily, unlike other parts of Italy, and this was one reason why no new political grouping or social class emerged to upset the existing structure of society. Hence the Allies, whose main interest was to keep Sicily quiet while war proceeded on the mainland, reinstated a class of political bosses who derived from the pre-fascist past; and, once done, there was no going back, for they quickly entrenched themselves. The almost illiterate Vizzini and his associates invoked all the old practices of clientelage, banditry, terrorism and *omertà* to build up enormous power and establish their profitable labyrinths of crime.

These sinister forces were helped to regain their influence by the fact that, in conditions of post-war chaos and starvation, the peasants again began occupying parts of the large estates; hence the *latifondisti* instinctively fell back on mafia protection. The landless labourers who formed most of the population had fared much worse than landlords or peasant proprietors during the war, and land occupation was a desperate though often fruitless attempt to redress the balance. Once again, as after 1918, successive governments tried to make landowners grant more equitable leases, and sometimes had to sanction illegal actions retrospectively. Such a trend was, however, resisted strongly by many landowners and the armed gangs at their disposal. In September 1944, communist and socialist leaders dared to break one taboo by challenging Vizzini's prestige and addressing the peasants in the central square of his own Villalba; the boss was forced to outface them, and his bodyguard opened fire to establish that this was forbidden territory. The criminal proceedings which followed this typical piece of mafia effrontery were allowed by the police to drag on until long after Vizzini's death ten years later; and were then dropped.

The restoration of free government revived the old techniques of boss rule and electoral gerrymandering, as different mafia groups began manœuvering and fighting for power. The winner would be the one who most quickly could establish close relations with whichever political party came to power at Palermo or Rome. Some mafia elements miscalculated and went back to supporting the right-wing liberals just as before 1922; others occasionally managed to infiltrate the parties of the Left; Vizzini, on the other hand, began by supporting the separatists, calculating that they were the men of money and influence.

Separatism was strong among the landowning classes, though there were also some utopian intellectuals on the Left who naively believed that winning independence from Italy would at last mean the end of exploitation and poverty. When the Allies handed Sicily over to Italian administration in February 1944, some of the more extremist groups formed a secret army and raised the yellow and red flag with the three-legged symbol of Trinacria in a civil war against the rest of Italy. Mafia elements and bandit gangs were freely recruited for the campaign, and a Mayor of Palermo justified this fact by quoting the example of Garibaldi, who in 1860 had not hesitated to employ the dregs of society in a noble cause. The separatist leaders thought that they were exploiting the bandits, but the exploitation went the other way. In any case the people of Sicily showed that they had no intention of fighting for independence, and the idealistic left wing of the separatist movement found that it had nothing in common with the *latifondisti* and the mercenary brigands in their employ.

As a means of defeating such a dangerous upsurge of separatist feeling, the Italian government in May 1946 granted a large measure of autonomy to Sicily. Einaudi and some other Italians thought this excessive, but in fact it reconciled many Sicilians to Italian rule, just as Cavour's denial of autonomy in 1861 had done something to qualify their feelings of national loyalty. Leading Sicilians now put forward the misguided but ardently held view that the economic decline of the island dated in fact from 1861, and that reparation was due to her from other Italians for wrongs done in the past. Autonomy, they said, would lead to the industrialisation of Sicily. More plausibly it was hoped that the existence of a distinct regional administration would give many more people a new political consciousness and sense of political responsibility. A legislative assembly of ninety deputies was therefore set up at Palermo with its own cabinet of ministers. This body was endowed with almost complete control over the vital areas of agriculture, mining and industry. It was also given fairly considerable power over communications, public order and many other fields of public life.

This grant of autonomy was especially pleasing to the inhabitants of Palermo, for in a sense it restored the old regional capital, greatly increasing the number of jobs available there and the authority of this one town over the rest of the island. Palermo doubled in size between 1861 and 1921, and trebled by 1961: the more it declined as a port, the more it needed to grow as a metropolis of bureaucracy. One general reason for satisfaction was that a special grant was to be paid to the region by the Italian government: this was to make up for Sicily having been inequitably treated in the past, and for the fact that her taxable income was much lower than the national average. The result was that, when the first regional parliament was elected in 1947, fewer than 10 per cent of the deputies were separatists, and by 1951 this party had been almost eliminated.

The first elections, however, caused a different kind of alarm, since communists and socialists together heavily outnumbered the Christian Democrats, while other parties had only a marginal importance. If only the Left could agree among themselves, it seemed likely that they would capture the regional government and carry out drastic reforms in society. This was the ominous possibility which caused many from both the Right and the Centre to rally to Christian Democracy. Vizzini and his friends quickly changed their allegiance: they saw that regional autonomy and a large regional budget opened up altogether new possibilities if only they could attach themselves to whatever party was in control of building licenses, import permits, and contracts for public works. The undoubted support of these people helps to explain how the Christian Democrats in 1948 doubled their representation and thereafter remained the majority party. It was also widely held to explain why subsequent governments, predominantly Christian Democrat as they were, firmly rejected the many requests for official action against the mafia. In the campaign of terrorism which ensued, dozens of trade union leaders were murdered, and the point was clearly made that organised labour was unwelcome. Franchetti's observation held good, for while the police on the one hand still used considerable severity against peasants who illegally ploughed up uncultivated land, on the other hand this kind of political murder never once led to a conviction but always to acquittal for 'lack of proof'.

The most notorious Sicilian of the post-war years, and a man who became very much involved in the campaign of violence against the Left, was the bandit Giuliano. This popular hero, subject of many admiring ballads, began his career by killing a policeman when smuggling flour to his family in 1943. Taking to the hills as an outlaw, he built up a band of other wanted men and financed the operation by imposing his protection on any who could be made to pay. At first his was just one of many such brigand gangs roaming the countryside; but owing to his ruthlessness, his ostentatious generosity to some of the poor, his good looks and whimsical flair for publicity, he soon became a legend and a familiar name even outside Italy. Considerable powers of leadership and some fortunate political involvements also helped to make him someone whose political support was cheap to those who could afford it, and, though a notorious murderer of many policemen, he received extraordinary favours from the authorities. He could freely give interviews to the press and even visit his family at Montelepre. He held up trains in broad daylight and kidnapped people in Palermo with equal ease; and releasing members of his band from prison presented only moderate difficulty.

Giuliano's political allegiance, like Vizzini's, was at first to the separatists, and in 1945 he was a colonel in the Sicilian army of independence; but when separatism could no longer guarantee him subsidies and high-level sponsorship, it was noticed that the pattern of voting in his zone of influence shifted significantly to the monarchists, and then, again like Vizzini's, to the Christian Democrats. By 1947 his considerable powers of intimidation were engaged in combating communism; and a few days after the elections of April 1947 had favoured the Left, he gave warning of his intentions when the spectators at a defiant May Day meeting outside Palermo were mowed down by the automatic rifles of his gang. In the next few weeks, many Communist Party offices were systematically wrecked.

By 1947 the central government was at last strong enough to put down the brigandage which had become serious just after the war, but Giuliano's band was mysteriously spared despite its ostentatious claim to responsibility for many outrageous crimes. Perhaps he was too strong to be touched, or perhaps there were political revelations which people feared he might make, or perhaps his help was still needed for the national elections of 1948. Enormous forces of police were arrayed against him, but with little success despite the fact that foreign journalists could easily visit his hiding place. Still unexplained is the fact that some senior police officers remained in fairly close touch with him and made it difficult for repressive operations to proceed, though the rivalry between different police forces may have been partly responsible. When Giuliano was killed in 1950, some policemen claimed the credit; but the official story was full of obvious untruths. Public opinion had to assume that the conspiracy of silence was again at work, and that certain elements of the mafia had decided that he was now becoming dangerous, or at least that he was no longer useful. By 1950 the village oligarchies were back in charge of the elections, and the scare of 1947 had been forgotten.

Chapter 58

SICILIAN AUTONOMY

The establishment of a semi-autonomous regional government did not bring all the advantages which its advocates had claimed, but it was followed by much bigger and more beneficial changes in the economy than those resulting from the union with Italy a century before. Not only were Sicilians given a larger say in their own affairs, but they received a vast increase in financial help from the rest of Italy, since at last it was recognised that, in the national interest, levels ought to be brought nearer to those prevailing in the north. Apart from a special grant of money to the region, the national ministries at Rome greatly increased their expenditure on Sicilian roads and other public works. A special organisation, the *Cassa per il mezzogiorno*, was also created to finance agricultural and industrial projects in the south, and this received ample support from the World Bank and later from other countries of the Common Market. Generous help also came from the United States.

Mussolini's belated plans for agrarian reform were now reactivated and taken a step further. Farm labourers had a vote under the new law of universal suffrage, so politicians at last had powerful reasons to compete for their favour. Despite changes in the pattern of landownership over the previous forty years, still in 1946 probably half the agricultural area of Sicily was owned by 1 per cent of the population, and at the other extreme a good deal of land was held in tiny fragments which defied profitable cultivation. Two decrees just after the war, one by a communist minister, the other by a Christian Democrat, aimed at creating an expansion of co-operatives and making landowners grant more equitable contracts of tenure. The abolition of the *latifondo* was even written into the Italian constitution as a solemn promise beyond doubt or discussion. To carry out this undertaking, a special department of the regional government was charged with compelling landowners to farm more productively. Any *latifondo* larger than 500 acres where proprietors were unwilling to carry out improvements might now be expropriated. The mere threat of this was often enough to cause change, and over the next fifteen years perhaps another half a million acres were transferred to small and medium holdings.

In many respects, however, this department for agrarian reform proved dilatory and improvident. It became a haven for job hunters, and at one point seems to have been spending nearly a third of its budget on administration. Once again, as under Mussolini, a publicity-seeking and inexpert bureaucracy wasted public money building new villages in which no one could be persuaded to live. Once again the acreage specified for grants of land was far too small to afford employment for more than half the year. In any case, since the bigger landowners still wielded enormous influence, the most barren and uncultivable areas were selected for redistribution, so that new tenants had an impossible task and the desperate ploughing of steep hillsides sometimes made erosion worse than ever.

One of the difficulties was that agricultural policy became involved in politics. Expert advice was not sufficiently consulted, and either too little financial help was given to farmers, or elsewhere an excessive distribution of credit helped to keep inefficient, high-cost farming in existence. Furthermore, the co-operative movement which might have made up for these deficiencies was still very hard to organise, and the very word 'co-operative', like the word 'planning', was thought to convey too direct a challenge to the values of private enterprise. Without proper technical assistance, without sufficient research being done by the region on methods of pest control or on finding the best varieties of seed, a third of the population was still abandoned to living by casual labour, unemployed for months at a stretch, and with no certainty of a job from one day to the next.

Some improvements in agriculture did take place. The area under wheat declined a little, though cereals continued to take up well over half the agricultural land, and much of this was in the hills or even the mountains where it could do real harm; the low yield per acre meant that subsidisation was required, and subsidies delayed the necessary processes of change which would otherwise have reduced still further this essentially precarious kind of employment. Hard wheat was still the only convenient crop in many areas, but the policy of the Common Market did not favour types of agriculture which depended on artificial help. When methods were developed for making good *pasta* from soft wheat, this struck another blow at what over the centuries had been the main prop of the Sicilian economy.

Nevertheless there was a further beneficial shift towards crops which needed more labour and could be cultivated more intensively. This happened as new land became irrigated and as the increase in agricultural wages made some areas unprofitable for wheat growing. A field under wheat, which needed only about ten days' work per acre a year, could sometimes be planted with vines to give five times as much work, or with tomatoes to provide ten times as much. In terms of value, tomatoes and vines might be five times as profitable a crop as cereals, and lemons five times as much again. It was therefore a positive gain that grape and wine production by the early 1960s was worth as much as that of cereals. The production of tomatoes tripled by 1960 over the pre-war figure, that of potatoes doubled, that of artichokes went up five times, as the region began to exploit the advantages of its early spring climate and higher standards of living in Italy.

Citrus growing improved a good deal, though not nearly so fast as in other Mediterranean states. Far too many varieties of fruit were produced. Farmers were unwilling to replant often enough, and showed none of the capacity of the Israelis to organise collectively so as to reap the advantage of mechanisation and establish a regular reputation for quality. Even inside the Common Market, with a 40 per cent tariff against Spanish or Israeli produce, other European countries still found Sicilian fruit too expensive. How much of this was due to the high cost of transport is hard to say. One important fact was that small orange groves of less than two acres, which was still about average in the Palermo region, required too much labour at a time when a new world of scientific knowledge and mechanisation was swinging the balance away from smallholdings; these small growers were too weak to withstand market pressures, and therefore had a standard of life very little above that found on the grainlands of the interior.

Any movement towards founding co-operatives among the citrus growers continued to encounter the obstacle of what government reports and even most farmers themselves referred to as 'excessive individualism'. Even in the much richer plantations of eastern Sicily, hardly a single serious co-operative could be found. In the west there was also the absolute veto of the mafia. Criminal interference with water supply, to say nothing of levies on transport and marketing, continued to affect lemon and orange prices; so did a campaign against the use of refrigerating processes which would have spread sales more evenly through the year at the same time as reducing mafia control over the wholesale market.

A little, though not enough, was done in these years about the fundamental matter of water supplies. A law was passed about irrigation as early as 1946, though powerful interests rendered it virtually inoperative. A number of dams and irrigation conduits were eventually built, but, whether because of ignorance or because of intimidation against individual farmers, the water was sometimes left for years to run uselessly into the sea. Other schemes for water control were projected but not carried out. A century had gone by since plans had been produced for irrigating the main plains of Catania, Syracuse, Gela and Licata, yet the work was still not completed. In other areas, where the engineering problems were more difficult, Danilo Dolci and his research team were among those who campaigned for action, and officials were ready to admit that, technically and financially, some of the plans were sound; but there was a pessimism and lethargy which prevented things being done. Some people put this down to the fact that many landowners feared the social consequences of economic progress. In particular the mafia feared any challenge to their control of water supplies unless they were allowed to allocate the contracts for a dam and take their cut out of land purchase and construction work.

Until electric power was more abundant and could be sold for a price nearer to that which prevailed in northern Italy, there was not much hope for any schemes of industrialisation in Sicily. The existing privately controlled electricity monopoly showed that it had no intention of trying to meet this demand, so in 1947, taking advantage of a momentary disarray in conservative machine politics, a public utility for electricity supply was set up at Catania, and this for the first time introduced a healthy degree of competition. Sicily by the early 1960s was consuming little more than 3 per cent of the electric power produced in Italy, yet production was ten times the figure which Mussolini had achieved, and it was at last expanding more quickly than on the mainland. An electric cable was also suspended over the straits of Messina. The idea of building an actual bridge over the straits went on being debated endlessly by a number of committees; and psychologically, as well as from the point of view of encouraging tourism and cheapening exports, such a bridge, while presenting considerable technical and financial problems, held out some hopes for the future.

The fascist government had given little encouragement to industrialisation in Sicily, and the regional authorities inherited a situation where the only sizeable industries were mining and fruit processing. Judged by the amount of capital invested, Sicily in 1949 had only 1.3 per cent of national industry though she had 10 per cent of the national population; and moreover her proportion of industrial to other workers was falling as it had done fairly continuously since 1861. Another significant figure was that between 1938 and 1949 the number and tonnage of cargo ships in Palermo harbour fell by more than half.

The results of regional self-government in this field were moderately encouraging, even though the pace of industrial and commercial expansion continued to be much faster in northern Italy. Regional laws giving certain tax exemptions and abolishing the compulsory registration of stock holdings, though challenged in the courts as unconstitutional, succeeded in attracting outside capital, and in fifteen years the number of limited companies in Sicily rose from 218 to 1,576; this, on paper at least, was a big change. The complaint, however, was still heard that too little investment came from inside Sicily itself. The census of 1961 showed that two-thirds of the industrial employees were still in small businesses which had only ten workers or less, and the larger factories were disproportionately in the non-labour-intensive field of chemical engineering. The new oil and chemical industries in fact gave work only to a few thousand people, and their profits largely went back to the north whence the original investment had been obtained. Furthermore, as tax laws were subsequently changed by the Italian government, as mafia activities became better understood elsewhere, and as the regional administration for one reason or another began to lose the confidence of other Italian investors, outside capital was becoming noticeably more timid and choosy. A sharp recession began in 1962, and industrial investment fell in the next two years. By 1965 it was clear that Sicily, alone in southern Italy, had a lower percentage of people employed in industry than fifteen years before, and this despite a massive injection of new capital.

Meanwhile the sulphur mines remained the same problem as ever. Working conditions were greatly improved, but higher wages only made it more obvious that the whole industry was uneconomic. Production fell by half in the 1950s as many mines stopped production, and Sicily then produced barely 2 per cent of the world's sulphur instead of 90 per cent a century before. The industry went on being subsidised as a concession to powerful interests of both capital and labour. When the other Common Market countries agreed to a short period of grace within which these subsidies would be reduced, the region assured them that the industry could be made to pay; but this was a very expensive piece of self-deception.

The discovery of oil was the most startling event in post-war Sicily. Where Mussolini had completely failed, the regional government sensibly encouraged foreign companies by a law much more favourable to prospectors than that which applied to the rest of Italy. In 1953 the Gulf Oil Company struck oil near Ragusa, and production began at the end of 1954. After the Italian company ENI discovered another field in the sea off Gela on the south coast, Sicily became responsible for nearly the whole of a quite considerable Italian oil industry. Four refineries were built in Sicily to deal with this and with great quantities of imported crude oil from Russia, the Near East and Libya. Once again a geographic position in the central Mediterranean was proving to have advantages as well as perils. The great hopes aroused a century earlier by the cutting of the Suez canal had been unfulfilled, but enthusiastic Sicilians now began to talk of the island as a bridgehead between the Common Market and the dramatically expanding world of North Africa.

The first refinery was the Standard Oil plant at Augusta, and this was later attached by pipeline to Ragusa. By 1966 it could deal with eight million tons of crude oil a year. Next to it grew up a thermo-electric plant, a cement works, and factories for producing fertilisers, plastics and other petrochemicals on a huge scale. At Gela the oil lay very deep and was expensive to extract, but a great deal of money was spent building another great petrochemical complex which was operating by 1964. This ancient town changed more in five years than in the previous thousand. For the first time a proper port was built on the south coast, and a three-mile jetty was extended to an island terminal where ships could load. A pipeline was also built to connect Gela with Gagliano where an important discovery of methane gas opened up the possibility of developing Enna, one of the poorest provinces in all Italy. The first quantity production of this gas was in 1963. Other pipelines were laid between Gagliano and Termini Imerese on the north coast, with further extensions planned to Porto Empedocle on the south coast, and above all to Palermo itself. From a second gas find at Bronte, a pipeline went eastwards to Catania. At last Sicily was within sight of possessing the cheap power which might make industrialisation feasible. The development of large potash deposits also opened up further exciting possibilities of making fertilisers for agriculture. These deposits had been known to exist for at least forty years, but the fascists had done little about them and had omitted to undertake the kind of serious geological survey which might have had a real impact on the economy.

A great variety of figures could be cited to indicate in rough outline the changes induced by these developments in the Sicilian economy and the minor industrial revolution they brought with them. The tonnage handled in Sicilian ports increased sixfold in the decade after 1953. Cement production went up tenfold. Sulphuric acid production rose from almost nothing to nearly half a million tons, and potash from nothing to over a million tons. Electricity production went up nearly 100 per cent in 1960–3. The number of tractors used in agriculture had still been well under a thousand at the end of Mussolini's regime; by 1955 it was five times as many, and by 1962 twice as many again. These figures are not large in the absolute, but relatively they mark a decisive break with the past.

Augusta emerged after the war as easily the busiest Sicilian port: a century earlier it had been almost permanently empty, but by 1964 it was ahead of Venice and Naples for tonnage handled, and gained ground on Genoa to become the foremost port in Italy. The next three most heavily used ports in Sicily were Milazzo (where there was another refinery), Priolo and Gela, all of which had been negligible even ten years before. Palermo came a long way behind these, despite the fact that it was still one of the largest towns in Italy. A new Sicily was coming into its own, replacing the historic Sicily of previous centuries, and the process was marked by a strong development of the eastern rather than the western districts. Syracuse, after several millennia, was again becoming the most dynamic area of Sicily as it had been under the Greeks. Attempts were made to industrialise Palermo in the west, but the results were strikingly unsuccessful. The failure to develop the Brancaccio industrial zone shows how little could be done here to change fundamental attitudes of mind and overcome the legacy of the past. At Palermo the slums were still terrible, the cost of food was often higher than in Rome or Milan, and any kind of change was slow and difficult.

The lack of development in western Sicily is one major qualification which must be made to the success story of Sicily during a period when Italy as a whole seemed to be undergoing a miracle of economic growth. Northern industrialists were afraid of moving to an area where transport costs were high, water was still short, skilled labour scarce, and the telephone system primitive. Psychologically, and even for practical purposes of communication, it could seriously be said at Catania that Palermo was as remote as Paris or London. All the more important, therefore, was the fact that the regional assembly and the various government offices were located in Palermo, and that the attitudes prevalent in this one town inevitably affected other parts of the island.

If industrialisation chiefly affected the areas round Catania and Syracuse in the already more developed and progressive east, one reason was mafia activity in the central and western provinces. The post-war outbreak of brigandage in eastern Sicily was brought under control, but in and around Palermo the mafia became ever more insolent and exorbitant as the regional government established itself. Many gangsters who had been made notorious by the Kefauver Crime Commission across the Atlantic now appeared in Palermo, after many hundreds of undesirables had been expelled and repatriated from the United States: these men at once fitted into the Sicilian kinship networks, and they demonstrated how the well-established techniques of gang warfare could be employed much more profitably in the big towns than in the villages. Mafia activity on an altogether new scale was soon to prove the quickest method of capital appreciation that the island had ever known. Most commercial and industrial enterprises at some stage in their operation seem to have been made to pay a tithe to the underworld, and this must have done as much as anything to keep Sicily poor. The mafia did not want industrialisation, because industrial workers would be relatively concentrated, educated, self-assured; and the result was that industrialists did not build factories at Palermo, just because they did not want to expose themselves to labour and protection rackets.

Because of the mafia's secrecy, and because of the illiteracy of many of its affiliates and the inevitable lack of documentary evidence, one must be guarded in assessing the present state of this scourge of Sicilian society. Even today many victims are either too terrified or have too perverted a sense of honour to give public evidence in the case of mafia crimes. It is very unlikely that it works or has ever worked as either a single unit or even a loose federation, though so long as Vizzini was alive the rivalries of the various gangs seem to have been kept under some check. Different groups seem to have staked out a special interest in the citrus plantations, the wholesale meat trade or the flour mills, while others specialised in dock labour, fishing, or cigarette smuggling. Some of them worked only in a single village. Certain places even in western Sicily were relatively free from these gangs, and on the east coast they were very little of a problem. As sociological studies of individual villages are beginning to show, only in some localities was a traditionally anarchic and individualistic way of life exploited by racketeers until it became an explosive criminal force. Elsewhere it might remain at a relatively innocuous level, as a mixture of fear, mild chicanery and an exaggerated respect for force and backstairs influence. The mafia in some villages might be just four or five groups contending for civic office and economic power: their number, composition and political colour might even be continually changing, and their involvement with crime could be a secondary matter or non-existent.

Many towns and villages, however, were the scene of gang war accompanied by political assassination and drug smuggling on a scale never before known. Palermo especially went through a terrible period. In an autonomous Sicily this town was the main source of official permits and government contracts. It was the financial axis, the centre of credit and justice, and hence was particularly exposed to this conflict for power and riches. Most of the magistrates in Sicily—something apparently unknown elsewhere in Italy—were of local origin, and so of course were all the politicians. At Palermo these men found themselves much more vulnerable to local pressures than their predecessors before 1946 had ever been at Rome. It was particularly difficult to eliminate administrative corruption, because politicians in this society were commonly considered to be corrupt, and hence they had little to lose from being corrupt in deed as well as in reputation.

The worst phase began in 1956, when open warfare broke out between a number of gangs for the control of the Palermo food markets. By a communist motion, this was forced on the attention of the regional assembly, but it was officially stated to be something so normal as to need no special enquiry, and meanwhile the government and the civic authorities watched the accumulation of murders with imperturbable complacency. Another field of combat was land speculation in the suburbs. Anyone who had both political influence and criminal friends could obtain credit on easy terms and then bully proprietors to sell cheaply. He found no difficulty in putting up tenement buildings just where the city planning authorities forbade any construction at all, or even where —as was seen most tragically at Agrigento in 1965—the danger of landslides made an area thoroughly unsafe for building. Control of labour would be relatively simple to such a man, and he could impose on the area the protection of his own private guards. In the end he might also possess a chain of supermarkets, garages and laundries, all backed by the ultimate sanction of violence and assassination.

Why the regional authorities repeatedly refused to investigate these matters is a perplexing question. Ordinary citizens preferred not to talk about the subject. Ministers at Rome and responsible Sicilians continued to repeat that the mafia did not exist, or that it was nothing peculiar to Sicily: for, on the one hand, ministers were unwilling to lose Sicilian votes or offend local susceptibilities; and on the other hand the regional government was perhaps too scared of possible revelations, too dependent on the Grand Electors, too anxious not to wash dirty linen in the full glare of national publicity. Meanwhile the murders continued. Genco Russo was able to stand as a Christian Democrat and obtain public office in his home town, while notorious friends of the gangsters became influential politicians at Palermo and even in Rome.

Nevertheless, even at its moment of greatest destructive power, some of the mafia's traditional prestige began to wear thin, and this must remain the chief hope for Sicily's future. Perhaps it never fully recovered from the loss of face which followed Mussolini's revelation of its essential weakness, and its legendary sense of honour became less credible to other Sicilians after exposure of its association with drugs and prostitution. Strong political opposition also developed after many union officials were assassinated for trying to organise labour on the *latifondi* and in the mines. The mother of Salvatore Carnevale, one of these murdered officials, broke with Sicilian custom and astonished everyone by giving evidence in open court.

Other individual Sicilians, and Dolci who was not a Sicilian, succeeded in showing by practical example that the mafia could be successfully resisted, and that ordinary men by co-operating against it could raise their standard of living as well as their self-respect. The increase of schools and roads, the much greater ease of movement inside Sicily and of emigration overseas, the spread of socialism and trade unions, and the first tentative steps towards the emancipation of women, all these helped to erode the mafia's power. Publicity above all helped, and the gang feuds, by becoming national news, increasingly prevented the mafia's political friends from giving it their customary protection in the corridors of power. When the Palermo left-wing daily *L'Ora* broke new ground in 1958 by printing names and photographs of the more dangerous *mafiosi*, at once the newspaper's office was damaged by an explosion; but this desperate act merely gave the facts an international notoriety, the last thing that had been intended.

Suddenly opinion showed signs of changing, as Sicilians became more sensitive to outside criticism and more aware of this brake on their economic development. In 1962, after years of intransigent refusal to hold an enquiry, the regional and national parliaments agreed to set up a commission with wide powers to investigate the mafia and suggest ways of eliminating it; and they did this with unusual and quite unexpected unanimity. This commission was long overdue. Once constituted, it worked very slowly; but in the meantime, after a number of police had been killed by bomb outrages, some of the firm measures which Mussolini had found easy and effective were again authorised. In a surprisingly short time, scores of people who for years had been declared untraceable were under arrest awaiting trial, and the public protests against such 'fascist' behaviour were not very loud. When Russo was banished from Sicily and placed under house arrest, this kind of treatment was a major loss of face to the mafia and an encouragement to some of those who had material evidence to give.

By 1960, one of the big problems of Sicily was once again that of emigration. In one sense this had never ceased to be a problem. Many rich Sicilians habitually lived on the mainland, and incomes deriving from Sicily went on being spent outside the island as they always had been. Likewise a great many of the best scholars, administrators and creative artists continued to leave for the north. Brancati and Vittorini among novelists, Guttuso and

Consagra among artists, Quasimodo the poet, La Malfa, La Pira, Scelba and Riccardo Lombardi among politicians, these are names which suggest that Sicily continued to contribute more than her full share to Italian life on the mainland. Most of her politicians preferred the metropolitan world of Rome to the provincial environment of Palermo, and those writers who, like Tomasi di Lampedusa and Sciascia, remained in Sicily seemed eccentric in their apparent indifference to worldly success. Nor was there any compensating movement in reverse, and any northerners who were obliged by their work to live in Sicily still spoke of their residence as either an apprenticeship or a punishment. University teachers from the mainland who received appointments in Sicily frequently lived elsewhere and merely commuted to work for several days a week. This helped to inculcate in their students a sense of isolation, of remoteness from national affairs, and of living in a depressed area.

A yet more serious kind of emigration, especially in the period 1955–60, concerned the population of the poorer agricultural areas who left in tens of thousands. Indeed the great economic development of Italy in the 1950s absolutely depended on this shift in manpower as Sicilians discovered that a job in Turin or Switzerland could earn as much in a single month as could be earned in a year back home. Possibly some half a million from a population of now nearly five millions left Sicily in ten years, and some villages again lost almost all their younger males. Obviously the island's economy was not developing nearly fast enough to absorb the annual increase in population. Emigration certainly relieved the population pressure and increased the wages of those who remained behind; mountain areas were consequently allowed to go back to pasture, greatly to the benefit of the community; money was also sent back by emigrants to their families at home. Yet the exodus of human capital and productive capacity was in other respects a great deprivation.

Though the discovery of oil and gas, the conquest of malaria and the appointment of the anti-mafia commission seemed to herald a new age in Sicilian history, it must be admitted that positive achievements were slower to materialise than had been hoped. Individual incomes, though rising, were little more than half the national average in the middle 1960s, and in some respects north and south were growing even farther apart. Under-employment was reduced, though the precariousness of jobs on the land remained a terrible psychological and economic burden. Over large areas it was true that most houses had no running water or drainage. Nearly a quarter of the population was officially registered as illiterate: in the interior the figure was yet larger, and there was still a primitive world of superstition, witches and magic to be overcome. A true sense of the state and an awareness of social and political obligation was often hard to find: not only was this shown in the figures for certain types of crime, but ascertained tax evasion among the rich was twice as high in Sicily as in Piedmont, and in many areas of public life a disproportionate regard was still paid to kinship and client-patron relationships.

Many Sicilians professed for these reasons that, although they might not want to renounce their new autonomy, twenty years of regional government left them less enthusiastic than they had been at first. According to Sciascia, indeed, a clear majority believed that autonomy was an experiment which had failed. It was a welcome change that shortage of money was no longer a major impediment, yet at the same time great sums voted for purposes of betterment continued to lie idle in the bank. Still in 1967 the region could not think how to spend the annual grant which the Rome government had been asked to concede as a matter of urgency.

Many of these problems suffered rather than gained from being caught up in local politics and political controversy; sometimes they suffered a great deal. Elections to the regional assembly regularly showed a 30 per cent vote for the extreme Left; but, though the Christian Democrats remained continuously the party of government, they possessed no outright majority, and to keep out communism they had no option but to form either a minority administration or else a series of coalitions. Either way, this made it expedient to avoid clear statements of policy and to shirk taking decisions in the more controversial fields where decisions were most needed. Each year there was a government 'crisis', and the consequent reluctance of the regional government to tackle some quite fundamental legislation was one reason given by the business community for the slowness of economic development.

Despite a number of negative points, there were many positive grounds for satisfaction with what was being achieved. The economy, which had improved very little indeed between 1861 and 1950, was now usually able to carry a growth rate of about 5 per cent a year. The great handicap of the *latifondi* had largely been removed, and that of the sulphur mines had at least been reduced, while the many other problems of the island were being studied more seriously and expertly than ever before and with resources which no previous generation had possessed. The development of North Africa and perhaps also the existence of the European Common Market were creating new economic possibilities. Moreover it could be hoped that the anti-mafia commission, when it finally reported, would outdo previous parliamentary investigations in its practical results—though many Sicilians had doubts on this score.

The concession of regional autonomy may have disappointed some people, but for others it could be seen as a major fact in Sicilian history. Even if not directly responsible for most of the material advances of the post-war years, at least it helped to remove many purely negative elements of frustration and placed a much greater degree of responsibility on Sicilians for their own future. Some important questions remained open, but that was inevitable. Whether the country could by its own unaided efforts achieve a balanced economy and a self-propelling process of development, was still in real doubt, though some economists now concluded that success was likely. Whether Sicily would ever cease to be a place of emigration from which people—especially the best people—were trying to escape; whether she would ever produce a new governing elite with a new code of political conduct less tied to traditions of personal patronage and boss rule; these were other questions which the grant of regional autonomy had still not been able to solve by 1967.

Bibliography

Bibliography

GENERAL

Of general histories, two old ones still read with great profit are G. E. di Blasi e Gambacorta, *Storia civile del regno di Sicilia* (17 vols., Palermo 1811–21), and R. Gregorio, *Considerazioni sopra la storia di Sicilia dai tempi Normanni sino ai presenti* (6 vols., Palermo 1805–16— plus other posthumous chapters in his *Opere scelte*, Palermo 1853). On economic history there is still nothing to replace L. Bianchini, *Storia economica e civile di Sicilia* (2 vols., the first published at Naples, the second at Palermo, 1841: vol. I takes the story as far as 1735); nor, on parliamentary history, A. Mongitore, *Parlamenti generali del regno di Sicilia dall'anno 1446 sino al 1748* (2 vols., Palermo 1749, and later editions with later supplementary chapters on parliaments up to 1786).

Useful for bibliography are G. M. Mira, *Bibliografia siciliana* (2 vols., Palermo 1875–81, full even though in many ways incorrect); I. Carini, *Gli archivi e le biblioteche di Spagna in rapporto alla storia d'Italia in generale e di Sicilia in particolare* (2 vols., Palermo 1884); I. Peri, *Studi e problemi di storia siciliana* (Florence 1959); F. Natale, *Avviamento allo studio del medio evo siciliano* (Florence 1959). A short modern outline that has an extensive bibliography is F. de Stefano, *Storia della Sicilia dal secolo XI al XIX* (Bari 1948).

The main periodical for consultation is the *Archivio storico siciliano*, stretching back nearly a hundred years; but also the *Archivio storico per la Sicilia orientale*, the *Archivio storico messinese*, and more recently the *Nuovi quaderni del meridione*. The *Società Siciliana di Storia Patria* has published many useful volumes of *Documenti per servire alla storia di Sicilia*.

MEDIEVAL SICILY: 800–1713

Part 1, Arab-Norman Sicily 800–1200

On the Arabs, the main source still remains the century-old M. Amari, *Storia dei musulmani di Sicilia* (but in the revised edition of 6 vols. by C. A. Nallino, Catania 1933–9), together with Amari's *Biblioteca arabo-sicula* (2 vols., Turin 1880–1, which gives the Arabic texts in Italian). Apart from the *Centenario di Michele Amari* (2 vols., Palermo 1910), additional material is listed in F. Gabriele, *Un secolo di studi arabo-siculi* (in *Studia Islamica*, 1954), and U. Rizzitano, *Nuove fonti arabe per la storia dei musulmani di Sicilia* (in *Rivista degli studi orientali*, 1957).

On the Normans, the most substantial work is F. Chalandon, *Histoire de la domination normande en Italie et en Sicile* (2 vols., Paris 1907).

There is a modern edition of Malaterra, *De rebus gestis Rogerii Calabriae et Siciliae comitis* (ed. E. Pontieri, Bologna 1927), and of Falcandus, *La historia o liber de regno Siciliae* (ed. G. B. Siragusa, Rome 1897). Some of the documentary material is only to be found in E. Caspar, *Roger II und die Gründung der normannisch-sicilischen Monarchie* (Innsbruck 1904), supplemented by *Atti del convegno internazionale di studi Ruggeriani* (2 vols., Palermo 1955). Also: W. Cohn, *Das Zeitalter der Normannen in Sizilien* (Bonn 1920); and John Julius Norwich, *The Normans in the South* (London 1967).

There are some excellent special studies: E. Jamison, *Admiral Eugenius of Sicily, His Life and Work* (London 1957); L. Genuardi, *Parlamento siciliano, 1034–1282* (Bologna 1924, of which only the first volume appeared); L. T. White, *Latin Monasticism in Norman Sicily* (Cambridge, Mass. 1938); E. Jordan, *La politique ecclésiastique de Roger I* (in *Le Moyen Age*, 1922–3); E. Besta, *Il diritto pubblico nell'Italia meridionale dai Normanni agli Svevi* (Padua 1929); F. Giunta, *Bizantini e bizantinismo nella Sicilia normanna* (Palermo 1950); G. B. Siragusa, *Il regno di Guglielmo I in Sicilia* (Palermo 1885); *Studi medievali in onore di Antonino de Stefano* (Palermo 1956); and Antonio Marongiù, *Il parlamento in Italia* (Milan 1962).

On art there is O. Demus, *The Mosaics of Norman Sicily* (London 1949); E. Kitzinger, *I mosaici di Monreale* (Palermo 1960); R. Salvini, *Il chiostro di Monreale e la scultura romanica in Sicilia* (Palermo 1962); and A. de Stefano, *La cultura in Sicilia nel periodo normanno* (Bologna 1954).

Two older books in English which are still useful: E. Curtis, *Roger of Sicily and the Normans in Lower Italy, 1016–1154* (London 1912); and C. Waern, *Mediaeval Sicily: Aspects of Life and Art in the Middle Ages* (London 1910).

Part 2, Hohenstaufen, Angevins and Aragonese 1200–1375

On the Hohenstaufen, apart from many general works about Frederick II, there is G. M. Monti, *Lo stato normanno svevo* (Trani 1943); W. Cohn, *Das Zeitalter der Hohenstaufen in Sizilien* (Breslau 1925); A. de Stefano, *La cultura alla corte di Federico II* (Bologna 1950); E. Pontieri, *Ricerche sulla crisi della monarchia siciliana nel secolo XIII* (Naples 1942); *Atti del convegno internazionale di studi Federiciani* (Palermo 1956); R. Morghen, *Il tramonto della potenza sveva in Italia* (Rome 1936).

The best book on the Angevin period is E. G. Léonard, *Les Angevins de Naples* (Paris 1954). In addition: V. Epifanio, *Gli Angioini di Napoli e la Sicilia* (Naples 1936); L. Cadier, *Essai sur l'administration du royaume de Sicile sous Charles I et Charles II d'Anjou* (Paris 1891); M. Amari, *History of the War of the Sicilian Vespers* (3 vols., London 1850); S. Runciman, *The Sicilian Vespers* (Cambridge 1958); O. Cartellieri, *Peter von Aragon und die sizilianische Vesper* (Heidelberg 1904).

There have lately been a number of books on the Aragonese and the thirteenth century. A. de Stefano has a good, though somewhat over-laudatory, volume on *Federico III d'Aragona, Re di Sicilia, 1296–1337* (Palermo 1937). Economic history is well treated in V. d'Alessandro, *Politica e società nella Sicilia aragonese* (Palermo 1963), and in F. Giunta's two volumes, *Aragonesi e Catalani nel Mediterraneo* (Palermo 1953), *Uomini e cose del medioevo mediterraneo* (Palermo 1964). Two older books, L. Genuardi, *Il comune del medioevo in Sicilia* (Palermo 1921), and S. V. Bozzo, *Note storiche siciliane del secolo XIV* (Palermo 1882), both contain a good deal of information not easily found elsewhere. Finally, there is S. Tramontana, *Michele da Piazza e il potere baronale in Sicilia* (Messina 1963).

Part 3, Submission to Spain 1375–1525

For the earlier part there is R. Moscati, *Per una storia della Sicilia nell'età dei Martini* (Messina 1953). For the fifteenth century, apart from Gregorio's *Considerazioni*, there is G. E. di Blasi e Gambacorta, *Storia cronologica dei vicerè, luogotenenti, e presidenti del regno di Sicilia* (5 vols., Palermo 1790–1, of which the first is on this period and contains a good deal not included in his *Storia civile*). More recently there has been: J. Vicens Vives, *Fernando el Catolico, principe de Aragon, rey de Sicilia* (Madrid 1952); C. Giardina, *L'istituto del vicerè di Sicilia, 1415–1798* (in *Archivio storico siciliano*, 1931); and Alfonso's relations with North Africa are considered in F. Giunta, *Medioevo mediterraneo* (Palermo 1954).

The history of Messina in this period is the subject of the second volume of C. D. Gallo, *Annali della città di Messina, capitale del regno di Sicilia* (Messina 1758). The main documents are in C. Giardina, *Capitoli e privilegi di Messina* (Palermo 1937); and there is also C. Trasselli, *La 'questione sociale' in Sicilia e la rivolta di Messina del 1464* (Palermo 1955). Trasselli has written many short articles on economic history at this time: e.g., two on the cloth trade (in *Annali della facoltà di economia e commercio dell'università di Palermo*, 1955; and in *Economia e storia*, 1957); one on the sugar industry (*Revista bimestre Cubana*, 1957); one on the expulsion of the Jews (*Annali della facoltà . . . di Palermo*, 1954); *La fine di due banchi siciliani del XV secolo* (in *Rassegna dell'associazione bancaria Italiana*, 1962). Among his other writings there are *Note per la storia dei banchi in Sicilia nel XV secolo* (2 vols., Palermo 1958–9), and *La pesca nella provincia di Trapani* (Trapani 1953).

Other useful works are the first volume of F. Testa, *Capitula regni Siciliae* (2 vols., Palermo 1741); F. Maggiore-Perni, *La popolazione di Sicilia e di Palermo dal X al XVIII secolo* (Palermo 1892); G. Fasoli, *Cronache medievali di Sicilia* (Catania 1950). For the *Capibrevi* of G. L. Barberi, see the edition by G. La Mantia (3 vols., Palermo 1879–1904), and the short introduction by I. Peri to an edition of *Beneficia ecclesiastica* (2 vols., Palermo 1962–3).

Part 4, Spanish Administration 1500–1650

Two interesting collections of studies are by V. Titone: *La Sicilia spagnuola, saggi storici* (Mazara 1948), and *La Sicilia dalla dominazione spagnuola all'unità d'Italia* (Bologna 1955). A good straightforward political narrative is I. La Lumia, *La Sicilia sotto Carlo V imperatore* (Palermo 1862). H. Koenigsberger studied a good deal in the Spanish archives for his *The Government of Sicily under Philip II of Spain* (London 1951), which deals very well with the machinery of government and with Spanish policy. Apart from the Archivio di Stato at Palermo, the archives at Simancas have the largest collection of unpublished material on Sicilian history, and a helpful catalogue was edited by R. Magdaleno, *Papeles de Estado, Sicilia, virreinato Español* (Valladolid 1951). In the British Museum, of particular interest is Additional MSS. 28,396.

Of published original sources, the most useful are: *Advertencias que el duque de Medinaceli dejò a D. Garcia de Toledo sobre el gobierno del reino de Sicilia* (in *Colección de documentos inéditos para la historia de España*, vol. XXVIII, Madrid 1856); the two following volumes XXIX, XXX, on military matters dealing with Malta and North Africa; *Carta de Juan de Vega al rey D. Felipe secundo, sobre cosas toccantes al gobierno de Sicilia* (ed. M. Ch. Weiss, *Papiers d'état du Cardinal de Granvelle*, vol. V, Paris 1844); *Registri di lettere di Ferrante Gonzaga vicerè di Sicilia* (Parma 1889); G. Capasso, *Il governo di don Ferrante Gonzaga in Sicilia dal 1535 al 1543* (in *Archivio storico siciliano*, 1905–6); *Avvertimenti di Don Scipio di Castro a Marco Antonio Colonna quando andò Vicerè di Sicilia* (ed. A. Saitta, Rome 1950); A. Ferramolino, *L'ordini di la fortificacioni di quista felichi chita di Palermo* (ed. V. di Giovanni, Palermo 1896); ed. G. V. Auria, *Notizie di successi varii nella città di Palermo . . . dall'anno 1516 sino all'anno 1606* (ed. G. di Marzo, *Biblioteca storica e letteraria di Sicilia*, vol. I, Palermo 1869).

For Church history, apart from Rocchi Pirri, *Siciliae sacrae celeberrimi* (ed. with additions by A. Mongitore, Palermo 1735), there is F. Scaduto, *Stato e chiesa nelle Due Sicilie dai Normanni ai giorni nostri* (Palermo 1887). A good work on local history is I. Scaturro, *Storia della città di Sciacca* (2 vols., Naples 1925–6).

Part 5, The Economy 1500–1650

On the history of Messina, apart from C. D. Gallo, *Annali della città di Messina* (vol. III, Messina 1804, covers this period), there is a short outline work by P. Pieri, *La storia di Messina nello sviluppo della sua vita comunale* (Messina 1939). The most comprehensive document on the rivalry between Messina and Palermo is *Razones apologeticas y fundamentos legales por el senado de la noble ciudad de Mecina contra el memorial de los deputados del reyno de Sicilia, y ciudad de Palermo* (Madrid 1630).

Documentary material of especial interest is contained in *Trattato di Sicilia* (Naples, Biblioteca Nazionale, MSS. X.D. 46); D. Ferrando Gonzaga, *Relazione delle cose di Sicilia fatta all'Imperatore Carlo V, 1546* (ed. F. C. Carreri, Palermo 1896); *Corrispondenza particolare di Carlo di Aragona, Duca di Terranova 1574–5* (ed. S. V. Bozzo, Palermo 1879); *Documentos relativos a Don Pedro Giron, tercer Duque de Osuna* (in *Colección de documentos inéditos para la historia de España*, vol. XLIV, Madrid 1864). An early essay on industry is C. Gallo, *Il seteficio in Sicilia* (in *Nuova raccolta di opuscoli di autori siciliani*, vol. I, Palermo 1788).

More general works, apart from the first volume of Bianchini, include G. B. Comandé, *Ricerche di storia siciliana* (Palermo 1956); F. Braudel, *La Méditerranée et le monde méditerranéen à l'époque de Philippe II* (Paris 1949); C. A. Garufi, *Per la storia dei comuni feudali in Sicilia* (Palermo 1907); L. Genuardi, *Terre comuni ed usi civici in Sicilia prima dell'abolizione della feudalità* (Palermo 1907).

On population, the census figures given by Maggiore-Perni have not all been accepted by K. J. Beloch, *Bevölkerungsgeschichte italiens* (Berlin 1937). See also A. Mori, *La distribuzione della popolazione in Sicilia e le sue variazioni negli ultimi quattro secoli* (Florence 1918), and Trasselli's article on the population of Palermo (in *Economia e Storia*, 1964).

Part 6, *The Disintegration of Spanish Sicily 1640–1713*

Di Blasi's *Storia civile* and *Storia cronologica* are both important for this period, and so is Mongitore's *Parlamenti generali*. The latter work should be read in conjunction with Genuardi's essay, and also with *Ordinazioni e regolamenti della deputazione del regno di Sicilia raccolti e pubblicati per ordine di Ferdinando III* (Palermo 1782). Archbishop Testa's *Capitula* is one of a number of collections of Sicilian laws, but more correct so far as it goes is F. P. di Blasi ed Angelo, *Pragmaticae Sanctiones Regni Siciliae* (2 vols., Palermo 1791–3).

There is a fair amount of documentary material in the Turin Archivio di Stato as well as the great bulk at Simancas. Published documents include D. V. Auria, *Diario delle cose occorse nella città di Palermo e nel regno di Sicilia* (ed. di Marzo, *Biblioteca storica e letteraria di Sicilia*, vol. III, Palermo 1869, and vol. V, 1870) which covers the period 1631–75; also *Diario Palermitano . . . dall'anno 1680*, ed. F. Serio e Mongitore (ed. di Marzo, *Biblioteca storica e letteraria*, vols. VII, VIII, IX, Palermo 1870–1); and B. Masbel, *Descritione e relatione del governo di stato e guerra del regno di Sicilia* (Palermo 1694).

On the 1647 revolution, Serio, *Veridica relatione di tumulti occorsi* (ed. di Marzo, *Biblioteca storica e letteraria*, vol. IV, Palermo 1869); I. La Lumia, *Giuseppe d'Alesi e la rivoluzione di Palermo del 1647* (Palermo 1863); A. Siciliano, *Sulla rivolta di Palermo del 1647* (in *Archivio storico siciliano*, 1938–9); H. Koenigsberger, *The Revolt of Palermo in 1647* (in *Cambridge Historical Journal*, 1946).

For the revolt of 1674, F. Laloy, *La révolte de Messina* (3 vols., Paris 1929–31); M. Petrocchi, *La rivoluzione cittadina messinese del 1674* (Florence 1954); also the volumes by G. Oliva in the new edition of Gallo's *Annali della città di Messina* (6 vols., Messina 1877–93). A number of other smaller manuscripts have also been published by G. di Marzo (*Biblioteca storica*, vol. VI, 1870).

MODERN SICILY: AFTER 1713

Part 7, Three Experiments in Foreign Government 1713–1765

The documents at Simancas for this period are much less important than for the previous century, but see the catalogue by R. Magdaleno, *Secretaria de estado, reino de la dos Sicilias, siglo XVIII* (Valladolid 1956). At Turin, and at Vienna in the Haus- Hof- und Staatsarchiv (Italien, Spanischer Rat, Sizilien), there are much smaller but better organized and therefore more useful collections, and they have suffered less damage than the archive material at Palermo and Naples. A selection of not very informative documents was published by V. E. Stellardi, *Il regno di Vittorio Amedeo II di Savoia in Sicilia dal 1713 al 1719* (3 vols., Turin 1862). Much more interesting are the various diaries edited in vol. XII of di Marzo's *Biblioteca storica e letteraria di Sicilia* (Palermo 1872); G. Giardina, *Memorie storiche del regno di Sicilia dall'anno 1718 al 1720* (Palermo 1873); and A. Apary, *Mémoire sur l'état politique de la Sicile presenté à Victor Amedée* (Amsterdam 1734). For the later years there is Emanuele e Gaetani, Marquis di Villabianca, *Diario palermitano* (ed. di Marzo, *Biblioteca storica*, vols. XVII and XVIII, Palermo 1874, which cover the period 1746–66). Di Blasi ended his history in 1774.

Useful secondary works include R. Martini, *La Sicilia sotto gli Austriaci, 1719–34* (Palermo 1907); P. Lanza di Scordia, *Considerazioni sulla storia di Sicilia dal 1532 al 1789* (Palermo 1836); G. Raffiotta, *Il supremo magistrato di commercio* (Palermo 1953); and the same author's *Gabelle e dogane a Palermo nel primo trentennio del settecento* (Palermo 1962); G. Falzone, *Carlo III e la Sicilia* (enlarged ed. Bologna 1964); G. Catalano, *Le ultime vicende della legazia apostolica in Sicilia* (Catania 1950).

Part 8, Society and the Enlightenment: The Eighteenth Century

A selection from the more important contemporary Sicilian writers, together with an excellent commentary by G. Giarrizzo, can be found in *Illuministi Italiani* (vol. VII, ed. Giarrizzo, Torcellan and Venturi, Naples 1965). Individually there are: T. Natale, *Riflessioni politiche intorno all'efficaccia e necessità delle leggi penali* (*Opuscoli di autori siciliani*, vol. XIII, Palermo 1772—the author said he wrote it in 1759, i.e. ahead of Beccaria); F. P. di Blasi ed Angelo, *Dissertazione sopra l'egualità e la disugguaglianza degli uomini* (in *Opuscoli di autori siciliani*, vol. XIX, 1778); the same author's *Saggio sopra la legislazione della Sicilia* (in *Nuova raccolta di opuscoli di autori siciliani*, vol. III, 1790); D. M. Giarrizzo, *Prospetto dei saggi politici ed economici su la pubblica e la privata felicità della Sicilia* (Palermo 1788); and the same writer's essay on roads in vol. III of *Nuova raccolta di opuscoli* (Palermo 1790). An interesting commentary is D. Scinà, *Prospetto della storia letteraria di Sicilia nel secolo XVIII* (3 vols., Palermo 1824–7).

Among general and recent books are R. de Mattei, *Il pensiero politico Siciliano fra il sette e l'ottocento* (Catania 1927); T. Mirabella, *Fortuna di Rousseau in Sicilia* (Caltanissetta 1957); and S. F. Romano, *Riformatori siciliani del settecento 1770–4* (Florence 1947). Useful is H. Tuzet, *La Sicile au XVIIIe siècle vue par les voyageurs étrangers* (Strasbourg 1955); and the best known of these foreign tourists was P. Brydone, *A Tour through Sicily and Malta* (2 vols., London 1773). On the aristocratic villas, the authority is G. Tomasi Lanza, *Le ville di Palermo* (Palermo 1965), which is fully illustrated.

On social and economic history, the main printed source, once again, is the Marquis di Villabianca, *Diario palermitano* (ed. di Marzo, *Biblioteca storica*, vol. XIX, Palermo 1875); also the same author's *Della Sicilia nobile* (5 vols., Palermo 1754–7). Contemporary commentators include G. A. Arnolfini, *Giornale di viaggio e quesiti sull' economia siciliana*, 1768 (ed. C. Trasselli, Caltanissetta 1962); A. Leanti, *Lo stato presente della Sicilia* (2 vols., Palermo 1761); G. Guerra, *Stato presente della città di Messina* (Naples 1781); the same author's *Memoria sulle strade pubbliche della Sicilia* (Naples 1784); V. E. Sergio, *Lettera sulla pulizia delle publiche strade di Sicilia* (Palermo 1777).

Recently there have been a number of special studies on aspects of economic history: A. Petino. *La questione del commercio dei grani in Sicilia nel settecento* (Catania 1946); V. Titone, *Economia e politica nella Sicilia del sette e dell'ottocento* (Palermo 1946); F. Brancato, *Il commercio dei grani nel settecento* (Palermo 1947).

Part 9, Revolution and Reform 1770–1800

A fundamental book on this period is E. Pontieri, *Il tramonto del baronaggio siciliano* (Florence 1943); and the same author's *Lettere del Marchese Caracciolo vicerè di Sicilia al ministro Acton, 1782–86* (in *Archivio storico napoletano*, 1929–32). On the events of 1773 in Palermo, see

N. Caeti, *La cacciata del vicerè Fogliani* (in *Archivio storico siciliano*, 1909–10), and a study by S. F. Romano in *Atti del comitato Trapanese dell' istituto per la storia del risorgimento* (ed. G. di Stefano, Trapani 1957). Another useful volume is F. Brancato, *Il Caracciolo e il suo tentativo di riforme in Sicilia* (Palermo 1946).

The published diaries of Villabianca continue from 1772 to 1784 (vols. XX, XXVI, XXVII and XXVIII of di Marzo, *Biblioteca storica*, 1875–86). On economic affairs and politics, P. Balsamo is an important witness: *Memorie economiche ed agrarie riguardanti il regno di Sicilia* (Palermo 1802); *Giornale del viaggio fatto in Sicilia* (Palermo 1809)—of which some appeared in English, ed. T. W. Vaughan, *A View of the Present State of Sicily* (London 1811); and *Sulla istoria moderna del regno di Sicilia. Memorie segrete* (Palermo 1848).

Part 10, Later Bourbon Sicily 1800–1837

On the period of the British occupation, the best study is J. Rosselli, *Lord William Bentinck and the British Occupation of Sicily 1811–14* (Cambridge 1956). Alongside this: G. Bianco, *La Sicilia durante l'occupazione inglese* (Palermo 1902); V. Titone, *La costituzione del 1812 e l'occupazione inglese della Sicilia* (Bologna 1936); and H. M. Lackland, *The Failure of the Constitutional Experiment in Sicily* (in *English Historical Review*, April 1926). A useful document is *Parlamento di Sicilia dell'anno 1810* (Palermo 1816). More recently: F. Renda, *La Sicilia nel 1812* (Caltanissetta 1963); G. Berti, *I democratici e l'iniziativa meridionale nel risorgimento* (Milan 1962); Enzo Sciacca, *Riflessi del costituzionalismo europeo in Sicilia, 1812–1815* (Catania 1966).

By contemporaries, apart from Balsamo's *Memorie segrete*, there is N. Palmeri, *Saggio storico e politico sulla costituzione del regno di Sicilia infino al 1816 con un appendice sulla rivoluzione del 1820* (which Amari edited anonymously, Lausanne 1847); M. Amari, *La Sicile et les Bourbons* (Paris 1849); G. F. Leckie, *An Historical Survey of the Foreign Affairs of Great Britain* (London 1808); and the continuation, by P. Insenga and G. Biundi, of di Blasi, *Storia cronologica* (Palermo 1842).

Important material is available in the Archivio di Stato at Palermo, and that of Naples; also in the British Foreign Office and consular papers; the Bentinck archive (Portland Papers, Nottingham University); that of A'Court (Heytesbury Papers, British Museum); and of slighter interest is Lord Valentia's diary in Sicily (also in the British Museum). The French consular and ambassadorial papers for 1830–47 are very interesting, and have been printed by A. Saitta, *Le riforme di Ferdinando II in Sicilia* (in *Annuario dell'istituto storico italiano per l'età moderna e contemporanea*, vol. VI, 1954).

There are some excellent modern studies: E. Pontieri, *Il riformismo borbonico nella Sicilia del sette e dell'ottocento, saggi storici* (Naples 1961);

R. Romeo, *La Sicilia nel risorgimento* (Bari 1950); N. Cortese, *La prima rivoluzione separatista siciliana 1820–1821* (Naples 1951); S. F. Romano, *Momenti del risorgimento in Sicilia* (Messina 1952).

Part 11, The Economy 1750–1850

Probably the most important contemporary writings are those of Balsamo, including his *Memorie inedite di pubblica economia ed agricoltura* (2 vols., Palermo 1845), and his report with the Abbé Piazza and D. Marabitti, *Sistema metrico per la Sicilia presentato a Sua Maestà dalla Deputazione de' pesi e misure* (Palermo 1809). Also note: N. Palmeri, *Cause e rimedi delle angustie dell'economia agraria in Sicilia, 1826* (ed. R. Giuffrida, Caltanissetta 1962); G. de Welz, *Saggio su i mezzi da moltiplicare prontamente le richezze della Sicilia* (Paris 1822, of which a new edition has now been made by F. Renda, Caltanissetta 1964); Afan de Rivera, *Pensieri sulla Sicilia al di là del faro* (Naples 1820); P. Lanza e Stella, *Sulla decadenza dell'agricoltura in Sicilia e sul modo di rimediarvi* (Naples 1786); G. La Loggia, *Saggio economico-politico per la facile introduzione delle principali manifatture . . . 1791* (ed. G. Falzone, Caltanissetta 1964); D. Scinà, *La topografia di Palermo e de' suoi contorni* (Palermo 1818); I. Sanfilippo, *Catechismo di agricoltura per la Sicilia compilato per ordine del governo* (Palermo 1836); R. Busacca, *Sullo istituto d'incoraggiamento e sulla industria siciliana* (Palermo 1835); L. Bianchini, *Storia economica e civile di Sicilia* (the second volume, published at Palermo 1841, covers the period after 1735); G. Perez, *La Sicilia e la sue strade* (originally published 1861, and now ed. C. Trasselli, Caltanissetta 1962); G. Schirò, *Attuale condizione forestale e solforifera di Sicilia* (Palermo 1860). A great deal of miscellaneous information can also be found in such contemporary Palermo magazines as the *Annali di Agricoltura*, the *Giornale di Statistica*, and the *Giornale di Scienze, Letteratura ed Arti per la Sicilia*.

The reports in the British consular papers from the Public Record Office are very full, and contain comparable statistics from year to year. Other reports by consul John Goodwin are in the British Museum and the library of the Royal Statistical Society. Some letters of Balsamo are in the University Library archives at Nottingham.

Recent studies on special subjects include: V. Titone, *Riveli e platee del regno di Sicilia* (Milan 1961); A. d'Arrigo, *Natura e tecnica nel mezzogiorno* (Florence 1956); A. Petino, *L'arte e il consolato della seta a Catania nei secoli XIV–XIX* (in *Bolletino storico catanese*, 1942–3); L. A. Pagano, *L'industria armatoriale siciliana dal 1816 al 1880* (Rome 1964); F. Squarzina, *Produzione e commercio dello zolfo in Sicilia nel secolo XIX* (Turin 1963). On agriculture there is A. Sartorius von Waltershausen, *Die sizilianische Agrarverfassung und ihre Wandlungen 1780–1912* (Leipzig 1913); A. Pupillo-Barresi, *Gli usi civici in Sicilia* (Catania 1903); and

D. Mack Smith, *The Latifundia in Modern Sicilian History* (in *Proceedings of the British Academy*, London 1966).

On society in general, apart from Nassau William Senior, *Journals Kept in France and Italy from 1848 to 1852* (vol. II, London 1871), there are G. Pitrè, *La vita in Palermo cento e più anni fa* (2 vols., Florence 1950); E. Loncao, *Considerazioni sulla genesi della borghesia in Sicilia* (Palermo 1900); and the same author's *Il lavoro e le classi rurali in Sicilia durante e dopo il feudalesimo* (Palermo 1900).

Part 12, The Risorgimento 1837–1860

The authoritative book on this period is R. Romeo, *La Sicilia nel risorgimento* (Bari 1950); and the same author has a bibliographical essay, *Gli studi sul risorgimento in Sicilia nell'ultimo trentennio, 1915–48* (in *Archivio storico siciliano*, 1948). A more recent bibliography is by S. Scibilia, *Il risorgimento in Sicilia* (in *Movimento operaio*, 1955). There are many important essays in *La Rassegna storica del risorgimento* published at Rome; others in *La Sicilia e l'unità d'Italia* (ed. S. M. Ganci and R. G. Scaglione, 2 vols., Milan 1962); also D. Mack Smith, *The Peasants' Revolt of Sicily in 1860* (in *Studi in onore di G. Luzzatto*, vol. III, Milan 1950).

On the 1848 revolution, apart from *Le Assemblee del risorgimento, Atti Raccolti* (vols. XII, XIII, XIV, XV, Rome 1911), there is G. La Farina, *Istoria documentata della rivoluzione siciliana, 1848–9* (2 vols., Capolago 1850–1), and his *Storia d'Italia dal 1815 al 1850* (6 vols., Turin 1851–2); P. Calvi, *Memorie storiche e critiche della rivoluzione siciliana del 1848* (2 vols., London 1851); V. Fardella, *Ricordi su la rivoluzione siciliana degli anni 1848 e 1849* (Palermo 1887); and M. Condorelli, *Stato e chiesa nella rivoluzione siciliana del 1848* (Catania 1965).

Other useful studies are C. Avarna di Gualtieri, *Ruggero Settimo nel risorgimento siciliano* (Bari 1928); G. Giarrizzo, *Un comune rurale della Sicilia Etnea* (Catania 1963); L. Tomeucci, *Messina nel risorgimento* (Milan 1963); S. Nicastro, *Dal quarantotto al sessanta* (Milan 1913); L. Natoli, *Rivendicazioni attraverso le rivoluzioni siciliani del 1848–60* (Treviso 1927); V. Mortillaro, *Notizie economiche statistiche ricavate sui catasti di Sicilia* (Palermo 1854); D. Mack Smith, *Cavour and Garibaldi, 1860* (Cambridge 1954); Benedetto Radice, *Nino Bixio a Bronte* (ed. L. Sciascia, Caltanissetta 1963); F. Brancato, *La Sicilia nel movimento per l'unità d'Italia* (Palermo 1947), and the same author's *La dittatura garibaldina nel mezzogiorno e in Sicilia* (Trapani 1965).

Part 13, Italian Sicily 1860–1890

A good modern outline history is F. de Stefano and F. L. Oddo,

Storia della Sicilia dal 1860 al 1910 (Bari 1963). In more detail there is
F. Brancato, *La Sicilia nel primo ventennio del regno d'Italia* (Bologna 1956),
and S. F. Romano, *La Sicilia nell'ultimo ventennio del secolo XIX* (Palermo
1958). Brancato has also written a good short life of *Francesco Perroni
Paladini* (Palermo 1962). Other important recent works are P. Alatri,
Lotte politiche in Sicilia sotto il governo della destra, 1866–74 (Turin 1954);
G. C. Marino, *L'opposizione mafiosa 1870–82* (Palermo 1964); R. Romeo,
Risorgimento e capitalismo (Bari 1959), and the discussion of Romeo's
thesis by A. Gerschenkron (*Rivista Storica Italiana*, 1959), and by
D. Tosi, *Sulle forme iniziali di sviluppo economico e i loro effetti* (in *Annali
del Istituto Giangiacomo Feltrinelli*, Milan 1962).

Of documentary material there is: *Relazione del consiglio straordinario
di stato, convocato in Sicilia per decreto dittatoriale del 19 ottobre 1860* (Palermo
1860); G. Scichilone, *Documenti sulle condizioni della Sicilia dal 1860 al
1870* (Rome 1952); *Relazione della commissione per l'inchiesta della città
e provincia di Palermo* (in *Atti parlamentari*, doc. CXI, 1867); R. Bonfadini,
Relazione della giunta per l'inchiesta sulle condizioni della Sicilia (Rome 1876);
A. Damiani, *Atti della giunta per l'inchiesta agraria e sulle condizioni della
classe agricola* (vol. XIII of Jacini's report, Rome 1885).

The most important contemporary study by far is that of L. Franchetti and Sidney Sonnino, *La Sicilia nel 1876* (2 vols., Florence 1877).
But in addition, C. Tommasi-Crudeli, *La Sicilia nel 1871* (Florence
1871); G. Ciotti, *I casi di Palermo: cenni storici sugli avvenimenti di set-
tembre 1866* (Palermo 1866); G. Pagano, *Avvenimenti del 1866: sette
giorni d'insurrezione a Palermo* (Palermo 1867); S. Corleo, *Storia della
enfiteusi dei terreni ecclesiastici di Sicilia* (Palermo 1871); P. Villari, *Scritti
sulla questione sociale in Italia* (Florence 1902); N. Colajanni, *La Sicilia
dai Borboni ai Sabaudi 1860–1900* (Milan 1951); ed. S. M. Ganci,
Democrazia e socialismo in Italia, carteggi di Napoleone Colajanni, 1878–1898
(Milan 1959); G. Bruzzo, *Sulle condizioni di sicurezza delle miniere di
Lercara in Sicilia* (Rome 1875); F. Maggiore-Perni, *Delle condizioni
economiche, politiche e morali della Sicilia dopo il 1860* (Palermo 1896).
On the revolt of 1866, see the *Nuovi Quaderni del Meridione* for 1966,
especially the articles by Ganci and Brancato.

A good deal can also be learnt from the occasional debates in
parliament (*Atti parlamentari, camera e senato*); as from *Un secolo di
statistiche italiane, nord e sud 1861–1961* (ed. Svimez, i.e., *Associazione
per lo sviluppo dell' industria nel mezzogiorno*, Rome 1961); from local
Palermo newspapers such as the *Giornale di Sicilia* and *L'Ora*, and from
Nuove effemeridi siciliane (ed. di Giovanni and G. Pitrè, Palermo 1875–81).

Part 14, The Failure of Parliamentarism 1880–1922

For the outline history of this period there is Romano's *La Sicilia
nell'ultimo ventennio del secolo XIX* (Palermo 1958), and G. Raffiotta,

La Sicilia nel primo ventennio del secolo XX (Palermo 1959). Also by Romano is *Storia dei fasci Siciliani* (Bari 1959).

On social and economic history, a vast amount of factual evidence is presented in G. Lorenzoni, *Inchiesta parlamentare sulle condizioni dei contadini nelle provincie meridionali e nella Sicilia* (Rome 1910, vol. VI of the Faina report), which should be compared with the Damiani report of 25 years before. Also: M. Basile, *Latifondi e poderi* (Messina 1898); A. Battaglia, *Studi sulla legislazione agraria in Sicilia* (Palermo 1904); N. Colajanni, *In Sicilia: gli avvenimenti e le cause* (Palermo 1894); A. di San Giuliano, *Le condizioni presenti della Sicilia* (Milan 1894); *Il commissariato civile del 1896 in Sicilia* (ed. S. Massimo Ganci, Palermo 1958); N. Ziino, *L'irrigazione e i suoi effetti economici agrarii nell'Italia meridionale* (Catania 1907); G. Bruccoleri, *La Sicilia di oggi, appunti economici* (Rome 1913); L. Granone, *Fattori e bisogni dell'economia siciliana* (Girgenti 1917); N. Prestianni, *La formazione di piccole proprietà coltivatrici in Sicilia* (Rome 1931). More recently there is C. Ruini, *Le vicende del latifondo siciliano* (Florence 1946); F. Renda, *Il movimento contadino nella società siciliana* (Palermo 1956), and the same author's *L'emigrazione in Sicilia* (Palermo 1963); L. Sciascia, *Pirandello e la Sicilia* (Caltanissetta 1961). An important work on intellectual history is G. Gentile, *Il tramonto della cultura siciliana* (Bologna 1917).

A great deal has been written on political corruption and the mafia: including M. Vaina, *Popolarismo e nasismo in Sicilia* (Florence 1911); N. Nasi, *Memorie* (Rome 1943); L. Notarbartolo, *Memorie della vita di mia padre Emanuele Notarbartolo* (Pistoia 1949); A. Nasalli Rocca, *Memorie di un prefetto* (Rome 1946); G. Alongi, *La maffia* (Florence 1886); T. Mercadante Carrara, *La delinquenza in Sicilia* (Palermo 1911); E. d'Alessandro, *Brigantaggio e mafia in Sicilia* (Messina 1959); D. Novacco, *Inchiesta sulla mafia* (Milan 1963), and the same author's bibliography (in *Nuovi Quaderni del Meridione*, 1964); also ed. N. Russo, *Antologia della mafia* (Palermo 1964).

Part 15, Sicily Since 1922

Many basic statistics can be found in *Statistiche sul mezzogiorno d'Italia, 1861–1953* (ed. Svimez, Rome 1954); *Un secolo di statistiche italiane, nord e sud, 1861–1961* (ed. Svimez, Rome 1961). Details on agricultural changes are in G. Molè, *Studio-inchiesta sui latifondi siciliani* (Rome 1929); G. Lorenzoni, *Dal diario di viaggio di un sociologo rurale attraverso la Sicilia, 1933* (in *Annali dell' Università di Ferrara*, 1937); G. Lorenzoni, *Trasformazione e colonizzazione del latifondo siciliano* (Florence 1940); N. Prestianni, *L'economia agraria della Sicilia* (Palermo 1946); S. Scrofani, *La questione agraria siciliana* (Caltanissetta 1961).

Most of the information on the fascist period in Italy is found in local, national and foreign newspapers. One of the few books is C. Mori,

Con la mafia ai ferri corti (Rome 1932), which was translated in a shortened version as *The Last Struggle with the Mafia* (London 1933). On the end of fascism, apart from the official war histories, there is G. Zingali, *L'invasione della Sicilia, 1943* (Catania 1962).

The best book on Giuliano is still Gavin Maxwell, *God Protect Me from My Friends* (London 1956), and the same writer has published an interesting social study on Sicily, *The Ten Pains of Death* (London 1959). Among other studies of social history, apart from unpublished reports by J. Boissevain, Ilys Booker and Michael Faber, there are a number of books by Danilo Dolci, notably *To Feed the Hungry, Enquiry in Palermo* (London 1959), and *Waste, an Eye-witness Report on Some Aspects of Waste in Western Sicily* (London 1963); also R. Rochefort, *Le travail en Sicile, étude de géographie sociale* (Paris 1961). There have been some excellent journalistic reports on Sicily by the Palermo daily *L'Ora*, and by the Rome weekly *L'Espresso*, and by *Il Ponte* (May 1959). Some of the best pieces of journalism have appeared in book form: F. Chilanti and M. Farinella, *Rapporto sulla mafia* (Palermo 1964); M. Pantaleone, *The Mafia and Politics* (London 1966).

An outstanding volume on present-day Sicily by a group of economists and sociologists is *Problemi dell'economia siciliana* (ed. P. Sylos-Labini, Milan 1966); and a vast amount of statistical material is now available through various bodies: e.g. *Informazioni Svimez; Bollettino di statistiche della regione siciliana; Bollettino d'informazioni Sicilcamere; Notiziario economico finanziario siciliano* (by the Banco de Sicilia). Something can also be learnt from the *Assemblea Regionale Siciliana, resoconti parlamentari*.

MAP OF SICILY

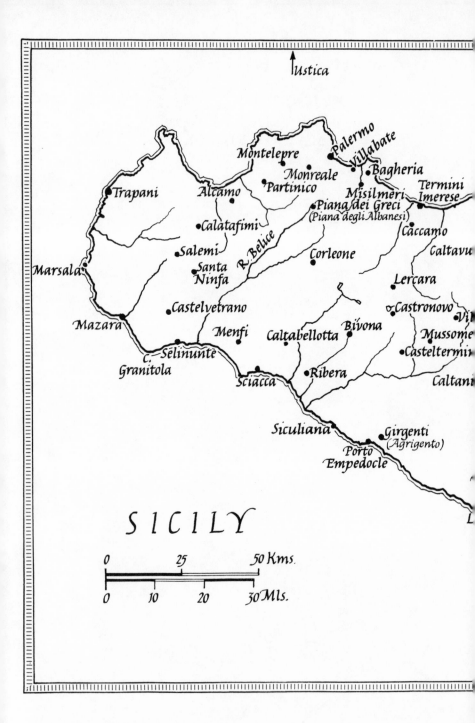

SICILY

0   25   50 Kms.

0   10   20   30 Mls.

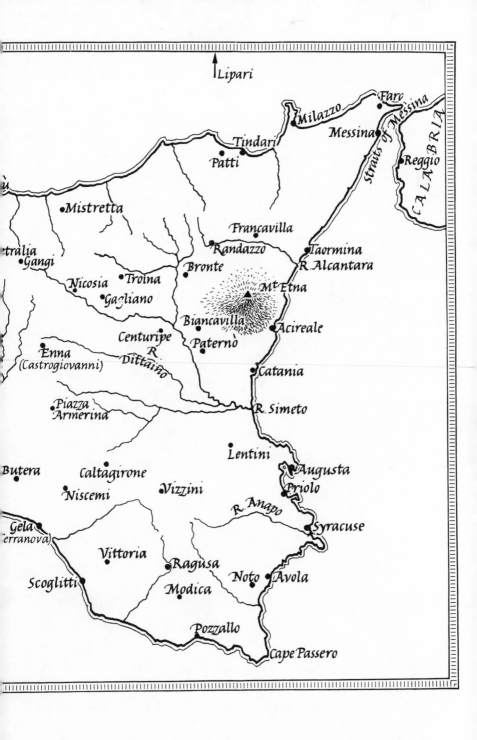

INDEX

References are to the two volumes, paged consecutively as follows:
Medieval Sicily, pp. 1–240; *Modern Sicily*, pp. 241–559.

AUG 2'95	DATE DUE	
FEB 11 '97		
JAN 16 1999		
MAR 3 1 1999		
JUL 20 2000		